Lloyds TSB

Tax Guide

2003/2004

Lloyds TSB

Tax Guide
2003/2004

SARA WILLIAMS AND
JONQUIL LOWE

Published by
Vitesse Media plc

This edition published 2003

Printed in Great Britain by The Bath Press

A CIP catalogue record for this book is available
from the British Library

ISBN 0-9540812-6-9

The Authors

Sara Williams is a former investment analyst and financial journalist. She has contributed many articles on tax and finance for national newspapers and for a number of years wrote for *Which?*, including the *Which? Tax-Saving Guide* and the *Which? Book of Tax*. She is also the author of the *Lloyds TSB Small Business Guide*. She is now the CEO of Aim-listed Vitesse Media, an online and print publisher, publishing magazines, directories, and newsletters, including *Business XL*, *Growth Company Investor*, *Tax-Effective Investor* and www.taxguide.co.uk.

Jonquil Lowe trained as an economist and worked for several years in the City as an investment analyst. She is a former head of the Money Group at Consumers' Association, a past editor of *The Which? Tax-Saving Guide* and was for many years a regular contributor to *Which? Way to Save Tax*. Jonquil now works as a freelance researcher and journalist. She writes extensively on all areas of personal finance for a diverse range of clients, including Consumers' Association, the Financial Services Authority and Butterworths-Tolley. Jonquil is author of several other books, including *Be Your Own Financial Adviser*, *The Which? Guide to Giving and Inheriting*, *The Which? Guide to Planning Your Pension*, *Take Control of Your Pension* (an Action Pack), *The Which? Guide to Money in Retirement* and *The Which? Guide to Shares*.

CONTENTS

A MESSAGE FROM MAARTEN VAN DEN BERGH, LLOYDS TSB GROUP CHAIRMAN

Lloyds TSB is proud to be associated with this *Tax Guide* and I am very pleased to welcome you to this, the 18th edition.

The Guide has proved very popular over the years, explaining the difficult subject of taxation using plain English, backed up by easy to follow examples and also tips on how you could minimise your tax bill.

This book is also invaluable when you are preparing your Self-Assessment Tax Return. It will help to make the task less onerous and provide advice on managing your tax affairs.

In addition to the *Tax Guide*, Lloyds TSB can offer you support through the broad range of financial services that we offer. If you ever wish to discuss any of our services or products we would welcome you at any of our branches throughout the UK.

I do hope that you find the *Lloyds TSB Tax Guide* provides you with a useful tool to aid your finances both now and in the future.

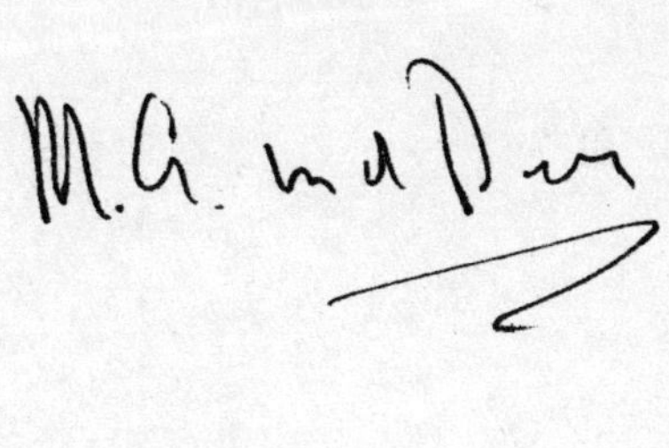

ACKNOWLEDGEMENTS

A tax guide of this type cannot appear without the help and hard work of a multitude of people. For this edition, Liz Lathwood, from the Chartered Institute of Taxation, has helped us on the technical side. On the production side, Jonathan Harley, Neill Purvis, Margaret Gudgeon and Alex Tomlin have worked long hours to perfect the guide. Moira Greenhalgh has again produced a very useful index.

Thank you

Sara Williams and Jonquil Lowe

NOTE

Both of us – along with everyone at Lloyds TSB and Vitesse Media plc – have made strenuous efforts to check the accuracy of the information. If by chance a mistake or omission has occurred, we are sorry that neither we, Lloyds TSB nor the Publisher can take responsibility if you suffer any loss or problem as a result of it. But please write to Sara Williams and Jonquil Lowe, Lloyds TSB Tax Guide, 95 Aldwych, London WC2B 4JF if you have any suggestions about how we can improve the content of the guide.

Dear Reader

The Lloyds TSB Tax Guide went to press shortly after the 2003 Budget on 9 April – and much may change before the chancellor's proposals become law. If you want to keep abreast of developments, there are two ways to do it:

- send for our free update, which will be issued in the autumn – see below for instructions on what to do

- log on to the Tax Guide website – at www.taxguide.co.uk

To get the paper version send an A4-sized self-addressed envelope with a 42p stamp on it to: Sara Williams and Jonquil Lowe, Lloyds TSB Tax Guide, 95 Aldwych, London WC2B 4JF.

Yours sincerely

Sara Williams
Jonquil Lowe

HOW INCOME TAX WORKS

CHAPTER 1

Under self-assessment you operate the tax collection system in part or fully. You provide the records, fill in the tax return, and you may also work out the tax bill. You must pay what you owe by sending a cheque (or by debit card), along with your tax return and your tax calculation, to the Inland Revenue by 31 January. If you prefer, you can send in your tax return to the Inland Revenue by 30 September. The tax you owe will be worked out by your tax inspector and you must pay it by 31 January.

However, around one in 10 taxpayers ends up paying a penalty for late delivery of their tax return. Remember that there are :

- dates by which you have to fill in your tax return (p. 19)
- penalties you have to pay if you don't stick to all the rules (p. 24)
- rules about records which you must keep (p. 17)
- dates to pay your tax bill (p. 21)
- rules about which income you will pay tax on (p. 3)
- dates for reporting income (p. 17)
- obligations which taxpayers must stick to (p. 17).

The taxes you might pay

There are a number of different ways in which the government raises money from taxpayers. Some of the taxes are as follows:

- income tax – some of your income is taxed at varying rates
- capital gains tax – some of the gains you make on investments or possessions may be taxed at varying rates
- inheritance tax – when you die, some of the money you leave to others could be taxed
- National Insurance – this is paid only by people who are earning, employees, employers, the self-employed or partners.

Other taxes include council tax, corporation tax, business rates, value added tax, stamp duty and excise duties.

The tax returns for the tax year ending 5 April 2003 should have landed on your doorstep during April 2003. These will cover your income and gains, reliefs and allowances. The information you provide will be used by you or your tax inspector to work out your income tax and capital gains tax bills.

How tax rules are changed

Strangely enough, income tax is a temporary tax and a new Act of Parliament is required each year to allow the government to go on collecting it. This provides the ideal opportunity for the government to ask Parliament to approve changes to the tax rules, so there is an annual cycle:

November before the start of the next tax year: Pre-Budget Report. The government announces complicated or tentative proposals to change the rules, often inviting experts and the public to make comments on the proposals.

March/April: Budget The government announces changes. Many apply from the start of the tax year (which means backdating them if the Budget is in April). Other changes may take effect from different dates.

6 April: start of the new tax year.

April/May: Finance Bill published. This is the draft legislation to implement the changes from the Pre-Budget Report and the Budget. Sometimes other last-minute government changes are slipped in too. Now Parliament sets about debating and amending the draft rules.

July: Finance Act passed. The measures in the act become law – many are backdated to the start of the tax year or even Budget Day.

What is in this guide?

This tax guide explains the rules for income tax, capital gains tax, inheritance tax and National Insurance. It covers most of the rules which the majority of taxpayers need to know, but it may not cover very specialised cases.

In Part I, the guide gives a broad outline of the rules and helps you to plan your affairs to minimise your tax bills. It covers what you need to know for the current tax year (ending 5 April 2004). It includes the changes proposed in the April 2003 Budget. By following its advice you should be able to save tax in the current and future tax years.

The guide went to the printers at the beginning of May 2003 and its advice is based on what was proposed in the Budget. Proposals are sometimes changed by debate in Parliament. You can receive notice of later changes by either:

- visiting our web site, www.taxguide.co.uk
- sending an A4 stamped (42p), self-addressed envelope to Sara Williams and Jonquil Lowe, Lloyds TSB Tax Guide, 95 Aldwych, London WC2B 4JF

In Part II, the guide helps you to fill in your tax return and has the information and figures for the tax year ending 5 April 2003. It includes lots of tax-saving tips which help you to cut your tax bill for the last tax year.

A simple guide to income tax

There are many complexities and exceptions in the way that income is taxed. What follows is a broad brush approach to how income is taxed. It gives some important relationships:

Taxable income = (Income − Reliefs − Allowances)
Total income = (Income − Reliefs)
Income tax = Taxable income × the rate(s) of tax

Income is made up of what you earn from your job or self-employment and what you receive as income from other sources, such as investments. But not all the money you receive is income (see p. 6) and some income you receive is tax-free (see p. 345). Some income you receive has had tax deducted (called *net* – see pp. 8 and 62) and some income is paid without tax deducted (called *gross* – see pp. 8 and 339).

Reliefs are amounts which you pay out and on which you get tax relief. Relief may be given in one of three ways:

EXAMPLE

Jessica Jones has income from employment of £20,000. She pays £1,000 into an occupational pension scheme and she can claim a personal allowance for the tax year ending 5 April 2004 of £4,615. Her taxable income is:

	£
Income	20,000.00
Less Reliefs: pension contributions	1,000.00
	19,000.00
Less personal allowance	4,615.00
Taxable income	14,385.00
Tax at 10 per cent on first £1,960	196.00
Tax at 22 per cent on next £12,425	2,733.50
Total tax bill	2,929.50

- a reduction in your income before tax is worked out. This gives relief at your highest rate of tax. Examples are occupational pension contributions and payroll giving to charity
- by deducting basic rate relief from the payment before handing it over. Any higher rate relief is given by raising the threshold at which you start to pay higher rate tax. Examples include stakeholder pension contributions and Gift Aid donations
- as a reduction in your tax bill – for example maintenance payments (available to older people only) and enterprise investment scheme investments. Relief is restricted to a percentage of the eligible payment.

Allowances are amounts to which you are entitled because of your personal circumstances. Personal allowance and blind person's allowance reduce your income before your tax bill is worked out, giving you relief at your highest rate of tax. But with married couple's allowance (available only to older people), relief is restricted and given as a deduction in your tax bill.

Taxable income is the figure on which your tax bill is largely based. The amount of income tax depends on how much taxable income you have and what rate of tax is paid on it (see below). From this initial amount, you then deduct any reliefs and allowances that are given as a reduction in your tax bill. The maximum reduction is the amount needed to reduce your tax bill to zero.

Total income is a figure that is not important for most taxpayers, but it is for older people in receipt of age-related allowances. The amount of total income determines whether you get these allowances in full or only a reduced amount (see pp. 11 and 48). Total income is the amount you have after you have deducted some reliefs from income, but before deducting allowances. The reliefs you deduct to arrive at total income include pension contributions, charitable donations under Gift Aid and gifts of shares or certain other investments to charity.

The rates of tax

There are different rates of tax:

- starting rate tax (10 per cent for tax years ending on 5 April 2003 and 5 April 2004)
- basic rate tax 22 per cent for the tax years ending on 5 April 2003 and 2004
- higher rate tax (40 per cent for tax years ending on 5 April 2003 and 2004)

The levels at which these rates apply can vary from year to year. Here are the levels of income for each of these rates for the tax years ending 5 April 2003 and 5 April 2004:

Tax year ending 5 April 2003

Income band	*Size of band*	*Tax rate*	*Tax on band*
£	£	%	£
0–1,920	1,920	10	192.00
1,921–29,900	27,980	22	6155.60
Over 29,900		40	

Tax year ending 5 April 2004

Income band	*Size of band*	*Tax rate*	*Tax on band*
£	£	%	£
0–1,960	1,960	10	196.00
1,961–30,500	28,540	22	6,278.80
Over 30,500		40	

Different tax rates apply to income from most savings and investments. The tax rates for savings income (for example, from building society accounts, gilts and corporate bonds) falling into each of the bands above are 10 per cent, 20 per cent (called the savings rate) and 40 per cent. Savings income is often paid with tax at the savings rate already deducted in which case starting rate taxpayers and non-taxpayers can reclaim half or all of the tax, respectively.

Dividends from shares, distributions from share-based unit trusts and similar investments are paid with tax at 10 per cent already deducted. Non-taxpayers cannot reclaim this tax. There is no further tax to pay unless you are a higher rate taxpayer, in which case you pay a further 22.5 per cent.

Tax credits

From 6 April 2003, two state benefits – the working tax credit and child tax credit – are integrated into the tax system, with the amount you get based broadly on your 'total income' (see opposite). If you do not have children, you are unlikely to qualify for tax credits if your income is more than about £11,000 a year (single) or £15,000 (couple). But credits may be payable to households with children that have incomes as high as £66,350 a year. For details see p. 12.

INCOME, RELIEFS, ALLOWANCES AND TAX CREDITS

CHAPTER 2

Income, reliefs and allowances are the three elements in determining your income tax bill – and the three ways in which you can minimise the size of it. Look for opportunities to arrange your income to be tax-free (see p. 345 for a comprehensive list). In the case of a couple, seek to distribute the income between the two of you to the greatest advantage. And don't forget to claim all your reliefs and allowances, including those from the past that you might have forgotten. You will find tax-saving tips throughout the guide; many of them are gathered together in Chapter 5.

INCOME

Your income will be made up of money or goods you receive or anything you get in return for a service – but not all payments you receive count as income (see below). The following will all normally be considered as income:

- what you earn from your work, including a job (see p. 209), a partnership (see p. 281) or self-employment (see p. 250). This includes salary, fringe benefits and business profits
- rent from letting out property (see p. 283)
- income from investments, such as interest, dividends and distributions (see pp. 61 and 155)
- pensions (from the state, your previous employer or your own plan)
- social security payments, such as jobseeker's allowance
- casual, occasional or miscellaneous income, such as freelance earnings, income received after you close a business, income from guaranteeing loans, dealing in futures, income from underwriting, certain capital payments from selling UK patent rights, gains on many discounted securities, accrued income in bond and gilt strip prices
- income from a trust.

Payments that are not income

Some payments you receive are not income. For example:

Main types of income (for tax year ending 5 April 2004)

Type of income	*Tax deducted?*	*At what rate?*	*More tax to pay?*
Earnings from a job	yes	StR, BR, HR	no(1)
Taxable fringe benefits	yes, from earnings	StR, BR, HR	no(1)
Occupational or personal pension	yes	StR, BR, HR	no(1)
Retirement annuity contract	yes(2)	BR	yes – HR
Bank, building society interest	yes(2)	SR	yes – HR
Gilts and most other bonds	no(3)		yes
Income from annuity (other than pension annuities)	yes(2) (4)	SR	yes – HR
Dividends from shares	yes(5)	10 per cent	yes(6)
Distributions from share-based unit trusts and oeics	yes(5)	10 per cent	yes(6)
Income from an executor before a will is sorted out	yes	10 per cent (5), SR and BR	yes – HR
Income from a trust	yes	10 per cent (5), SR and BR or 34 per cent (see p. 308)	yes – HR
Income from self-employment or a partnership	no		yes
Social security benefits	no(7)		yes
Rent from property	no		yes(8)

Key: StR = starting rate; BR = basic rate; HR = higher rate; SR = savings rate

(1) There could, of course, be more tax to pay if insufficient has been deducted.
(2) Non-taxpayers can have this income paid without tax deducted – see p. 64.
(3) But you can choose to have interest from gilts paid with tax deducted at the savings rate of 20 per cent.
(4) Tax is deducted from the part of the annuity which counts as income, not the part which counts as a return of the capital.
(5) But non-taxpayers cannot claim back the tax deducted.
(6) Higher rate tax payers will pay taxes at the rate of 32.5 per cent (after 10 per cent tax credit, further tax of 22.5 per cent, see p. 67).
(7) But if you return to work, tax if due will be deducted from your earnings.
(8) But rent in the Rent a Room scheme is tax-free up to a limit. (For more details see p. 283).

- presents and gifts
- loans
- lottery prizes
- gambling winnings (unless it is your way of making a living)
- what you make from selling an asset (unless this is how you make a living)
- maintenance from an ex-spouse or former partner
- money you inherit.

Although these payments are not income, there may be other tax to pay on some of them – for example, capital gains tax or inheritance tax

Tax-free income

There are many examples of income that is completely tax-free, including premium bond prizes, interest on National Savings Certificates and income from savings or investments held in an individual savings account (ISA). A comprehensive list is given on p. 345.

How is income paid to you

Income can be paid to you without any tax deducted (*gross*) or with tax deducted (*net*). The tax can be deducted at the savings rate, the basic rate and/or some other rate. If it's savings income, tax will usually be deducted at the savings rate (currently 20 per cent). Tax at 10 per cent is deducted from dividends from shares and similar income. The table on p. 7 lists types of income, whether or not they are paid with tax deducted and if any further tax will be due. There are more details of income in Chapter 13.

If you need to give a figure for gross income when you have received net income, there are ready reckoners which help you to gross it up in Appendix B on p. 348.

RELIEFS

You make certain choices in life but sometimes the government gives a helping hand to encourage particular courses of action, such as saving for retirement or giving to charity. It does this by letting you have tax relief on what you pay. The items which qualify for this tax relief are known as reliefs, outgoings or deductions.

You can get a double boost from making some payments if they also reduce your 'total income'. This may save you extra tax if you qualify for age allowance (see p. 11) or entitle you to extra tax credits (see p. 15).

Main types of relief (for the tax year ending 5 April 2004)

Type of relief	*Amount of relief*	*How do you get tax relief?*
Business losses not already set against profits	St, BR or HR	through your PAYE code or tax bill
Charity(1): Gift Aid(2), gifts of shares, land or buildings	StR, BR or HR	BR: make lower payments HR: either PAYE code or tax bill
EIS and VCT (up to limits)	20%	through your PAYE code or tax bill
Community investment tax relief	5%	through your PAYE code or tax bill
Home income plan(3)	23%	lower payments through MIRAS
Interest on a loan to personal representative to pay inheritance tax	StR, BR or HR	through your PAYE code or tax bill
Interest on business loans	StR, BR or HR	through your PAYE code or tax bill
Job expenses	StR, BR or HR	through your PAYE code or tax bill
Maintenance payments(4)	10% of £2,150	through your PAYE code or tax bill
Mortgage interest on a property you let	StR, BR or HR	lower tax bill on rental income
Pension contributions to employers' schemes	StR, BR or HR	through PAYE system
Personal pension payments (including stakeholder pensions)	BR or HR	BR: make lower payments HR: through PAYE code or tax bill

Key: StR = starting rate; BR = basic rate; HR = higher rate

(1) And community amateur sports clubs that meet certain conditions.
(2) You make lower payments by deducting relief at the basic rate. If your tax bill is less than the relief deducted, the Inland Revenue may claw back some of the relief.
(3) Relief not available for loans made on or after 9 March 1999.
(4) Since 6 April 2000, available only where one or both parties was born before 6 April 1935.

> **EXAMPLE**
> Peter Atwell wants to put £2,400 into a stakeholder pension scheme. He makes the payment net – in other words, after deducting tax relief at the basic rate which comes to 22 per cent × £2,400 = £528. Peter is a higher rate taxpayer, so can claim extra relief of (40 per cent × £2,400) – £528 = £432. His pension contribution of £2,400 has cost him only £2,400 – £528 – £432 = £1,440.

> **TAX-SAVING IDEA**
> You have until the 31 January five years after the end of a tax year to correct your tax bill if, say, you've forgotten to claim a relief or allowance. This means by 31 January 2004 you can go back as far as the tax year starting 6 April 1997 to claim tax relief for a deduction or allowance which occurred in that year. You get the tax relief at the rates which applied in the tax year for which you are claiming not the current one.

How you get tax relief

There are three ways in which you can get tax relief:

- you can make a lower payment by deducting the amount of the tax relief from the payment and keeping it yourself – for example, if you want a charity to receive £50 under the Gift Aid scheme, you hand over just £39
- you can get your tax relief through the PAYE system. It will be included in your Notice of Coding and thus you will pay less tax on your salary each month
- you can get your tax relief by claiming it in your tax return. If you are going to work out your own tax bill you would deduct the amount in your calculation and pay less tax. Or your tax inspector will work out the bill allowing for the deduction.

The table on p. 9 lists the main types of reliefs and how you get them. There are more details about reliefs in Chapter 14.

ALLOWANCES

Everyone is entitled to an allowance to deduct from their income to ensure that some income is tax-free. This is called the personal allowance. But the amount of the allowance varies with age. There are a few other allowances that you might be able to claim – but these depend on your personal circumstances. There are details of allowances in the table opposite and in Chapter 15.

Details of allowances

Allowance	*Age*	*Tax year ending 5 April*	*Amount*
Personal	up to 65	2003	£4,615
		2004	£4,615
	65-74	2003	£6,100(1)
		2004	£6,610(1)
	75 plus	2003	£6,370(1)
		2004	£6,720(1)
Married couple's(2)	67–74	2003	10% of £5,465(1)
	68–74	2004	10% of £5,565(1)
	75 plus	2003	10% of £5,535(1)
		2004	10% of £5,635(1)
Blind person's	any	2003	£1,480
		2004	£1,510
Children's tax credit	any	2003	10% of £5,290(3) (4)
		2004	no longer available(5)

(1) The amount of these allowances is reduced if total income is above a certain amount. In the tax year ending 5 April 2003 the allowances were reduced if total income was over £17,900 and in the tax year ending 5 April 2004 the income limit is £18,300. For more details see p. 48.

(2) From April 2000, this allowance was abolished for people born on or after 6 April 1935. Where the allowance received by an older person is restricted because of income – see note 1 above – it will not be reduced below £2,110 in the tax year ending 5 April 2003 and £2,150 in the tax year ending 5 April 2004.

(3) But the credit is reduced by £2 for every £3 by which your income exceeds the higher-rate tax threshold.

(4) Increased to £10,490 if you had a new baby in the year ending 5 April 2003.

(5) You may instead be able to claim child tax credit which is given as a cash benefit rather than a reduction in tax – see p. 12.

TAX CREDITS

From 6 April 2003, two new state benefits have been introduced: working tax credit (WTC) and child tax credit (CTC). They replace working families' tax credit, disabled person's tax credit, children's tax credit and the child additions formerly payable with income support and income-based jobseeker's allowance.

The two new tax credits are integrated into the tax system in the sense that the amount of credit you can get depends on broadly your income for tax purposes and, in some cases, the credit is paid through the PAYE system. The credits are administered by the Inland Revenue.

WTC and CTC are not paid automatically – you must claim them. If you are married or living with someone as husband and wife, you must claim jointly and the amount you get will be based on your joint incomes.

> **TAX-SAVING IDEA**
> In the tax year ending 5 April 2003, you may have qualified for the old children's tax credit (see p. 202) which was given as a reduction in your tax bill but is now no longer available. If so, you will see a jump in your tax bill for the year ending 5 April 2004 compared with the previous year. Make sure you claim the new CTC – although paid in a different way, the amount you get should roughly replace the children's tax credit you have lost.

Tax credits if you have no children

You may be able to claim WTC if you are in work but on a low income or unable to work because of disability. You must either be: aged 25 or more and working at least 30 hours a week; 16 or more, working at least 16 hours and disabled; or aged 50 or more and have recently started work after a period claiming certain state benefits. You are unlikely to be eligible in the year ending 5 April 2004 if your income comes to more than about £11,000 a year (single) or £15,000 (couple).

Tax credits if you have children

You may be eligible for both the new credits or just the CTC. For the year ending 5 April 2004, you can get at least some CTC provided your household income does not exceed £58,175 (or £66,350 if you have a child under one).

To qualify for WTC, you must be working at least 16 hours a week if you have children or a disability, 30 hours a week otherwise. WTC is made up of eight elements – see the table. Your claim is based on as many of these elements as apply to you and you add on the relevant individual element of CTC for each child you look after. However, for every £1 by which your income (see below) exceeds the first threshold (£5,060 in the year ending 5 April 2004), the credits are reduced by 37p. WTC is reduced first with the childcare element being the last to go, then the CTC.

If you qualify only for CTC and no WTC, the first threshold at which you start to lose the individual elements of CTC is higher (£13,230 in the year ending 5 April 2004).

Every household with children also qualifies for the family element of CTC. This is not reduced at all until the household income reaches the second threshold (£50,000 in the year ending 5 April 2004). You then lose £1 of credit for every £15 of income over the threshold.

Rate of tax credits (for the tax year ending 5 April 2004)

Element	*Who qualifies*(1)	*Amount*
Working Tax Credit (WTC)		
Basic	Everyone eligible for WTC	£1,525
Lone parent	Single, caring for a child	£1,500
Second adult	Most couples	£1,500
30-hour	Working at least 30 hours a week	£620
Disability	Satisfy range of disability conditions	£2,040
Severe disability	Eligible for highest rate of disability benefit	£865
50-plus	Aged 50 or more and returning to work. Higher rate applies if work at least 30 hours a week	£1,045 or £1,565
Childcare	Incurring eligible childcare costs	70% of eligible costs(2)
Child Tax Credit (CTC)		
Individual element	For each child in your care	£1,445(3)
Family element – child under one	First year following new birth	£1,090
Family element	Families without a newborn child	£545

(1) The rules are complicated and just a brief indication is given here.

(2) Eligible costs are up to £135 a week for one child and £200 a week for two or more.

(3) Increased to £3,600 or £4,465 for a disabled child depending on severity of disability.

EXAMPLE

Julie Brown is a single parent, working full-time and earning £13,000 a year. She has two children both at primary school and spends £84 a week (£4,368 a year) on childcare. She qualifies for both WTC and CTC as follows:

Income in excess of first threshold	
(£13,000 – £5,060)	£7,940
Taper (37p for each £1 of excess)	£2,937
WTC	
Basic element	£1,525
Lone parent element	£1,500
30-hour element	£620
Childcare element (70% × £4,368)	£3,058
WTC before taper	£6,703
WTC after deducting taper (£2,937)	£3,766
CTC	
Individual elements (2 x £1,445)	£2,890
Family element	£545
Total CTC	£3,435
Total credits after taper	£7,201

Julie receives £7,201 in tax credits taking her income to £20,201 a year.

How to claim tax credits

You make a single claim for both credits. Claim either using the online form at www.inlandrevenue.gov.uk/taxcredits or the paper-based claim pack available from tel: 0800 500 222. Claims can be backdated no more than three months so, to get credits for a full tax year, you need to submit your claim by 6 July during the tax year.

Income on which your claim is based

Tax credits for a year are based on your income for that same year. However, the tax credit system works in a similar way to the self assessment tax collection system: so payments for the current year are based initially on income for an earlier year but an adjustment is made once your current year's income figure is known.

For the year ending 5 April 2004, your tax credits are initially based on income for the year ended 5 April 2002. But, in future years, credits in one year will initially be based on income for the immediately preceding year. This creates a problem if you are self-employed as your accounts may not have

TAX-SAVING IDEAS

If your income for the initial basis year was over the limit for tax credits but you do not know what your income for the year ending 5 April 2004 will be and so do not know whether you will be eligible for credits this year, you should nevertheless put in a claim by 6 July 2003. Otherwise, if you do turn out to be eligible, it will be too late to backdate your claim to the start of the tax year. This might apply if, for example, you are self-employed and your income varies from year-to-year, or you are an employee and think you might be made redundant.

Any payment that qualifies for tax relief can be super tax-efficient if it also reduces your income and so increases the amount of CTC or WTC you can claim. This applies to, for example, pension contributions, Gift Aid donations, and purchases through your business if you are self-employed. See Example.

been drawn up in time for the 6 July deadline for claiming. In this case, you will have to submit estimated income figures and ask the Inland Revenue to adjust your claim once the actual figures are available.

The rules are complex but broadly income includes earnings from employment and self-employment, pensions, taxable state benefits, rents (but not under the rent-a-room scheme), taxable investment income, and income treated as yours such as income received by a settlor-interested trust. It does not include maintenance from an ex-spouse or former partner. And you can deduct the gross amounts paid into pension arrangements or donated under Gift Aid. (Carry back rules are ignored for this purpose, so amounts are deducted in the year they are actually paid.)

EXAMPLE

Douglas and Angela Adams have two children and a household income of £55,000. They qualify for the family element of CTC. The basic amount is £545 in the year ending 5 April 2004, but the couple lose £1 of credit for every £15 by which their income exceeds £50,000. The credit is reduced by (£55,000 – £50,000) ÷ 15 = £333 to £212.

However, Douglas pays £5,000 into his personal pension. He is a higher-rate taxpayer, so in total he gets 40% × £5,000 = £2,000 tax relief on the payment. The pension contribution is also deducted from the household income for the purpose of CTC. This reduces Douglas' and Audrey's income to £50,000 and increases their CTC to £545. Effectively, Doug has had tax relief of (£2,000 + £333) ÷ £5000 = 46.7 per cent on the contribution.

YOU AND YOUR TAX INSPECTOR

CHAPTER 3

The Inland Revenue has been working hard in recent years to develop a more user-friendly relationship with you, the 'customer'. You normally have one office to send out your tax return, process it when you send it back and issue your PAYE code. A network of high-street Taxpayer Enquiry Centres provides a face-to-face service where taxpayers can talk to tax staff who can call up their records on computer screens and deal with queries. The Revenue has also set up a range of telephone helplines dealing with particular areas of tax – for example, a helpline for new and small employers to help them with PAYE and related matters.

Along with other government departments, the Inland Revenue is trying to become an increasingly electronic business. It aims to receive half of all self assessment tax returns by Internet by 2005. After a slow start and some unfortunate breakdowns in the service, e-tax seems finally to be catching on. By the 31 January 2003 deadline, nearly 325,000 tax returns had been filed by Internet. That's four times as many as in the previous year, though it's still a far cry from the 4.5 million the Revenue hopes will be e-filing by 2005. However, some 4.4 million taxpayers have registered with the Internet service and are perhaps getting ready to dip a toe in the electronic water. Filing by Internet is unlikely to save you much time, but it does have some plus points. The service automatically calculates your tax bill for you, picks up common errors, such as leaving mandatory boxes empty or forgetting to add the date, delivery is faster and more secure than using the post and tax repayments are faster. There are several ways to sign up:

- follow the instructions supplied, if you have received a 'Getting started' letter from the Inland Revenue
- register through *www.inlandrevenue.gov.uk* or *www.gateway.gov.uk*. You will be sent an ID and password by post or you can use a digital certificate
- ask a tax adviser or accountant to register to file your tax return for you.

You can complete your tax return using the Inland Revenue's free service, SA Online. You must complete it while online but you do not have to complete it all in one go – you can save what you have done so far and come back to it later. When you've completed the whole form, you have the option to send it over the Internet and/or to save it and print off a paper version. The form covers only the ten-page basic return, the Employment supplementary pages, the Self Employment and Partnership supplements, and the Land and Property pages.

If you need other supplements, you can still send in your tax return electronically, but you'll need to buy alternative software. The Inland Revenue website lists commercial software that has passed the test of working with Inland Revenue procedures. Some of the products available include the additional supplementary pages that you might need.

You can also pay tax electronically. You'll either need to arrange a direct payment from your bank account or use a debit card. The Inland Revenue does not accept credit card payments.

For more information, contact the Inland Revenue, telephone 0845 60 55 999 or website www.inlandrevenue.gov.uk/sa.

YOUR OBLIGATIONS

New source of income or capital

If you don't receive a tax return, you must notify your tax inspector of any income or capital gains, which have not been previously declared, within six months from the end of the tax year in which you make the income or gain. This applies even if you don't yet know the amount of the income or gain.

There are certain circumstances in which you don't have to notify your tax office. This applies, for example, if all the income comes under the PAYE system or if the income is dividends from shares which is paid with tax deducted at 10 per cent and you pay tax at no more than the basic rate.

Note that, quite apart from the rules above, if you become newly self-employed, you must normally register with the Inland Revenue within three months of the end of the month you start up or face a £100 fine (see p. 252).

Records

You are required to keep records, such as original copies of dividend vouchers, bank statements, certificates of interest received and any certificates showing foreign tax deductions, which you need to complete your tax return. If you don't have the original certificates, you can complete your tax return using information that can be verified by an external source. You don't have to send in your vouchers and other documents in order to get a tax refund. You must keep the originals in case of Inland Revenue enquiry, but if they are lost you will not be penalised providing you can produce other evidence for the information. You also need to keep a copy of the working papers that you used to work out your calculations.

> **EXAMPLE**
>
> Roger Rose (a basic-rate taxpayer) is an employee paying tax under the PAYE system. He buys some shares in a UK company in October 2002 and receives a dividend of £84 some two months later. He also decides to do some freelance consulting on the side, as well as his job. He doesn't know how much income that will bring in, since part of his payment will be in the form of commission.
>
> As a basic-rate taxpayer, Roger has no further tax to pay on the dividend. So, if this had been his only extra income in the tax year ending 5 April 2003, he would not have needed to take any action. But he also has the freelance income on which tax will be due. Even though he does not yet know how much the income will be, he must tell his tax office about it by 5 October 2003 (that is within six months of the end of the tax year). His tax office will then send him a tax return to complete.

If you don't run your own business or have letting income, the period to keep records is one year from the date by which you must send back the tax return (31 January). However, this period is extended if there should be an enquiry into your affairs. Records must be kept until the enquiry is complete.

The period to keep records is also extended if you send in your return late or need to correct it after you have sent it in. The documents need to be kept until one year after the end of the quarter in which you amended the return or sent it in late. Quarters end on 31 January, 30 April, 31 July and 31 October.

> **TAX-SAVING IDEA**
>
> Make sure you keep all your records and your working papers. If you don't, you may end up paying more tax than you should because you can't provide the evidence to back up your tax return. And don't forget you can be fined for not keeping your records.

If you run your own business or receive any income from letting, you need to keep records for five years from the date by which you should send in your tax return (31 January). The records should include what you receive and spend in your business, for example, sales and purchase invoices.

The failure to keep records can result in a swingeing penalty (see p. 25).

THE TAX RETURN

Your tax return asks you for details of your income, deductions and allowances for the tax year just ended, that is the year ending on 5 April 2003. There is one basic tax return of ten pages sent to everyone who should receive a tax return. But there are also a lot of supplementary pages for particular types of income – self-employment, trusts, employment, share schemes, partnerships, land and property, foreign, capital gains and non-residence. You may not receive any of these or, in an extreme case, you might receive nine different supplements to the basic return. For more details about these supplements see p. 149.

In the past, it was acceptable to use such phrases as 'as returned' or 'as agreed' for income or the value of benefits. But you are now required to fill in the correct figure – otherwise you will not be able to work out how much income tax or capital gains tax you owe. This means you must get hold of the documents you need, including forms P60 (your income from your job and the tax you have paid on it), P45 part 1A (your income and tax to date when you leave your job), P11D or P9D (your fringe benefits and expenses for the year), P2 (your notice of coding). Your employer has the responsibility to supply you with these forms (but not P2) by certain dates (see p. 28).

> **EXAMPLE**
>
> Ashley Hickie is a self-employed journalist. He also has some savings, such as unit trusts and a building society account. He completes his tax return for the year ended 5 April 2003, including carrying out the calculation of his own tax bill, and returns it by 31 January 2004. Ashley must keep all the records on which his tax return is based, including personal records as well as those relating to his business, until 31 January 2009.

Deadlines for your tax return

There are two important dates to bear in mind. If you want to ask the Inland Revenue to work out your tax bill on your behalf your tax return must be sent in by 30 September. Unless you are using a tax adviser, we recommend that you do this. Unless you file by Internet, this is also the date by which you must submit your return even if you do your own tax calculation if you owe tax of less than £2,000 and want it deducted through the PAYE system, rather than your paying it as a single lump sum. But, if you e-file, the deadline is end-December.

There is a different date set for returning your tax return if you or your tax adviser choose to calculate what you owe in income tax. This is 31 January.

If you have missed the 30 September deadline and decide that after all you want the Revenue to calculate the tax due, you can still ask for this to happen. But your tax inspector won't guarantee to do this by the 31 January slot, so you may have to estimate the tax due or end up paying a penalty if any is paid late.

Where a tax return has been issued after 31 October, you are given three months to complete it and send it back to your tax office. If the return is issued after 31 July and you want your tax inspector to calculate the tax due, it must be returned within two months.

> **TAX-SAVING IDEA**
>
> If you are an employee paying tax under the PAYE system and you have some other income, for example from investments, on which you will need to pay tax, you should send in your tax return with your tax calculation by 30 September or end-December if you file by Internet. If you do this, and the amount of tax due is less than £2,000, you will not have to pay tax on this extra income by 31 January. Instead, it will be included in your PAYE code for the following tax year and you will pay tax on it with your monthly salary, thus spreading out and delaying the payment of your tax bill.

If you don't send in your tax return

Failing to send back your completed tax return means you can be charged a penalty (see p. 25) and allows the Inland Revenue to issue what's called a determination. Your tax inspector produces an estimate, to the best of his or her belief and using the best information available, of how much tax you should pay. The tax shown on this determination is payable; you cannot appeal against it or postpone it. The only way you can overturn this estimate is to complete your tax return and tax calculation. You must do this within five years of the date by which you should have sent it in, or, if it is later, within a year of the determination by your tax inspector.

Your tax inspector cannot normally make a determination if five years have passed since the date by which you should have sent in your tax return. But there will be penalties and interest to pay (see p. 22). If there is reason to believe you have been fraudulent or negligent, the inspector can go back 20 years.

Short tax returns

The Inland Revenue is reviewing the self assessment system to see whether so many people need to be within the system and whether there is scope for issuing shorter tax returns to at least some taxpayers. Under a pilot scheme, 50,000 taxpayers have received a short, four-page tax return in April 2003 instead of the usual ten-page return and supplements. The short return is aimed at people with simple tax affairs and does not include any facility to work out the tax bill, so recipients are being encouraged to file by 30 September 2003. They can also opt to fill in the form by phone. If the pilot goes well, the scheme could be rolled out nationally but probably not before April 2005.

TAX PAYMENTS

Self assessment is used to collect income tax, capital gains tax and, if you are in business, Class 4 National Insurance contributions (NICs). You, your adviser or your tax inspector works out the total amount due. The tax is usually paid in three instalments.

Interim and final payments

Self assessment requires two interim payments on account. The first is due on 31 January during the tax year; the second on 31 July following the tax year. Each payment is normally half the amount of your income tax and Class 4 NICs bill for the previous year less any tax paid through the PAYE system, dividend tax credits, and so on. There is no adjustment for changes in tax rates and allowances from one year to the next. However, if say you expect your income to be lower this year than last, you can ask for a reduction in the payments on account (see p. 344) – but, if you turn out to be wrong, you'll have to pay interest on the tax paid late.

The final balancing income tax payment or repayment will be made after completion of the tax return on 31 January following the end of the tax year. Any capital gains tax due will also be paid with this third instalment.

There are rules which mean that interim payments will not be required if they are small. Working on the basis of the tax due for the previous tax year, if the total tax payable, net of tax deducted at source (including PAYE), is less than £500 or if tax deducted at source (including PAYE) is more than 80 per cent of the total income tax plus Class 4 National Insurance due, then interim payments won't be required.

> **TAX-SAVING IDEA**
> Always check your Statement of Account (see next page) to see if you can claim a reduction in interim payments. But if in doubt, it is better to pay slightly more rather than ask for a reduction – you will be charged interest if you pay too little, whereas tax you have overpaid will earn interest. The rate of interest charged on underpaid tax is over twice as much as that added on overpaid tax.

Employees can put off paying a final

tax bill of less than £2,000 by asking for it to be included in next year's PAYE code. To achieve this, you have to send in your tax return by 30 September (or end-December if you e-file).

An effect of the self assessment payment system is that, if your income increases from one tax year to the next, you may face a hefty tax bill in the following January. This is because the jump in income produces a final payment to scoop up tax underpaid in the last tax year plus an increased payment on account for the current tax year – see Example. Make sure you set aside enough money to cover the tax bills.

EXAMPLE

Shalini Edwards is self-employed. Her profits are usually around £32,000 but, for the tax year ending 5 April 2003, they jumped to £40,000. During 2003, her tax bills were £4,484 in January and £3,796 in July. Of these, 2 × £3,796 = £7,592 were payments on account for the year ending 5 April 2003. But due to the profit increase, the total bill for the year is £10,348. Shalini must make a final payment on 31 January 2004 of £10,348 – £7,592 = £2,756. The increased total bill feeds through to a higher first payment on account for the year ending 5 April 2004 (½ × £10,348 = £5,174), also due on 31 January 2003. Her total tax bill for January 2004 is £7,930. This is nearly double the previous January's bill, even though her profits increased by only a quarter.

Statement of account

During January 2003, you may have received a statement of account showing what you should pay on 31 January 2003. In June 2003, you should receive a second statement showing the amount to be paid on 31 July. For how to check these statements and for how to appeal against them, see p. 342.

Interest and surcharges

Interest is payable on tax which is paid late. On the other hand, any tax you have overpaid also earns interest. Any interest charged or received will be shown on your statement of account. Interest is automatically charged on any tax left unpaid by 31 January or 31 July following a statement of account. However, if the statement of account was issued late, although you sent in your tax return on time, the interest will only start 30 days after the date on the statement. Interest is also charged on any tax left unpaid by 31 January following the end of the tax year – that is by 31 January 2004 for the tax year ending 5 April 2003 – unless your tax return was issued late. If the tax is still not paid by 28 February 2004, there is a surcharge of 5 per cent of the unpaid tax. A further 5 per cent surcharge of the amount of tax still unpaid after 31 July 2004 is imposed. Interest will be added to any unpaid surcharge, starting 30 days after the notice of the surcharge.

CHANGES TO YOUR TAX RETURN

Estimates, mistakes and corrections

Sometimes you may not know a figure with 100 per cent accuracy by the time it comes to fill in your tax return. What you have to do is to put in your best estimate and work out the tax due on that. Say on your tax return when you expect to have the final figure. You should supply this as soon as possible. If there is more tax to pay, you will have to pay interest (or will receive interest if a refund is due) but no surcharges or penalties unless you have been negligent or fraudulent.

It's also possible that you might make a mistake when you complete the return. You have 12 months from the filing date within which you can amend your return with a minimum of fuss. And if, within nine months of the date you sent in the return, the Inland Revenue picks up any obvious errors, it too can amend the return. You also have five years from the date the tax return had to be in by – for example 31 January 2009 in the case of the tax return for the year ending 5 April 2003 – to correct any mistakes and claim back any tax overpaid as a result. You should notify your tax office in writing.

Any tax due as a result of a revised self-assessment should be paid either by the normal payment date or 30 days after the making of the self-assessment (but this does not put off the date from which interest is charged).

Enquiries

Your tax inspector has the right to enquire into your tax return. A small proportion of all returns is selected at random for enquiry. But most are chosen because the inspector thinks there may be something wrong. Your tax inspector must tell you if the enquiry is into your whole return or just some aspect of it (such as a particular expense you have claimed or your calculation of capital allowances).

Your tax inspector must give you written notice of an enquiry. If you sent in your tax return on time, the notice must be made by 31 January the following year. If you sent in your return late, the notice of an enquiry can be issued up to a year after the end of the quarter in which you sent in your return (quarter ends are 31 January, 30 April, 31 July and 31 October). With an amended tax return, the notice can be issued up to a year after the end of the quarter in which you amended it.

Your tax inspector has the right to demand that you produce certain documents. When you receive a notice of an enquiry, you may also receive a notice to produce these within 30 days. You can produce copies, but your tax inspector may insist on seeing the originals. You can appeal within 30 days against this notice to produce documents.

You can also appeal to the general commissioners (see p. 26) if you consider that an enquiry should not have been undertaken or is being continued unnecessarily. If it agrees, the general commissioners can issue a notice to the Inland Revenue requiring it to close the enquiry.

When the subject of an enquiry is complete, your tax inspector will issue you with a formal notice telling you so, how much tax you are considered to owe (if any) and requiring you to amend your self-assessment. You can appeal against it, if you don't agree. For more information about enquiry procedures and your rights, see Inland Revenue booklet IR160 *Inland Revenue enquiries under self assessment* or www.inlandrevenue.gov.uk/compliance.

What your tax inspector can do if an enquiry has been completed
Although a second enquiry into the same return cannot take place, the law allows a discovery assessment if you have been acting fraudulently or negligently and in some other limited circumstances.

A discovery means that your tax inspector has discovered that some income or gain on which you should have paid tax has not been included in your self-assessment, or the assessment is too low, or the amount of relief given is too much. A discovery assessment would be to collect the tax due. You can appeal against a discovery assessment (see p. 26).

A discovery assessment cannot be made if the correct information was available to the Inland Revenue and it should have been possible to work out the correct tax. If the tax lost results from an error in the taxpayer's return but the return was made in accordance with prevailing practice at the time, no discovery assessment can be made.

PENALTIES, APPEALS AND COMPLAINTS

Penalties

The self assessment system is underpinned by a range of penalties, the most important of which are summarised in the table. In addition, interest is added to overdue tax and also to penalties that remain unpaid. The tax inspector has discretion to reduce penalties based on the amount of tax due based, for example, on the gravity of your case and the extent of your co-operation.

Action/omission triggering penalty	*Penalty*	*Deadline for tax year ending 5 April 2003*
Notifying tax office of liability to pay tax		
Failure to tell your tax office (if you have had no tax return) within six months of the end of the tax year about income or gains on which tax is due	Equal to the amount of tax due and unpaid by 31 January following end of tax year	5 October 2003
Tax return		
1. Failure to send in tax return by the due date	£100 or, if less, penalty equal to amount of tax due	31 January 2004
2. Tax return still not sent in six months after due date	Further £100 or, if less, penalty equal to amount of tax due	31 July 2004
3. Tax return still not sent in one year after due date	Equal to amount of tax due	31 January 2005
4. Instead of 2 and 3 above, for continued failure to submit return	Up to £60 a day	
5. Fraudulently or negligently sending incorrect return	Equal to amount of tax due on income or gains undeclared	
Records		
1. Failure to keep records for a tax or accounting year and to preserve them for required period	£3,000	
2. Failure to produce documents on request	£50	
3. Continuing failure to produce documents	Up to £30 a day or, with permission of commissioners, up to £150 a day	
Paying tax		
1. Final payment unpaid more than 28 days after the due date	Equal to 5% of the unpaid tax	28 February 2004
2. Final payment unpaid more than six months after due date	Further 5% of unpaid tax	31 July 2004

From 1 January 2001, a new criminal offence was introduced of being *'knowingly concerned in the fraudulent evasion of income tax'*. This is aimed at catching people who deliberately dodge tax, for example, employers and employees colluding to pay less through PAYE, or householders and tradesmen

deliberately negotiating a cash price so they benefit from tax saved. The maximum penalty for serious cases is an unlimited fine and/or seven years in prison.

Appeals and complaints

You can appeal against an assessment which is not a self-assessment, an amendment to your self-assessment by the Inland Revenue after an enquiry, an amendment of a partnership statement where a loss of tax is discovered, a disallowance in whole or in part of a claim or election included in a tax return, penalty determinations, or a formal notice requesting documents etc.

You have to give written notice of appeal within 30 days after the issue of the notice of assessment, amendment or disallowance. But you may not appeal against an amendment as a result of an enquiry until you've had notice that the enquiry is complete, although certain questions may be referred for decision to the Special Commissioners or the courts while an enquiry is in process.

If you disagree about the amount of the tax bill, you should first of all exhaust the avenues within the Inland Revenue. Appeal to your tax inspector – he or she may not have made the original decision. However, if it becomes clear that the two of you are not going to agree, there remains the option of appealing to the commissioners – and if that doesn't work you could appeal to the High Court, then to the Appeal Court and ultimately to the House of Lords.

There are two types of commissioners. The general commissioners are not tax experts, but often local people acting in the same way as magistrates. There will be a clerk with expert knowledge on hand to advise them. The second group are known as special commissioners. These are part of the Civil Service and tax experts in their own right.

If you are dissatisfied with the way the Inland Revenue handles your tax affairs, you should first complain to your tax inspector. If you get no satisfaction, you should direct your complaints to the regional controller responsible for your tax office (ask the tax office for the name and address). If this doesn't work, you should channel your next communication to the independent Revenue Adjudicator. The Adjudicator's remit covers matters such as excessive

> **TAX-SAVING IDEA**
>
> You can appeal against the £100 penalty for missing the deadline for sending in your tax return. A reasonable excuse would be, for example, an unexpected postal strike, serious illness, the death of a close relative, or loss of records due to fire, flood or theft. Pressure of work, a failure by your tax adviser or lack of information would not be regarded as a reasonable excuse.

delay, errors, discourtesy or the way your tax inspector has exercised his or her discretion.

THE PAYE SYSTEM

Your employer is an unpaid tax collector for the Inland Revenue using the PAYE system – Pay As You Earn. Every time employees are paid, income tax and National Insurance contributions (NICs) are deducted from the earnings and sent in a batch to the collector of taxes. Your employer is also responsible for paying certain tax credits (see p. 12) along with your pay packet and collecting student loan repayments on behalf of the government (see p. 233).

Your employer needs various bits of information to operate the PAYE system. The aim is that at the end of the tax year, each employee will have had the correct amount of tax deducted, although this does not always happen. Underpayments of tax might be collected in the following year through the PAYE system or in a tax bill at the end of the year.

The Inland Revenue will tell your employer what your PAYE code is and will also supply tax tables so that your employer can deduct the right amount of tax. The PAYE system is flexible and can be adjusted during the tax year. If your circumstances change, you should tell your tax inspector who should issue a new PAYE code. Your monthly after-tax earnings should change once the new code has been received by your employer. See Chapter 25 for more information about PAYE and your tax code.

Your employer must give you certain forms by required dates so that you can use them to fill in your tax return. You should receive your P60 for the tax year ending 5 April 2003 by 31 May 2003. Form P9D or Form P11D should be received by 6 July 2003. Chase your employer if you don't receive them.

CLAIMING A TAX REFUND

If you have paid too much tax through PAYE because you have stopped doing a job part way through the tax year, a refund will automatically be arranged by your new employer or the Job Centre/other office handling your benefit claim. But, if you are neither going to a new job nor getting benefit, claim a tax rebate using form P50.

In other cases where you have paid too much tax – for example, because tax has been deducted from your savings income but you are a non-taxpayer –

claim a refund using form R40. Do not send any documents, such as certificates of tax deducted, with the form but keep them safe in case your tax inspector asks to see them. The Inland Revenue aims normally to process your claim within 28 days. Refunds are based on the information you provide, but the Inland Revenue can open an enquiry either before or after paying the refund. You do not have to wait until the end of the tax year to make a claim but repayments of less than £50 are not usually made mid-year.

Either ask your tax office for the relevant claim form or download it from www.inlandrevenue.gov.uk.

DEADLINES

Within 60 days

- Tell your tax office if you disagree with the statement of taxable social security benefits you receive from the benefit office

On or before 31 May 2003

- Form P60 should have been given to all employees by employer

On or before 4 June 2003

- Choose to pay tax in instalments on exercise of option in the tax year ending 5 April 2003 to acquire shares through an approved scheme

On or before 6 July 2003

- Form P9D (or Form P11D) should have been given to employees receiving fringe benefits by employer, plus details of other benefits provided by someone else
- Send in your tax credit claim form to get credits for the full tax year

On or before 31 July 2003

- Second interim payment of tax due for tax year ending 5 April 2003

On or before 30 September 2003

- Send in tax return if you want Inland Revenue to work out tax due
- Employees who owe less than £2,000 tax should send in their tax return so that tax will be collected through the PAYE system (unless they e-file)

On or before 5 October 2003

- Tell your tax inspector about any new source of income or capital gain for year ending 5 April 2003

On or before 30 December 2003

- Employees who owe less than £2,000 should e-file their tax return, so that the tax will be collected through the PAYE system

On or before 31 January 2004

- Claim to reduce payments on account for the tax year ending 5 April 2004 (see p. 344)
- Tell your tax inspector if you have reduced your payments on account by too little
- Send in your tax return, along with calculation of any tax due, plus payment for any unpaid tax for the year ending 5 April 2003
- Make first interim payment on account of tax due for tax year ending 5 April 2004 (statement received from Inland Revenue based on previous year's tax bill or your own self-assessment calculation)
- Choose to carry back retirement annuity contract payments made in the tax year ending 5 April 2003 to the tax year ending 5 April 2002
- Choose to carry back payments to personal pensions (including stakeholder schemes) made in the period 6 April 2003 to 31 January 2004 to the tax year ending 5 April 2003 (election must be made at the same time as the payment)
- Choose to carry back Gift Aid donations made in year ending 5 April 2004 to previous year (unless you have already sent in your tax return)
- Claim for allowances and deductions for tax year ending 5 April 1998

On or before 6 July 2004

- Provide details of actual income for the year ending 5 April 2004 in order to finalise tax credit claim for that year
- Send in claim to get tax credits for the full year ending 5 April 2005

On or before 31 January 2005

- Set losses made in a new business for the tax year ending 5 April 2003 against other income for the previous three tax years
- Set business losses made in the tax year ending 5 April 2003 against other income

On or before 31 January 2009

- Claim for allowances and deductions left out of tax return by mistake for the tax year ending 5 April 2003
- Set business losses made in the tax year ending 5 April 2003 against future profits of the same business

On or before 5 April 2009

- Claim unused relief for retirement annuity contracts for tax year ending 5 April 2003.

TAX CHANGES FOR THE TAX YEAR ENDING 5 APRIL 2004

CHAPTER 4

In 2003, the Budget was for the second year running held in April after the start of the new tax year. There were relatively few tax changes with the main focus on increasing employment and work skills, extra benefits for pensioners, and encouraging small business creation especially in deprived regions. Many of the tax changes are sticks to close fairly esoteric tax loopholes, but there are a few small carrots too, particularly for employees.

The most innovative Budget measure is the introduction of child trust funds. These have been trailed through consultation and are underpinned by the idea that equality cannot be fostered simply through income measures. To grasp opportunities, people need assets as well. The amount the government plans to pay into each child's fund at birth is modest but is intended to prompt parents and others to add to the fund. In this way, the child trust fund may be the seed corn to grow a nationwide savings habit.

These and other tax changes for the year ending 5 April 2004 are summarised below.

Income tax
For the year ending 5 April 2004, tax rates are unchanged. Thresholds are increased in line with inflation. The starting rate becomes £1,960 (was £1,920) and higher rate tax starts at £30,500 (was £29,900).

Allowances
Allowances for the year ending 5 April 2004 were announced in November 2002. The under-65s personal allowance is frozen at £4,615, but the age-related personal allowances rise by more than inflation to £6,610 for the 65-74 age group (was £6,100) and £6,720 for people aged 75 (was £6,370).

Tax credits
From 6 April 2003, new tax credits start (see p. 12).

Reliefs
The maximum amount of maintenance payments that qualify for tax relief increases in line with inflation to £2,150 (from £2,110) for the year ending 5 April 2004. To qualify, one or both parties to the marriage must have been born before 6 April 1935.

As previously announced, from the tax return for the year ending 5 April 2004 onwards, through your tax return, you will be able to direct that part or all of any tax rebate due is paid by the Inland Revenue to a charity of your choice. You will also be able to specify whether Gift Aid should apply.

Savings and investments
The earnings cap which limits benefits from occupational pension schemes and payments to most types of pension arrangement is raised in line with inflation to £99,000 (from £97,200). The government has clarified that contributions to which the cap applies include any made by your employer.

Every child born from September 2002 onwards is to have a child trust fund (CTF). Under this new scheme which aims to promote a savings culture, the government will pay £250 into an account for the child at birth (£500 if the family qualifies for full child tax credit) and is considering whether it might add further sums when the child is of school age. Parents, relatives and friends will be able to add to the account up to a maximum £1,000 a year. The child will be unable to touch the fund until age 18 but can then use the money for any purpose or roll it over into other savings products. Details of the accounts, tax treatment, and so on are to be published in summer 2003. It is expected the accounts will start in 2005 with payments backdated to birth.

A new consultation on improving small business' access to finance will look at the scope for enhancing the enterprise investment scheme and venture capital trusts.

Changes to the taxation of life insurance aim to stop tax avoidance. For example, you used to be able to defer any tax on a maturing policy if you exercised an option to reinvest the proceeds in a new policy with the same company. You could then make 5 per cent a year tax-deferred withdrawals based on the reinvested sum instead of just the amount invested in the original policy. To counter this, tax is now charged on the maturing policy.

Inheritance tax
The threshold at which tax starts to be paid is increased in line with inflation to £255,000 for the tax year ending 5 April 2004 (from £250,000).

Capital gains tax

The amount of net capital gains which an individual can make without paying capital gains tax is increased to £7,900 for the tax year ending 5 April 2004 (was £7,700). Most trusts are exempt on the first £3,950 of gains.

From 6 April 2004, the definition of business assets for the purpose of taper relief will be extended to assets you own which are used in someone else's business. (At present, they must either be used in your own trade or employment or by a company to which you are connected.) This means you will be able to claim the higher rates of business taper relief on, for example, property you let out to a sole trader.

The reporting requirements for CGT are changed for self assessment returns for the tax year ending 5 April 2004 onwards. You will not need to fill in the Capital gains supplementary pages if your chargeable gains after deducting taper relief come to no more than the annual tax-free allowance, unless either the proceeds from your disposals of all assets (except those which are tax-free) exceed four times the annual allowance, or you are claiming allowable losses.

Employees

The IR35 legislation (see p. 211) is extended from 9 April 2003 to people whose clients are individuals rather than businesses. This will catch, for example, domestic workers such as nannies and butlers. The IR35 rules apply if you work for clients through your own personal service company. They ensure you pay both income tax and National Insurance on your fees even if you arrange to draw them as dividends from your company.

The (currently very light) tax treatment of company vans available for private use is being reviewed. Changes are likely to encourage the use of smaller, more fuel-efficient models (for example, by linking taxable value to CO2 emissions).

Company cars are already taxed on the basis of their CO2 emissions. The lowest standard taxable value of 15 per cent is available in the year ending 5 April 2004 for cars which emit no more than 155g/km. This falls to 145g/km in the following year and 140g/km in the tax year ending 5 April 2006.

From 6 April 2003 onwards, payments up to £2 a week from your employer to cover additional household costs if you work from home are tax-free and there is no need to keep records. Higher amounts can also be tax-free, but your employer must then have evidence to show the extra costs that have been incurred.

The limits on several minor tax-free fringe benefits are being raised: long service awards – you may receive up to £50 for each year (was £20); annual parties – the limit is raised to £150 per head per year (was £75); small non-cash gifts from someone other than your employer may be up to £250 a year (was £150); and breakfast if you take part in a cycle-to-work day, which was limited to six times a year, can now be provided on an unlimited number of occasions.

Employee share schemes
Changes to the rules for employee share schemes include:

- **Approved discretionary share options** From 9 April 2003, the requirement that an option under a company share option plan should not be exercised within three years of a previous exercise is abolished (see p. 240)
- **Approved share incentive plans** To simplify the administration involved, the three-year minimum period of time for which you must leave dividend shares in the plan (see p. 245) is to be abolished. Instead you must hold them for the period that applies to the shares which gave rise to the dividends
- **Approved share incentive plans** Purchases of partnership shares need no longer be made through a monthly (or equivalent) deduction from salary. Instead purchases up to the yearly limit (which is unchanged) can be made at any time.

Businesses
The 100 per cent first year allowance for spending on information and communications technology (computers, Internet, and so on) is extended for a further year until 31 March 2004.

100 per cent first year allowances for environmentally friendly spending have been extended to some new technology groups, including those that reduce water use or improve water quality (for example, metering equipment, leakage detectors and efficient toilets and taps). For more information, see www.eca.gov.uk or call the Environment and Energy Helpline 0800 585 794.

In summer 2003, the European Union is due to announce new, higher thresholds for defining small and medium-sized enterprises (SMEs). The Chancellor has said these will be adopted as soon as possible into UK legislation meaning that more small businesses will qualify for some of the higher first-year capital allowances available.

The VAT registration limit increases to £56,000 from 10 April 2003 (previously £55,000).

Several VAT anti-avoidance measures are being introduced. They include making all the suppliers in a chain jointly and severally liable for payment of VAT. This means if a supplier to your business failed to hand over the VAT he charged you, Customs & Excise could demand that you pay it instead.

A new tax relief is introduced for people who foster children. From 6 April 2003, receipts up to £10,000 a year per residence plus up to £200 (under 11s) or £250 (age 11 and over) per week per child is tax-free. Where income from fostering exceeds this limit, you can opt simply to be taxed on the excess instead of working out your taxable profits in the normal way.

National Insurance

The earnings limit (primary threshold) below which no employee (or employer) pays Class 1 National Insurance contributions remains at £4,615 (£89 a week) for the year ending 5 April 2004. The upper earnings limit increases in line with inflation to £30,940 (£595 a week). Class 1 rates rise by 1 per cent from 6 April 2003 to 11 per cent on earnings between the primary threshold and upper earnings limit. In addition, you will pay 1 per cent on earnings above the upper earnings limit.

In the year ending 5 April 2004, Class 2 contributions paid by the self-employed are unchanged at £2 a week. The earnings below which payment is optional rises to £4,095. The lower profit limit for Class 4 contributions remains at £4,615 and the upper limit increases to £30,940. The Class 4 rate increases to 8 per cent on profits between the lower and upper profit limits (was 7 per cent). A new rate of 1 per cent applies to profits above the upper limit.

Self assessment

The Inland Revenue is to start a new crackdown on anti-avoidance. Areas it will focus on include non-payment of taxes through failure to file tax returns and failing to declare income from offshore savings accounts.

Other

The government is still consulting on changes to the rules on residence and domicile and has published a background paper to inform the debate but no firm proposals.

A review will look at ways of increasing the use of long-term fixed rate mortgages for house purchase. The dominance of variable rate mortgages in the UK is thought to contribute to economic instability.

A consultation will consider specific measures to improve households' energy efficiency.

ONE HUNDRED WAYS TO SAVE TAX

CHAPTER 5

Here are 100 tips to cut your tax bill. None of them requires you to turn your life upside down in search of tax savings.

All taxpayers

- Keep careful records – apart from the legal requirement, it could help you pay less tax. Note down all the expenses you could claim: if you are an employee (see p. 228); if you are self-employed (see p. 266); if you let out property (see p. 286).

- Don't be late sending in your tax return. The 2003 tax return must be sent back by 30 September 2003 if you want the Inland Revenue to work out your bill (p. 19) and by 31 January 2004 if you want to avoid an automatic £100 penalty (see p. 25).

- Always check your tax forms. As soon as you receive a Tax Calculation or PAYE Coding Notice make sure your tax inspector has got the sums right (see Chapter 25).

- If you have provided all the required information but the Inland Revenue makes a mistake, you cannot be charged penalties or interest on any tax paid late as a result.

- If you are asked to make payments on account, check that you're not paying more than you need to. The figures will be based on last year's tax bill. If you expect your income to be lower this year or your allowances and reliefs to be higher, you can make reduced payments (see p. 344).

- Investigate the past. It may not be too late to claim an allowance or deduction you have forgotten about. Some of the more important deadlines for claims are given on pp. 28–29.

- If you want to give money to charity, think about payroll-giving schemes and Gift Aid – you'll get tax relief on the gifts, large or small, regular or one-off. There are more details on pp. 216 and 195.

- Higher rate relief on Gift Aid donations made during the year ending 5 April 2004 onwards can be carried back to the previous tax year. This is worth doing, if you were a higher rate taxpayer last year but not this, or if it would increase the amount of age allowance or children's tax credit you can claim for last year.

- Think about giving quoted shares to charity. You will get income tax relief at your highest rate of tax and there's no capital gains tax on the gift.

- From 6 April 2002, you can claim income tax relief on gifts of land or buildings to charity. There's no capital gains tax either on these gifts.

- From 6 April 2002, many of the tax reliefs on donations to charity are also available on donations to community amateur sports associations.

Married

- If you are married, consider reorganising your investments so your investment income is paid to the partner who pays least tax on it.

- If a husband's income is too low to use all the married couple's allowance, even the age-related part can be transferred to the wife (see p. 50).

- If your income is too low to use all your allowances, blind person's allowance can be transferred to your husband or wife (see p. 51).

- You can pay into a personal pension or stakeholder scheme for your husband or wife even if they have no earnings. You get basic rate tax relief on the contributions.

Parents

- If your tax bill has gone up because of the abolition of children's tax credit, bear in mind you may be able to claim the new child tax credit instead (see p. 12). Households with children and income up to £58,175 (£66,350 for the year a new child is born) are eligible for the new credit.

- If you are self-employed and your income varies from year-to-year, or you are an employee and might be made redundant, put in a claim for tax credits by the 6 July 2003 deadline (see p. 15) even if your income presently seems too high for you to qualify. Otherwise, if you do turn out to be eligible, it will be too late to backdate your claim to the start of the tax year.

- If you have a baby from September 2002 onwards, your child qualifies for a cash gift of at least £250 from the government under the new child trust fund scheme. Do nothing yet – the government is still working out the details but will backdate the awards once the scheme is up and running. (The birth will also entitle you to higher tax credits – see pp. 12 and 202.)

- Any payment that qualifies for tax relief can be super tax-efficient if it also reduces your income and so increases the amount of tax credits you can claim (see p. 15). This applies to, for example, pension contributions, Gift Aid donations, and purchases through your business if self-employed.

- Backdating pension contributions is ignored for the purpose of calculating child tax credit but not the old children's tax credit. Therefore a contribution paid in the year ending 5 April 2004 and carried back to the previous year could increase both a claim to children's tax credit last year and child tax credit this year. The same applies to backdated Gift Aid donations.

Employees

- If you are taxed mainly through PAYE but owe tax of less than £2,000 on other income (for example, from investments), send in your tax return by 30 September 2003 (or end-December if you e-file). The tax will then be deducted through PAYE from your earnings during the tax year ending 5 April 2005 instead of as a lump sum on 31 January 2004.

- There is a long list of fringe benefits which are tax-free whatever your level of earnings – try to take advantage of them in your negotiations with your boss. These perks are still free of tax: entertainment by your suppliers or customers at cultural or sporting events (within certain rules); air miles (which enable you to make cheap flights); and non-cash gifts costing up to £250 from a third party (see p. 89).

- From 6 April 2002, any mileage allowance you get for using your own transport on business is tax-free provided it comes to no more than the authorised mileage rate set by the Inland Revenue (see p. 92). Similarly, you can claim tax relief on eligible expenses up to the authorised mileage rate. If you're changing your car or motorbike soon, think about choosing an economical one whose running costs will not exceed the authorised rate.

- Fringe benefits which are not tax-free can still be a tax-efficient way of being paid. The taxable value put on them may be lower than the value to you. There is a rundown of how they are taxed in Chapter 9.

- Choosing a new company car? From April 2002, the tax is linked to its carbon dioxide emissions (see p. 97). Pick a low-polluting car to keep the tax bill down.

- If you are in a position to choose, you could save tax by opting for a van rather than a company car.

- Cycling to work? A bike or safety equipment provided by your employer is a tax-free benefit.

- Working parents should try to persuade their employers to provide child-care facilities, as this fringe benefit is tax-free. Your private childcare arrangements are not eligible for tax relief, but may enable you to increase your claim for tax credits (see p. 12).

- If you often work away from home or your normal workplace, you may be able to claim the costs of travel (see p. 229). Start keeping a note now – but don't include your costs of normal commuting.

- If you work from home, you might be able to claim relief for the costs of running your home-office and the cost of travel between home and work, but only if it is necessary for you to work from home – for example, there is no space at your employer's premises, and no other workplace (for example, a local library) is acceptable because of, say, the confidential nature of your work. Get your employer to confirm in writing that this is the case.

- From 6 April 2003, you can receive up to £104 a year tax free from your employer towards household costs if you work from home without the need to keep any records of your costs.

- If you can arrange your work so you count as self-employed rather than an employee, you will be able to claim a wider range of expenses (see p. 266). But remember there may be disadvantages in not having the protection of employment law. For more about the distinction between employees and the self-employed, see pp. 209 and 250.

- Persuade your employer to set up a share incentive plan. Your employer can give you up to £6,000 of shares a year tax-free so long as you keep them in the scheme for five years (p. 244).

- See if you can negotiate the introduction of a share option scheme (p. 237).

- Instead of a pay rise, see if your employer would agree to pay extra for you direct to an occupational pension scheme or personal pension. You get a tax-free benefit and your employer escapes National Insurance on this type of 'pay'.

- If you become unemployed and are not claiming social security benefits, ask your tax inspector for a rebate of tax paid when you were working.

Self-employed

- As a result of reductions in corporation tax from April 2002 and increases in National Insurance from April 2003, unless you would be caught by the IR35 rules (see p. 211), you are likely to pay less tax if you operate as a company rather than as a sole trader or partnership.

- If you switch from being an employee to self-employment (or vice versa) during the tax year, you may pay too much in Class 1,2 and 4 National Insurance contributions. Claim a refund or ask to defer some payments until the position becomes clear (see p. 279).

- You can still claim as an expense for your business something you use partly for business and partly in your private life, for example, using your home for work, sharing the car (p. 267).

- If your turnover is less than the VAT threshold (£56,000 for the year starting 10 April 2003), you can opt to use Inland Revenue authorised mileage rates as a basis for claiming car expenses. This saves some record-keeping and saves tax if your actual expenses would be less.

- You might qualify for a 100 per cent capital allowance in the year that you buy information technology and communications equipment. This concession, for four years up to 31 March 2004, covers things like computers, software and internet-enabled mobile telephones (p. 258).

- You may be able to claim a 100 per cent capital allowance in the year you buy new energy-saving or water-saving equipment for your business (see p. 259 and p. 33).

- If between 17 April 2002 and 31 March 2008, you buy a new, low-emission car (defined as producing no more than 120 g/km of carbon dioxide) for use in your business or by your employees, you can claim a 100 per cent first-year capital allowance.

- When you first start your business, claim capital allowances on any equipment you already own but take into the business, for example, a car, desk and so on (see p. 257).

- You do not have to claim all the capital allowances you are entitled to. It may save you more tax to claim less and carry forward a higher value to the next year when your profits may be higher or your personal allowances lower (p. 259).

- If you are married and run your own business, consider employing your spouse if he or she does not work. It could save money if your spouse's tax rate would be lower than yours.

- If you employ someone, there is no income tax or National Insurance on their earnings up to the primary threshold (£89 a week in the year ending 5 April 2004). Provided they earn at least the lower earnings limit (£77 a week in the year ending 5 April 2004), they will build up state pension.

- If you make a tax loss in your business, there are several ways this can be used to reduce tax on other income or gains (see p. 275).

- From April 2003, businesses with a VAT-exclusive taxable turnover up to £150,000 can opt to join the VAT flat-rate scheme. It's unlikely the scheme will save you administration as the government intended (see p. 264) but you might save some tax.

- If you have fewer than 50 employees, you can get an incentive payment up to £250 if you switch to electronic filing and payment for PAYE in the tax year ending 5 April 2005.

Investments

- The government offers lots of tax incentives to persuade you to save for a pension. Take advantage of them. Chapter 8 tells you how to take them up.

- Consider starting a stakeholder scheme for your children or grandchildren. Pensions savings made early in life are especially valuable because they have plenty of time to grow.

- What you can pay into a stakeholder scheme or personal pension can be linked to your earnings in any of the previous five tax years. To maximise your contributions, choose the year with the highest earnings.

- Even if retired, provided you are under age 75, a stakeholder scheme or personal pension can still be a tax-efficient way to invest.

- Take advantage of the rules that allow you to backdate contributions to a stakeholder scheme or personal pension (see p. 76). You may be able to get a higher rate of tax relief – for example, if you paid tax at the higher rate in the previous tax year – or claim extra tax credit (see p. 12).
- If you haven't made the maximum contributions to a retirement annuity contract in the last six tax years, you can claim the unused relief this year (see p. 78).
- If you pay tax at the top rate of 40 per cent, tax-free investments can be attractive. Even if you could get a higher advertised rate of return on a taxable investment, the after-tax return could be considerably lower.
- Non-taxpayers investing in banks, building societies and other investments where tax is deducted from the income should claim it back from the Inland Revenue or arrange for it to be paid without deduction of tax (see p. 64).
- If you give capital to your children, any income it produces over £100 a year will be counted as yours (see p. 309). Choose investments that produce a tax-free income or capital gain (see pp. 309 and 67).
- If you are elderly, watch out for the income trap – the level of income where age-related allowances are reduced. You are effectively taxed at 33 per cent on each extra £1 of income (see p. 50). Consider tax-free investments if this is the case.
- If you have invested in shares, investment trusts or unit trusts through personal equity plans (PEPs) before they were replaced by individual savings accounts, try not to sell them. There's no tax to pay on the income or gains and you can keep PEPs going even if you have ISAs.
- If you have a tax exempt special savings account (TESSA) opened before the closing date for new accounts of 5 April 1999, you can get tax-free interest on up to £9,000 of savings until the end of the five-year term. You can go on adding to it up to the maximum each year – see p. 84.
- Saving through an ISA means no tax to pay on income or gains on the investments (see p. 81). You won't lose the tax relief if you withdraw your money, so you can use an ISA even for short-term savings.
- If you receive shares through an employee profit-sharing scheme, a savings-related share option scheme or share incentive plan you can

transfer them into an ISA (see p. 82). This will mean no income tax on the dividends and no capital gains tax when you eventually sell the shares.

- If you receive shares through an employee profit-sharing scheme, a savings-related share option scheme or share incentive plan, you can transfer them to a stakeholder pension scheme. Future capital growth in the shares will be tax-free and dividends are taxed at just 10 per cent.

- From 6 April 2000, unquoted shares in trading companies – including those listed on the Alternative Investment Market (AIM) – and employee shares count as business assets. This means normally only a quarter of any gain is taxable provided you have held the shares for two years.

- Even non-taxpayers might benefit from using an ISA to invest in shares or unit trusts. Normally, the 10 per cent tax deducted from dividends and distributions can't be reclaimed by non-taxpayers, but it can if the shares or unit trusts are held within an ISA. But check that any charges for the ISA will not outweigh the tax advantage.

- Investors should consider having some investments which give a capital gain rather than income. There is a capital gains tax-free allowance (£7,900 in the tax year ending 5 April 2004) which is often wasted (see p. 118).

- If you get income from trusts, it comes with a tax credit – you can reclaim some or all of this if it is more than you should have paid (see p. 308). Unless you pay tax at the higher rates, you will be entitled to a tax rebate on income from discretionary trusts.

- People investing in growing businesses can claim tax relief on up to £150,000 in a tax year through the Enterprise Investment Scheme – and the minimum period for an investment is just three years (p. 85). There is also tax relief for investing in venture capital trusts (see p. 87).

- If you get income from investments abroad on which you have paid foreign tax, tax credit relief can reduce the UK tax you pay (see p. 305).

Homeowners

- If you are away from your home for quite long periods keep an eye on the capital gains tax position – don't lose private residence relief which means you pay no capital gains tax on your only or main home (see p. 58).

- Do you have more than one home? You may have to pay capital gains tax when you sell your second home (p. 57). But you can choose which of your homes counts as your main one, make sure you nominate the home that is likely to incur the biggest capital gains tax bill. Unmarried couples who have two homes can each elect a different one as their main residence even if, say, one is used only for weekends.

- Do you want an income of over £80 a week tax-free? If you let out a room in your home under the rent a room scheme, you can take £4,250 of gross rent a year tax-free. This relief can reduce your tax bill even if the income is higher (see p. 283).

- If you let out your home, don't forget to claim the interest you pay on the mortgage as an expense against letting income. You get the tax relief at your highest rate of tax (see p. 287).

- If you let out your second home, try to make sure you meet the conditions for the rent to be taxed as income from furnished holiday lettings (p. 285). You can claim a wider variety of deductions against tax, and you may be able to avoid capital gains tax when you sell the home.

- You can claim a tax allowance for the wear and tear incurred in letting out furnished property (see p. 294).

- Work on a let property or business premises that once counted as an improvement (capital expenditure) may due to technological advances now be accepted as a repair (allowable expense) – for example, replacing old windows with double glazing. If you are replacing an old feature with a modern equivalent, try claiming and ask your tax office to confirm that the expense is allowable. See p. 287.

- If you have made a loss letting out property which qualifies as furnished holiday letting, you may be able to use this to reduce other parts of your tax bill (see p. 290).

- If you've let out part or all of your home, lettings relief could mean no capital gains tax to pay when you dispose of it (see p. 59).

Capital gains tax

- Try to use the tax-free allowance for capital gains tax every year – you can't carry over unused allowances to other years. Think about selling some shares showing a profit and buying them back within an ISA to make a gain that uses up the allowance or choosing investments, such as investment trust zero-dividend shares, designed to produce a capital gain on a set maturity date.

- Husband and wife are each entitled to the tax-free allowance of net capital gains – £7,900 for the tax year ending 5 April 2004 (see p. 118). Consider reorganising your possessions so each of you can use up the limit before either starts paying capital gains tax.

- If you are going to dispose of assets, split the disposals over several years. You can then claim the tax-free allowance for capital gains to reduce the bill each year.

- If you are facing a capital gains tax bill on the disposal of one large asset, you could sell assets that are showing losses to set against the gain. If you don't really want to get rid of these other assets, you can buy them back some time later (see p. 117).

- Selling shares in the company you work for? From 5 April 2000, you can claim taper relief at the rate for business assets, so you may be able to reduce the gain on which you pay tax to just a quarter after two years (see p. 120). But bear in mind, if you get shares every year, that any sale will be matched first with the most recently acquired shares (see p. 122).

- If you acquire shares on or after 6 April 2002 on the same day from more than one employee share scheme, or from one share scheme and also from a purchase on the open market, if you dispose of some of them, instead of the shares being pooled together, you can elect to have the disposal matched to the shares showing the smallest capital gain (see p. 127).

- If you accept cash for shares when a company is taken over, this counts as a disposal of the shares. However, sometimes you can opt for loan notes instead. If so, the disposal is deferred until you cash in the notes. So loan notes can be used to put off any taxable gain until a year when you have more unused allowances, more taper relief or a lower tax rate. Get professional advice if you are considering this.

- If you own valuables such as antiques, a second home or collectables, keep careful records of what they cost you to buy and maintain. You could face a capital gains tax bill when you dispose of them – allowable expenses can reduce the tax bill (p. 112).

- If you are thinking of making a gift to charity of an asset which is showing a loss, think again. It might be better to sell the asset and give the money to the charity (see p. 197).

- Do not forget to claim losses if you dispose of something like shares or valuables. Losses are set off against taxable gains, but, if unused, can be carried over to later years. But you must claim them within time limits (see p. 119). Keep careful records so you don't forget them later!

- From 6 April 2003 onwards, unused capital losses you personally make must be set against any gains from a settlor-interested trust that are attributed to you.For the tax years ending 5 April 2001, 2002 and 2003, you can choose whether to use your personal losses in this way (instead of carrying them forward). Make the election by 31 January 2005.

- You can set business losses against capital gains. For losses made in the tax year ending 5 April 2005 onwards, you set the loss against capital gains before (instead of after) taper relief allowing more of the gain to be relieved. For losses made in the tax years ending 5 April 2003 and 2004, you can elect for this treatment.

- If you face a big capital gains tax bill, think about investing the gain in growing companies. Deferral relief can defer the bill (see p. 132).

- For spending on or after 11 May 2001, you can claim a 100 per cent capital allowance on the cost of converting space above shops and businesses into flats (see p. 295).

- From 6 April 2004 onwards, when you dispose of an asset used in a business it can qualify for business asset taper relief even if it was not your own business.

Inheritance tax

- Draw up a will. There are simple steps you can take to minimise the tax payable on your estate when you die and to reduce the complications for those you leave behind (see p. 138). However, there are steps you can take to reduce an inheritance tax bill after a death (see p. 145). In particular, you can rearrange inheritances in ways that reduce the amount of tax.

- Make as full use as possible of the gifts you can make which do not fall into the inheritance tax net. Gifts on marriage and those made out of normal income are tax-free (p. 136). There is also an annual exemption for life-time gifts of £3,000.

- Share your wealth with your husband or wife so you can each make tax-free gifts. There is no capital gains tax to pay on gifts between a married couple (p. 130).
- Use life insurance to blunt the impact of inheritance tax. Policies written in trust go straight to the beneficiary and don't form part of your estate (see p. 140). If you pay the premiums out of your normal income, they are tax-free gifts (see p. 137).
- If you own a small business or farm, take professional tax advice. There are extensive tax reliefs which can mean you pay little or no capital gains tax (p. 132) or inheritance tax (p. 141), but they are complicated and need careful planning.

MARRIAGE AND DIVORCE

CHAPTER 6

Married couples are treated as two independent entities for the purpose of paying tax (though not when it comes to claiming tax credits – see p. 12). They are taxed on their own income and gains and have their own allowances. Each is responsible for filling in their own tax return and paying their own tax bills. There is no longer a tax allowance for married couples unless either or both husband and wife were born before 6 April 1935.

However, there are some aspects of the tax system which recognise that husband and wife are more than just two individuals living together. One is that they can transfer some allowances between them in certain circumstances. Gifts between husband and wife don't normally fall into the net for capital gains tax or inheritance tax. And by sharing their wealth, a couple can each use their tax-free allowances to reduce the amounts paid in tax.

This chapter explains the opportunities to save tax in marriage. It also sets out the rules for what happens when marriages come to an end. And it gives some brief guidance on what happens if you are widowed. For how marriage affects home ownership, see p. 57; information about capital gains tax is on p. 130, and on inheritance tax on p. 139.

> **TAX-SAVING IDEA**
>
> If one of you pays tax at a higher rate than the other, you should consider giving investments which produce a taxable income to the spouse who would pay least tax on the income.
>
> Gifts between married couples must be genuine – you can't hand them over with strings attached. If you are reluctant to give away the investments completely, consider putting them into joint names with your spouse so the income is shared equally (see p. 51).

MARRIAGE

Personal allowances

A husband and wife are each entitled to a personal tax allowance in the same way as single people – £4,615 for the tax year ending 5 April 2004. This personal allowance is deducted from income in arriving at the taxable income on which the individual's tax bill is calculated (see p. 4).

Married people aged 65 and over can claim the higher amounts of personal allowance for older people in the same way as single people. The rates are £6,610 for the tax year ending 5 April 2004, rising to £6,720 for those aged 75 and over. The additional amount is gradually reduced if 'total income' is above a certain level – £18,300 for the tax year ending 5 April 2004. The personal allowance is reduced by £1 for every £2 over the limit until it reaches the amount for under-65s. Total income is broadly all your income less deductions such as pension contributions (see p. 4).

EXAMPLE

Janet Lardon is on a salary of £60,000 a year and interest from savings accounts of £5,000 a year before tax. She pays tax at the higher rate of 40 per cent on her earnings – and that will be the rate for any savings interest.

She decides to share the savings accounts with her husband Ted, who pays tax at the basic rate only. She puts them in their joint names, so £2,500 of the interest is taxed as his. He has to pay tax on interest at 20 per cent (see p. 62), so they save higher rate tax of 20 per cent of £2,500, that is £500 a year.

Married couple's allowance

Until 6 April 2000 all married couples could claim an extra tax allowance that could be allocated to either partner or split between them. But from that date the married couple's allowance ended except where one (or both) of the couple was born before 6 April 1935.

For the tax year ending 5 April 2004, a couple qualifies for married couple's allowance if either husband or wife, or both, were born before 6 April 1935. The allowance gives tax relief at 10 per cent as a reduction in the tax bill.

Married couple's allowance has two elements: a basic amount of £2,150 and an additional age-related amount – see table opposite. The allowance is automatically awarded to the husband, but half or all of the basic amount can be transferred to the wife. The age-related addition stays with the husband (unless his income is too low to use it – see p. 50).

Normally, you must elect to transfer half or all of the basic allowance to the wife before the start of the tax year, so an election for the tax year beginning 6 April 2004 must be made before that date. (But the rules are different for the year in which you marry – see p. 51.) An election to transfer half the basic allowance can be made by the wife alone. An election to transfer the whole basic amount must be made jointly (though the husband alone can then elect to have half the amount transferred back to him). Whatever you elect continues year after year until you make a new election.

The married couple's allowance for this tax year and the last tax year is given in the table below. The table also gives the maximum tax savings with the relief given at 10 per cent.

	Tax year ending 5 April 2003		*Tax year ending 5 April 2004*	
Age of older partner during tax year	*maximum allowance* £	*maximum tax-saving* £	*maximum allowance* £	*maximum tax-saving* £
66/67–74	5,465	546.50	5,565	556.50
75 and over	5,535	553.50	5,635	563.50

This allowance is gradually reduced if the husband's 'total income' is above a certain level – even if the couple are getting the allowance because of the wife's age. However, it never falls below the basic amount – £2,150 for the tax year ending 5 April 2004.

If the husband's total income in the tax year ending 5 April 2004 is £18,300 or more, his personal allowance is first reduced by £1 for each extra £2 over the limit until he is getting the same allowance as the under-65s. So if he is 65-74, his personal allowance falls to the £4,615 for under-65s when his 'total income' reaches £22,290. If he is 75 or over, the personal allowance falls to the under-65s level when his 'total income' reaches £22,510. If his income is higher, the married couple's allowance is next reduced until it falls to the basic amount. The table on the next page shows the husband's income level at which the age-related addition is completely lost – this depends both on the husband's age and the age of his wife. If the husband is under 65, he won't get any age-related *personal* allowance, so, if his total income is above £18,300, this will immediately start to reduce the married couple's allowance.

> **TAX-SAVING IDEA**
>
> If one of you is 68 or over and the husband's 'total income' is high enough to lose age allowance (see table on p. 50) see if you would save tax by giving investments that produce a taxable income to the wife. Even if the husband is under 68, his total income could be reducing the amount of married couple's allowance you get.

Husband's income level at which age-related addition to married couple's allowance is completely lost in year ending 5 April 2004

Age of husband during tax year	*Age of wife during tax year*	*Income level at which married couple's allowance reduced to the basic amount (£2,150)*
Under 65	68–74	£25,130
Under 65	75 and over	£25,270
65–67	Any age under 68	£22,290
65–67	68–74	£29,120
65–67	75 and over	£29,260
68–74	Any age under 75	£29,120
68–74	75 and over	£29,260
75 and over	Any age	£29,480

Transfer of allowances because of low income

If either husband or wife has a tax bill which is too low to use up all their married couple's allowance, they can ask to have the unused part deducted from the tax bill of their spouse. Even the husband's age-related addition can be transferred to the wife in these circumstances. You can do this after the end of the tax year in which you got the allowance – see p. 207 for how to claim this.

You have up to five years and ten months after the end of the tax year to transfer the unused allowances. So for the tax year ending 5 April 2004, you can make a claim any time up to 31 January 2010. But if you know in advance that your income will not be big enough to benefit from these allowances, you can ask your tax inspector to transfer the part you estimate will be unused to your spouse's PAYE code.

EXAMPLE

Jasper Duffy, 69, has a total income of £24,000 – of which £11,400 a year is from savings and investments. Because his total income is well over the £18,300 limit, it reduces the amount of personal allowance he gets to the amount for under-65s. But it is also high enough to reduce the married couple's allowance the Duffys get from £5,565 to £4,710.

He decides to share his savings and investments equally with his wife Ellen, whose total income is well below the £18,300 limit. He puts them all into their joint names, which means only half the income they produce is his. This reduces his total income by half of £11,400 = £5,700 to £18,300.

The Duffys will thus get the full amount of married couple's allowance for people aged 68 to 74. And Jasper will get the full higher personal allowance for those aged 65 to 74.

Only older couples qualify for married couple's allowance and, therefore, the right to transfer any unused part of it. But married couples of any age can transfer blind person's allowance if the spouse receiving the allowance is unable to fully use it because their income is too low. The unused part can be transferred to the husband or wife even if they themselves are not blind.

Allowances in the year of marriage

If you get married and either you or your husband or wife was born before 6 April 1935, you qualify for married couple's allowance. In the tax year of your marriage, you get one-twelfth of the married couple's allowance for each month or part-month you are married during the tax year. The proportion depends on the date of the wedding – the table below shows the amounts for the tax year ending 5 April 2004.

	Tax year ending 5 April 2004					
Date of marriage before	*Older partner aged 68 to 74*		*Older partner aged 75 or more*		*Basic amount (where age-related addition lost)*	
	Maximum allowance	*Maximum tax-saving*	*Maximum allowance*	*Maximum tax-saving*	*Maximum allowance*	*Maximum tax-saving*
6 May	£5,565	£556.50	£5,635	£563.50	£2,150	£215.00
6 June	£5,102	£510.20	£5,166	£516.60	£1,971	£197.10
6 July	£4,638	£463.80	£4,696	£469.60	£1,792	£179.20
6 August	£4,174	£417.40	£4,227	£422.70	£1,613	£161.30
6 September	£3,710	£371.00	£3,757	£375.70	£1,434	£143.40
6 October	£3,247	£324.70	£3,288	£328.80	£1,255	£125.50
6 November	£2,783	£278.30	£2,818	£281.80	£1,075	£107.50
6 December	£2,319	£231.90	£2,348	£234.80	£896	£89.60
6 January	£1,855	£185.50	£1,879	£187.90	£717	£71.70
6 February	£1,392	£139.20	£1,409	£140.90	£538	£53.80
6 March	£928	£92.80	£940	£94.00	£359	£35.90
6 April	£464	£46.40	£470	£47.00	£180	£18.00

In the year of marriage, the married couple's allowance is initially given to the husband, but the couple can elect to transfer the basic amount of the allowance (reduced as shown in the table according to the date of the marriage) as described on p. 48. In the year of marriage only, you have until the end of the year (in other words, 5 April following your marriage) to elect for the transfer. So, if you marry between 6 April 2003 and 5 April 2004 inclusive, you have until 5 April 2004 to elect how the allowance is allocated between you for the tax year ending 5 April 2004.

Jointly owned assets

If you have investments which are jointly owned, your tax inspector will assume the income from them is split equally between you. If the investments are not owned in equal proportions, you can have the income divided between you to reflect your actual shares of it. You do this by both signing a declaration of beneficial interests on form 17 (available from tax offices) and sending it to your tax inspector.

The new split of joint income applies from when the declaration is signed – it can't be backdated. If you acquire new assets on which the 50:50 split is not to apply, you must make a further declaration. Note the split for income will also be used to allocate any gain on selling an asset between you when you dispose of it (see p. 108).

SEPARATION AND DIVORCE

Separation or divorce may affect:

- the tax allowances you get in the year you separate or divorce, but only if you or your husband or wife were born before 6 April 1935
- tax relief on maintenance you pay, but only if you or your husband or wife were born before 6 April 1935
- National Insurance contributions you pay if you are a married woman who has been paying contributions at the married women's reduced rate
- your entitlement to tax credits (see p. 54 and p. 206).

If any of the above apply to you, you should tell your tax inspector when you separate, even if you have not yet made a formal deed of separation or sought a court order. The Inland Revenue will then treat you as no longer living with your husband or wife, provided your circumstances suggest that the separation will be permanent.

Married couple's allowance

Each of you retains your personal allowances. And each of you will retain any married couple's allowance you were getting before the separation – but only for the rest of the tax year.

Maintenance payments

Maintenance can take several forms, including direct payments of cash or the provision of support such as a home to live in. The person receiving maintenance does not pay any tax on the amount they get. This means they can have other income up to the amount of their personal allowance (£4,615 in the tax year ending 5 April 2004 for someone under age 65 and more for an older person) before paying income tax.

Where the maintenance is provided voluntarily – that is, the payment cannot be enforced – the person paying it gets no tax relief. This is also true for enforceable maintenance payments, except where you or your husband or wife were born before 6 April 1935.

Provided you or your former (or separated) wife or husband were born before 6 April 1935, you can claim relief for payments made under a legally binding agreement, such as a court order, a Child Support Agency assessment, or a written agreement.

Only payments up to a set limit qualify for relief. The limit is £2,150 in the year ending 5 April 2004. Relief is given at a fixed rate of 10 per cent.

The tax relief is available only on regular payments made direct to someone you were married to (so not to children). It ends if the ex-spouse remarries. The maximum is the same however many former spouses you are paying, but the tax relief is in addition to any married couple's allowance you get in the year of separation.

You get the tax relief on these maintenance payments through your PAYE code (see Chapter 25) or through an adjustment to your tax bill.

National Insurance contributions

Paying certain types of National Insurance contributions entitles you to some state benefits, such as state retirement pension. If you are a woman and you married before May 1977, you may have opted to pay contributions at the 'married women's reduced rate'. In return for paying less National Insurance, you gave up the right to those state benefits and instead relied on your husband. Although, from May 1977 onwards, wives could not newly opt to pay married women's reduced rate contributions, anyone who had already made the option could continue with it.

Your right to pay National Insurance at the reduced rate ends at the time your marriage ends – generally, on the date of the decree absolute. If you are an employee, tell your employer so that he can arrange for you to pay full rate contributions. If you are self-employed, notify your tax office.

For more information, see Inland Revenue leaflet *CA10 National Insurance contributions for divorced women*.

Capital gains tax and inheritance tax on separation

You can carry on making gifts to your ex-husband or ex-wife in the year of separation without falling into the net for capital gains tax. After this, gifts may lead to a capital gains tax bill in the same way as for any other gifts (see p. 131).

However, if one of you moves out of the family home and gives or sells it to the other within three years of the separation, there will be no capital gains tax to pay. Even after that, there may be no capital gains tax if your ex-spouse is still living there and you have not claimed any other property as your only or main home.

Gifts between a separated husband and wife are free of inheritance tax (see p. 137). Once you are divorced, gifts may fall into the inheritance tax net unless they are for the maintenance of the ex-spouse or any children.

WIDOWED

If your husband or wife dies, you carry on getting your own personal allowance as usual. If you have been claiming tax credits, you need to make a new claim as a single person (see below).

If you or your husband or wife were born before 6 April 1935, you keep any married couple's allowance you were getting for the rest of the tax year in which death occurs. Any married couple's allowance unused in the year of death by the person who has died can be transferred to the surviving husband or wife. Married couple's allowance ceases from the following year.

TAX CREDITS

A claim for tax credits (see p. 12) is based on your household circumstances and income. If you are claiming credits and you marry, separate or divorce, become widowed, or start or stop living with someone as if you were husband and wife, you must tell the Inland Revenue about your change in circumstances within three months. You can be fined up to £300 if you fail to do so.

If you have not previously been claiming tax credits, you may find that you become eligible following a change in marital status and any consequent change in household income. Claim as soon as possible – claims can be backdated only three months.

HOME AND TAX

CHAPTER 7

Buying a home is probably the biggest purchase you will make. Your mortgage payments are almost certainly the largest outgoing in your household budget. And your home is also likely to be your most valuable asset.

This chapter explains the limited situations in which you can still get tax relief on mortgage interest and how to make sure you don't pay a hefty capital gains tax bill if you sell your home for a lot more than you paid for it.

MORTGAGE INTEREST TAX RELIEF

Home income schemes

People aged 65 or over can still get tax relief on the interest paid on a mortgage loan taken out as part of a home income scheme before 9 March 1999. Under such schemes, an insurance company lends against the security of the home. The loan may be used to buy an annuity which pays a regular income that leaves the homeowner with money to spend after making the mortgage payments.

Provided 90 per cent or more of the loan was used to buy the annuity, tax relief is given on the interest payments on up to £30,000 of the loan at a rate of 23 per cent. Provided you took out the scheme before 9 March 1999, you go on getting tax relief even though mortgage interest tax relief ended on 6 April 2000 – even if you move house or take out a new mortgage.

Usually tax relief is automatically deducted from the interest payments. If unusually it is not, call the Inland Revenue on 0151 472 6155.

Running a business from home

If you use your home for business purposes, you may be able to set off some of the interest against business income – see p. 269).

If you let your home

If you let part or all of your home, you may be able to deduct mortgage interest from rental income when working out the profit or loss of your letting business (see pp. 287 and 293).

CAPITAL GAINS TAX ON HOMES

If you sell most types of investments (including property) for more than you paid for them, there may be capital gains tax to pay (see Chapter 10). But if you sell your only or main home, there is normally no capital gains tax to pay unless the garden is excessively large (see overleaf) or you are making a business out of buying and selling homes. This exemption from capital gains tax is known as private residence relief.

However, if you own more than one home, only one of them qualifies for private residence relief. And you might lose the relief if you use the home for business, leave it for prolonged periods or let it out. If you do have to pay capital gains tax on selling a home, it can mean a hefty tax bill – the gain, adjusted for inflation and other reliefs, can be taxed at up to 40 per cent.

Which homes?

Private residence relief is given for your only or main home, whether it is a house or flat, freehold or leasehold, and wherever in the world it is situated.

You must occupy the home exclusively as your residence if it is to be free of capital gains tax. If part of the home is used exclusively for business, you may have to pay tax on part of the gain (see p. 58). And letting out some or all of your home can also mean a capital gains tax bill (see p. 59).

If you live in a caravan or houseboat, there's normally no capital gains tax to pay on it, even if it is not your only or main home. Caravans and boats count as wasting assets with a useful life of 50 years or less – and are thus outside the net for capital gains tax (see p. 107). But if you own the land on which a caravan stands, you might have to pay capital gains tax if you sell it, unless the caravan was your only or main home.

Gains on a former home that continues to be occupied by your ex-spouse are tax-free if you sell within three years of your leaving. A longer exemption period applies if this is your ex-spouse's only or main home and you have not nominated any other property as your own only or main home.

A home which a dependent relative lives in rent-free is also free of capital gains tax provided it fell into this category on or before 5 April 1988. This exemption lasts only as long as the relative continues to live in the home. Dependent relatives are:

- your mother or mother-in-law if widowed, separated or divorced
- any relative of yours or your spouse who is unable to look after themselves because of permanent illness, disablement or old age (usually 65 or over).

Gardens

Private residence relief applies to both your home and garden. But there are rules to stop people taking advantage of it to avoid capital gains tax on dealing in land.

If the area of your home and garden exceeds half a hectare (about 1¼ acres), there may be tax to pay on the gain you make on the excess. The gain on any excess will be free of tax only if you can convince your tax inspector that a garden of that size is appropriate for the home.

If the area of the home and garden is less than half a hectare, you can sell part of the garden without having to pay capital gains tax, even if you have obtained planning permission to build on the land. But if you actually build a new property and then sell, the gain will be subject to tax (either capital gains tax or, if you are deemed to be earning a living from development, income tax). And if you sell the home and keep some of the land, there may be capital gains tax to pay when you eventually sell the land.

If you own more than one home

If you own more than one home, you can choose which of your homes is your main one and thus free of capital gains tax. It doesn't have to be the one you live in most of the time.

So you should think about which home is likely to make the largest gain and nominate it for private residence relief. You must make your choice and tell your tax inspector in writing within two years of acquiring the second home. Newlyweds who have kept the two homes they owned while single should tell their tax inspector which is to get private residence relief within two years of the marriage. Note that, even if you spend a lot of time living in a different home from your husband or wife (for example, because you live apart during the week for work purposes), for the tax rules you are still deemed to share one of the homes as your joint main residence. You can't each claim a separate main residence. However, unmarried couples can each have a different main residence.

You can alter your choice at any time, but you cannot backdate the change by more than two years. Again, write and tell your tax inspector that you wish to change your choice and when you want the change to run from.

If you don't nominate one of your homes for private residence relief, your tax inspector will decide – probably on the basis of which home you spend the most time at. You can appeal against this decision in the normal way (see p. 26), but you will have to produce proof that the other home really is your main one.

Working from home

If any part of your home is used exclusively for business, there may be a capital gains tax bill when you sell the home. This will not usually apply if you are an employee working from home, but could do if a substantial part of your home is set aside exclusively for the work.

If you use one or more rooms entirely for business (as an office or workshop, for example), there will be tax on a proportion of the gain when you sell the home. You will have to agree the proportion with the tax inspector, who may base it on the number of rooms you use or their floor area. If you claim a proportion of the rent or mortgage interest as a business expense (see p. 269), the same proportion of the gain is likely to be taxable.

For details of how the taxable gain will be worked out – and ways to reduce the tax bill – see Chapter 10.

Away from home

If you don't live in your home for all the time you own it, you might lose some of the private residence relief – even though it is the only home you own or you have nominated it as your main home. Normally you will have to pay capital gains tax on the following proportion of the taxable gain:

$$\frac{\text{Number of complete months of absence}}{\text{Number of complete months of ownership}}$$

Only months of ownership or absence since 31 March 1982 count in working out the proportion – earlier gains are outside the scope of the tax (see p. 115).

In practice, you can be away from the home for considerable spells of absence without losing any private residence relief. You can retain it during absence for the following periods:

- the first year of ownership while you are building, rebuilding or modernising the home. This can be extended for another year if you can convince the tax inspector it is necessary. To retain the exemption, you must move in within the one-year (or two-year) period

- the last three years of ownership – even if you have already moved out
- any other absences totalling up to three years, provided you live in the home both before the first absence and after the last.

You may also be able to retain private residence relief if work takes you or your spouse away from home. If you work for an employer who requires you to live away from home in the UK, you can go on getting private residence relief for up to four years of absence. If your employer requires you to work abroad, you can get private residence relief indefinitely. But you must live in the home before the first absence and normally also after the final absence.

Provided you intend to live in your home in the future, private residence relief continues if you or your spouse are required to live in job-related accommodation (see p. 90). Self-employed people who have to live in work-related accommodation (for example, over the shop or at the club) can go on getting private residence relief on their own homes as long as they intend to live in them eventually.

EXAMPLE

Linda March bought a house on 24 June 1992. On 6 July 1995 her employer sent her on an overseas posting lasting until 10 November 1997. On Linda's return to the UK, her employer sent her to work away from home until 15 August 2001. She lived in the home until 22 October 2001, when she bought a new home, eventually selling her old home on 27 February 2003.

During the ten years and eight months Linda owned the home, she was absent for three periods totalling seven years and three months. But she will get private residence relief for the entire time she owned the house:

- the two years and four months from July 1995 to November 1997 count for private residence relief because they are a period of employment spent entirely abroad
- the three years and nine months from November 1997 to August 2001 are less than the four years of employment elsewhere in the UK possible without losing private residence relief
- the year and four months from October 2001 to February 2003 are part of the last three years of ownership.

Capital gains tax on lettings

There is no capital gains tax to pay if you take in a lodger who is treated as a member of the family – sharing your living rooms and eating with you. But in other circumstances, there may be capital gains tax to pay when you sell a home that has been let out wholly or in part.

If you let out the whole house for a period, the gain attributable to that period is taxable.

If you let part of your home, you may have to pay capital gains tax on the part that is not occupied by you. If you let two of your six rooms, for example, one-third of the gain on selling the home is taxable (less if you haven't let the two rooms for all the time that you've owned the home).

However, there may still be no capital gains tax to pay if you can claim lettings relief, for homes which have been wholly or partly eligible for private residence relief. Lettings relief reduces the taxable gain by £40,000, or the amount of private residence relief if this is lower – see the example.

EXAMPLE

Jane Mortimer lived in a home for four years and then let it out for six. She sold it making a taxable gain of £50,000.

Jane qualifies for private residence relief for the four years she lived in it, plus the last three years of ownership – seven years in all. The gain attributable to the remaining three years is ³⁄₁₀ of the £50,000. This £15,000 is taxable.

Jane next works out how much lettings relief she is entitled to. The amount is the lower of £40,000 or the value of private residence relief on the house, which is £50,000 – £15,000 = £35,000. She can reduce the gain by £35,000; that means no taxable gain on the letting.

Property dealings

If you regularly buy and sell houses for profit, there might be a capital gains tax bill when you sell one – even if you have been living in it as your only or main home. This is meant to catch people who are making a business out of doing up unmodernised homes for sale.

If your property dealings are on a substantial scale, you could find yourself classified as a dealer in land. You would then have to pay income tax on the profits like any other self-employed person (see Chapter 18).

Inheritance

If you inherit a property – for example, a family home on the death of your parents – you are deemed to have acquired it at its market value on the date of death. If you do not take up residence, there could be capital gains tax to pay if you sell the property and its value has risen since the date of death.

SAVING AND INVESTING

CHAPTER 8

The ordinary saver faces a wider choice of investments than ever before. Banks, building societies and National Savings & Investments (NS&I) are vying to look after your spare cash. Many more people have become shareholders through employee share-ownership schemes, privatisations and the conversion of building societies into companies. Millions are saving for their retirement through personal pensions and stakeholder schemes.

To encourage savings, the government has introduced a series of tax incentives for investors, including a lower tax rate on savings income for basic-rate taxpayers and tax relief on pension contributions. There are also special tax rules to persuade you to build up some savings (individual savings accounts – ISAs), take out long-term life insurance policies, and invest in new businesses (for example the enterprise investment scheme – EIS). If you still have some earlier tax-efficient schemes – such as personal equity plans (PEPs) and tax-exempt special savings accounts (TESSAs) – you can continue to enjoy the benefits even though the schemes are no longer open to new investors. The government's latest incentive to saving is the child trust fund for children born from September 2002 onwards (see p. 31).

This chapter guides you through the various types of savings and investments and how they are taxed. It explains the rules and tells you how to cash in on the tax breaks offered by the government.

INCOME TAX ON INVESTMENTS

Income from some investments is tax-free (that is, there is no income tax to pay). For a list of these, see p. 346.

All other investment income is taxable. With more and more investments, tax is deducted from the income before it is paid to you. There is no further tax to pay on such income unless you pay tax at the higher rate. If you should have paid less tax than was deducted, you will normally be able to get a refund.

Interest paid after deduction of tax
Interest on most kinds of savings is now normally paid after tax has been deducted from it. This applies to building society accounts, bank accounts, annuities (other than pension annuities) local authority loans and bonds and NS&I fixed rate savings bonds.

On these types of interest, tax is deducted at 20 per cent from the gross income before handing it over to you. There is no further tax bill if you pay tax at the basic rate on your income – which is the case for the vast majority of taxpayers. If you pay tax at the higher rate, there will be extra tax to pay on this income (see opposite). If your income is too low to pay tax or you pay tax on the rest of your income at the starting rate of 10 per cent only, you can reclaim all or some of the tax which has been deducted (see p. 64).

EXAMPLE

Sonny Dasgupta pays tax at 40 per cent on his income. NS&I certificates offer him an average return of 2.7 per cent a year tax-free over five years. He could get 4.1 per cent a year over the same period in a bank term account.

Sonny invests in the NS&I certificates, since that will give him 2.7 per cent a year whatever his tax rate. The interest rate he would get on the bank account after paying tax at 40 per cent would be slightly lower: 60 per cent of 4.1 per cent, that is 2.46 per cent a year.

GROSSING-UP

If you receive investment income after some tax has been deducted from it, what you receive is known as the net income. But you may need to work out how much the income was before tax was deducted from it (the gross income).

You can find the gross income by grossing-up the net income using the ready reckoners in Appendix B (p. 248), or by using the following formula:

$$\text{Amount paid to you} \times \left(\frac{100}{100 - \text{rate of tax}}\right)$$

For example, if you receive £50 of income after tax has been deducted at 20 per cent, the grossed-up amount of the income is:

$$£50 \times \left(\frac{100}{100 - 20}\right)$$
$$= £50 \times \frac{100}{80}$$
$$= £62.50$$

The savings income is treated as an upper slice of your income. This means it does not reduce the amount of earnings or other income that can be taxed at the starting rate – the £1,960 taxable at 10 per cent in the tax year ending 5 April 2004.

> **TAX-SAVING IDEA**
>
> If you pay tax at the top rate of 40 per cent, tax-free investments can be very attractive. Even if you could get a higher advertised rate of return on a taxable investment, the after-tax return could be considerably lower.

Higher rate tax on income paid after deduction of tax

If you get interest after tax has been deducted and pay tax at the higher rate of 40 per cent, there will be a further tax bill to pay – as the example below shows. The higher rate tax will be collected by the Inland Revenue in one of two ways:

- by increasing the amount of tax you pay on your earnings through PAYE (see Chapter 25)
- through the payments you have to make in January and July under the self-assessment system (see p. 21).

> **EXAMPLE**
>
> Niamh Fagan gets £80 interest on her building society account in the tax year ending 5 April 2004. Tax has already been deducted from the interest at 20 per cent before it is credited to her account, so this £80 is the net (that is, after deduction of tax) amount.
>
> To work out the gross (before deduction of tax) amount of interest, Niamh must add the tax back to the net amount. The grossed-up amount of interest is:
>
> $$\pounds 80 \times \left(\frac{100}{100 - 20}\right)$$
> $$= \pounds 80 \times \frac{100}{80}$$
> $$= \pounds 100$$
>
> In other words, Niamh has paid £100 – £80 = £20 in tax and this covers her basic rate tax on the interest.
>
> If Niamh should pay tax at 40 per cent on this interest, her overall tax liability is 40 per cent of £100 = £40. Since she has already paid £20 in tax, she has to pay only £40 – £20 = £20 in higher rate tax. This leaves her with £80 – £20 = £60 of interest after higher rate tax has been paid.

Too much tax deducted?

If too much tax has been deducted from your interest, the excess can be claimed back. This would happen if the rest of your income is below the level at which you pay tax or you pay tax at the lower rate of 10 per cent only on the rest of your income – as the next example shows. For how to claim back tax, see p. 27.

> **EXAMPLE**
>
> Niall O'Halloran has earnings of £5,000 in the tax year ending 5 April 2004 and received interest from his savings of £400. The correct tax has already been paid on his earnings. Tax has been deducted from this interest at 20 per cent but Niall reckons he should be paying tax on it at the lower rate of 10 per cent only. He checks to see if he is due a rebate.
>
> First he works out the gross amount of interest he received – the amount before deduction of tax at 20 per cent:
>
> $$£400 \times \left(\frac{100}{100 - 20}\right)$$
>
> $$= £400 \times \frac{100}{80}$$
>
> $$= £500$$
>
> This means he has been paid a gross amount of £500 from which £100 of tax has been deducted.
>
> He adds the £500 to the £5,000 of earnings to find his total income of £5,500. Like all taxpayers, he is entitled to a personal allowance of £4,615 for the tax year, so his taxable income is £5,500 − £4,615 = £885.
>
> Lower rate tax of 10 per cent is due on the first £1,960 of taxable income, so that is the rate he should have paid on the £500 of gross interest. 10 per cent of £500 is £50, so he is due a rebate of £100 − £50 = £50 on the interest.

Not a taxpayer?

If your income is too low to pay tax, you can arrange with the bank or building society to be paid interest without deduction of tax. Fill in form R85 which is available from banks, building societies and post offices, as well as from tax offices and www.inlandrevenue.gov.uk. A copy is in Inland Revenue leaflet *IR110 A guide for people with savings*, which also contains useful hints on checking whether you will pay tax or not. The Inland Revenue website can help you do the sums – see www.inlandrevenue.gov.uk/taxback.

Arranging for interest to be paid without deduction of tax not only saves you claiming back the tax which has been deducted, you also get the money much earlier. However, interest on joint accounts can be paid without deduction of tax to just one of the two account-holders only if the bank or building society can arrange it. There are hefty penalties for making a false declaration.

Gilt-edged stock

Since 6 April 1998, interest on all British government stocks (gilts) is usually paid gross – ie without any tax already deducted. But, if interest you started to receive before 6 April 1998 was originally paid net, it will continue to be paid with tax at 20 per cent already deducted unless you ask the Bank of England to pay it gross instead. Similarly, if you are receiving the interest gross, but would prefer to receive the interest net of tax, you can ask the Bank of England to change the way you are paid.

Corporate bonds

Interest on corporate bonds used to be paid with 20 per cent tax already deducted. However, from 1 April 2001, interest from bonds listed on a stock exchange is paid gross (without any tax deducted). If you have not received a tax return, do not forget to declare this untaxed income by 5 October following the end of the tax year (see p. 17).

Bond-based unit trusts

Unit trusts and open-ended investment companies (oeics) that invest wholly or mainly in gilts and/or corporate bonds pay 'income distributions'. They are taxed like other savings income and paid with 20 per cent tax deducted. Distributions from share-based unit trusts are taxed differently (see below).

Shares and unit trusts

Dividends from UK companies and distributions from share-based unit trusts are paid with a tax credit – the amount is given on the tax voucher which comes with the dividend or distribution. There is no further tax bill if you pay tax at the lower or basic rate only on your income – which is the case for the vast majority of taxpayers.

For dividends and distributions paid on or after 6 April 1999, the tax credit is 10 per cent of the gross amount. So if you receive a dividend of £80, the grossed-up amount of this dividend is:

$$£80 \times \left(\frac{100}{100 - 10}\right)$$
$$= £80 \times \frac{100}{90}$$
$$= £88.89$$

The tax credit is £88.89 – £80 = £8.89.

The tax on the grossed up amount of dividends and distributions is 10 per cent for starting rate and basic rate taxpayers. Since this is the same amount as the tax credit, they need pay nothing extra. Note that the 10 per cent tax credit does not eat up any of your starting rate band: you can still have up to £1,960 of other income taxed at the 10 per cent starting rate in the tax year ending 5 April 2004.

EXAMPLE

Maggie East has income of £12,000 in the year ending 5 April 2004 made up of £7,000 pension, £1,500 building society interest (grossed up to include the 20 per cent tax) and £3,500 in dividends (grossed up to include the 10 per cent tax credit). She has a personal allowance of £6,610 and wonders how the tax bill is allocated between these different types of income.

Her allowances and tax bands are set against her income in the following order: income other than from savings and investments, savings income, dividend income (but bearing in mind that allowances cannot be used to reclaim dividend tax credits). So her tax position is as follows:

	'Other' income	*Savings income*	*Dividend income*
Income	£7,000	£1,500	£3,500
Less personal allowance	£6,610	£0	£0
Taxable income	£390	£1,500	£3,500
Starting rate band	£390	£1,500	£70
Basic rate band	£0	£0	£3430
Tax at 10%	£39.00	£150.00	£350.00
Tax at 20%	n/a	£0	n/a
Tax at 22%	£0	n/a	n/a
Less tax already paid	£39.00	£300.00	£350.00
Tax refund/extra to pay	£0	£150 refund	£0

The allowance reduces Maggie's taxable income other than savings and investments (her 'other' income) to just £390 and this is all taxed via PAYE at the starting rate. Her 'other' income is too low to use up all the starting rate band, so the unused part is next set against her savings income. This means £1,500 of her savings income should have been taxed at 10 per cent rather than the 20 per cent already deducted. Therefore Maggie can claim a tax refund of £300 – £150 = £150. Tax due on the dividend income matches the tax credit so there is nothing further to pay.

If you pay tax at the higher rate, there is extra tax to pay. Higher rate taxpayers pay tax on the grossed-up amount of dividends and distributions at 32.5 per cent. So on a net dividend of £80, your total tax bill is 32.5 per cent of the grossed-up amount of £88.89 = £28.89. Since you have a tax credit of £8.89, the higher rate tax due is £28.89 – £8.89 = £20. That leaves you with £80 – £20 = £60 after paying the higher rate tax.

The effect of this arrangement is that there is no difference for a higher rate taxpayer between dividends and distributions which come with a 10 per cent tax credit and interest paid after deduction of tax at 20 per cent. If the net income received is £80, a higher rate taxpayer ends up with £60 whether it is a dividend or interest.

The tax credit cannot be claimed back if the income is not taxable in your hands. So if your income is too low to pay tax you cannot claim it back, and you could be better off investing in shares and unit trusts through an individual savings account (ISA) which can reclaim the tax credit (see p. 81).

This also means that if most or all of your income is dividends and distributions, you might not get the full value of your tax allowance. There is no refund of the tax credit even if some of the allowance could otherwise be set against the dividend income.

INVESTING FOR CAPITAL GAINS

One way of reducing your income tax bill is to invest for capital gains rather than income. Capital gains tax is paid on increases in the value of investments – for example if the value of shares rises and then the shares are sold. The chargeable gain is added to your income and taxed at the same rate as savings (interest) income.

But there's no tax to pay if your total net capital gains in the tax year ending 5 April 2004 are below £7,900. A husband and wife can each make total net capital gains of this amount before paying capital gains tax. And you can often make gains of

> **TAX-SAVING IDEA**
> Many people are careful to make the most of their income tax-free allowances each year, but overlook the tax-free capital gains limit. To make regular use of the limit, you could consider investments that are designed to produce a capital gain on a set maturity date – for example, investment trust zero-dividend shares. Alternatively, consider selling assets each year and buying them back later or immediately buying similar assets (see p. 124).

more than the £7,900 limit, because of the deductions you can make in calculating your net capital gains. These include expenses incurred in acquiring, owning or disposing of the investment and losses on other investments. You can also deduct indexation allowance for gains due to inflation between 1982 and 1998. And taper relief reduces the tax bill according to how long you have owned the investment since 6 April 1998. A few investments – shares in unquoted trading companies including those listed on the Alternative Investment Market (AIM) and employee shares – count as business assets and so benefit from higher relief (see p. 120).

For more about capital gains tax and how to minimise it, see Chapter 10.

LIFE INSURANCE POLICIES

Many types of life insurance build up a cash-in value which makes them suitable as a form of investment. With most, the insurance company has paid tax on the investment income and gains before paying out the return to you. This is deemed to be equivalent to tax at the basic rate but you cannot reclaim any of it even if you pay tax at less than the basic rate. However, provided certain rules are met, higher-rate taxpayers do not have any further tax to pay on the return. There may be higher tax to pay if you cash in a savings-type life insurance policy after less than ten years or three-quarters of the term, if this is shorter (see p. 173).

Tax relief on life insurance premiums

With certain types of life insurance policies taken out before 14 March 1984, you were able to get tax relief on the premiums (within limits). Provided you haven't substantially changed the policy, you can go on getting the tax relief which is now 12½ per cent of the premiums. In most cases you get it by paying reduced premiums to the insurance company – you pay 87½ per cent of the gross premium and the insurance company reclaims the 12½ per cent tax relief from the Inland Revenue. You can get tax relief on no more than £1,500 of gross premiums. If you change the policy, such as extending the term, increasing the cover or converting it to a different type of

> **TAX-SAVING IDEA**
>
> Although there is often no tax for you to pay when you cash in a life insurance policy, the insurance company has already paid tax which you can't reclaim. Unless you are a higher rate taxpayer, other investments will usually be a more tax-efficient way for you to save or invest. For example, consider unit trusts, investment trusts or open-ended investment companies as alternatives to unit-linked life insurance policies.

policy, you may lose the tax relief. But you won't lose the tax relief if the value of the policy increases automatically as part of the policy (for example, if it increases by 5 per cent every year). Check with the insurance company.

PENSIONS

The government offers tax incentives to encourage you to provide for your retirement by saving with an employer's occupational pension scheme or through your own personal pension or stakeholder scheme. These mean that saving for the future through a pension often provides a better return than any other type of investment:

> **TAX-SAVING IDEA**
>
> Everyone should try to make sure that they are saving for retirement through a pension – and the earlier you start, the better the pension you should get at the end. Don't delay. You can get tax relief at your highest rate of tax. This means a contribution of £1,000 costs you just £600 if you are a higher rate taxpayer, and just £780 if you are a basic rate taxpayer for the year ending 5 April 2004. The fund into which you pay your contributions pays no capital gains tax and some of the income builds up tax-free.

- there is tax relief on your contributions to the scheme (within limits)
- any employer's contributions made for you are not taxable as your income or as a fringe benefit
- the fund the money goes into pays no capital gains tax and some of the income builds up tax-free
- you can trade in some pension to get a tax-free lump sum when you retire.

Occupational pension schemes

The tax incentives for saving through an occupational pension scheme are available only if it is approved by the Inland Revenue. At present, approved schemes must normally offer benefits within set limits:

- the maximum pension is two-thirds of your final salary
- the maximum tax-free lump sum is 1½ times your final salary
- the maximum lump sum payment which can be made on death in service (the life insurance cover) is four times your final salary
- the maximum widow's or widower's pension is two-thirds the pension you would have got.

There is a further restriction on the pension benefits from an approved scheme set up on or after 14 March 1989, or if you joined an older scheme on or after 1 June 1989. The amount of final salary which can be taken into account is limited by the pension scheme earnings cap which is £99,000 for the tax year ending 5 April 2004 (£97,200 for the tax year ending 5 April 2003). If the cap applies to you, the maximum you can draw in the tax year ending 5 April 2004 are:

- a maximum pension of £66,000 a year (two-thirds of £99,000)
- a maximum lump sum of £148,500 (1½ times £99,000)
- a maximum payment for death in service of £396,000 (four times £99,000).

Other benefits such as widow's and widower's pensions are also subject to the pension scheme earnings cap.

> **EXAMPLES**
>
> Marion Mould is an employee. Her monthly contributions of £50 to an employer's occupational pension scheme are deducted from her salary before tax is worked out under the PAYE scheme.
>
> Margaret May is an employee. She doesn't contribute to an occupational pension scheme, but saves in a stakeholder scheme instead. She saves £50 a month, but hands over only £39 to the pension provider, because she has deducted £11 (basic rate tax at 22 per cent for the year ending 5 April 2004). The scheme provider claims back the £11 from the Inland Revenue.
>
> Marcia Mumps is self-employed, saving £50 a month in a retirement annuity contract. She hands over £50 each month to the pension provider. She claims tax relief through her tax return, deducting the contributions from her income before working out how much tax she should pay on 31 January.

Contributions to an occupational scheme

The amount you are required to contribute to an occupational pension scheme is decided by your employer, but under current rules cannot exceed 15 per cent of your earnings (this can include the value of fringe benefits). Provided the pension scheme is approved by the Inland Revenue, you get tax relief at your highest rate of tax on these contributions. Your contributions will be deducted from your income before working out how much tax has to be paid under PAYE (although your National Insurance contributions are worked out on your full pay, that is, before deduction of pension contributions).

If the earnings cap applies to you (see above), your contributions are restricted to 15 per cent of earnings up to the cap. For the tax year ending 5 April 2004, that means you can get tax relief on maximum contributions of 15 per cent of £99,000, that is £14,850.

If you leave an approved pension scheme within two years of joining, your pension contributions can be repaid only after tax has been deducted at a flat rate of 20 per cent, to recover the tax relief you have had.

From 6 April 2001 onwards, some types of occupational scheme can opt to be treated under the same tax rules as personal pensions (called the 'DC regime'). If you belong to this type of scheme, the maximum you can pay into the scheme and any stakeholder schemes and personal pensions is either a total of £3,600 or a percentage of your earnings, as described on p. 75. Your employer does not have to pay anything into this type of scheme; anything your employer does pay counts towards the contribution limit.

Topping up your pension

An occupational pension scheme is usually the best way to save for retirement, if there is a scheme you can join, because in most cases your employer must pay a substantial part of the cost of providing your pension and other benefits. But you might want to save extra. Provided your scheme has not opted into the DC regime, there are several ways you can do this:

- your employer must offer an in-house additional voluntary contribution (AVC) scheme. This might be an 'added years' scheme or a 'money purchase' scheme (see below)
- you may be able to pay into a free-standing scheme called an FSAVC scheme (see below), and
- from 6 April 2001 onwards, if you earn no more than £30,000 a year and you are not a controlling director of the firm you work for, you can invest up to £3,600 in stakeholder pension schemes and/or personal pensions (see p. 73).

You count as earning £30,000 a year or less, if in any of the five tax years preceding the one in which you pay into the personal pension or personal stakeholder scheme, you have earned £30,000 or less. But you can't refer to years before the tax year ending 5 April 2001.

> **TAX-SAVING IDEA**
>
> If you belong to an occupational pension scheme and you want to top up your savings, the best way to do this will often be a stakeholder pension scheme. This type of scheme has low charges, lets you stop and start contributions without penalty and provides a tax-free lump sum at retirement as well as a pension.

If your scheme has opted into the DC regime, you can increase the ordinary contributions you make to your employer's scheme and/or pay into stakeholder schemes and/or personal pensions. But your total contributions to all these schemes must not exceed the £3,600 a year limit or, if applicable, percentage of your earnings (see p. 75). You are not eligible to pay AVCs or FSAVCs.

TAX-SAVING IDEA

Pension schemes and plans are a good way to save for retirement because they benefit from various tax reliefs. But saving through an ISA can be just as tax efficient in some cases and almost as tax efficient in others – see table. And an ISA is much more flexible than a pension scheme, because you can withdraw your money whenever you like. With pension schemes, you must normally leave your money invested until at least age 50 under current rules. For more about ISAs, see p. 81.

Which options you choose depend, in part, on how each of the different schemes is taxed – see table.

How different ways to save for retirement are taxed

Type of scheme	*Tax relief on your contributions*	*Tax-free gains on invested savings*	*Tax-free income from invested savings*	*Proceeds can usually be taken as a tax-free lump sum*
Most occupational schemes	yes	yes	partly	partly
Occupational schemes that have opted into the 'DC regime'	yes	yes	partly	partly
In-house 'added years' AVC scheme	yes	yes	partly	partly
In-house 'money purchase' AVC scheme	yes	yes	partly	no
FSAVC scheme	yes	yes	partly	no
Stakeholder pension scheme	yes	yes	partly	partly
Personal pension	yes	yes	partly	partly
ISA	no	yes	yes(1)	yes

(1) But dividend income is tax-free only until 5 April 2004.

Additional voluntary contributions

You can choose between two different ways of investing your AVCs:

- through your employer's pension scheme (in-house AVCs), which should be considered first. This could be an 'added-years scheme' where your AVCs buy extra notional years of scheme membership, so that your pension and all other benefits are increased. Or it could be a 'money purchase scheme' where your AVCs are invested and the fund that has built up by retirement is used to provide extra pension or certain other benefits

- by making your own arrangements with an insurance company, bank, building society or unit trust manager (free-standing AVCs).

You get full tax relief on AVCs, provided the total amount you contribute, together with your normal contributions to your employer's scheme, does not exceed the 15 per cent limit. So if your employer's pension scheme contributions are 6 per cent, you can pay up to 15 – 6 = 9 per cent in AVCs.

You cannot use AVCs to buy pension benefits greater than the maximum limits set by the Inland Revenue for approved schemes. If you inadvertently contribute so much that the benefits would exceed the limits, some of the AVCs will be paid back when you retire, with a deduction to cover the tax relief you have had.

Within the limits, AVCs and FSAVCs can be used to increase any benefits from your employer's scheme except money purchase AVCs to an in-house scheme you started on or after 8 April 1987 and FSAVCs can't be used to increase the tax-free lump sum.

Stakeholder pension schemes and personal pensions

From 6 April 2001, a new system of tax rules, called the 'DC regime', applies to personal pensions, including those which qualify as stakeholder schemes. (A stakeholder scheme is a pension scheme which meets certain conditions, such as low charges and flexible contributions. Although some occupational schemes can qualify as stakeholder schemes, this book uses the term 'stakeholder pension scheme' to mean a personal pensions registered as stakeholder scheme.)

The 'DC' in DC regime stands for 'defined contribution'. This describes the type of pension schemes involved and is another name for 'money purchase'. All money purchase schemes work in basically the same way. They are all like savings schemes: what you pay in is invested and builds up a fund that is used later on to buy your retirement pension and any other benefits.

If you save through a stakeholder scheme or personal pension, you can build up a fund with an insurance company or other pension provider and use it to provide you with an income for retirement. Your employer can also contribute to your scheme, as will the government if you use it to contract out of the state additional pension. Under present rules, you can begin to draw this pension any time after the age of 50 (younger for certain professions such as sports-playing).

A quarter of the accumulated fund can be taken as a tax-free lump sum, with a cash limit of £150,000 for a personal pension taken out on or before 26 July 1989.

How much tax relief?

Nearly everyone can get tax relief on up to £3,600 a year of contributions to any schemes within the DC regime. That limit applies to your total contributions to:

- stakeholder schemes
- personal pensions
- a money purchase occupational scheme that has opted into the DC regime.

> **TAX-SAVING TIP**
>
> Nearly everyone can pay up to £3,600 a year into personal stakeholder pension schemes and certain other pension schemes. You can contribute up to £3,600 regardless of the amount you earn and even if you have no earnings at all. Even a child can pay up to £3,600 a year into a pension scheme.

The only people who cannot get this relief are employees earning more than £30,000 a year and controlling directors who are members of an occupational pension scheme that is not within the DC regime.

If you do not belong to an occupational pension scheme at all – because, say, you are self-employed or you are an employee but there is no occupational scheme for you to join – and you have moderate or high earnings, you can pay more than £3,600 into schemes within the DC regime. The amount you can pay depends on:

- your net relevant earnings, and
- your age.

Net relevant earnings for employees are earnings from non-pensionable jobs, including the taxable value of fringe benefits but after deduction of allowable expenses. For self-employed people, it is taxable profits after deducting certain payments made by your business under deduction of tax (for example, patent royalties or covenant payments). In the case of a partnership, it is your share of the partnership profits. With furnished holiday lettings, net relevant earnings are your profits from the lettings.

> **EXAMPLE**
>
> Mark Fisher is aged 55 and has net relevant earnings for the year ending 5 April 2004 of £120,000. He wants to pay the maximum he can into a stakeholder pension scheme. Under the rules for the DC regime, the most he can pay is 30 per cent of his earnings up to the earnings cap of £99,000, in other words 30% × £99,000 = £29,700.

Your contributions can be based on your current tax year's net relevant earnings. Alternatively, under the DC regime, you can use the earnings from any of the previous five tax years.

The table shows the maximum contributions on which you can get tax relief and the income level at which they come to more than the basic £3,600 that everyone can contribute:

TAX-SAVING TIP

If your earnings have fallen – say, because of a career break – there's no need to reduce your pension contributions. What you pay into your stakeholder scheme or personal pension can be linked to your earnings in any of the previous five tax years. To maximise your contributions, choose the year with the highest earnings.

Age at 6 April	*Percentage of net relevant earnings* you can pay in contributions*	*Net relevant earnings at which you can contribute more than £3,600*
35 or less	17½	£20,572
36–45	20	£18,000
46–50	25	£14,400
51–55	30	£12,000
56–60	35	£10,286
61–74	40	£9,000

* But you must ignore earnings above the earnings cap for the year in which contributions are paid or treated as paid – £99,000 in the year ending 5 April 2004.

Any contributions made by your employer to a scheme in the DC regime count towards the limits above. And the maximum net relevant earnings that can be used to calculate the amount you can get tax relief on is the pension scheme earnings cap. For the tax year ending 5 April 2004, the pension scheme earnings cap is £99,000 – so the maximum for someone aged 35 or less is 17½ per cent of £99,000 – that is, £17,325.

Other people can pay into your pension scheme on your behalf. For example, a parent or grandparent can pay into a pension scheme for a child, a husband can pay into a scheme for his wife, an elderly person can pay into a scheme for their carer. Whatever they pay counts towards the overall contribution limit.

How you get tax relief

You get tax relief on contributions to pension schemes in the DC regime by making payments from which you have deducted tax relief at the basic rate (22 per cent in the year ending 5 April 2004). For example, if you want to pay the full £3,600 into a pension scheme, you first deduct 22% × £3,600 = £792 and hand over £3,600 − £792 = £2,808 to the pension company. The

> **TAX-SAVING IDEA**
> Usually, any income in excess of £100 that a child gets as a result of a gift from a parent counts as the parent's income (see p. 309). But this does not apply where a parent pays money into a pension scheme – for example, a stakeholder scheme – for a child. By using one of the inheritance tax exemptions – for example, regular gifts out of normal income (see p. 137) – you can ensure that the gift is free of inheritance tax too.

company then claims back £792 from the Inland Revenue and adds it to your plan. In this way, £3,600 is paid into your plan at a cost to you of just £2,808.

If you are a higher rate taxpayer, you can get extra tax relief on contributions you make to your own pension scheme through PAYE, your tax return or by sending your tax office claim form PP120. In the example above, higher rate relief on a £3,600 contribution would be 40% × £3,600 = £1,440. But you have already had basic rate relief of £792, so the extra relief due is £1,440 − £792 = £648.

If you are a starting rate taxpayer or non-taxpayer, you still hand over contributions after deducting tax relief at the basic rate and the pension company still claims the relief from the Inland Revenue and adds it to your pension scheme. In this way, you are getting a bonus added to your pension savings. For every £10 a non-taxpayer saves, a bonus of £2.82 is added.

Life insurance cover

If you die before drawing a pension from a scheme in the DC regime, the contributions are normally paid into your estate – usually with interest. But many pension providers also offer some sort of optional life insurance cover, and you can get tax relief on the premiums for this up to:

- a maximum of 5 per cent of your net relevant earnings in the case of a pension scheme started before 6 April 2001. Whatever you pay counts towards the overall contribution limit
- a maximum of 10 per cent of the actual contributions you actually make in the case of a pension scheme started on or after 6 April 2001.

Backdating contributions

You can elect to have a contribution paid at any time up to 31 January in one tax year treated as if it had been paid in the previous tax year. You must make the election either before or at the time you pay the contribution (see p. 185). This is known as 'carrying back' a contribution. You get tax relief at the rates applying to the earlier tax year.

> **EXAMPLE**
> Sheila Fitzherbert is a non-taxpayer. In May 2003, she pays £20 into a stakeholder pension scheme. This is treated as a contribution from which tax relief at the basic rate has already been deducted. The pension provider claims £20 × 22/(100 − 22) = £5.64 from the Inland Revenue and adds it to her stakeholder scheme. So at a cost to Sheila of £20, £25.64 is invested in her scheme.

Retirement annuity contracts

A retirement annuity contract is a type of money purchase pension scheme taken out before 1 July 1988. From that date, no new contracts could be started but you can carry on paying into an existing one. Retirement annuity contracts are very similar to personal pensions but they do not come within the DC regime. Different tax rules apply.

The main differences between retirement annuity contracts and personal pensions are:

- you can't pay into a retirement annuity contract if you belong to an occupational pension scheme (unless the scheme has opted into the DC regime). However, you can pay simultaneously into a retirement annuity contract and pension schemes within the DC regime
- the contribution rules (see below)
- the tax-free lump sum at retirement. With a retirement annuity contract, the maximum lump sum is three times the pension the remaining fund will buy
- the minimum age at which you can draw your pension. With retirement annuity contracts, this is 60. You can transfer very simply to a personal pension at any time in order to benefit from the lower age of 50, but then you lose all the other features of the retirement annuity contract
- employers' contributions. Your employer (if you have one) does not get tax relief on amounts he pays into your retirement annuity contract, so is unlikely to make any contributions to it.

How much tax relief?

The amount of contributions you can get tax relief on depends on: your net relevant earnings (see p. 74), and your age.

If you have no earnings, you can't

> **EXAMPLE**
> Brenda Robertson, 55, is self-employed and has been saving through a retirement annuity contract since 1980. In the tax year ending 5 April 2004, she has net relevant earnings of £100,000. The maximum she can pay into her pension contract is 20 per cent × £100,000 = £20,000.

pay into a retirement annuity contract. To work out the maximum you can pay, take all your earnings without limit – the earnings cap (see p. 75) does not apply to retirement annuity contracts. The table shows the maximum you can pay.

Age at 6 April	*Percentage of net relevant earnings you can pay in contributions*
50 or less	17½
51–55	20
56–60	22½
61–74	27½

Anything you pay into a retirement annuity contract during the tax year reduces the amount you can pay into pension schemes within the DC regime.

How you get tax relief

You pay contributions gross (in other words, without any tax relief deducted). You must claim the tax relief through your tax return (see p. 183). Your PAYE code may be adjusted to give you the tax relief through lower tax deductions from your earnings (see Chapter 25).

If you are a non-taxpayer you do not get any tax relief on contributions to a retirement annuity contract. If you are a starting rate taxpayer, relief is given only at 10 per cent. You will probably be better off contributing to a stakeholder pension scheme (or other scheme within the DC regime), because with these schemes the government adds a bonus to your savings equal to tax relief at the basic rate (see p. 76).

Backdating contributions and unused tax relief

You can claim extra tax relief on payments to a retirement annuity contract by using the 'carry-back' and 'carry-forward' rules. They allow you to make maximum use of the available tax relief even if you do not have enough cash to save in a particular year.

TAX-SAVING IDEA

If you are a high earner and have a retirement annuity contract, you may be able to save more through the contract (because the earnings cap does not apply) than you would through a personal stakeholder scheme or personal pension. But charges for the retirement annuity contract may be higher than for a stakeholder scheme, so you'll need to weigh up carefully which is the best way for you to save. Consider getting advice from an independent financial adviser or accountant.

You can choose to carry back payments made in one tax year to the previous tax year. For example, you could carry back payments made in the tax year ending 5 April 2004 to the tax year ending 5 April 2003. And if you had no net relevant earnings in the year ending 5 April 2003, you could carry the payments back to the year ending 5 April 2002 – but no further. You might choose to carry back payments if your rate of tax in the previous year was higher than your current rate of tax, thus saving money – see the example below. You must make the claim for carry-back either on form 43 or in your tax return by 31 January following the year of payment.

You can carry forward unused tax relief from the previous six tax years. You can do this only if you have already made your maximum contribution for the current year, and the tax relief will be at the tax rates for the year in which you use it up. Unused relief from the earliest years is used first, as the example above shows. The carry back and carry forward rules can be combined to use up relief from seven years ago.

New rules for pensions?

At the time of writing, the government was consulting on simplifying the tax system for pensions. Instead of different rules for occupational schemes, personal pensions, retirement annuity contracts, and so on, under the proposals there would be a

TAX-SAVING IDEA

If you haven't made the maximum contributions for the last six years, you can use the carry-forward rules to get relief on an extra-large contribution paid now.

EXAMPLE

Alan Perry is 37 and has a retirement annuity contract into which he pays £5,000 a year – normally well within his limits for tax relief. But the year ending 5 April 2004 is a bad one and he earns only £20,000 – so his maximum contribution is 17½ per cent of that, or £3,500. He gets tax relief for that year at 22 per cent, his top rate of tax – 22 per cent of £3,500 saves him £770.

But the previous year he had earnings of £45,000, and could have made contributions to his retirement annuity of 17½ per cent of that figure, or £7,875. Since he had paid in his usual £5,000, he has £7,875 − £5,000 = £2,875 of unused allowance.

By using the carry-back rule, he can keep his contribution at £5,000 and also boost the tax relief he gets. He pays £5,000 now and carries back £2,875 to the year ending 5 April 2003. On this, he gets tax relief of 40% × £2,875 = £1,150. The remaining £5,000 − £2,875 = £2,125 stays in the current tax year and qualifies for tax relief of 22% × £2,125 = £467.50. Alan must make the carry-back claim by 31 January 2005.

EXAMPLE

James Loch's net relevant earnings for the last six complete tax years are set out below. He has his 51st birthday in February 2002, which means the maximum retirement annuity contract contributions on which he can get tax relief rose from 17½ per cent of net relevant earnings to 20 per cent on 6 April 2002.

Tax year ending 5 April	*Net relevant earnings* £	*Maximum premiums* £	*Premiums paid* £	*Unused relief* £
1998	20,000	3,500	2,000	1,500
1999	15,000	2,625	2,000	625
2000	20,000	3,500	2,000	1,500
2001	22,000	3,850	2,000	1,850
2002	24,000	4,200	2,000	2,200
2003	22,000	4,400	2,000	2,400

James contributed £2,000 a year to his contract, which means that by the end of the tax year ending 5 April 2003, he had unused relief for the previous six years of £10,075. If, having used all his relief for the tax year ending 5 April 2004, he wanted to pay an extra £5,000, he would use the unused tax relief, starting with the tax year ending 5 April 1998 (£1,500), then the following two years (£625 + £1,500 = £2,125) and £1,375 from the tax year ending 5 April 2001. Relief is given at his tax rate for the year he makes the payments – the one ending 5 April 2004.

single regime. The new regime could be introduced as early as 6 April 2004. The main features would be:

- a lifetime limit on pension savings of £1.4 million per person. This limit would be indexed to increase each year, say, in line with price inflation
- the yearly 'inflow' (from contributions and investment growth) into all your pension savings would be capped at £200,000 a year (also indexed)
- tax relief would still be given on contributions and much of the investment growth and you would be able to take a quarter of the fund up to the lifetime limit as a tax-free lump sum
- savings in excess of the lifetime limit would be taxed to claw back the relief
- the minimum age at which you could draw a pension would be raised to 55 from 2010. This would apply to all occupations.

INDIVIDUAL SAVINGS ACCOUNTS

The individual savings account (ISA) was introduced from 6 April 1999 for anyone aged 18 or over. It allows you to save in three ways without paying tax on the income and capital gains:

> **TAX-SAVING TIP**
> Invest as much as you can each year in an ISA – up to £7,000 each tax year until 5 April 2006. This maximises the amount you are saving free of income tax and capital gains tax.

- cash savings accounts with banks, building societies or National Savings
- stockmarket investments such as shares, unit trusts and gilt-edged stock
- specially designed life insurance policies.

From 6 April 2001, the age limit for investing in a cash ISA was reduced to 16.

The accounts are provided by ISA managers – banks, building societies, insurance companies, investment managers and other financial institutions. You can save up to £7,000 in ISAs in the tax year ending 5 April 2004. The government has promised that this limit will be retained until 5 April 2006. A husband and wife can each save through ISAs, so a married couple can save £14,000 in the tax year ending 5 April 2004.

Any interest, dividends or distributions paid are free of income tax – you don't need to declare them on your tax return. You can take your money out at any time and there will be no capital gains tax to pay when you cash in part or all of an ISA.

There's an added benefit for people whose income is too low to pay tax. ISA managers can claim back the 10 per cent tax credit that comes with dividends and distributions paid until 5 April 2004 and add them to your account. Non-taxpayers cannot claim back the tax credit if they own the shares or unit trusts outside an ISA (see p. 67).

Note that you have to be resident in the UK (unless you are a Crown servant working abroad, or, from 6 April 2001, their husband or wife) to put money into an ISA, but if you go abroad after starting one, you don't have to cash it in – it still goes on getting tax relief.

Investing in ISAs

You can put all your investment for the year in a single ISA which can combine cash savings accounts, stockmarket investments and life insurance

– this is known as a maxi-ISA. Or you can have up to three mini-ISAs, one for each of the three types of savings. You can't change your mind about which option to go for after you have started your ISA savings for the tax year.

The most you can invest in a cash savings account in the tax year ending 5 April 2004 is £3,000. The maximum for life insurance policies is £1,000 a year. So this means if you have three mini-ISAs, the most you can have in the stockmarket investment one is £3,000. With a single maxi-ISA, you can save more than £3,000 in stockmarket investments if you invest less than the maximum in the cash savings part and life insurance – up to the maximum of £7,000 a year.

If you receive shares from employee share-ownership schemes – such as savings-related share option schemes (see p. 237), share incentive plans (see p. 244) and employee profit-sharing schemes (see p. 236) – you can transfer them into an ISA up to the maximum you are allowed to invest. So for the tax year ending 5 April 2004, you can transfer £7,000 of such shares into an ISA provided you made no other ISA investments in the tax year. There will be no capital gains tax to pay on the transfer, no income tax on the dividends and no capital gains tax on any profits on selling the shares. You must make the transfer within 90 days of the shares being issued.

You can save more than the normal maximum amount in ISAs if you have a tax-exempt special savings account (TESSA) taken out on or before 5 April 1999 which reaches the end of its five-year term. The capital – what you invested – can be invested in the cash savings account part of an ISA or a special TESSA-only ISA, up to the maximum TESSA investment of £9,000. The money must be paid into the ISA within six months of the TESSA maturing. You don't have to transfer the money straight from the TESSA to the ISA and you don't have to stay with the same provider for both investments. Make sure you get a certificate from the TESSA provider when you cash it in and hand this to the ISA provider when you open the ISA.

If by mistake you realise you have taken out too many ISAs, tell the manager of the last one you bought. The tax due on any income or gains on it will have to be paid by the manager and you will be sent details for entering on your tax return.

Switching ISAs

If in any tax year you decide to go for two or three mini-ISAs, you can have a different manager for each one. Whether you have mini-ISAs or a maxi-ISA, next year you do not have to stick with the same ISA manager(s) you chose this year.

You can transfer your existing ISAs from one manager to another. In the year the ISA was taken out, however, you can do this only by closing the old ISA and switching everything in it to a new one. Once the tax year in which you took out the ISA has ended, you can switch just part without closing the old one. Ask the ISA managers to organise the switch – you may lose tax relief if you withdraw cash yourself from one ISA to pay into another. Note that there may be charges for switching.

PERSONAL EQUITY PLANS (PEPS)

A personal equity plan (PEP) is a way of investing in various stockmarket investments such as shares and unit trusts without paying income tax or capital gains tax on the proceeds. PEPs came to an end on 5 April 1999, so you can no longer invest new money in them. But you can continue to own PEPs taken out on or before that date and get the tax benefits.

> **TAX-SAVING TIP**
>
> Keep your old PEPs going if you can afford to – together with saving through ISAs, you can build up a sizeable chunk of savings with no tax to pay on income or gains.

From 6 April 2001, many of the rules applying to PEPs were relaxed to bring them in line with ISAs, for example:

- if you have different types of PEP (for example, general PEPs and single company PEPs), they can be merged
- the range of investments eligible for PEPs is now the same as that for stocks-and-shares ISAs
- you can transfer part of a PEP (instead of just the whole PEP) to another manager.

There is one circumstance under which tax might be due on PEP proceeds: if some of your money is held as cash on deposit and earns interest which is paid out to you. If more than £180 of interest is paid out to you in a year, the plan manager must deduct tax at 20 per cent and hand this over to the Inland Revenue. The net interest is treated in the same way as any other interest you receive after deduction of tax – higher-rate taxpayers face an additional tax bill (see p. 63).

TAX EXEMPT SPECIAL SAVINGS ACCOUNTS (TESSAS)

TAX-SAVING TIP

Remaining TESSAs will end in the tax year ending 5 April 2004. Pay in the maximum you can in this last year and, when it ends, transfer the TESSA capital to an ISA so that it can continue to grow tax-free.

A tax exempt special savings account (TESSA) allows you to save with a bank or building society without paying income tax on the interest, provided you save for five years. The last date for starting a TESSA was 5 April 1999, but if you started one on or before that date it can continue until its five-year term is up.

The maximum you can save is £9,000 over five years which you can build up by regular savings (up to £150 a month), by lump sum deposits or a combination of both. No more than £3,000 could be invested in the first year of your first TESSA, and the maximum in each of the remaining years is £1,800.

If you need income from your TESSA, you can draw out up to 80 per cent of the interest. But you must leave at least 20 per cent – the equivalent of the tax which would have been deducted from the interest with a normal savings account. If you draw out more than this – or withdraw any of the capital – the TESSA comes to an end and all the interest will be taxed.

When a TESSA reaches the end of its five-year term, some or all of the capital – what you invested – can be invested in the cash savings account part of an ISA or a special TESSA-only ISA. This could be up to the maximum you can invest in a TESSA of £9,000, and doesn't count against the maximum you are allowed to invest in ISAs for the tax year. The money must be transferred within six months of the end of the TESSA. If you also want to invest the accumulated interest on your TESSA in an ISA, this counts as part of the annual ISA limit of £7,000.

INVESTING IN GROWING BUSINESSES

The government offers a variety of incentives to encourage you to invest in small and growing companies. The tax breaks are welcome, but bear in mind these are by their nature high-risk investments, so losses could outweigh any up-front tax relief and returns might not materialise to become tax-free. However, if the company does take off, your handsome profits will be sheltered from tax and at least losses can be set off against other capital or income. The main tax incentives are:

- loss relief
- Enterprise investment scheme
- Venture capital trusts.

The table broadly summarises the tax incentives you can get.

Tax reliefs for investment in unquoted trading companies

Type of investment	*Income tax relief on amount you invest*	*Capital gains deferral relief*	*Tax-free income*	*Tax-free gains*	*Can set losses against taxable gains on other assets*	*Income tax relief on losses*
Investing direct in unquoted trading company shares	No	No	No	No(1)	Yes	Yes
Enterprise investment scheme	Yes at 20%	Yes	No	Yes	Yes	Yes
Venture capital trusts	Yes at 20%	Yes	Yes	Yes	No	No

(1) But gains qualify for business asset taper relief (see p. 120).

Income tax loss relief

If you buy newly issued shares in an unquoted trading company and subsequently sell them at a loss, you can under the normal capital gains tax rules set the loss against capital gains you make on other assets (see p. 117). Alternatively, you can deduct the loss from:

- your income for the tax year in which you make the loss, and/or
- your income for the tax year before the one in which you make the loss.

To be eligible for this relief, the shares must match the definition of shares that can qualify for the EIS (see below) and meet certain other conditions, but you do not have to have invested in the shares through an EIS.

You must claim loss relief in writing within one year of 31 January following the year in which you make the loss. For example, if you make a loss in the year ending 5 April 2004, you must make your claim by 31 January 2006.

Enterprise investment scheme (EIS)

If you invest £500 or more in new shares issued by certain unquoted trading companies, you can get tax relief on the investment – provided you hold the shares for a minimum period. For investments on or before 5 April 2000, the minimum period was five years, but from 6 April 2000 it is three years from the issue of the shares (or when the company starts trading if this is later). In the past, you could not complete the minimum period if within the three (or five) years the company floated on a stock exchange. But for shares issued from 7 March 2001 onwards (or, in the case of shares already issued, for events occurring on or after 7 March 2001), the period is not broken provided the flotation had not been arranged at the time you invested in the shares.

Investments in EIS approved investment funds which invest in such companies also qualify – even if less than £500.

If you dispose of the investments after the minimum period, there will be no capital gains tax to pay when you sell your investment. To further encourage you to invest in growing companies, a series of investments in EIS shares will be treated as a single investment when working out taper relief for capital gains tax – see p. 119. This means that 'serial investors' can still reduce the capital gains tax bill on EIS shares held for less than the minimum period.

You get income tax relief at 20 per cent on up to £150,000 of EIS investments in any tax year. But if you make the investment between 6 April and 5 October inclusive, half the investment up to a maximum of £25,000 can be set off against your income for the previous tax year. With a married couple, husband and wife can each invest up to these limits.

Making EIS investments can also allow you to put off paying capital gains tax made on other assets if you are able to claim capital gains deferral relief (see p. 132). To get the relief, you must reinvest at least part of the proceeds within a period starting one year before and ending three years after receiving them.

The companies you can invest in must be unquoted; this includes those with shares traded on the Alternative Investment Market (AIM). They have to be trading companies, which excludes those engaged in banking, insurance, share-dealing, dealing in land or property, farming, market gardening, forestry, managing hotels, leasing and legal or accountancy services. The company must be trading in the UK, but it does not have to be registered or resident in the UK. Investments in schemes where a substantial part of the return is guaranteed or backed by property made on or after 2 July 1997 are also excluded because they do not carry the degree of risk envisaged when the EIS was introduced.

You won't get tax relief on investments if you are connected with the companies – broadly this means being an employee or director or owning over 30 per cent of the shares. In deciding how much of a company you own, you must include the holdings of connected persons – your spouse and you and your spouse's children, parents and grandparents (but not brothers or sisters) – and associates such as business partners. Once you have made your EIS investment, however, you can take part in the active management of the company as a paid director (or 'business angel') provided you had not been connected with the company before you made the EIS investment.

You can't claim the tax relief until the company has carried out its qualifying trade for at least four months, and you lose it if it ceases to do so within three years. If you sell the shares within the minimum period, you lose tax relief on the amount you sell them for (that is, if you sell them for more than they cost you, you have to pay back all the relief). If you sell the shares after the minimum period and the company still qualifies under the scheme there will be no capital gains tax to pay on any gain you make. If you make a loss, this can be set off against other income or capital gains (see loss relief on p. 85) – reducing your overall tax bill for the year.

Business Expansion Scheme

The Business Expansion Scheme (BES), which used to offer tax relief on a wider range of investments than the EIS, came to an end on 31 December 1993. But although no new investments have been possible under the BES since, there is still no capital gains tax to pay when you sell BES investments which you made after 18 March 1986.

Venture capital trusts (VCTs)

VCTs are a type of investment trust listed on the stock exchange whose business is investing in the shares of unquoted trading companies. By buying VCT shares, you are investing in a spread of different small, growing companies. This should help to spread your risks, and the fact that the VCT is itself quoted should make it easier to find buyers if you want to sell your investment later on.

You must be aged at least 18 to invest in a VCT and you must buy the VCT shares when they are newly issued. The shares must give you no preferential rights to dividends or a share of the assets if the VCT is wound up, and there must be no promise or guarantee that you'll get your money back.

The unquoted trading shares in which the VCT invests must meet basically the same definition as shares eligible for EIS (see opposite).

Provided you hold the shares for at least three years (five years in the case of shares issued before 6 April 2000), you get income tax relief at a rate of 20 per cent on up to £100,000 invested in VCT shares in the tax year ending 5 April 2004.

You get tax relief on any dividends paid by the VCT provided certain conditions are met.

Provided you've held the shares for three (or five) years, there is no tax on any gain you make when you sell VCT shares. But any loss you make is also ignored – so it can't be used to reduce capital gains tax on other assets or set off against your income.

But making VCT investments does allow you to put off paying a capital gains tax bill on the disposal of other assets if you claim capital gains deferral relief (see p. 132). To get the relief, you must reinvest the proceeds in VCT shares within one year before or one year after making the gain (and you must receive some income tax relief on the VCT investment).

Community investment tax relief

Since January 2003, a new scheme offers tax relief on money you invest or lend that is used to set up small businesses or community projects in socially deprived areas. You cannot invest direct in these ventures – only via an accredited community development finance institution.

The businesses and community projects are such that the likelihood of your making a profit is very slim. So this tax relief scheme should more properly be viewed as an incentive to philanthropic giving rather than investment. Although open to individuals, it is likely to be of more interest to firms wishing to 'put something back' into their local communities.

For details of the tax relief, see p. 191.

FRINGE BENEFITS

CHAPTER 9

Many employers give their employees non-cash fringe benefits as part of their pay package. Typical examples are employer's contributions to a pension scheme, company cars, luncheon vouchers or interest-free loans to buy your season ticket for the railway.

Many fringe-benefits are tax-free, and even those which are not can remain good value for employees because the taxable value put on them may be less than it would cost you to pay for the benefit yourself.

However, the government has been steadily raising the tax it charges you on benefits connected with motoring as part of its wider policies on the environment. If you drive a large, inefficient car (either your own or a company car) and/or run up substantial business mileage, since April 2002 you will be taxed heavily.

Most benefits that are subject to income tax are now also subject to employers' (but not usually employees') National Insurance contributions.

TAX-FREE FOR ALL

There are many fringe benefits which are tax-free for all employees regardless of what you are paid – see the list below. There are also a number of other benefits which are tax-free for some employees, but not all. There are more details of these on p. 96.

> **TAX-SAVING IDEA**
> There is a long list of fringe benefits which are tax-free whatever your level of earnings – try to take advantage of them in your negotiations with your boss.

Your employer's own products or services provided to you at less than the price to the general public are tax-free as long as providing them does not cost your employer anything; for example, goods sold to you at the wholesale price, cheap conveyancing for solicitors which does not require the firm to take on extra staff, or free bus travel for bus company employees which does not displace fare-paying customers. The courts have decided that something costs your employer nothing to provide if the extra cost (rather than the average cost) is nil – for example, a private school educating one of its teacher's children at no charge was deemed to be a tax-free benefit because the extra cost to the employer was nothing.

> **TAX-SAVING IDEA**
> Working parents should try to persuade their employers to provide childcare facilities, as this fringe benefit is tax-free. Your private childcare arrangements are not eligible for tax relief though you might be able to claim tax credits (see p. 12).

The following are also tax-free:

- free or subsidised meals at work, provided they are available to all employees and are not provided in a public restaurant
- changing room and shower facilities at work, provided they are available to all employees
- luncheon vouchers (or equivalent) up to a maximum of 15p a day
- your employer's contributions to a pension, life insurance or sick pay insurance policy for you (but premiums to a private medical insurance policy for you do count as a taxable fringe benefit)
- loans on preferential terms where the total loan outstanding is not more than £5,000
- routine medical check-ups or medical screening for you or your family
- the costs of medical treatment while you are working abroad (or insurance to cover it)
- nurseries and playschemes run by your employer. Under current rules, if the childcare is not on your employer's premises, then the employer must participate in financing and arranging the care. At the time of writing, the government was consulting on proposals to make a wider range of employer-funded (but not necessarily employer-run) childcare arrangements tax-free
- living accommodation provided it is either necessary for you to do your job, or beneficial and customary for someone in your line of work (for example, a caretaker). This benefit is not tax-free if you are a director, unless you have no material interest in the company, and you are either a full-time working director, or a director of a non-profit-making company or charity
- living accommodation provided as part of special security arrangements, and other security precautions, if there is a threat to your security because of your job
- if you live in accommodation which is tax-free for one of the two reasons

above, any council tax paid by your employer is also a tax-free benefit

- a car-parking or bicycle-parking space at or near your work (although some local councils are proposing to tax parking spaces and employers might pass this cost on to employees)
- free breakfast if you participate in a cycle-to-work day (limited to six days a year but unlimited once Budget 2003 changes come into effect
- mileage allowances up the authorised rates, if you use your own car for work (see overleaf)
- mileage allowance of 20p per mile if you use your own bicycle for business
- mileage allowance of 24p per mile if you use your own motorbike for business
- passenger mileage allowance of 5p per passenger per mile if on business trips colleagues travel with you in your car
- travelling expenses paid for your spouse if he or she accompanies you when you go to work abroad subject to certain conditions
- reasonable extra travel or overnight subsistence expenses paid to you because of disruption to public transport by industrial action
- the cost of transport home if you are occasionally required to work late after public transport has shut down or cannot reasonably be used
- financial help with the cost of travelling between home and work if you are severely and permanently disabled and cannot use public transport
- equipment – for example a hearing aid or wheelchair – provided if you are disabled and which is primarily to enable you to do your job, even if you also use it privately
- some retraining and counselling costs paid for by your employer when you leave your job, providing you have worked for your employer for at least two years
- the cost of fees and books for further education or training courses paid for by your employer if the course is either necessary or directly beneficial for your work, or if you are under 21 when starting a general educational course. If you have to be away from your normal workplace for not more than 12 months, and will return to it after training, some travel and subsistence costs may be tax-free
- truly personal gifts from your employer of an appropriate size and nature (excluding cash), including gifts on marriage, and long-service awards of things or shares in the company. However, long-service awards are tax-free only if they are to mark service of 20 years or more, they do not cost

> **TAX-SAVING IDEA**
>
> These perks are also still free of tax: entertainment by your suppliers or customers at cultural or sporting events (within certain rules); air miles (which enable you to make cheap flights); and non-cash gifts costing up to £250 from a third party.

more than £20 for each year of service (increasing to £50 per year from 2003), and you have received no similar award in the previous ten years

- suggestion scheme awards (see Incentive awards on p. 217)
- entertainment for you or your family provided by someone other than your employer purely as a gesture of goodwill – but not if there are any strings attached, or if it counts as payment for your services
- small non-cash gifts from someone other than your employer. To qualify, the total cost of all gifts you received from the same donor must not be more than £150 in any tax year (increasing to £250 from 2003), and they must not be provided on any sort of condition, for example, that you will provide some particular service
- annual parties or similar functions, such as a Christmas dinner or summer party, which are open to staff generally and together cost no more than £75 a head per year (increasing to £150 from 2003) to provide
- sports facilities generally available to all staff and their families (and not available to the general public)
- incidental overnight expenses paid or reimbursed by your employer if you are away overnight on business, such as newspapers and phone calls home. The maximum payment is £5 a night (£10 outside the UK); if more is paid, the whole of the payment becomes taxable, not just the excess
- relocation expenses if you move house for your job, such as the costs of buying and selling homes, some travel and subsistence expenses, and bridging loan expenses. There is a maximum of £8,000 per move; you will be taxed on anything over this figure
- private use of a mobile phone provided by employer
- work buses which can transport nine or more employees, discounted or free travel on public bus services subsidised by your employer, bicycles and cycling safety equipment for employees to get between home and work
- the loan of a computer from your employer even if for private use
- from 6 April 2003, up to £2 a week towards household expenses if you work from home (and more if your employer has evidence to show you incur higher extra costs).

Tax-free car mileage allowances

If you use your own car for work, most employers pay you a mileage allowance. Your employer decides what mileage allowance to give you, but the amount must be compared with the Inland Revenue's mileage scale. Provided the allowance does not exceed the authorised rates, it is tax-free. (See p. 96 for what happens with more generous allowances.)

The authorised scale is the same for all cars. For the year ending 5 April 2004, the rates are:

- 40p per mile for the first 10,000 business miles, and
- 25p per mile for each additional business mile.

The scale takes into account depreciation (so you can't claim any capital allowances on what you paid for the car). For what counts as business travel see p. 229 – note that it usually excludes travel between home and work.

> **TAX-SAVING IDEA**
> The tax-free authorised mileage rates, if you use your own car for work, will not cover all your costs if you drive a fuel-thirsty car. You can save most tax by using a relatively small, fuel-efficient vehicle.

If your employer pays mileage allowance at less than the authorised rates and your actual motoring costs are higher than the allowance you get, you can claim the difference between the authorised rate and what you get as an allowable expense. If you don't get any mileage allowance, you can claim your actual costs up to the authorised rate as an allowable expense. You can't get tax relief on any motoring costs in excess of the Inland Revenue scale.

TAXABLE FOR ALL

There are four types of benefits which are always taxable. These are:

- assets transferred to you or payments made for you
- vouchers (with a few exceptions – see p. 95) and any goods or services paid for by credit card
- living accommodation provided by your employer (apart from the few exceptions listed on p. 90)
- mileage allowances in excess of the authorised rate if you use your own transport for work.

Assets transferred to you or payments made for you

Your employer may give you as a present, or allow you to buy it cheap, an item such as a television set, furniture, groceries or your employer's own product. These payments in kind may be taxed in a number of ways depending on how much you earn and whether you have the alternative of cash instead.

If you earn less than £8,500 (see p. 96)

The taxable value is the second-hand value of the payment in kind (whether or not you actually sell it). Since many assets have a much lower second-hand value than the cost of buying them new this can be advantageous to you.

If you earn at the rate of £8,500 or more (see p. 96)
The tax rules are tougher for those who earn at a rate of £8,500 or more, or directors. They pay tax on the larger of:

- the second-hand value, or
- the cost to the employer of providing the asset, including ancillary costs such as installation or servicing. Remember, though, that if it is the employer's own product, you pay only the extra cost to the employer. So if it does not cost the employer anything (after taking into account anything you have paid for it) it should be tax-free.

If you are being given something you have already had the use of (apart from a car), the taxable value is the larger of the following, less any amount you have paid:

- the market value when you are given it, or
- the market value of the asset when it was first loaned out (either to you or to anyone else), less the total amount on which tax has already been charged. This is because assets which have been on loan will already have had some tax paid on them.

> **TAX-SAVING IDEA**
> Fringe benefits which are not tax-free can still be a tax-efficient way of being paid. The taxable value put on them may be much lower than the value to you.

If you are given a car, for example on leaving a job, you are taxed on its second-hand value when you are given it, less anything you pay for it. If you buy your company car for a low price, you may have to pay tax on the difference between the price you paid and what your tax office reckons it would fetch on the open market.

Cash or perks?
You may be given the alternative of either a particular payment in kind, such as free board and lodging, or cash. If you have a perk you can convert into money either immediately or at short notice, you have to pay tax on the value of the cash alternative, even if you opt for the perk. However, note that there is a concession for some workers, including farm workers, and for cash alternatives to cars. And you usually will not be taxed on a reduction in salary in exchange for your employer paying for work-related training.

Payments made for you
However much you earn, you pay tax on the full amount of any bill paid directly by your employer on your behalf, such as:

- your phone bill
- your personal credit card bill
- your council tax (unless it is tax-free because you live in tax-free accommodation, see p. 90)
- rent paid direct to your landlord
- a tax bill.

Note, though, that this normally applies only to payments settled directly by your employer, for example to the telephone company, the credit card company or your landlord. If you were given cash to settle the bill yourself, it should already have been added to your other pay on your payslip and taxed through PAYE.

Vouchers and credit cards

You may be given a voucher for a particular service (for example, a season ticket), a credit token or a company credit or charge card. If so, you are taxed on their cash equivalent unless they appear in the list of tax-free fringe benefits on pp. 90–92 (for example, luncheon vouchers, gift vouchers which count as a small gift), or the voucher gives you access to certain minor benefits that are in the tax-free list, such as a pass for an employer-subsidised bus service. Cash vouchers worth a specified amount of cash will usually be taxed under PAYE.

For vouchers and cards which do count as a taxable fringe benefit, broadly speaking you pay tax on the expense incurred by the person who provided them, less any amount that you have paid yourself. You will not have to pay tax on any annual card fee or interest paid by your employer.

Company credit cards and charge cards are often provided as a convenient way of paying business expenses. But you will have to pay tax on anything which is not an allowable business expense.

Living accommodation

In some cases living accommodation may count as a tax-free fringe benefit – see the list on p. 90. But if it does not, it counts as a taxable perk however much you earn. It includes houses, flats, houseboats and holiday homes but not board and lodging or hotel-type accommodation where typically you get food and other services.

The taxable value of the accommodation is based on the higher of:

- the rateable value of the property, or
- if the property is let, the rent paid for it.

From the taxable value, you can deduct anything you pay for the accommodation, and also, if part of the property is used exclusively for your work, a proportion for that.

Rateable values are still used, although rates are no longer payable. However, for properties in Scotland, where rateable values were revalued more recently than elsewhere, only a percentage of the rateable value is used (found by multiplying the rateable value by 100 and dividing by 270). If there is no rateable value your employer will have to agree a value with your tax office.

If the tax is based on the rateable value, there may be an extra charge if the property cost more than £75,000, including the cost of any improvements made before the current tax year, but deducting anything you paid towards the cost. Broadly, you pay interest at the Inland Revenue's official rate at the start of the tax year (5 per cent for the year ending 5 April 2004) on the excess over £75,000, reduced in line with the number of days you do not have the property if it is provided for only part of the year. You can deduct any rent you pay not already deducted when working out the basic taxable value, and an amount for business use.

Mileage allowances

If, when you use your own transport for work, your employer pays you a mileage allowance that is more than the Inland Revenue authorised rates which apply from 6 April 2002 onwards (see p. 93), the excess is taxable. This is the case even if your actual costs are so high that you do not make any profit from your mileage allowance.

TAXABLE FOR SOME, TAX-FREE FOR OTHERS

The following benefits are tax-free if you earn at a rate of less than £8,500 and are not a director:

- a company car or van
- private medical or dental insurance
- services without a second-hand value, such as hairdressing at work
- loans of things or money.

However, these benefits are taxable for employees who earn at the rate of £8,500 or more. You cannot get around this by asking to be paid under £8,500 and getting substantial perks instead. To work out whether you earn at a rate of £8,500 a year, you need to take into account two rules:

Rule 1
Your earnings for this purpose are any kind of pay you receive for the job – that is, including your expenses and the taxable value of any perks worked out as if you earned £8,500 or more. However, you can exclude any contributions you make to an employer's pension scheme, and payroll giving donations.

Rule 2
The earnings are worked out assuming you work full-time for a whole year. So if you leave a job half-way through the year, having earned £5,000, you will still count as earning more than £8,500 – because in the second part of the year you would have earned another £5,000, that is, £10,000 in total.

If you are a director you are automatically counted as earning £8,500 or more unless all of the following three conditions apply:

- you are either a full-time working director or a director of a charity or non-profit-making concern
- you do not own or control more than 5 per cent of the share capital
- you earn under £8,500.

Your employer should take account of your rate of earnings when filling in your taxable benefits and their cash equivalent: you can tell what category you fall into depending on whether you get a form P11D (which is the form for people who earn at a rate of £8,500 or more) or P9D (the alternative form if you earn under £8,500).

Company cars
Some employers provide a company car that is also available for your private use (including travel between home and work). Since 6 April 2002, a new way of taxing this benefit has been introduced. The new system aims to cut polluting emissions and is much less favourable than the previous system if you drive a gas-guzzler. Some employers are offering employees cash instead of a car and requiring you to use your own car for business – but changes to the mileage allowance (see p. 92) aim to stop you or your employer profiting from this move. If you only need a car for work occasionally, note that a 'pool car' is tax-free. To qualify it must not normally be kept overnight near your home, it must be used by more than one employee, and any private use must be a consequence of business use. But before you can work out which option is better for you, you need to be

> **TAX-SAVING IDEA**
> The taxation of large and inefficient company cars is becoming more onerous. If you are about to get a new car, consider a smaller, more fuel-efficient model.

able to work out the taxable value of a company car and any free fuel you get.

Working out the tax on a company car

In the tax year ending 5 April 2004, the taxable value of your company car is usually its price when new multiplied by a percentage based on the carbon dioxide (CO2) emissions figure for your type of car. There are five steps to arrive at the taxable value:

- take the list price of your car when new
- find out the CO2 emissions figure for your car
- use Inland Revenue tables to find out the percentage corresponding to that CO2 emissions figure
- Increase or reduce the percentage by any supplement or discount (but only if the car was registered on or after 1 January 1998)
- Multiply the list price by the percentage.

If you had the car for only part of the year, you can scale down the taxable value in proportion to the number of days in the tax year it was not available. And, you can deduct anything you pay yourself for use of the car.

The car's list price when new

This is the list price of the car at registration (not the dealer's price), including delivery charges, VAT and car tax. Any contribution you make towards the cost of the car is deducted from its price, up to a limit of £5,000, and the maximum price for tax purposes is capped at £80,000. For cars without a list price, your employer will have to reach agreement with the Revenue, usually on the basis of published car price guides. The market value is used for classic cars worth at least £15,000 and aged 15 years or more at the end of the tax year.

You cannot create an artificially low price by getting a basic model and adding accessories. The price includes any accessories fitted before the car was made available to you, and any accessories or set of accessories worth more than £100 which are fitted after that. Accessories needed because you are disabled are excluded.

The CO2 emissions figure

Cars registered in the UK from 1 March 2001 onwards have an official CO2 emissions figure which is shown on the vehicle registration document. You can also get the figure for your car from the Vehicle Certification Agency: VCA (FCB requests), 1 The Eastgate Office Centre, Eastgate Road, Bristol BS5 6XX Tel: 0117 951 5151 *www.vca.gov.uk*.

Cars registered between 1 January 1998 and 28 February 2001 also usually have an emissions figure but this is not shown on the registration document.

You can get the figure either free from the Society for Motor Manufacturers and Traders website (*www.smmt.co.uk*) or from the car manufacturer or importer (there may be a small charge).

Cars registered before 1998 – and a few other more recent but unusual models – do not have a CO2 emissions figure. Instead, the taxable value is the list price multiplied by a percentage based on the car's engine size (see table).

The percentage charge

The CO2 emissions figure is given in grams per kilometre. The minimum percentage of list price that you will be taxed on is normally 15 per cent (for cars emitting 165 g/km and 155 g/km in the years ending 5 April 2003 and 2004, respectively). The percentage increases in steps of 1 per cent for every extra 5 g/km up to a normal maximum percentage of 35 per cent – see table. If the emissions figure for your car does not end in '0' or '5' you round it down to the nearest amount that does.

CO2-related car benefit percentage charges for the year ending 5 April 2003 and 2004

% of car's price to be taxed	*Given CO2 emission figure (g/km) in tax year ending 5 April 2003*	*2004*	*% of car's price to be taxed*	*Given CO2 emission figure (g/km) in tax year ending 5 April 2003*	*2004*
15%	165	155	26%	220	210
16%	170	160	27%	225	215
17%	175	165	28%	230	220
18%	180	170	29%	235	225
19%	185	175	30%	240	230
20%	190	180	31%	245	235
21%	195	185	32%	250	240
22%	200	190	33%	255	245
23%	205	195	34%	260	250
24%	210	200	35%	265*	255*
25%	215	205			

*or more

TAX-SAVING IDEA

If you drive a company car or van in central London, the taxable value of your vehicle already includes any congestion charges (or related penalty charges) that are reimbursed by your employer. There is no need to declare these amounts separately and no further tax to pay on them.

Car benefit percentage charges for cars without a CO2 emissions figure

Engine size	*Percentage of car's price to be taxed*	
	Cars registered before January 1998	*Cars registered on or after 1 January 1998*
Up to 1,400 cc	15%	15%
1,401–2,000 cc	22%	25%
Over 2000 cc	32%	35%
Cars without a cylinder capacity	32%	35%

EXAMPLE

Sanjay O'Rourke chose a new company car in March 2003. He could have any make or model up to a cost of £16,000. He was thinking about an Alfa Romeo 156. He checked its CO2 emissions figure which was 202 g/km. The table (see above) told him that at this level of emissions, in the year ending 5 April 2004 he would be taxed on 24 per cent of the car's list price: 24% × £16,000 = £3,840. As Sanjay is a higher rate taxpayer, the car would cost him 40% × £3,840 = £1,536 in tax. Instead Sanjay opted for a Vauxhall Vectra. It cost the same, but with an emissions figure of 171 g/km, he is taxed on just 18 per cent of the list price, giving a taxable value of 18% × £16,000 = £2,880 and a tax bill of 40% × £2,880 = £1,152. Choosing a more fuel-efficient car saves Sanjay £384 tax this year.

Supplements and discounts for cars registered on or after 1 January 1998

If your company car is a diesel, you must add an extra 3 per cent to percentage charge unless the car meets EU standards for cleaner diesels. But the overall percentage is still capped at 35 per cent.

Some alternatively fuelled cars (for example, LPG or electric cars) qualify you for a discount which reduces the overall percentage to less than the normal 15 per cent minimum.

Fuel for company cars

If you get a company car, you may get free fuel for private use as well. In the year ending 5 April 2003, this was taxed according to a fixed scale of charges added to your taxable income. The only reduction you got was if you had the car for only part of the year, in which case the scale charge was worked out in line with the number of days the car was available to you. If the car was provided throughout the tax year, but the free fuel was only provided for part of the year the full scale charge applied.

Car fuel scale charges in the tax year ending 5 April 2003

	Engine size, cc		
	0-1,400	*1,401-2,000*	*2,001+*
Petrol			
2001–02	£1,930	£2,460	£3,620(1)
2002–03	£2,240	£2,850	£4,200(1)
Diesel			
2001–02	£2,460	£2,460	£3,620
2002–03	£2,850	£2,850	£4,200

(1) These figures also apply for cars without a cylinder capacity

From 6 April 2003 onwards, the taxation of free fuel has been brought into line with that for company cars. The taxable value of fuel is a percentage of a set figure which is £14,400 in the year ending 5 April 2004. The percentage is the same as that used to find the taxable value of the company car (see p. 99). Therefore in the year ending 5 April 2004, the taxable value of fuel will normally lie between 15% × £14,400 = £2,160 and 35% × £14,400 = £5,040. But it will be lower if you drive a fuel-efficient car running on alternative fuel and higher if you drive a standard diesel. The fuel charge is proportionately reduced if you stop receiving free fuel for part of the tax year or your company car is not available for the full year. There is no fuel charge for an electrically powered company car.

Under both the old and new systems, you can avoid the fuel charge if you are required by your employer to reimburse the full cost of fuel used for private purposes and you actually do so. Bear in mind that commuting between home and work normally counts as private use. But fuel provided for travel between home and work for disabled employees is tax-free.

Vans

A van provided by your employer for your private use is currently very lightly taxed, compared with a company car. The basic taxable value of a van is £500, and there is no tax charge for free fuel. You may also qualify for these reductions:

- the taxable value is reduced to £350 if the van is aged four years or more at the end of the tax year
- if the van is shared with other employees and is not exclusively yours for any period of more than 30 days at a stretch, the taxable value is split between all the employees concerned
- the taxable value is reduced in line with the number of days within the tax year for which it is unavailable (as for company cars, see above)

- any amount you have to pay for the use of the van is deducted from the taxable value.

Cheap or free loans

The basic rule is that if your employer provides a cheap or interest-free loan, you have to pay tax on the difference between the interest you pay and the interest worked out at an official rate – 5 per cent for the tax year ending 5 April 2004. You do not need to worry about any of this, however, if:

- your employer lends money as part of its normal business, comparable loans were available to members of the general public (a substantial proportion actually being sold to them), and the loan was made to you on the same terms as those comparable loans. Such loans are tax-free from 6 April 1994, even if they were first taken out before then, and
- the total loans you have outstanding are no more than £5,000 throughout the tax year. If you have several loans, one of which qualifies for tax relief, then the qualifying loan is ignored when deciding whether the other loans fall within the limit.

EXAMPLE

Lene Mikkelsen has a £10,000 loan from her employer to help buy a flat, at a special low interest rate of 4 per cent (compared with the official interest rate of 5 per cent). She paid off £1,000 of the loan halfway through the year. The taxable value of the perk is £95 in the tax year ending 5 April 2004, worked out as follows:

Amount outstanding:		
At start of tax year	£10,000	
At end of tax year	£9,000	
Average:	£19,000 ÷ 2 = £9,500.	
Interest payable at official rate	£9,500 × 5% =	£475
Actual interest payable		£380
Difference (taxable value)		£95

Lene is a basic rate taxpayer, so the loan costs her 22% × £95 = £20.90 in tax in the year ending 5 April 2004.

To work out the tax on a loan, you take the average amount owing during the year (the whole amount, not just the amount above £5,000), adjusted if the loan was only outstanding for part of the year. You then multiply the average loan by the average official rate of interest for the period in the year during which the loan was outstanding (your tax office should be able to tell you this). Lastly, you deduct the interest you were actually liable to pay during the tax year, to find the amount on which you will be taxed.

If you think that you will lose out under this averaging method, you can choose to calculate the figures using the daily amounts of the loan and official rates of interest. However, you have to use the same method for all your taxable loans, and the calculations can get quite complex. If you want to make this choice, you have to tell your tax office within roughly 21 months of the end of the tax year in question.

Note that under either method, if the loan qualifies for tax relief, you get tax relief on both the interest you actually paid and the difference between that and the official rate of interest. Effectively, the tax relief is worked out assuming you paid the official rate of interest.

Private medical or dental insurance

If your employer pays premiums for a private medical expenses policy for you (for example, through a group scheme for all employees), the amount is a taxable benefit. The same applies to dental insurance schemes. You pay tax on the cost to your employer, less any amount you pay for the benefit.

Other benefits

There is a variety of other perks taxable only if you earn at the rate of £8,500 a year or more. These include:

- relocation expenses which would normally be tax-free but which are above the £8,000 tax-free limit for each move
- childcare provided by your employer – workplace nurseries and playschemes – should be tax-free, but if your employer just pays for you to arrange your own childcare, this will count as a taxable benefit. However, you might then be able to claim the childcare element of working tax credit (see p. 12).
- services supplied, such as free hairdressing, holidays, gardening or a free chauffeur – but remember that you pay tax only on the extra cost to your employer, so services that your employer provides as part of their normal business may be tax-free
- share schemes or share options which are not tax-free – see Chapter 17
- subscriptions and fees paid for by your employer for you to join professional bodies, societies, leisure or sports clubs etc. Note that if you had paid a professional subscription yourself and could have claimed the cost against your tax because it was necessary for your work (see p. 231), there will be no tax charge
- any income tax paid for you by your employer, other than through PAYE.

This may sometimes apply if PAYE was not deducted from your pay at the proper time, and the tax was later paid for you or if there was insufficient pay from which to deduct the tax under PAYE.

- the value of anything provided for your use, except for cars, vans, mobile phones and living accommodation (for example, a television, furniture, a yacht or aircraft). The value is 20 per cent of the market value when it was first provided (to you or to anyone else), plus any expense of providing it met by your employer. If you are later given whatever it is, you will be taxed as explained on p. 93.
- help with educating your children (unless this is nothing to do with your job, for example it is pure coincidence that your child gets one of the generally available scholarships your employer's firm provides).

MINIMISING CAPITAL GAINS TAX

CHAPTER 10

If you own items which increase in value, you may find yourself paying capital gains tax. For example, shares, unit trusts, land, property and antiques can increase in price, giving you a capital gain. If you sell them – or even give them away – you may be faced with a tax bill at up to 40 per cent of the chargeable gain.

The average taxpayer is unlikely to pay capital gains tax, however. There is a long list of assets on which gains are tax-free, including your only or main home, private cars and other personal belongings (see opposite). If you do part with an asset which falls into the capital gains tax net, you can deduct from the gain any money you've spent acquiring and owning it. You also deduct any losses you've made on other assets.

Then there is indexation allowance to reduce the part of the gain caused by inflation between 1982 and 1998 and taper relief reduces the gain still further by taking into account how long you have owned the asset since 6 April 1998. There are special reliefs which can reduce or eliminate the gain made on selling business assets, farms or growing businesses. And if there is still any chargeable gain left after all these deductions, there is an annual tax-free allowance that can swallow up another £7,700 of chargeable gains in the tax year ending 5 April 2003, £7,900 for the tax year ending 5 April 2004.

This chapter explains how capital gains tax works and the details of the various reliefs and allowances. It tells you how to keep your capital gains tax to a minimum. And it sets out the complicated rules for calculating the tax when you buy and sell shares. But it begins with a guide to when you might face this tax.

When do you have to pay capital gains tax?
You may have to pay this tax whenever you dispose of an asset. What is meant by dispose is not defined by law. But if you sell an asset, swap one asset for another or give something away, this will normally count as a disposal. So will the loss or destruction of an asset (although not if you replace or restore it by claiming on an insurance policy, or by using compensation received).

TAX-SAVING IDEA

If you are thinking of making a gift to charity of an asset which is showing a loss, think again. You won't be able to claim the loss to reduce other taxable gains (though with gifts of quoted shares or property, you may be able to claim income tax relief – see p. 197). Ideally, find something which is showing a taxable gain to give – there will be no tax to pay on the disposal. Alternatively, sell the asset which is showing a loss and give the proceeds to the charity. That would create an allowable loss which could reduce your tax bill on other disposals.

EXAMPLE

Leonie Dale is trying to decide whether to give some shares worth £12,000 to a charity or whether to make a cash donation. If she sells the shares on the stock market, they would produce an allowable loss of £10,000. But she sold her share of a rental property earlier this tax year, making a chargeable gain of £10,000, so her best course of action would be to sell the shares and give the resulting proceeds to charity. She can then deduct the loss on the shares from the gain on the property sale, saving herself £4,000 capital gains tax.

There are some occasions when there is no capital gains tax to pay, regardless of what is being disposed of or how much it is worth:

- assets passed on when someone dies
- gifts to a husband or wife, unless separated
- gifts to charity and community amateur sports clubs.

Although there are no taxable gains in these circumstances, there are also no losses if the asset is worth less than when you acquired it.

Tax-free gains

There is no capital gains tax to pay on any gain you make on the following assets:

- your home (though not a second home in most cases – see p. 57)
- private cars
- personal belongings – known as chattels – sold for less than £6,000 (see p. 117)

TAX-SAVING IDEA

If your husband or wife is terminally ill, consider giving them any assets you own that are showing large taxable gains, assuming your spouse plans to leave you their estate in their will. There is capital gains tax neither on the transfer to your spouse nor on death. Moreover, you inherit the assets at their market value at the time of death, wiping out the previous gains. Bear in mind that the initial gift will not be accepted as genuine and will not save the intended tax, if leaving the assets back to you in the will is a condition of the gift.

- wasting assets with a useful life of 50 years or less (for example, a boat or caravan), so long as you could not have claimed a capital allowance on it
- British money, including sovereigns dated after 1837
- foreign currency for your personal spending abroad (including what you spend on maintaining a home abroad), but not foreign currency accounts
- gains on insurance policies, unless you bought them and were not the original holder, or your wife did so and gave them to you (though you may have to pay part of the insurance company's capital gains tax bill – see p. 173)
- betting, pools or lottery winnings
- National Savings & Investments such as NS&I Certificates and Capital Bonds
- Individual savings accounts (ISAs) – see p. 81
- Personal equity plans (PEPs) – see p. 83
- Business Expansion Scheme (BES) shares bought after 18 March 1986 (see p. 87)
- Enterprise Investment Scheme (EIS) shares, provided you have owned them for a minimum period and they carried on their qualifying activity for at least three years – see p. 85
- shares in venture capital trusts (VCTs) – see p. 87
- terminal bonuses on Save-As-You-Earn (SAYE) contracts
- British Government stock and any options to buy and sell such stock
- certain corporate bonds such as company loan stock and debentures issued after 13 March 1984 and options to buy and sell such bonds
- interests in trusts or settlements, unless you bought them
- decorations for bravery, unless you bought them
- gifts to certain bodies (such as museums) and gifts of certain heritage property in line with the inheritance tax exemptions (see p. 137)
- gifts to charity and to community amateur sports clubs
- damages or compensation for a personal injury or wrong to yourself or in your personal capacity (for example, libel)
- compensation for being given bad investment advice that left you worse off after being persuaded to buy a personal pension between 29 April 1988 and 30 June 1994.

Disposals of land to housing associations may also be free of capital gains tax.

If an asset is one where there is no capital gains tax to pay on disposal, any loss you make on it cannot normally be used to reduce your overall tax bill. Exceptions are enterprise investment scheme shares (see p. 87) and chattels worth £6,000 or less (see p. 117).

Who has to pay?

Capital gains tax applies to you as an individual in your private life or in your business whether self-employed or in partnership. Trustees may also have to pay capital gains tax on the assets that are held in trust (see below).

Any capital gains tax for the tax year ending 5 April 2003 will have to be paid by 31 January 2004, along with the final payment for any income tax still unpaid from the same tax year. Capital gains tax for the tax year ending 5 April 2004 will have to be paid by 31 January 2005.

Married couples

A husband and wife are treated as two single people for capital gains tax purposes, and each is responsible for paying their own capital gains tax bills. With assets jointly owned by husband and wife – second homes, shares, valuables and so on – the gain or loss should be split 50:50 between you unless you have told your tax inspector that they are not owned equally.

If assets are held in your joint names unequally, you need to complete a declaration of beneficial interests using form 17. If the asset produces income, you may already have filled in form 17 to allocate the income other than 50:50 (see p. 51). There is no need to fill in another for capital gains tax purposes.

Trusts

Where assets are held in trust, the trustees are liable for capital gains tax on disposals of the assets in the trust, in much the same way as individuals. The rate of capital gains tax paid by trustees is 34 per cent.

Trusts are entitled to a tax-free capital gains tax allowance in the same way as individual taxpayers. For most trusts, the allowance is half the figure that applies to individuals. So for the tax year ending 5 April 2003, the first £3,850 of net chargeable gains is free of tax for a trust; for the tax year ending 5 April 2004, the tax-free allowance for trusts is £3,950. Trusts for certain disabled people get the same tax-exemption as individuals: £7,700 for the tax year ending 5 April 2003; £7,900 for the tax year ending 5 April 2004.

HOW TO WORK OUT THE GAIN OR LOSS

The gain or loss on an asset disposed of in the tax year ending 5 April 2004 is worked out broadly as follows (and see the example on pp. 110–111):

Step 1: Find the final value of the asset – what you get for selling it or its market value if given away.

Step 2: Find its initial value – normally what you paid for it or its market value (see p. 110). There are special rules for valuing assets owned on or before 31 March 1982 (p. 115) and for shares and unit trusts (p. 122).

Step 3: Deduct the initial value from the final value to find the gross capital gain or gross capital loss.

Step 4: If you incurred any allowable expenses in acquiring, owning or disposing of the asset (p. 112), these can be deducted from the gross capital gain or loss to give the net capital gain or net allowable loss.

Step 5: If you have made a net capital gain on an asset owned on or before 5 April 1998, you can reduce this by claiming indexation allowance which reflects the impact of inflation before that date on the figures (p. 114).

Step 6: You may be able to claim special reliefs to reduce a gain further or increase a net allowable loss – for example, when disposing of your only or main home (p. 56) or retiring from your business (p. 133).

Step 7: Subtract your total allowable losses for the year from the total of your chargeable gains to find your net chargeable gain or your net allowable loss. If the losses exceed the gains, there is no capital gains tax to pay and your net allowable loss can be carried forward to set against gains in future years (p. 117).

Step 8: If you have made a net chargeable gain, you can deduct any losses carried over from previous years (p. 118). If the result is equal to or less than the tax-free capital gains tax allowance for the tax year (£7,900 for the tax year ending 5 April 2004), there is no capital gains tax to pay.

Step 9: If the result of deducting losses from previous years from your net chargeable gain is more than the tax-free allowance, you must next work out if you are entitled to taper relief on any of the gains you have made in this tax year. If you have owned an asset since 5 April 1998, taper relief reduces the net capital gain on it according to the number of whole years it was owned after that date (p. 119). Personal (but not business) assets owned before 17 March 1998 and sold on or after 6 April 1998 qualify for one bonus year of taper relief (see p. 120).

Step 10: Now deduct your losses for the tax year and previous tax years from the net capital gains made on each asset, starting with those that do not qualify for taper relief, going on to those with the lowest rate of taper relief, then to those with the next lowest rate and so on.

EXAMPLE

Ben Barber bought a small paddock for £7,000 in April 1987 paying a valuation fee of £100. In the same week, he spent £500 laying a water supply to the field. The paddock was sold in May 2003 for £26,000 with an estate agent's fee of £250. Ben calculates the tax due as follows:

Step 1: The final value of the paddock is what he sold it for – £26,000.

Step 2: The initial value is what he paid for it – £7,000.

Step 3: He deducts the initial value from the final value to find the gross capital gain of £19,000.

Step 4: He incurred allowable expenses of £850: the £100 fee paid for valuing the paddock, the £500 spent on the water supply and the £250 fee paid when selling it. He deducts this from the £19,000 gross capital gain to get the net capital gain of £18,150.

Step 5: He can claim indexation allowance for the £7,000 cost of buying the paddock, the £100 valuation fee and the £500 cost of installing the water supply. The allowance is £4,538 (for how he calculated this, see p. 114). Ben subtracts this indexation allowance from the net capital gain of £18,150 to get a chargeable gain of £13,612.

Step 6: Ben can claim none of the special reliefs against capital gains tax.

Step 7: This is his only chargeable gain for the tax year and he has no allowable losses from the same tax year to deduct from it.

Step 11: When all the losses are used up, you can reduce each of the remaining chargeable gains by the appropriate rate of taper relief.

Step 12: Add the net tapered gains together to get the total net tapered gain for the tax year. Deduct the tax-free capital gains tax allowance for the tax year from the total – this was £7,900 for the tax year ending 5 April 2004.

Step 13: Add the result to your taxable income for the year. If the total is less than £1,960, the gain is taxed at 10 per cent. If the total is less than £30,500 for the tax year ending 5 April 2004, the rate of tax on the capital gain is 20 per cent (or a mix of 10 and 20 per cent). If the total is more than £30,500 tax on the amount over the limit is charged at 40 per cent.

Initial and final value

In most cases, the value of an asset when you acquire or sell it is what it cost you to acquire it or what you get on selling it. If you acquired something by inheritance, its initial value is its probate value.

Step 8: Ben has £3,500 of allowable losses from previous tax years to set off against this chargeable gain. Deducting this from his £13,612 net chargeable gain gives £10,112 – well above the £7,900 capital gains tax-free allowance for the tax year, so he will pay capital gains tax.

Step 9: He will be entitled to taper relief on the chargeable gain made on the paddock. He has owned it for five full years after 5 April 1998 and he gets a bonus year for having owned it before 17 March 1998. This is a personal asset rather than a business asset, so five years entitles Ben to 20 per cent taper relief (see p. 120).

Step 10: Ben deducts the £3,500 loss from previous tax years from his net chargeable gains of £13,612 to get £10,112.

Step 11: Ben now deducts taper relief to arrive at a tapered gain of 80% × £10,112 = £8,089.

Step 12: The tax-free allowance for the tax year ending 5 April 2004 is £7,900. He subtracts this from the total chargeable gain to get £189.

Step 13: The £189 is added to Ben's taxable income for the tax year ending 5 April 2004 and tax is charged on it. His income is already high enough for him to be paying tax at the higher rate of 40 per cent, so that is the rate he pays on the gain.

So Ben must pay 40 per cent of £189 – a capital gains tax bill of £75.60.

With a gift, the value is its market value: what anyone selling it at the time of the gift would get for it on the open market. However, in certain circumstances, the initial value of a gift may be what the giver acquired it for if you agreed at the time of the gift to take over the giver's capital gain (see below).

The market value is also the final value if you dispose of an asset to a connected person, however much you sell it for. For capital gains tax, a connected person includes your husband or wife, your business partner and their spouse, a relative of yours or these others (brother, sister, parents, child, grandchild) and the spouse of one of these relatives.

When a person (the settlor) puts money or assets into trust, the trustees become connected with the settlor (and any people connected to the settlor).

There are special rules for valuing assets owned before April 1982 (see p. 115).

Gifts

With some things you are given, you may have agreed to take over the giver's capital gains tax bill by agreeing to a claim for hold-over relief (see p. 131). Since 14 March 1989, this can be done for only a limited range of gifts, but before that date it could be done with almost anything.

When you come to dispose of an asset on which hold-over relief has been claimed when you got it, its initial value is what the giver acquired it for, not its market value when you were given it.

> **EXAMPLE**
>
> In December 1988 Suzy Richmond gave an antique diamond ring valued at £8,500 to her daughter Emma. Suzy had bought the ring herself four years previously at a cost of £4,000. They claimed hold-over relief. This means there was no capital gains tax for Suzy to pay at the time she made the gift, but there may be extra tax for Emma when she eventually disposes of the ring.
>
> In December 2003 Emma sold the ring for £12,000. Because hold-over relief had been claimed on the gift, her net gain was not £12,000 − £8,500 = £3,500 (less indexation allowance and taper relief). Instead, Suzy's original purchase price of £4,000 is taken as the initial value. And Emma can claim as an allowable expense a £200 bill for restoring the ring paid by Suzy in June 1986.
>
> So Emma's net gain (ignoring indexation allowance and taper relief) was £12,000 − £4,000 − £200 = £7,800.

Allowable expenses

Deducting the initial value of an asset from its final value gives you the gross capital gain or gross capital loss. However, you can then deduct certain allowable expenses in computing the gain on an asset for capital gains tax. These include:

- acquisition costs, such as payments to a professional adviser (for example, surveyor, accountant, solicitor), conveyancing costs and stamp duty, and advertising to find a seller
- what you spend improving the asset (though not your own time) provided the improvement is still reflected in the asset when you come to dispose of it
- what you spend establishing or defending your rights or title to the asset
- disposal costs, similar to acquisition costs, but including the cost of valuing it for capital gains tax.

Deducting these expenses gives you the net capital gain or net allowable loss.

EXAMPLE

When Melanie Hill sold her holiday cottage in September 2003 for £108,000, she feared an enormous capital gains tax bill – she had bought it in August 1990 for £52,000. But she soon realised there were a lot of expenses she could claim to reduce the capital gain:

- acquisition costs of £1,735 – the £790 legal bill incurred in buying it, the £520 stamp duty and the £425 surveyor's fee for inspecting and valuing it
- improvement costs of £18,750 – the cost of installing modern plumbing and central heating, rewiring and building an extension which were all paid for in May 1991
- disposal costs of £3,575 – legal bills for the sale of £1,725 and £1,850 commission paid to the estate agent.

The net capital gain is worked out as follows:

Final value		£108,000
minus allowable expenses:		
original cost	£52,000	
acquisition costs	£1,735	
improvement costs	£18,750	
disposal costs	£3,575	
Total allowable expenses		£76,060
Net capital gain		**£31,940**

However, Melanie won't pay capital gains tax even on this net capital gain of £31,940 – she can claim indexation allowance (see overleaf) and taper relief (p. 119).

If the asset was a gift to you and the giver got hold-over relief (see above), you can also claim any allowable expenses incurred while the giver owned it.

Part disposals

If you dispose of part of an asset, you will need to allocate expenses between the part you are getting rid of and the part you have kept.

Any expense connected only with the part being disposed of can be fully deducted from the proceeds in working out the gain. Anything connected only with the part you are keeping cannot be deducted. But some of the expenditure will be impossible to allocate in this way, and will thus have to be divided between the two parts, in proportion to their value. The proportion of such a cost that you can deduct from the gain is as follows:

EXAMPLE

Martin Thompson buys a house which he converts into a pair of flats. He spends £5,000 converting one into a weekend retreat for himself and £3,000 on doing up the other one to sell off.

Each of the flats is given identical valuations at the time of the sale. So any money spent on the whole house can be divided equally between the two flats. He can therefore claim the following expenses to reduce the gain on the flat he sells off:

- the £3,000 spent improving the flat he sells off
- the expenses of selling the flat
- half the expenses of buying the house including the purchase price.

$$\frac{\text{Disposal proceeds}}{\text{Disposal proceeds} + \text{Value of the part retained}}$$

There are special rules for allocating costs to shares and unit trusts where holdings are divided or added to (see p. 125).

Indexation allowance

If you end up with a net capital gain after deducting allowable expenses from the gross capital gain, you can claim indexation allowance to remove some or all of the gain created by inflation if you owned it between 1 April 1982 and 31 March 1998. If there is a net capital loss, you can't claim indexation allowance, however – indexation allowance cannot be used to create or increase a loss.

EXAMPLE

Ben Barber works out the indexation allowance he can claim on the paddock he disposed of in May 2003 (see p. 109). He can claim the allowance for the original cost of £7,000, the valuation fee of £100 and the cost of laying on the water supply of £500 – all of this £7,600 was spent in April 1987 when the indexation factor was 0.597.

The indexation allowance is as follows:

$$\begin{aligned}&\pounds 7{,}600 \times 0.597\\ &= \pounds 4{,}538\end{aligned}$$

Ben's chargeable gain net of indexation allowance on the paddock is therefore £18,150 – £4,538 = £13,612.

INDEXATION FACTORS

Year	Jan	Feb	Mar	Apr	May	Jun	Jul	Aug	Sep	Oct	Nov	Dec
						Month						
1982			1.047	1.006	0.992	0.987	0.986	0.985	0.987	0.977	0.967	0.971
1983	0.968	0.960	0.956	0.929	0.921	0.917	0.906	0.898	0.889	0.883	0.876	0.871
1984	0.872	0.865	0.859	0.834	0.828	0.823	0.825	0.808	0.804	0.793	0.788	0.789
1985	0.783	0.769	0.752	0.716	0.708	0.704	0.707	0.703	0.704	0.701	0.695	0.693
1986	0.689	0.683	0.681	0.665	0.662	0.663	0.667	0.662	0.654	0.652	0.638	0.632
1987	0.626	0.620	0.616	0.597	0.596	0.596	0.597	0.593	0.588	0.580	0.573	0.574
1988	0.574	0.568	0.562	0.537	0.531	0.525	0.524	0.507	0.500	0.485	0.478	0.474
1989	0.465	0.454	0.448	0.423	0.414	0.409	0.408	0.404	0.395	0.384	0.372	0.369
1990	0.361	0.353	0.339	0.300	0.288	0.283	0.282	0.269	0.258	0.248	0.251	0.252
1991	0.249	0.242	0.237	0.222	0.218	0.213	0.215	0.213	0.208	0.204	0.199	0.198
1992	0.199	0.193	0.189	0.171	0.167	0.167	0.171	0.171	0.166	0.162	0.164	0.168
1993	0.179	0.171	0.167	0.156	0.152	0.153	0.156	0.151	0.146	0.147	0.148	0.146
1994	0.151	0.144	0.141	0.128	0.124	0.124	0.129	0.124	0.121	0.120	0.119	0.114
1995	0.114	0.107	0.102	0.091	0.087	0.085	0.091	0.085	0.080	0.085	0.085	0.079
1996	0.083	0.078	0.073	0.066	0.063	0.063	0.067	0.062	0.057	0.057	0.057	0.053
1997	0.053	0.049	0.046	0.040	0.036	0.032	0.032	0.026	0.021	0.019	0.019	0.016
1998	0.019	0.014	0.011									

To calculate indexation allowance for assets held on 5 April 1998, the initial value and each allowable expense is multiplied by the indexation factor for the month in which the money was spent. The factors are in the table above – for example, if the money was spent in June 1994, the factor is 0.124.

Assets owned on or before 31 March 1982

If you owned an asset on or before 31 March 1982, only the gain since that date is liable to capital gains tax. Any gain made before 1 April 1982 is effectively tax-free. With such assets, the initial value is normally its market value on 31 March 1982. You cannot deduct expenses incurred on or before that date. Indexation allowance runs from March 1982.

In some circumstances, using the 31 March 1982 value could artificially inflate your gain or loss. Suppose, for example, you bought something in 1978 which fell in value before 31 March 1982 and has risen in value since. Basing the gain on the 31 March 1982 value would make the gain larger than the amount you've actually made since that date. Similarly, if you dispose of something which rose in value while you owned it before 31 March 1982 and fell in value afterwards, this could produce a bigger loss than you actually made.

Thus when calculating the gain or loss on assets owned before 1 April 1982, you need to work out the sums using two different methods:

- the rebased chargeable gain – using the value on 31 March 1982 and ignoring costs incurred on or before that date
- the actual gain – using the original cost you paid for it and allowing for allowable expenses incurred on or before 31 March 1982 (with indexation allowance on them running from that date).

The two answers are then compared in what the Inland Revenue calls the kink test:

- if both methods produce a gain, the smaller gain is used to calculate your tax bill
- if both methods produce a loss, the smaller loss is allowable
- if one produces a gain and the other a loss, the disposal is assumed to produce no gain or loss.

To avoid all this palaver, you can make a rebasing election, which means all your gains and losses on assets owned on or before 31 March 1982 will be based on their market value on that date. This will avoid having to keep complicated records (although it could mean paying more tax if you have assets which fell in value before 31 March 1982 and have risen in value since).

If you want to make a rebasing election, tell your tax inspector in writing

EXAMPLE

Jim Brooke carries out the kink test on a home he rents out which he sold for £120,000 in December 2003.

He had bought it in June 1979 when he had paid £20,000 for it, with acquisition costs and other allowable expenses before 1 April 1982 of £2,000. Its value at 31 March 1982 was £16,300.

The net capital gain using the 31 March 1982 value as the initial value would be £120,000 − £16,300 = £103,700. The net capital gain based on what he paid for it in June 1979 and expenses before 1 April 1982 would be £120,000 − £20,000 − £2,000 = £98,000.

Both methods produce a gain, so the capital gains tax bill will be based on what Jim paid for it in June 1979 since that produces the smaller gain. If Jim had already opted for all his pre-1 April 1982 assets to be treated as if they were acquired on that date, his tax bill would be based on the larger figure produced by using the market value on 31 March 1982.

within two years of the first disposal of such an asset. This is likely to be the first disposal to which the rebasing rules apply. The election is irrevocable – so make sure it will pay for you. For more details, see Help Sheet *IR280 Rebasing – assets held at 31 March 1982.*

Special rules for personal belongings – chattels

If personal belongings, known as chattels by the Inland Revenue, are sold for less than £6,000, the gain is tax-free. Chattels are defined as tangible, movable property and include furniture, silver, paintings and so on. A set (for example, a silver tea-set) counts as one chattel for this exemption.

If a chattel is sold for more than the tax-free limit, the taxable gain is restricted to $\frac{5}{3}$ of the amount of the disposal value over the limit. So the maximum gain on a chattel sold for £7,200 would be $\frac{5}{3}$ of £7,200 − £6,000 = $\frac{5}{3}$ of £1,200 = £2,000.

EXAMPLE

William Baxter bought a piece of furniture for £4,000 and sold it for £7,500 in the tax year ending 5 April 2004. This produces a gain of £7,500 − £4,000 = £3,500. The sale price is over the £6,000 chattels limit so the gain is not tax-free. But for capital gains tax purposes, the gain cannot be more than $\frac{5}{3}$ of £7,500 − £6,000. This is $\frac{5}{3}$ of £1,500 = £2,500, thus reducing William's taxable gain by £1,000.

In most cases, disposing of an asset that would produce a tax-free gain means that you cannot claim any allowable loss made on such an asset. With a chattel, you can claim a loss even if it is sold for less than £6,000 – but the loss is calculated as if it had fetched £6,000.

EXAMPLE

William Baxter sold a painting for £4,500 which he had bought for £9,500. His gross loss is calculated as if he had sold it for £6,000: it is therefore £9,500 − £6,000 = £3,500 – rather than the £5,000 loss William actually made.

For more about chattels, ask for Help Sheet *IR295 Chattels and capital gains tax.*

Capital losses

If the initial cost of an asset and its expenses add up to more than its final value, you have made a net capital loss on that asset. Net capital losses are deducted from your chargeable gains to find the total chargeable gain on which your capital gains tax bill is based. If your net capital losses are bigger than your total chargeable gains, the difference – your net allowable loss – can be carried over to reduce your chargeable gains in later tax years.

Note that a loss made when you dispose of an asset to a connected person (p. 111) can be set off only against a gain made on a disposal to the same connected person. This is called a 'clogged loss' and applies even if the loss was made when you disposed of the asset for a genuine commercial value.

The tax-free allowance

The first slice of total chargeable gain in any tax year is free of capital gains tax. For the tax year ending 5 April 2003, the tax-free allowance was £7,700; for the tax year ending 5 April 2004, the allowance is £7,900.

If you don't use all your tax-free allowance in one year, you can't carry the unused part over to another year. So try not to reduce your total chargeable gain below the level of the tax-free allowance by claiming too much by way of losses. You usually have to deduct losses from gains made in the same tax year, even if this reduces your net chargeable gain below the tax-free level. However a loss made on a disposal to a connected person can't be set off against the same year's gains unless they too were made on a disposal to the same connected person.

EXAMPLE

Gus Henry made chargeable gains of £8,100 in the tax year ending 5 April 2004 and allowable losses of £3,250 in the same year. All the losses have to be set off against the gains for this tax year, even though this brings the net chargeable gain below the tax-free allowance of £7,900 for the tax year.

So his net chargeable gain is £8,100 – £3,250 = £4,850 – on which no tax is payable.

Losses from previous years

If your net chargeable gain for the tax year is bigger than the tax-free allowance, you must use any losses from previous tax years to reduce your tax bill. If you have enough such losses, you must reduce your total chargeable gain to the level of the tax-free allowance and pay no capital gains tax at all. Note that – unlike with losses from the same tax year – you don't have to deduct more than is necessary to get down to the tax-free amount.

If your losses from previous tax years are not sufficient to reduce your total chargeable gain below the level of the tax-free allowance, then they can be used to reduce your capital gains tax bill. The carried-forward losses are subtracted from the chargeable gains on individual assets in a way that ensures the biggest possible reduction in your tax bill by maximising the amount of taper relief you can claim – see below.

Losses can never be carried back to an earlier tax year, except in the year when you die and, since 10 April 2003, where you make a loss on the disposal of certain rights to future payments, in which case you may be able to set the loss against any gain on the earlier sale of the asset that gave rise to the rights. On death, your executors can carry back losses to set against gains you made in the three previous tax years – starting with the gains in the most recent year. There is further information in Help Sheet *IR282 Death, personal representatives and legatees.*

Claiming losses

You have to claim losses within five years and ten months of the end of the tax year in which they were made. So losses made in the tax year ending 5 April 2004 must be claimed by 31 January 2010.

You can claim the losses by giving details on the Capital gains pages of the tax return (see pp. 316 and 321). If you haven't been sent these pages, write and tell your tax inspector about your losses.

> **EXAMPLE**
>
> Elizabeth Ong has a total chargeable gain for the tax year ending 5 April 2004 of £8,400. The tax-free amount for that tax year is £7,900, which would mean paying capital gains tax on £8,400 – £7,900 = £500. But she has losses of £3,500 carried over from previous years and she can use £500 of this amount to reduce her total chargeable gain to nil – with no capital gains tax to pay.
>
> This still leaves her with £3,500 – £500 = £3,000 of unused losses to be carried forward to the tax year ending 5 April 2005 and beyond.

Taper relief

Taper relief is designed to encourage you to invest for the longer term. It reduces the amount of the gain according to the number of complete years the asset has been owned after 5 April 1998. The reduction is bigger for business assets (see overleaf).

For a non-business asset owned for three full years, taper relief reduces the gain by 5 per cent – so 95 per cent of the gain on it is chargeable. After 10 years, taper relief rises to 40 per cent, leaving 60 per cent of the gain chargeable.

	Non-business assets		*Business assets*					
Number of complete years asset owned after 5 April 1998			*Disposal before 6 April 2000*		*Disposal on or after 6 April 2000 and before 6 April 2002*		*Disposal on or after 6 April 2002*	
	Taper relief	*% of gain chargeable*	*Taper relief*	*% of gain chargeable*	*Taper relief*	*% of gain chargeable*	*Taper relief*	*% of gain chargeable*
0	0	100	0	100	0	100	100	0
1	0	100	7.5	92.5	12.5	87.5	50	50
2	0	100	15	85	25	75	75	25
3	5	95	22.5	77.5	50	50	75	25
4	10	90	30	70	75	25	75	25
5	15	85	37.5	62.5	75	25	75	25
6	20	80	45	55	75	25	75	25
7	25	75	52.5	47.5	75	25	75	25
8	30	70	60	40	75	25	75	25
9	35	65	67.5	32.5	75	25	75	25
10	40	60	75	25	75	25	75	25

For business assets, the rate of taper relief is higher – a maximum of 75 per cent that leaves just 25 per cent of the gain chargeable. For disposals on or before 5 April 2000, this maximum was reached after 10 years; for disposals between 6 April 2000 and 5 April 2002, the maximum is reached after four years; and, for disposals from 6 April 2002 onwards, the maximum is reached after just two years.

If you owned a non-business asset before 17 March 1998, you will be given one bonus year of ownership if you sell it after 5 April 1998. So if you bought the asset on 1 January 1998 and sold it on 1 July 2003, you would be treated as having owned it for six years after 5 April 1998 – the five complete years after that date plus the one bonus year. Business assets disposed of on or after 6 April 2000 no longer qualify for a bonus year because taper relief was enhanced for such assets.

Taper relief is calculated on the chargeable gain after deducting any losses for the tax year and previous tax years. To maximise the amount of taper relief you can claim, losses are deducted first from the gains that qualify for least taper relief, then the next least and so on. So, for example, if you have a non-business asset that qualifies for 10 per cent taper relief and one that qualifies for 20 per cent, the losses are deducted from the first gain – if it is too small to use up all the losses, they are then deducted from the second gain. Note that a business asset owned for just a few years qualifies for a higher rate of

What counts as a qualifying company for business asset taper relief

Period to which definition applies	*Definition of qualifying company* — *Your relationship with the company (apart from holding shares)*	*Type of company*	*Nature of your shareholding*
6 April 1998 to 5 April 2000	None required	Trading company(1)	Shares giving you at least 25% of the voting rights
	Full-time working officer or employee	Trading company(1)	Shares giving you at least 5% of the voting rights
6 April 2000 onwards	None required	Unquoted trading company(1) (2)	Any
	None required	Quoted trading company(2)	Shares giving you at least 5% of the voting rights
	Officer or employee (full- or part-time)	Quoted trading company(2)	Any
	Officer or employee (full- or part-time)	Non-trading company	No more than 10% of any class of shares or 10% of the voting rights or rights to no more than 10% of distributable income or assets

(1) Or holding company of trading group.
(2) Quoted means listed on the London Stock Exchange or a recognised overseas exchange. Other companies are unquoted.

taper relief than a non-business asset owned rather longer, so may come behind the non-business asset in the queue for losses.

Business assets

The definition of 'business asset' was changed from 6 April 2000 onwards (see below). The definition now includes shareholdings in most unquoted trading companies and most employee shares. 'Unquoted' includes shares listed on the Alternative Investment Market (AIM) and, from 28 November 2001, shares on various European junior markets, such as NASDAQ Europe (formerly EASDAQ), the Nouveau Marché and Neue Markt Frankfurt.

If you have an asset that was a business asset for only part of the time you owned it (perhaps because of the changes to the definition), you must apportion any gain into two parts: a business part and a non-business part. Different rates of taper relief will apply to each part (see Example opposite).

A business asset is:

- any item you use in your trade or profession
- from 6 April 2004 onwards, any item used in a trade or profession carried on by someone else
- until 5 April 2000, any item you held for the purpose of your employment (including as a director) by a trading company, provided you were required to devote at least 75 per cent of your working hours to that job
- from 6 April 2000 onwards, any item you hold for the purpose of your employment (including as a director) by a trading company
- shares or securities in a qualifying company – see table for what counts as a qualifying company.

Calculating your capital gains tax bill

If there is anything left after deducting expenses, indexation allowance, losses, taper relief and the tax-free allowance, there is capital gains tax to pay.

For the tax year ending 5 April 2003, your total net tapered gains minus the tax-free allowance of £7,700 is added to your taxable income for the year and taxed as if it was savings income. So if the combined total comes to less than £1,920, the tax rate on the gains is 10 per cent. Any amount over £29,900, the upper limit for the basic rate of income tax, is taxed at the top rate of 40 per cent. Between the upper and lower limit for the basic rate, gains are taxed at 20 per cent.

Similarly, for the tax year ending 5 April 2004, if adding your taxable gains to your taxable income comes to no more than £1,960, the gain is taxed at 10 per cent. If it comes to more than £30,500, the gain is taxed at 40 per cent. In between those limits, the gain is taxed at 20 per cent.

SHARES AND UNIT TRUSTS

Shares and unit trusts are treated in the same way as other assets for capital gains tax purposes. But if you buy and sell identical shares in a particular company or units in a particular unit trust at different times, how do you decide which you have bought or sold when working out the gain? And there are further complications when companies merge, are taken over or otherwise reorganise their capital. This section explains the special rules for working out the gains and losses on share transactions. Help sheet *IR284 Shares and capital gains tax* has more details.

Valuing shares

The market value of shares bought and sold on a stock exchange is normally the amount you paid for them or got for selling them.

But you should use the market value when valuing gifts or disposals to a connected person (see p. 111). If they are traded on the London Stock Exchange use the prices recorded in the Stock Exchange Daily Official List (which can be supplied by a stockbroker or bank). The market value is the lower of the following two figures, calculated using prices on the date of the gift or disposal:

- the selling price, plus a quarter of the difference between the selling price and the (higher) buying price – the quarter-up rule
- the half-way point between the highest and lowest prices of recorded bargains for the day.

EXAMPLE

Reg Parsons and Jack Gill both hold 10 per cent of the shares of a company (which they do not work for). Reg got his shares in 1990 and Jack got his ten years later on 6 April 2000. They both sell their shares on 6 April 2003, realising a profit of £60,000.

Jack's shares have counted as a business asset throughout the three years he has owned them and qualify for maximum taper relief of 75 per cent. This means only 25% × £60,000 = £15,000 of Jack's gain is taxable.

Reg has owned his shares for 13 years – ten years longer than Jack. However taper relief was introduced from 6 April 1998 and this is the period which counts for taper relief purposes. The shares only became business assets when the rules changed from 6 April 2000. So for three of the five years, the shares count as business assets. Using the apportionment rules means that ³⁄₅ the shares count as business assets, so ³⁄₅ × £60,000 = £36,000 of the gain qualifies for 75 per cent business taper relief, giving a taxable gain of 25% × £36,000 = £9,000. The remaining ²⁄₅ of the shares count as a non-business asset. As they have been held for five years since 6 April 1998, non-business taper relief of 20% is due (five years plus the bonus year). The gain of ³⁄₅ × £60,000 = £24,000 is tapered 80% to £19,200. Reg's total taxable gain is £9,000 + £19,200 = £28,200.

Despite owning his shares for longer, Reg has a much higher taxable gain than Jack.

With any disposal of unquoted shares, the market value must be agreed with the Share Valuation Division of the Inland Revenue. This cannot be negotiated in advance and reaching agreement can be a lengthy business. For more about the Share Valuation Division, see Inland Revenue leaflet SVD1.

Unit trusts and investment trusts

The gain on disposing of unit trusts and investment trusts is worked out in the same way as for shares. If you receive an equalisation payment with your first distribution from a unit trust, this is a return of part of your original investment and should be deducted from the acquisition price in working out your gain or loss.

Which shares or unit trusts have you sold?

If you buy one batch of shares in a company and later sell it without any other dealings in the shares, it is quite simple to calculate the gain or loss. But if you buy shares in the same company on different occasions and then sell them – together or in parcels, disposals will be matched with acquisitions in the following order:

- first, shares acquired the same day
- second, shares acquired at any time in the next 30 days (see below)
- third shares acquired before the day of sale and after 5 April 1998 – with the most recent acquisitions first (last in, first out, or LIFO)
- fourth, shares acquired between 6 April 1982 and 5 April 1998 – see p. 126 for how their initial cost and indexation allowance are calculated
- fifth, shares acquired between 6 April 1965 and 5 April 1982
- finally, shares acquired on or before 5 April 1965.

> **TAX-SAVING IDEA**
>
> It could still pay you to sell some shares towards the end of the tax year to use up the tax-free allowance. In the tax year ending 5 April 2004, you can have chargeable gains of up to £7,900 tax-free – saving up to £3,160 in capital gains tax. You could buy the same shares back after the 30 days – taking the risk that the shares shoot up in price during the 30 day-period. Or you could buy different shares – perhaps in a similar company. Another option is to sell shares you own directly and buy them back within a stocks and shares ISA or get your spouse to buy the shares back – these are effective for tax purposes without waiting 30 days. Remember to take the costs of buying and selling shares into account.

Shares acquired at any time in the next 30 days

Shares bought in the 30 days after a sale are treated as those sold in the sale before those bought earlier – to stop a practice that was known as 'bed and breakfasting'. This involved selling some shares towards the end of the tax year and buying them back the next day to realise a gain which could help use up the tax-free allowance or realise a loss for offsetting gains made on other assets.

This can no longer be done. If you sell shares and buy them back within 30 days of the sale, the shares you sell are matched to those you buy back, not shares bought earlier. So if you sell some shares for £5 each which you originally bought for £3 and then buy them back for £5 the next day, the initial value of the shares you sold will be £5 each not £3 – and there would be no gain realised.

Shares acquired before 6 April 1998 and after 5 April 1982

Shares you acquired between these two dates qualify for indexation allowance, according to when the acquisition was made. If you acquired more than one batch of the same shares at different times between the two dates, they are pooled when working out the gain or loss – this means they are treated as a single asset. Each share is given the average initial value of all the shares in the pool, and each is entitled to the average indexation allowance. The example overleaf shows how pooling works.

Shares bought on or before 5 April 1982

Shares owned on or before 5 April 1982 and on or after 6 April 1965 are kept in a separate pool, and treated like other assets owned before 1 April 1982:

- the gain is based on their value on 31 March 1982, unless it is to your advantage to base it on their cost when you bought them (see p. 115)
- indexation allowance runs only from March 1982.

Shares bought before 6 April 1965

Shares acquired before 6 April 1965 are kept completely separate. They are the last to be sold if you have bought batches since that date – all shares bought after that date are sold first. When you come to sell pre-April 1965 quoted shares, it is assumed the last to be bought are the first to be sold.

However, you can elect for your shares acquired before 6 April 1965 to be added to your pre-April 1982 pool. This is usually to your advantage, as their value on 31 March 1982 is likely to be higher than what you paid for them more than 17 years before.

Employee share schemes

Employee share schemes allow employees to acquire shares in their companies free or cheaply – and if they are certain types approved by the Inland Revenue, without an income tax bill. There could be a capital gains tax bill

EXAMPLE

Diana Nichols bought 2,000 ordinary shares in United Enterprises plc in June 1983 at a cost of £7,000. In December 1988, she added another 2,000 United Enterprises shares for £10,000. That gave her a pool of 4,000 United Enterprises shares bought before 6 April 1998 and after 5 April 1982. She works out the average cost and indexation allowance of the shares in the pool using the following figures for indexation factor:

- June 1983 – 0.917
- December 1988 – 0.474

First Diana calculates the average initial cost of the shares in the pool. The total cost is £7,000 + £10,000 = £17,000, which bought her 4,000 shares. So the average cost is:

$$\frac{£17,000}{4,000} = £4.25$$

Then she works out the indexation allowance on the 2,000 shares bought in June 1983:

$$£7,000 \times 0.917 = £6,419$$

The indexation allowance on the 2,000 shares bought in December 1988 is:

$$£10,000 \times 0.474 = £4,740$$

Total indexation allowance on the 4,000 shares is:

$$£6,419 + £4,740 = £11,159$$

Average indexation allowance for each share in the pool is:

$$\frac{£11,159}{4,000} = £2.79$$

So if she sells 1,000 shares in the pool, the initial cost is taken to be 1,000 × £4.25 = £4,250. The indexation allowance is 1,000 × £2.79 = £2,790.

when the shares are disposed of, though from 6 April 2000 onwards the gain will qualify for the higher rates of taper relief for business assets (see p. 120).

The initial cost of the shares and when you are deemed to have received them depends on the type of scheme:

- approved savings-related share option schemes – you acquire the shares at the price you paid on the day that you opted to buy them
- approved profit-sharing schemes – you acquire the shares at the market

value on the day they are allocated to you, even though you can't sell them for three years

- approved discretionary share option schemes – you acquire the shares at the price you pay for them on the day you exercise the option. If you paid anything for the option, this an allowable expense
- share incentive plan – when the shares are first awarded to you or, in the case of partnership shares, first acquired on your behalf, even though you have to hold them for a minimum period (see p. 244).

You can transfer shares from an approved profit-sharing scheme, savings-related share option scheme or share incentive plan direct to an ISA (see p. 82) or stakeholder pension scheme (see p. 73). Shares transferred in this way are free of capital gains tax on transfer and when they are subsequently sold.

Identical shares acquired on the same day are normally pooled together. But, if you acquire shares from two employee schemes on the same day (or from one employee scheme and buy a second batch on the open market on the same day), you can opt to match a disposal with the shares that have the higher initial value (ie produce the lowest gain).

Help Sheet *IR287 Employee share schemes and capital gains tax* has more details.

Rights issues

If you get extra shares through a rights issue or a bonus issue, they are allocated to the relevant shares or pool. So if half your shares were bought in May 1990 and half in July 1998, the rights issue is split 50:50 between the July 1998 shares and the pool of 1982-1998 shares. Whatever you pay for the rights issue is added to the initial costs of the two lots of shares, with any indexation allowance running from the time the payment was made. Taper relief on the new shares is calculated from the time the shares they relate to were acquired, since rights and bonus issues are treated as share reorganisations.

Stock dividends and accumulation unit trusts

If you get extra shares instead of dividends, this is known as a stock dividend (or scrip dividend). The value of the new shares is the amount of dividend foregone excluding the value of the tax credit – the cash equivalent. Any indexation allowance or taper relief runs from the date of the dividend. Accumulation unit trusts work in a similar way, with extra units allocated to the appropriate pool.

Takeovers and mergers

If you own shares in a company which is taken over, you may get shares in the new parent company in exchange for your old shares. This exchange does not count as a disposal. The new shares are assumed to have been acquired at the cost of the old ones and on the same dates.

If part of the price for the old shares is cash, this is a disposal. For example, if you get half cash, half shares, you have disposed of half the old shares.

Sometimes you are offered loan notes as an alternative to taking cash. Usually, these are treated as the same asset as the shares you have given up, so no disposal takes place until you cash in the loan notes. Accepting loan notes in place of cash is useful if deferring the disposal until a later date would reduce the capital gains tax you'll pay (for example, by taking you into a new tax year or increasing the taper relief you can claim).

When mutuals become PLCs

Some building societies and mutual insurance companies convert to public limited companies or are involved in other organisational changes that may produce benefits for members. If you receive shares or cash – or both – in such circumstances, there may be a bill for income tax or capital gains tax. Ask the building society or insurance company for guidance.

Payment by instalments

If you have bought newly issued shares, you may have paid for them in instalments. Indexation allowance and taper relief on the full purchase price runs from when the shares were acquired only if all the instalments were paid within 12 months of acquisition. If instalments are paid more than 12 months after the shares were acquired, indexation allowance and taper relief on those instalments runs from when the payments were made.

However, if you paid in instalments when buying newly issued shares in a privatised state enterprise, indexation allowance and taper relief run from the date you acquired the shares (even though you hand over some of the money months or even years later).

Monthly savings schemes

If you have invested in unit trusts or investment trusts through a monthly savings scheme since before 6 April 1998, working out your gains and losses could be very complicated. (But because of changes to the share identification rules the complications disappear for investments made on or after 6 April 1998.) For these pre-April 1998 savings, you would have to work out the gain, indexation allowance and taper relief for each instalment you invested when making a disposal. If you have been investing in a monthly savings scheme since before 6 April 1998, you can opt for a simplified method of working out the initial costs and indexation allowance for instalments invested up to the end of the accounting year of the fund after that date.

For each year the simplified method applies, it assumes that all 12 monthly instalments for a year were made in the seventh month. So if you invested £100 a month in a fund with an accounting year that runs from 1 January to 31 December, you could assume that you invested 12 × £100 = £1,200 in July, the seventh month.

You may have to add in or deduct extra amounts:

- any distribution or dividend reinvested during the year is added to your investment. So a £50 dividend added to your fund in the above example would take the amount you had invested in July to £1,200 + £50 = £1,250
- extra savings over and above the regular instalments are included, provided you don't add more than twice the monthly instalment in any month – a bigger payment is treated as a separate investment
- if you increase the monthly instalments, the extra is added to the year's investment so long as the increase is in or before the seventh month (if later, it is added to next year's fund)
- small withdrawals are deducted if they are less than a quarter of the amount invested in the year by regular instalments (if withdrawals exceed this amount, the simplified calculation cannot be used).

To opt for this simplified method, you must write to your tax inspector within two years of the end of the first tax year after 6 April 1998 in which you dispose of the units or shares and any of the following applies:

- you face a capital gains tax bill
- the disposal proceeds are more than twice the amount of the tax-free band for the year (more than £15,400 for the tax year ending 5 April 2003, more than £15,800 for the tax year ending 5 April 2004)
- your other disposals in the year create net losses.

Details are contained in Inland Revenue statement of practice SP2/99 available from tax offices and www.inlandrevenue.gov.uk. In 2003, the Revenue will be publishing a new guidance note on this subject.

HOW TO REDUCE OR DELAY YOUR CAPITAL GAINS TAX BILL

There are a number of ways to reduce or delay a CGT bill. For a start, it is important to claim all the allowable expenses you can (p. 112), indexation allowance (p. 114) and taper relief (p. 119). Also, take advantage of the special rules for disposing of assets owned before 31 March 1982 (p. 115). Then use the tax-free capital gains allowance you can make each year (see p. 118) and don't overlook losses which you can set off against gains (see p. 117).

These are all ways to minimise your tax bill once you have made a disposal. But there are several steps you can take before reaching a disposal to keep your tax bill down:

- take advantage of the allowances of your husband or wife (below)
- make the best use of losses (see opposite)
- pass the tax bill for gifts of business assets and certain other gifts on to the recipient if possible, or pay it in instalments if not (see opposite)
- invest the gains from any disposals in growing businesses if you don't need the proceeds immediately – you may be able to defer the tax bill by claiming capital gains deferral relief on buying shares through the EIS or VCT schemes (see p. 132)
- claim the special reliefs which can reduce your tax bill if you are disposing of a business or farm (see p. 132).

It will help in minimising your capital gains tax bill if you keep a record of the assets you have acquired which may fall into the tax net, together with relevant receipts (for example, for allowable expenses).

Husbands and wives

Husbands and wives are treated as separate individuals for capital gains tax. They pay tax on their own gains and can deduct their losses only from their own gains. They have their own tax-free allowances to deduct from their own net chargeable gains.

But if a married couple living together dispose of assets to each other, this is ignored for the purposes of capital gains tax. For example, if a husband buys shares worth £10,000 in June 2002 and gives them to his wife at a later date, her gain or loss when she sells them will be calculated as if she had bought them for £10,000 in June 2002. Anything they pay each other on such transfers is ignored.

> **TAX-SAVING IDEA**
>
> Since there is no capital gains tax on gifts between husband and wife, you can effectively double your tax-free band if you are married by giving assets to your spouse to dispose of. So in the tax year ending 5 April 2004, a married couple can effectively make £15,800 of disposals.

A married couple is treated as living together unless legally separated or where the separation appears to be permanent. Gifts between husband and wife in the year of separation are free of capital gains tax, but after this, tax may be payable. For more about marriage and capital gains tax, see Help Sheet *IR281 Husband and wife, divorce and separation.*

Making the best use of losses

If your allowable losses in a tax year look likely to mean you will not be able to use the whole tax-free allowance for the year, there are two options:

- make more disposals to increase your chargeable gains – by selling some shares that have done well, for example
- hold back on loss-making disposals to a later year when there are no gains or they can be used to reduce future gains.

Gifts

If you give away certain assets or sell them for less than their market value, you can avoid paying capital gains tax by claiming hold-over relief. This means the recipient is treated as having acquired the assets when you did and having paid the costs you paid (less anything paid to you). The recipient's agreement is necessary, since he or she is taking over the tax bill for your period of ownership.

Hold-over relief is available only for the following gifts, however:

- business assets
- heritage property
- gifts to political parties
- gifts which result in an immediate inheritance tax bill (mainly gifts to certain trusts and companies).

If the person you have made the gift to becomes non-resident without having sold or given it away, you might have to pay a capital gains tax bill.

There is no point in claiming hold-over relief if your net taxable gains for the year, including the gift, will be within the tax-free band (£7,700 for the tax year ending 5 April 2003, £7,900 for the tax year ending 5 April 2004). There would be no capital gains tax for you to pay, but you might add to the tax the person you are making the gift to has to pay eventually.

Business assets include land or buildings used by the business, goodwill, fixed plant and machinery, and shares or securities of a trading company, where the company is unlisted or is the transferer's personal company.

If you make a gift of land or certain types of shareholdings which do not qualify for hold-over relief, you may be able to pay the capital gains tax in ten annual instalments. The shareholdings in question are a controlling shareholding in a company or minority holdings in unquoted companies. Interest is charged on the unpaid tax in the usual way. For more about hold-over relief, see Help Sheet *IR295 Relief for gifts and similar transactions*.

Capital gains deferral relief

If you're facing a capital gains tax bill that you can't reduce by claiming losses or other reliefs, consider investing the gain in the shares of certain types of small companies through either the EIS or VCT schemes (see pp. 85–8). You can claim deferral relief which allows you to put off the tax bill.

To get the relief you have to invest through an EIS in the ordinary shares of unquoted companies – companies which are not listed on the UK Stock Exchange or any other recognised stock exchange – or in the shares of a VCT – an investment trust that invests in such companies. Investments in companies quoted on the Alternative Investment Market (AIM) are eligible, provided they meet the other requirements for deferral relief. The main one is that the company must be trading in certain qualifying sectors or be a holding company for such trading companies. The shares must be newly issued.

In the case of an EIS, you must make the investment any time between one year before and three years after the disposal that produces the gain. The amount of the gain that you reinvest will generally be taxed only when you eventually sell the shares. If there is a gain when you dispose of EIS shares and you reinvest in shares in another EIS company, you can treat this as a single investment in calculating taper relief when you sell the second lot. This is designed to encourage 'serial entrepreneurs' by giving an incentive to reinvest gains on successful EIS companies in new ones.

In the case of a VCT, you must make the investment at any time between one year before and one year after the disposal that produces the gain. Once again, the gain that you reinvest will generally only be taxed when you eventually sell the VCT shares.

Businesses and farms

If you are disposing of a business or farm, you could face an enormous tax bill on the gain. There are two reliefs to reduce the impact on entrepreneurs and others who create small businesses:

- retirement relief when you retire from your business (see opposite)
- roll-over relief if you replace business assets (see p. 134).

What follows is a brief introduction to indicate their scope. But with large sums at stake, it would pay to seek professional advice on these reliefs to ensure you meet the complex requirements.

Retirement relief

This relief has now been phased out and superseded by business asset taper relief (see p. 120). The tax year ending 5 April 2003 is the last for which you can claim retirement relief.

Retirement relief reduces your taxable gain if you dispose of a business (or part of it) when aged 50, or more or less if you are retiring because of ill health. To get the maximum relief, you must have owned the business for at least ten years. In the year ending 5 April 2003, you get tax relief in full on the first £50,000 of the gain and on half of the next £150,000.

EXAMPLE

Harry Singh, aged 65, started a business 30 years ago and sold it in May 2002. The gain after indexation allowance was £500,000. He is entitled to the maximum retirement relief as he had the business for more than ten years.

Harry can claim full relief on the first £50,000 plus relief on half the gain between £50,000 and £150,000:

£50,000 + (50 per cent of £150,000)
= £50,000 + £75,000
= £125,000

Harry's taxable gain is:

£500,000 – £125,000 = £375,000

This £375,000 gain is Harry's only chargeable gain for the tax year and he has no losses to set off against it. But he is entitled to taper relief: four years for owning it since 5 April 1998. Four years for a business asset means only 25 per cent of the gain is taxable – that is, 25 per cent of £375,000 = £93,750.

The first £7,700 of taxable gains in the tax year ending 5 April 2003 is free of capital gains tax, so tax is charged on:

£93,750 – £7,700 = £86,050

Harry's taxable income is £45,000 on which he pays tax at the higher rate of 40 per cent. His capital gains tax bill is therefore:

40 per cent of £86,050 = £34,420

With retirement relief, a husband and wife can each make claims if they are eligible – effectively doubling the limits for a married couple who share ownership of the business. And you do not have to retire to claim it unless you are making your claim when aged under 50.

Retirement relief applies to business assets, and to shares in a company in which you have at least 5 per cent of the voting rights, providing you have been a full-time director or an employee of the company for the past ten years, and the company is a trading company.

You can still get retirement relief if you have owned several different businesses in the last ten years. Providing that each business qualifies for the relief, and the gap between each is not more than two years, you can add together the separate periods of business activity over the past ten years to calculate the total period that counts for the relief.

Roll-over relief

Roll-over relief allows you to defer the capital gains tax bill when you sell or otherwise dispose of assets from your business, providing you replace them in the three years after the sale or the one year before it. You can claim this roll-over relief even if you do not buy an identical replacement as long as you use the proceeds to buy another qualifying business asset. Assets which qualify include land or buildings used by the business, goodwill, fixed plant and machinery.

You usually get the relief by deducting the gain for the old asset from the acquisition cost of the new one. So when you come to sell the new asset, the gain on it has been increased by the gain on the old asset. However, if you replace again, you can claim further roll-over relief, and currently capital gains tax will not have to be paid until you fail to replace the business asset.

You can make a claim for roll-over relief up to five years after the 31 January following the end of the tax year in which you dispose of the asset or the year in which you replace it if this is later. You must reinvest all of the sale proceeds from the disposal of the first asset to get full relief.

For more information see Inland Revenue Helpsheet *IR290 Business asset rollover relief*.

INHERITANCE TAX

CHAPTER 11

There is no space on the 2003 tax return for inheritance tax. This is because it is largely a tax on what you leave when you die (including gifts made in the seven years before). The number of estates which are taxed has been rising in recent years and now stands at around one estate in 20.

The tax rate is a hefty 40 per cent of anything over £255,000 for the tax year ending 5 April 2004. There is plenty that can be done to reduce the amount paid – as long as you plan carefully. As one former chancellor said a few years ago: 'It is largely paid by people of modest means who either cannot or simply do not make careful plans to avoid it.'

This chapter tells you how inheritance tax works and how to reduce the amount that goes to the Inland Revenue. It also has some guidance on what can be done to reduce an inheritance tax bill after the event.

HOW INHERITANCE TAX WORKS

When you die, everything you own – your home, possessions, investments and savings – goes into your estate. So does money paid out by life insurance policies unless they are written in trust (see p. 140), and the value of things you have given away but reserved the right to use for yourself (gifts with reservation – see p. 142). Debts such as outstanding mortgages and funeral expenses are deducted from the total to find the value of your estate.

Inheritance tax is worked out on a rolling total of gifts you have made over the last seven years. What you leave on death is in effect your final gift. So to the estate you leave are added any gifts you made in the seven years before death unless they were tax-free gifts (see overleaf).

Some or all of your estate may be free of inheritance tax: anything left to your husband or wife, or to a UK charity, for example (for a full list of what is tax-free, see opposite). These tax-free bequests and legacies are deducted from the value of your estate before the tax bill is worked out.

If the resulting total exceeds a certain limit – £255,000 for deaths on or after 6 April 2003 – inheritance tax is payable on the amount over the limit at 40 per cent. (For deaths in the tax year ending 5 April 2003, the limit was £250,000.)

So if the total is £300,000, tax is payable on £300,000 – £255,000 = £45,000. This gives a tax bill of 40 per cent of £45,000, that is £18,000.

Quite separately from tax on your estate, potentially exempt transfers (see p. 139) and taxable gifts you made in the last seven years are reassessed on death and tax (or extra tax) may be due on them. Initially the person you made the gift to will be asked to pay. If they can't or won't, tax is paid from your estate. But taper relief can be claimed to reduce the tax bill if the gift was made more than three years before death (see below). Note that taper relief does not reduce the tax bill on the estate, and will only be useful if the life-time gifts exceed the nil band of £255,000.

Years between gift and death	*% of inheritance tax payable*
Up to 3	100%
More than 3 and up to 4	80%
More than 4 and up to 5	60%
More than 5 and up to 6	40%
More than 6 and up to 7	20%

EXAMPLE

Angela Framing died in May 2003, leaving an estate worth £287,000 (largely the value of her home). In December 1997, she had made a taxable gift of £10,000 to help a grandchild with the cost of studying. Subsequently, in August 1998, she gave another grandchild a taxable gift of £5,000 to start a business.

In calculating the tax due on Angela's estate, the £15,000 of taxable lifetime gifts is added to the £287,000 left on death to produce a total of £302,000. The first £255,000 of that is free of tax, leaving £302,000 – £255,000 = £47,000 on which tax is due.

Tax at 40 per cent on £47,000 is £18,800 – tax that will be entirely paid out of Angela's estate, since the life-time gifts are deemed to use up the £255,000 before the balance is used to calculate the tax on the estate.

Gifts free of inheritance tax

Gifts that are always tax-free:

- gifts between husband and wife – even if the two are legally separated. But only the first £55,000 is tax-free if the gifts are to someone who is not domiciled in the UK (domicile reflects the individual's natural home, see p. 330)
- gifts to UK charities and community amateur sports clubs
- gifts to certain national institutions such as the National Trust, National Gallery, British Museum (and their Scottish, Welsh and Northern Ireland equivalents)
- gifts of certain types of heritage property such as paintings, archives, land or historic buildings to non-profit-making concerns like local museums
- gifts of land in the UK to registered housing associations
- gifts of shares in a company into a trust for the benefit of most or all of the employees which will control the company
- gifts to established political parties.

Gifts that are tax-free on death only:

- lump sums paid out on your death by a pension scheme provided the trustees of the scheme have discretion about who gets the money
- refunds of personal pension contributions (and interest) paid directly to someone else or a trust – in other words, not paid into your estate
- the estate of anyone killed on active military service in war or whose death was hastened by such service
- £10,000 ex gratia payments received by survivors (and their spouses) held as Japanese prisoners of war during World War Two and amounts from other specified schemes that also provide compensation for wrongs suffered during the war.

Gifts that are tax-free in lifetime only:

- anything given to an individual more than seven years before your death – unless there are strings attached (see p. 142)
- small gifts worth up to £250 to any number of people in any tax year. But you can't give anyone more than this limit and claim exemption on the first £250 – if you give someone £500, the whole £500 will be taxable unless it is tax-free for one of the other reasons below
- regular gifts made out of normal income. The gifts must come out of your usual after-tax income and not from your capital. After paying for the gifts, you should have enough income to maintain your normal standard of living
- gifts on marriage to a bride or groom: each parent of the bride or groom can give £5,000, grandparents or remoter relatives and the bride or groom themselves can give £2,500 and anyone else £1,000. The gifts must be made before the big day – and if the marriage is called off, the gift becomes taxable

- gifts for the maintenance of your family – an ex-husband or wife, certain dependent relatives and children under 18 or still in full-time education. The children can be yours, stepchildren, adopted children or any other children in your care
- up to £3,000 in total a year of other gifts. If you don't use the whole £3,000 annual exemption in one year, you can carry forward the unused part to the next tax year only. You can't use the annual exemption to top up the small gifts exemption. If you give someone more than £250 in a year, all of it must come off the annual exemption if it is to be free of inheritance tax.

PLANNING FOR INHERITANCE TAX

If your estate is likely to be well below the threshold for paying inheritance tax, there is no need to worry about it. But if it looks as if you are above it, there is much you can do to reduce the tax bill. An important first step is to draw up a will which will make you think about what you own and how you want it to be disposed of after you die.

Most of the ways of minimising inheritance tax involve making gifts which are free of tax or making potentially taxable gifts more than seven years before your death. But remember your heirs will still gain from what you leave them even if tax is due on your estate. Don't give away so much that you or your spouse are left impoverished in old age, merely to cheat the Inland Revenue of every last penny of tax.

> **TAX-SAVING IDEA**
> Draw up a will. There are simple steps you can take to minimise the tax payable on your estate when you die and to reduce the complications for those you leave behind.

Tax-free gifts

If you do have some resources to spare, make as full use as possible of the annual £3,000 exemption, gifts out of normal income and such like. And make sure your spouse has enough to make similar gifts tax-free.

> **TAX-SAVING IDEA**
> Make as full use as possible of the gifts you can make which do not fall into the inheritance tax net. For example, gifts on marriage and those made out of normal income are tax-free.

If you want to make larger gifts, the earlier you make them the better – because inheritance tax may have to be paid on a gift if you die within seven years of making it. For this reason, lifetime gifts are often described as potentially exempt transfers (PETs). They are potentially free of inheritance tax but you must survive for seven years after they are made for the tax to be avoided.

Even if you die within seven years of making a gift, the inheritance tax paid by the person you made the gift to will be reduced by taper relief (see p. 136) if the gift is made more than three years before your death and it is not fully covered by the nil band. Note that gifts in your lifetime, other than cash, may mean a capital gains tax bill – see Chapter 10.

Share your wealth

A married couple can share their wealth – what they give to each other is free of inheritance tax. Each can then make tax-free gifts and leave a taxable estate of up to £255,000 without paying inheritance tax.

In practice, it may not be easy to split your worldly goods and give them away during your lifetime. It may make more sense to pass all or most of them on to the survivor so he or she has enough to live on. But this principle of estate-splitting is a basic strategy to be followed where possible.

EXAMPLE

Veronica McGough wants to give away as much as possible free of inheritance tax before she dies.

First, she gives £1,000 a year to each of her three children – taking advantage of the £3,000 a year annual exemption. Then she makes £250 gifts every year to each of her ten grandchildren – a total of £2,500 a year free of inheritance tax as small gifts. She also gives the maximum £2,500 to any of her grandchildren who get married.

She can afford to pay the premiums on insurance policies on her own life out of her normal income. So she takes out policies written in trust (see opposite) for each of her three children. The premiums come to £60 a month each and will be tax-free as regular gifts made out of normal income (when she dies, the money from the insurance policies will be paid straight to the children without being taxable).

Overall, Veronica manages to give away almost £7,660 every year free of inheritance tax. Even if she dies within seven years of making the gifts, there will be no inheritance tax to pay on them because they are all exempt gifts.

Your home

Your home is almost certainly your most valuable possession – and may be the main reason why your estate ends up over the threshold for paying inheritance tax. But it is one of the hardest assets to remove from the tax net – assuming you intend to go on living in it until you die.

For example, you can't make a lifetime gift of it to your children on condition you can continue to live in it. That would count as a gift with reservation (see p. 142), and the home would still be treated as yours.

You might be able to reduce the size of your estate somewhat by sharing the ownership of the house. If your home is jointly owned with someone under a joint tenancy, your share automatically goes to the survivor when one of you dies. But if you jointly own your home with someone else as a tenancy in common, you can bequeath your half-share to anyone you please.

For example, if you had a tenancy in common with your spouse, you could bequeath half of your half-share to your spouse and the other half to the next generation. This would reduce the size of your spouse's estate but leave him or her in control of at least part of the home.

There is no inheritance tax to pay if you leave part or all of a home to your spouse, since gifts between husband and wife are always tax-free. But a gift to anyone who is not your husband or wife is taxable, unless it falls within the £255,000 tax-free limit.

EXAMPLE

Alan and Meg Riordan realise there could be a hefty inheritance tax bill when they die, since most of their assets are in Alan's name. They decide to start an active programme of making tax-free gifts and estate-splitting.

They adopt a similar approach to Veronica McGough in making gifts. Since each of them can make these tax-free gifts, they are soon passing on around £100,000 to their children and grandchildren every seven years.

They also divide their assets between them, and bequeath a further £200,000 each to their children in their wills, with the rest to each other. When the first dies, the £200,000 bequest to the children will be below the threshold for inheritance tax.

The second to die will thus leave £200,000 less to fall into the tax net. And the Riordans will have saved £100,000 from inheritance tax for each seven years of the lifetime gifts programme.

By starting 15 years before their deaths, the Riordans manage to pass on £400,000 more without tax than if they had left it all in Alan's name. This saves their heirs £160,000 in inheritance tax.

Life insurance

If you want to make sure there is enough money to pay an inheritance tax bill on a home or business, you can take out a term life insurance policy which pays out if you die within seven years of giving it away. And if you plan to leave a large asset on death, whole life insurance policies pay out whenever you die, again providing cash to pay the inheritance tax.

Make sure you have any such policies written in trust to the person you want to have the money. The proceeds will then be paid directly to that person on your death and be free of inheritance tax. If the policy is not written in trust, the money will be added to your estate and inheritance tax charged on it (there will also be a delay before your heirs can get their hands on it until probate is granted).

The premiums for a policy written in trust count as gifts, but will be free of inheritance tax if the policy is for your spouse. And if you pay the premiums out of your normal spending, they will be tax-free whoever benefits.

> **TAX-SAVING IDEA**
> Use life insurance to blunt the impact of inheritance tax. Policies written in trust go straight to the beneficiary and don't form part of your estate. If you pay the premiums out of your normal spending they are tax-free gifts.

Shares

The market value of any shares left on death must normally be included in your estate in working out the inheritance tax bill. But some sorts of shares qualify for business relief (also available on lifetime gifts). This reduces the value for inheritance tax purposes – or even removes them from the calculation altogether:

- shares in a listed company which form a controlling interest, the value of the shares is halved
- unquoted shares in most companies – including those listed on the Alternative Investment Market (AIM) – qualify for full relief
- unquoted securities which either alone or with other securities and unquoted shares give you a controlling interest qualify for full relief.

To prevent 'death-bed' purchases of business property, all these shares and securities must have been owned for at least two years.

Your own business or farm

If you own or have an interest in a small business or a farm, seek professional advice on inheritance tax, since there are substantial concessions which can reduce or eliminate the tax:

- business relief means there will be no inheritance tax to pay on business assets such as goodwill, land, buildings, plant, stock, patents and so on (reduced by debts incurred in the business)
- agricultural relief can mean no inheritance tax on the agricultural value of owner-occupied farmlands and farm tenancies (including cottages, farm buildings and farm houses). There are also reliefs for landowners who let farmland.

Estate freezing

Estate freezing is a way of freezing some of the value of your wealth now so the increase in value in future years benefits someone else.

A simple way of doing this is by investing in an endowment or unit-linked life insurance policy written in trust for your children or grandchildren (see Life insurance, above). Any growth in its value accumulates in the policy free of inheritance tax. Some unit trust managers can do something similar with investments in unit trusts.

A more ambitious approach is to set up an accumulation and maintenance trust for your children or grandchildren. You put some capital in and any income from it is either reinvested or used for the maintenance, education or benefit of the beneficiaries at the discretion of the trustees. When the beneficiaries reach the age of 25, either the capital is shared out or they become entitled to the income from it. If you live for more than seven years after making gifts to such trusts, there is no inheritance tax to pay.

If you are thinking of setting up a family trust, consult a professional tax adviser such as a solicitor or accountant.

INHERITANCE TAX PLANNING PITFALLS

You might think that there are some rather obvious wheezes that will help you avoid inheritance tax. It is unlikely that the Inland Revenue will not have thought of them and blocked their use.

Gifts with strings attached

If you give something away but reserve the right to use it, it counts as a gift with reservation – and is treated as remaining your property. The gift would not be recognised for inheritance tax purposes and its value would be added to your estate when you died.

For example, if you give your home to a child on condition that you can go on living in it until your death, this would count as a gift with reservation. This could apply even if there was no formal agreement that you go on living in the home. If the gift was made after 17 March 1986, it counts as subject to a reservation if you go on using it.

Associated operations

If you try to get round the inheritance tax rules by making a series of gifts, the

Inland Revenue is allowed to treat them as associated operations which form a single direct gift.

For example, you might think you could give an extra £2,500 to an adult child by making ten tax-free gifts of £250 to friends which they pass on. The taxman will treat this as a single £2,500 gift, however – and potentially subject to tax.

Related property

In working out the value of a bequest or gift, the Inland Revenue may treat as yours property which it reckons is related to yours – in particular, anything owned by your husband or wife. This means you can't reduce its value by splitting it up with your spouse.

Suppose, for example, you own 30 per cent of the shares in a company and your spouse owns another 30 per cent. The Inland Revenue will value your 30 per cent as worth half the value of a 60 per cent controlling interest, which is generally higher than the value of a 30 per cent minority interest.

Property will also be treated as related if it has been owned at any time in the previous five years by a charity, political party or national institution to which you or your spouse gave it.

PAYMENT OF INHERITANCE TAX

Inheritance tax is due six months after the end of the month in which death occurred. In general, the property in the estate cannot be distributed until probate has been granted, but probate will not be granted until the tax has been paid. Therefore, the personal representatives may have to borrow to pay the tax bill. However, certain National Savings & Investments products can be used before probate solely for paying tax and, from 2003, the balances in the deceased's bank and building society accounts can also be used in this way.

Interest is charged if the tax is paid after the six-month deadline, running from the time the tax was due. Likewise, if you pay too much inheritance tax, you will get interest on the over-payment from the Inland Revenue.

If you take out a loan to pay inheritance tax before probate is granted, you can get tax relief on the interest on it for up to 12 months.

Payment by instalments

You can spread the pain of paying inheritance tax over ten equal yearly instalments with two sorts of assets:

- land and property
- a business, including certain holdings of unquoted shares.

This option is allowed only with bequests on death and lifetime gifts where the recipient still owns the property when the death occurs. Interest has to be paid on the delayed tax with land and property, unless it is business property or agricultural land.

If you want to pay in instalments, tell the Inland Revenue before the normal payment date for the tax. The first instalment is due on the date the whole tax would have been payable.

Reducing the tax on bequests that have fallen in value

If you inherit investments or land and buildings which fall in value after the death of the person who bequeathed them, you might be able to reduce your inheritance tax bill.

For investments, this applies to quoted shares and authorised unit trusts which fall in value or become worthless in the year after death:

- if sold during this period for less than they were worth on death, the sale price can be used to value them for inheritance tax purposes instead of their value on death
- if cancelled without replacement, they are treated as having been sold immediately before the date of cancellation for the nominal sum of £1
- if suspended and remaining suspended a year after the death, their value at the first anniversary can be used for inheritance tax purposes instead of their value on death.

When this relief is claimed, however, all such investments sold in the year after death are revalued in this way. So if some shares or unit trusts have been sold for more than they were worth on death, this would offset any loss made on other shares or unit trusts.

For land or buildings, you can ask for the inheritance tax bill to be recalculated if you sell them within four years of the death for less than their probate value. The inheritance tax bill will be worked out on the actual sale proceeds instead. Again, if this relief is claimed, all land or property sold during the four-year period is revalued for inheritance tax purposes at what it was sold for, rather than what it was worth on death (although there are special rules for sales in the fourth year and sales where the difference from the value at death is small).

Facing a second inheritance tax bill within five years?

If you inherit something that has only recently been subject to inheritance tax, the tax due on this second change of ownership is reduced by what is known as quick succession relief. Provided the death which led to the first payment was within five years of the death that has led to a second tax bill, the second bill can be reduced by a fraction of the first bill.

If the first death was within one year of the second death, the second bill is reduced by the following fraction of the first bill:

$$\frac{\text{Value of inheritance at the time of first transfer}}{\text{Value of inheritance at transfer + tax paid on first transfer}}$$

If the first death was more than one year before the second death, the fraction is reduced by 20 per cent for each complete year between the two deaths. The example, right, shows how quick succession relief works.

EXAMPLE

Maurice Thornton inherits a half-share of his mother's estate, worth £150,000. Inheritance tax of £10,600 is due on this share.

However, Maurice's mother had inherited £80,000 from her father only two and a half years earlier – an inheritance on which tax of £20,000 had been paid. Because Maurice's legacy is within five years of his mother's own legacy, he is entitled to reduce the inheritance tax on his legacy by a fraction of what was paid on hers.

The fraction of the tax bill on his mother's legacy which can be taken into account is worked out as follows:

$$\frac{£80{,}000}{£80{,}000 + £20{,}000} = \frac{£80{,}000}{£100{,}000} = \frac{4}{5}$$

This means if the second death had occurred within one year of the first, the tax bill would be reduced to ⅘ × £20,000 = £16,000. However, the period between the two deaths is two-and-a-half years, so the fraction is reduced to just 60 per cent (100 per cent less 20 per cent for each complete year) of ⅘. This means the tax bill is 60% × £16,000 = £9,600.

Changing inheritances after a death

If you are facing an inheritance tax bill, one option to reduce it is to vary the inheritances covered. Whether or not there is a will, those who are entitled to a share of a dead person's estate can agree to vary the way the estate is divided up. For example, the variation could direct some of the estate towards tax-free bequests – from the children to the dead person's husband or wife, for example.

The procedure is to draw up a deed of variation in writing, which must be signed within two years of the death by all those who will lose out. If it increases the amount of tax, the personal representatives of the dead person must also sign it. A variation can be carried out only once, so it is important to get it right. A solicitor can advise on drawing up the document – if children under 18 and unmarried are involved, it will be necessary to obtain a court order. If you want inheritance tax to be calculated on the basis of the varied bequests, the deed must make this clear.

HOW TO FILL IN YOUR TAX RETURN

CHAPTER 12

When you receive your tax return for the tax year ending 5 April 2003, this is what you should have:

- a ten-page booklet entitled Tax Return. We show you how to complete these pages in Chapters 13 to 15
- supplementary pages for the tax return to cater for your individual circumstances – there are nine sets of supplementary pages (see below). If your tax office knows that a supplement is relevant to you it may be bound into your tax return. We explain how to complete these pages in Chapters 16 to 24
- a Tax Return Guide. This consists of 34 pages which explain how to complete the ten pages of the tax return (see above) plus extra pages on how to fill in any supplements bound into your tax return
- a 16-page Tax Calculation Guide. But if your tax affairs are complex, you'll need to ask for the 34-page Comprehensive Tax Calculation Guide or use the Inland Revenue's Internet Service (see p. 16).

What you should do next

Step 1

Make sure you have the correct supplementary pages.

Step 2

If one or more of the supplementary pages you need are missing, contact the Inland Revenue. The Orderline is open every day from 8 am to 10 pm, except Christmas Day, Boxing Day and New Year's Day. The phone number is 0845 9000 404, fax number is 0845 9000 604, the e-mail address is saorderline.ir@gtnet.gov.uk or you can write to PO Box 37, St Austell, PL25 5YN. Alternatively, you can download the pages you need from the Inland Revenue website http://www.inlandrevenue.gov.uk/sa.

Step 3

Gather together all your records and supporting documentation, which you need to fill in the tax return.

Step 4
Fill in your supplementary pages FIRST, using the advice in Chapters 16 to 24 of this Guide. If you need further help, contact your tax office (see p. 16) or, if that is closed, the Inland Revenue helpline on 0845 9000 444. The helpline is open evenings and weekends and can give general advice.

Step 5
After filling in the supplementary pages, complete the tax return.

Step 6
If you are not going to work out your tax bill yourself, send in your tax return and supplementary pages by 30 September 2003.

Step 7
If you want to calculate your own tax – and we recommend that you don't – use your Tax Calculation Guide. But if any of the following apply, you will not be able to use the guide sent with your tax return:

- you have filled in any of the supplementary pages other than the Employment pages, Self-employment pages or Land and property pages
- you received any scrip dividends or non-qualifying distributions (boxes 10.21 to 10.26 on page 3 of the main tax return)
- you received any gains on UK life insurance policies or refund of additional voluntary contributions (question 12 on the main return)
- you received any taxable lump sums (box 1.29 in the Employment supplement)
- you can claim higher rate relief on annuity or covenant payments you make for commercial reasons connected to your business (box 15.9 on page 5 of the main tax return)
- you have made a compulsory payment to an employer's scheme to provide death benefits for your widow, widower or children and unusually you did not get relief through PAYE (box 15.11)
- you are claiming an allowance against higher rate tax on cash received from the redemption of bonus shares (box 15.12).

If any of these apply and you want to calculate your own tax, contact the Orderline on 0845 9000 404 and ask for the Comprehensive Tax Calculation Guide or consider using software to file by Internet (see p. 17).

Step 8
If you are an employee and the tax you owe is less than £2,000, choose to send in your tax return, supplementary pages and tax calculation by 30 September, or, if you use the Internet, by 30 December. Then you can ask to pay your tax

bill through the PAYE system on a monthly basis starting in April 2004.

Step 9

Otherwise send in your tax return, supplementary pages and tax calculation by 31 January 2004. Send your final tax payment for the tax year ending 5 April 2003 by the same date. If you pay tax by making payments on account (see Chapter 25), you must also make your first payment for the tax year ending 5 April 2004 at this time.

THE SUPPLEMENTARY PAGES

On page 2 of the basic tax return you are asked nine questions. If you answer YES to a question you will need to fill in the corresponding supplementary pages. If you have not been sent those pages automatically you will need to ask for them from the Orderline (see p. 147).

Employment

Q1 Were you an employee, or office holder, or director, or agency worker or did you receive payments or benefits from a former employer (excluding a pension) in the year ended 5 April 2003?
If you were a non-resident director of a UK company but received no remuneration, see the notes to the Employment Pages, page EN3, box 1.6. **YES** ☐ **EMPLOYMENT** ☐

You are required to fill in the Employment supplementary pages if you answer YES to this question. If you have more than one job, you will need a set of Employment pages for each job. The Inland Revenue will regard you as an employee even if you work on a part-time or casual basis. There are more guidelines on who counts as an employee in Chapter 16 (p. 209).

Share schemes

Q2 Did you have any taxable income from share options, shares or share related benefits in the year? (This does not include
- dividends, **or**
- dividend shares ceasing to be subject to an Inland Revenue approved share incentive plan within three years of acquisition

they go in Question 10.) **YES** ☐ **SHARE SCHEMES** ☐

If you receive shares or options under one of the special approved schemes which are tax-free and you kept to the rules of scheme, you aren't required to complete this supplement. You will have to fill it in if in the tax year ending 5 April 2003 you have received shares or options in any other way or you have broken the rules of an approved scheme. Chapter 17 on p. 234 gives a lot of background information on share schemes and guides you through the completion of this supplement.

Self-employment

Q3 Were you self-employed (but not in partnership)? (You should also tick 'Yes' if you were a Name at Lloyd's.)	YES ☐	SELF-EMPLOYMENT ☐

If you carried on a trade, profession or vocation as a self-employed person during the tax year ending on 5 April 2003 you need to complete this supplementary section. Chapter 18 on p. 250 has guidelines on who counts as self-employed.

If you are in partnership you need to complete a different set of supplementary pages (see below).

Partnership

Q4 Were you in partnership?	YES ☐	PARTNERSHIP ☐

If you are in business with one or more partners, you should answer YES to this question and complete a set of supplementary pages. There is a short version and a long version. You will find guidance on which version you should complete in Chapter 19 (p. 281).

Land and Property

Q5 Did you receive any rent or other income from land and property in the UK?	YES ☐	LAND & PROPERTY ☐

You need to complete these supplementary pages if you receive income from land and property, furnished holiday accommodation, or providing furnished accommodation in your home during the tax year ending 5 April 2003. However, if you provide additional services, such as meals, you will need to complete the Self-employment supplementary pages instead, as you are considered to be carrying on a trade. You can get more guidance by turning to Chapter 20 (p. 283).

Foreign

Q6 Did you have any taxable income from overseas pensions or benefits, or from foreign companies or savings institutions, offshore funds or trusts abroad, or from land and property abroad or gains on foreign insurance policies?	YES ☐	
Have you or could you have received, or enjoyed directly or indirectly, or benefited in any way from, income of a foreign entity as a result of a transfer of assets made in this or earlier years?	YES ☐	
Do you want to claim foreign tax credit relief for foreign tax paid on foreign income or gains?	YES ☐	FOREIGN ☐

There are five supplementary pages which have space to give details about your foreign savings, pensions and benefits, income from offshore trusts, gains on foreign life policies, property income and other investment income from abroad. Ask for it if you received any such income or benefit in the tax year ending 5 April 2003 or if you answered yes to any of the three questions above. If you turn to Chapter 21 (p. 298) you will find more information on what is foreign income and how it is taxed.

Trusts etc

Q7 Did you receive, or are you deemed to have, income from a trust, settlement or the residue of a deceased person's estate? *YES* ☐ *TRUSTS ETC* ☐

You need to complete this supplement if you were a beneficiary, a settlor or had income from the estates of someone who has died. You can find more information and guidance on filling in the supplementary page in Chapter 22 (p. 307) A beneficiary of a bare trust enters the income in the basic tax return, see p. 156.

Capital gains

Q8 Capital gains - read the guidance on page 7 of the Tax Return Guide.

- If you have disposed of your only or main residence do you need the Capital Gains Pages? *YES* ☐
- Did you dispose of other chargeable assets worth more than £15,400 in total? *YES* ☐
- Were your total chargeable gains more than £7,700 or do you want to make a claim or election for the year? *YES* ☐ *CAPITAL GAINS* ☐

You must complete these supplementary pages if you have made a capital gain (with some exceptions – see below) or you wish to claim an allowable capital loss for the tax year ending 5 April 2003.

You won't need to return the supplementary page if your gains were £7,700 or less (which is the tax free slice for the year). Nor do you need to fill it in if any gain was from selling your home (and it is free of tax) and the other assets which you disposed of (leaving out assets on which gains are tax-free) totalled £15,400 or less for the year. For more information on which gains are tax-free and guidance on whether the gain on selling your home will be taxable or not, see Chapter 10 (p. 105).

Non-residence etc

If at any time during the tax year ending 5 April 2003, you consider yourself to be non-resident, not ordinarily resident or not domiciled in the UK, or resident in the UK at the same time as being resident in a country with which the

Q9	Are you claiming that you were not resident, or not ordinarily resident, or not domiciled, in the UK, or dual resident in the UK and another country, for all or part of the year?	YES	NON-RESIDENCE ETC

UK has a double taxation agreement, then you will need to complete this supplement. Chapter 24 (p. 329) will give you guidance.

COMPLETING THE TAX RETURN

You can fill in the first seven pages of the tax return, using Chapters 13–15 of this guide. Chapter 13 completes the Income pages, Chapter 14 explains the Reliefs page and Chapter 15 deals with the Allowances pages.

In the last three pages of the tax return, you are asked for information about student loan repayments, your tax bill, tax repayments and refunds.

Q17	**Are you liable to make Student Loan Repayments for 2002-03 on an Income Contingent Student Loan?** *You must read the note on page 31 of your Tax Return Guide before ticking the 'Yes' box.*	YES	If yes, tick this box. If not applicable, go to Question 18.
	If yes, and you are calculating your tax enter in Question 18, box 18.2A the amount you work out is repayable in 2002-03		

Student loans taken out from August 1998 onwards are 'income contingent'. This means that you start to repay them once you're earning and your income exceeds £10,000 a year. If your income for the year ending 5 April 2003 exceeds this threshold, you are required to make a loan repayment equal to 9 per cent of the income in excess of £10,000. Some income is ignored, for example, unearned income (from savings, pensions, benefits, and so on) unless it comes to more than £2,000, and benefits in kind. In calculating your income, relief is given for pension contributions and some types of losses that qualify for tax relief.

If the Student Loan Company has notified you that repayment of your loan started before 6 April 2003 (and you had not fully repaid the loan before the start of the tax year on 6 April 2002), tick YES. Provided you send in your tax return by 30 September 2003, your tax office will work out the repayment due. If you are calculating the payment yourself, enter the amount later in Box 18.2A. Any amounts you've already paid back through PAYE (see p. 233) are deducted to arrive at the amount due.

Q18 **Do you want to calculate your tax and, if appropriate, any Student Loan Repayment?** YES [ ] Use your Tax Calculation Guide then fill in boxes 18.1 to 18.8 as appropriate.

Tick YES if you intend to work out your own tax bill, although we recommend that you send in your return by 30 September to let the Inland Revenue work out the sum for you.

If you are not going to work out your own tax bill, move on to Q19.

Q19 **Do you want to claim a repayment if you have paid too much tax?** *(If you do not tick 'Yes' or the tax you have overpaid is below £10, I will use the amount you are owed to reduce your next tax bill.)* YES [ ] If yes, tick this box and then fill in boxes 19.1 to 19.12 as appropriate. If not applicable, go to Question 20.

Tick YES to claim a repayment and complete the subsequent boxes as appropriate.

Q20 **Have you already had any 2002-03 tax refunded or set off by your Inland Revenue office or the Benefits Agency (in Northern Ireland, the Social Security Agency)?** *Read the notes on page 32 of your Tax Return Guide* YES [ ] If yes, tick this box and then enter the amount of the refund in box 20.1.

20.1 £

If this does not apply to you, go direct to Q21.

If YES enter the amount you were refunded, either directly from your tax office (including repayments of tax deducted from investments) or from your Benefits Agency (such as refunds of tax deducted from jobseeker's allowance). You should also include similar amounts which, rather than being repaid directly to you, have been set against payments of tax you owe.

Enter the amount refunded for the tax year ending 5 April 2003 in box 20.1.

Q22 **Please give other personal details in boxes 22.1 to 22.7.** *This information helps us to be more efficient and effective.*

Your daytime telephone number

22.1

Your agent's telephone number

22.2

and their name and address

22.3

Postcode

Your first two forenames

22.4

Say if you are single, married, widowed, divorced or separated

22.5

Your date of birth (If you were born before 6 April 1938, you may get a higher age-related allowance.)

22.6 / /

Your National Insurance number (if known and not on page 1 of your Tax Return)

22.7

If you are self-employed, you need to give your first two forenames in box 22.4 and, if you know it, your National Insurance number in box 22.7. Everyone should complete the other boxes in question 22.

Tick box 23.1 if you do **not** want any tax you owe for 2002-03 collected through your tax code.	23.1

If you are on PAYE and owe tax of less than £2,000, it will normally be collected through the PAYE system. You are asked to tick box 23.1 if you do not want this to happen, but do not do so without some thought. PAYE spreads out and delays the payment of your tax.

Please tick box 23.2 if this Tax Return contains figures that are provisional because you do not yet have final figures. Pages 32 and 33 of the Tax Return Guide explain the circumstances in which provisional figures may be used and asks for some additional information to be provided in box 23.5 below.	23.2

In box 23.2, you have to say whether any of the figures are provisional. If they are, don't delay sending in your tax return. In the Additional information box, explain which figures are provisional (including the box numbers), why they are provisional and when they will be finalised. If you know you are not going to be able to give reliable figures, because you have lost information or have had to estimate a valuation, for example, explain what they are and how you have arrived at the estimates.

Be warned that, if you negligently submit a provisional figure which is inaccurate or unnecessary, you may be liable to a penalty.

And finally

At Q24, tick any additional pages you are sending with the basic tax return. In the case of employment, self-employment and partnership, you might be including more than one set of supplementary pages (if you have changed job during the year or you have more than one job or business). If this applies to you, write in the relevant box the number of supplements you are sending back. Don't forget to sign and date the declaration. One of the commonest mistakes made by taxpayers is to forget to sign the tax return. If you are signing for someone else, state in what capacity you are doing this.

INCOME

CHAPTER 13

The first stage in working out your income tax bill for the tax year ending 5 April 2003 is to find your taxable income. Pages 3 and 4 of the basic tax return set out various different types of income, such as income from savings and investments, pensions and benefits, life insurance gains and other bits and pieces. You should complete this income section to tell your tax inspector what types of income and how much of each type you received. You may find it helpful to read Chapter 8.

This is not the only way in which your tax inspector will find out about your income. There are also supplementary pages, including Employment, Self-employment and Land and property, where you must give details of other sorts of income. And these should be filled in before you tackle the basic tax return.

You don't need to enter in the tax return any income which is tax-free. A comprehensive list is given in Appendix A (see p. 345).

INCOME *for the year ended 5 April 2003*

When entering your income in the tax return, you should enter the amount you received in the year ending on 5 April 2003 (although in a few cases there are special rules for what counts as received). If you receive income of the same type from more than one source – for example, you have several savings accounts – enter the overall total for each type, but keep records for each separate account in case your tax office asks to see them.

When you enter amounts of income, round any odd pence down to the nearest £. When you enter amounts of tax credits or tax already deducted, round any odd pence up to the nearest £. If you are entering the total of income or tax from several sources (several savings accounts, say), add up each amount including the pence and round just the total.

SAVINGS AND INVESTMENT INCOME

Q10 Did you receive any income from UK savings and investments? YES [ ] If yes, tick this box and then fill in boxes 10.1 to 10.26 as appropriate. Include only your share from any joint savings and investments. If not applicable, go to Question 11.

You can get an income from your investments or savings in the form of interest, dividends or distributions (which are treated in the same way as dividends); for example, interest on a building society account, dividends from shares or distributions from unit trusts. Although the income from these sources can be paid out to you, this is not always the case. For example, interest can be added to your account rather than paid out, and with distributions from unit trusts it can be reinvested if you choose. It counts as income whether it is paid out to you or not. If you have any investment income (unless it is tax-free, see p. 346), you should tick the YES box at Q10 and fill in boxes 10.1 to 10.26.

Only enter details of investments you own. If you own an investment jointly, you need to enter only the amount in the tax return which is your share. If you are married, the income from a jointly-owned investment normally will be split equally. But if you own an investment in a different proportion, the income can be split to reflect ownership (see p. 51).

> **TAX-SAVING IDEA**
>
> Take advantage of the many ways you can save which are free of tax: pensions, ISAs and many National Savings & Investment products. These are especially helpful if you are a higher rate taxpayer. If you are a basic rate taxpayer, check to see that any expenses, for example for managing an ISA, are not more than the tax saved.

There are many opportunities for tax saving and tax planning with investments. Turn to Chapters 5 and 8 which should help you maximise your tax-efficient investing.

If you are the beneficiary of a bare trust, that is one in which you have an immediate absolute title to the capital and income, you should enter the amount of (or your share of) the income on this page of the return. Your trustee will be able to give you the details of your share. Which boxes you complete on this page depends on the type of income concerned.

Your income from investments includes income from investments which you have given to your children aged 18 or less and unmarried. You need to enter details if the amount of income for the tax year is more than £100 before tax. This tax treatment now applies even to a bare trust you have set up for your child, where the trust was set up on or after 9 March 1999. If you make additional gifts on or after that date to an existing trust, income from the extra gifts is also treated in the same way. This tax treatment also applies to money you have given your child to invest in a cash ISA, even though interest from the ISA would otherwise be tax-free.

Which investment income should not be included on page 3 of your tax return?

You shouldn't include in your tax return any investment income which is tax-free (see box overleaf). If all your investment income is tax-free, you can skip Q10 and go straight to Q11.

These other types of income may be taxable but should go elsewhere in the tax return:

- income from an annuity under a personal pension plan or retirement annuity contract or trust scheme. Enter on page 4 under Q11
- gains on UK life insurance policies or life annuities or capital redemption policies. These should be included on page 4 under Q12
- a share of any partnership investment income should be entered in the Partnership supplement
- annual payments from UK unauthorised unit trusts. Enter under Q13.

The documents you need

Get together all your interest statements, tax deduction certificates, dividend and distribution tax vouchers and trust vouchers. Keep them safe; don't send with your tax return.

EXAMPLE

Sidney Barrow has the following investments and accounts: NS&I Certificates, a stocks and shares ISA, a TESSA account and a bank current account which pays interest on credit balances. If he didn't have the bank current account Q10 would not apply to him. But the interest payable on his bank current account means that he has to tick the YES box.

TAX-SAVING IDEA

Couples, where one person pays tax at the higher rate and the other does not, can adjust their investments between them, so that more investments are in the name of the lower taxpayer. Thus less of the return will be taxed at the higher rate. Couples, where one pays tax at the starting rate or pays no tax at all and the other pays at the basic rate, can save tax in the same way by shifting interest-earning investments (but not shares or unit trusts) to the lower taxpayer.

TAX-FREE INVESTMENT INCOME

Some investment income is free of income tax. This income does not have to be entered in the tax return. Income from the following investments is tax-free:

- prizes from premium bonds, National Lottery and gambling
- an ISA (individual savings account)
- a TESSA account (tax exempt special savings account), but not if you closed your account before the five years was up
- a PEP (personal equity plan), but not if you withdraw more than £180 in interest
- SAYE schemes
- National Savings & Investments (NS&I) Ordinary account (but only up to the first £70 of interest, or up to £140 in the case of a joint account)
- NS&I Certificates, including the index-linked ones
- NS&I Children's Bonus Bonds
- Ulster Savings Certificates, if you normally live in Northern Ireland and you bought the certificates or they were repaid while you were living there
- dividends on shares in venture capital trusts (up to £100,000 of shares for each tax year).

There are other less obvious forms of investment income which are also tax-free and don't need to be entered in the tax return:

- interest awarded by a UK court as part of a claim for damages for personal injury or death. There is an extra-statutory concession which means that this can also apply to awards from a foreign court
- interest awarded as part of compensation for being mis-sold a personal pension or free-standing AVC scheme
- lump sum compensation made in accordance with Financial Services Authority policies relating to being mis-sold a free-standing AVC scheme
- compensation (which would normally count as interest for tax purposes) paid by banks on dormant accounts opened by Holocaust victims and frozen during World War II
- adoption allowances paid under the Adoption Allowance Regulations 1991 (or the Scottish equivalent)
- if you are a trustee, before-tax interest which is paid out direct to beneficiaries from the payer, but through your authority. But beneficiaries should declare this income.

INTEREST

Banks and building societies

- Interest from UK banks, building societies and deposit takers (interest from UK Internet accounts must be included) - *If you have more than one bank or building society etc account enter **totals** in the boxes.*

Most saving income is now paid with tax deducted and the rate of tax for the tax year ending 5 April 2003 is 20 per cent. Income from most accounts in UK banks, building societies, finance houses, organisations offering high-interest cheque accounts and other licensed deposit takers is paid after deduction of tax. There is no further tax bill to pay if you pay tax at the basic rate only on your income, which applies to most taxpayers. If you pay tax at the higher rate, there will be extra tax to pay, at the rate of 20 per cent (see p. 63). If your top rate of tax is the starting rate, tax due on your savings income is reduced to 10 per cent – you can claim back the excess tax already deducted. If you are a non-taxpayer, you can claim back all of any tax already deducted. If you expect to carry on being a non-taxpayer, you should register to receive your interest before any tax is deducted – see Chapter 8 (p. 64).

- enter any bank, building society etc interest that **has not** had tax taken off. (Most interest is taxed by your bank or building society etc. so make sure you should be filling in box 10.1, rather than boxes 10.2 to 10.4)

	Taxable amount
10.1	£

You may have received interest from your bank or building society paid gross, that is without tax deducted. The most common circumstance where this might apply is if you have registered to receive interest gross because you are a non-taxpayer (see p. 64). If you get gross interest from an offshore bank account, do not enter it here – it goes on the Foreign supplement.

Add up all the interest you have received without tax deducted from your bank, building society or deposit taker in the tax year ending 5 April 2003 and enter it in box 10.1.

If you are a beneficiary of a trust and you are entitled to income as it arises, you should include in box 10.1 any untaxed interest paid direct to you because the trustee has authorised the payer to do so.

Don't include NS&I interest here (it goes in box 10.8).

- enter details of your **taxed** bank or building society etc interest. *The Working Sheet on page 10 of your Tax Return Guide will help you fill in boxes 10.2 to 10.4.*

Amount **after** tax deducted	Tax deducted	Gross amount **before** tax
10.2 £	10.3 £	10.4 £

You can get the information for these boxes from your statements or pass books or ask your bank, building society or deposit taker direct to give you a tax deduction certificate. Enter the totals for all three figures in the boxes.

If your statement only shows the after-tax figure, you will need to gross it up, see Appendix B on p. 348.

You may have received cash or shares when two or more building societies have merged or a building society has converted to a bank or been taken over by a bank. You may have to pay either income or capital gains tax and your building society should be able to tell you this. If you have received a cash payment on which you should pay income tax, put the details in boxes 10.2 to 10.4. If you don't know whether you have to pay income tax, put the details under Q13 on page 4, but also tick box 23.2 on page 9 and explain the situation in the Additional information box. Any capital gain should be entered in the Capital gains supplementary pages. If you have received shares, you may not need to supply details until you dispose of the shares.

Unit trusts

	Amount after tax deducted	Tax deducted	Gross amount before tax
• Interest distributions from UK authorised unit trusts and open-ended investment companies (dividend distributions go below)	10.5 £	10.6 £	10.7 £

Some types of unit trusts and open-ended investment companies pay interest rather than dividends. These include unit trusts which invest in gilts and other fixed-interest investments. In these cases, 20 per cent tax has been deducted from the income before you get it in the same way as for bank or building society interest (see p. 62) and you will get a tax voucher telling you the amount paid. You may be able to claim some or all of it back, or you may have to pay more tax in the same way as for bank or building society interest.

The interest might not be paid out to you but automatically reinvested in accumulation or other units. However, you still have to enter the interest in your tax return.

Add up all the interest you receive after tax has been deducted and enter the total in box 10.5. Put the tax deducted in box 10.6. Then add together boxes 10.5 and 10.6 and enter the sum in box 10.7 (gross amount before tax). If you received interest without any tax deducted, enter nil in boxes 10.5 and 10.6 and enter the before-tax amount in box 10.7.

When you buy units in a unit trust, part of the purchase price includes an amount of income which the trust has received but not yet paid out. The first payment you receive will include an equalisation payment, which is not income, but a refund of part of the original purchase price you paid. It is not taxable, so do not enter it here. (Note that it is deducted for CGT purposes.)

Don't enter dividend distributions from unit trusts here, but in boxes 10.18 to 10.20.

National Savings & Investments

• National Savings & Investments (other than First Option Bonds and Fixed Rate Savings Bonds and the first £70 of interest from an Ordinary Account)	Taxable amount 10.8 £

You will receive or be credited with interest paid before deduction of tax from the following NS&I investments:

- Ordinary Account
- Investment Account
- Deposit Bonds
- Income Bonds
- Capital Bonds
- Pensioners' Guaranteed Income Bonds

Tot up the before-tax interest you received (or added to your account) in the tax year ending 5 April 2003. You don't include the first £70 of interest on an NS&I Ordinary Account, as this is tax-free (as are many other NS&I investments – see box on p. 158). Do not include interest from FIRST option bonds or fixed rate savings bonds (see below).

The return from NS&I guaranteed equity bonds is usually taxable only at the end of the five-year term. But if the holder died in the year ending 5 April 2003, any gain is paid without deduction of tax and should be entered in box 10.14 (see overleaf), not here. Enter a loss in box 15.8.

Enter the total amount you received in box 10.8.

	Amount **after** tax deducted	Tax deducted	Gross amount **before** tax
• National Savings & Investments First Option Bonds and Fixed Rate Savings Bonds	10.9 £	10.10 £	10.11 £

You receive interest after tax at the savings rate has already been deducted, if you invest in FIRST option bonds or fixed rate savings bonds. Enter in box

10.9 the amount you received, in box 10.10 the amount of tax deducted and in box 10.11 the amount of interest before tax.

British Government stock and other interest-paying investments

	Amount **after** tax deducted	Tax deducted	Gross amount **before** tax
• Other income from UK savings and investments (except dividends)	10.12 £	10.13 £	10.14 £

There is a hotch-potch of interest from other investments which should be entered here. Depending on the nature of the interest, it may be paid without tax being deducted or after tax is deducted. Tot up the relevant amounts and enter in boxes 10.12 to 10.14. If no tax has been deducted, put the interest in box 10.14 only and put nil in boxes 10.12 and 10.13. If tax has been deducted fill in all the boxes.

Here are examples of the investments to include:

- certificates of tax deposit when the certificate is applied to payment of a tax bill
- British Government stock (see below)
- other loan stocks, such as corporate bonds and local authority loans and stocks
- permanent interest bearing shares (PIBS) of building societies
- loans to an individual or organisation
- income from credit unions and friendly societies
- interest from Enterprise Zone trusts
- discount on relevant discounted securities (enter in box 10.14)
- discount from gilt strips (enter in box 10.14)
- income from securities to which you have sold or transferred the right to the income, but not the security – even if you have not received the income (enter in box 10.14)
- purchased life annuities (see below).

Corporate bonds

From 1 April 2001 onwards, corporate bonds listed on a recognised stock exchange pay interest gross – in other words, without any tax deducted. Before that date, interest was usually paid with tax at the savings rate already deducted. This means that bondholders who have not had to complete a tax return in the past may now need to do so.

British Government stock (gilts)

Tax at the rate of 20 per cent for the tax year ending 5 April 2003 may have been deducted from the interest on your British Government stocks before you receive it. Note that you can arrange to have the interest paid in future without tax deducted.

If tax has been deducted, your interest payment should be accompanied by a tax voucher which lets you know how much tax has been paid. If you are a non-taxpayer, you should be able to claim back the amount deducted. If you are a basic rate taxpayer, there is no more tax to pay. Enter the appropriate amounts in the three boxes 10.12, 10.13 and 10.14.

Accrued income scheme
If you own fixed-interest securities with a nominal value in excess of £5,000, and you buy or sell them, there are special tax rules designed to stop tax avoidance by turning income into capital gains. Ask your tax inspector to send you Inland Revenue leaflet *IR68 Accrued income scheme.*

Relevant discounted securities
Some corporate and other bonds do not pay interest. Instead you get a return by selling or redeeming the bond at a higher price than you paid – the difference is called the 'discount'. (In the past, these investments were often called 'deep discount bonds'.) Usually, you are taxed on the proceeds only when you sell the bond or it is redeemed (but see below for different rules applying to gilt strips). In box 10.14, enter the sale or redemption proceeds less the price you originally paid. Note that NS&I guaranteed equity bonds count as relevant discounted securities.

If you made a loss, you will get tax relief if you have other taxable income in the year ending 5 April 2003 against which the loss can be set. If you don't have enough other taxable income, you lose the loss relief – you cannot carry it forward or back to another year. Do not enter any loss in box 10.14. Instead enter it in box 15.8 on page 5 of the return.

Gilt strips
A traditional British Government stock provides regular interest payments (usually twice a year) and possibly a capital sum at the end of its lifespan. Each of these payments can be stripped out and sold as a separate investment, called a gilt strip. A gilt strip entitles you to one payment on a specified future date. Strips can be bought and sold before the payment falls due at a market price which is at a discount to the payment. For each gilt strip you hold on 5 April 2003, you will be treated as if you had sold the strip on 5 April and bought it back the next day. Income tax is due on any increase in the market value of the strip between 6 April 2002 (or, if later, the date you bought the strip) and 5 April 2003. The relevant market values are available from your tax office. Enter the change in value in box 10.14. Enter

any loss on actual disposal or redemption in box 15.8 on page 5 of the return.

Annuities

An annuity is an investment made with a life insurance company. You invest a lump sum and in return the insurance company will pay you an income. Sometimes this could be for a particular period, say ten years, or it could be until you die. The income which you receive is considered to be in two parts: some of it is your original investment being returned to you. There is tax to pay only on the interest.

The annuity payment is made to you with tax at the rate of 20 per cent of the interest part already deducted. The tax voucher which accompanies the payment will tell you how much tax has been deducted. If you are a non-taxpayer you can claim back the tax deducted.

With an annuity which you buy as part of your pension, the tax treatment is different. Tax will be deducted from the whole payment through the PAYE system. Details of annuities bought under personal pension schemes or retirement annuity contracts should be entered on page 4 of the tax return under Q11.

DIVIDENDS

■ *Dividends*

You will receive share dividends from UK companies and distributions from authorised unit trusts with no more basic rate tax to pay because you also receive a tax credit. The payments are accompanied by a tax voucher which sets out the amount of the tax credit (10 per cent for the year ending 5 April 2003). You work out the gross amount of dividend by adding together the net dividend and the tax credit (see p. 65).

Since 6 April 1999, non-taxpayers cannot claim back the tax credit. Starting rate and basic rate taxpayers have no further tax to pay, but higher rate taxpayers pay extra bringing the rate they pay up to 32.5 per cent (see p. 67).

If you are a beneficiary of a trust and you are entitled to income as it arises, include in these boxes any dividends or distributions shown on your trust voucher.

Shares in UK companies

Your dividend voucher should show the amount of the dividend and the tax credit. Put these in boxes 10.15 and 10.16 and add them together to enter the sum in box 10.17. Note that scrip dividends are included below in boxes 10.21 to 10.23.

	Dividend/distribution	Tax credit	Dividend/distribution plus credit
• Dividends and other qualifying distributions from UK companies	10.15 £	10.16 £	10.17 £

Include dividends you get from shares acquired through employee share schemes, unless the dividends were used to buy more shares through a share incentive plan (see p. 245). However, if during the year you've sold shares bought with dividends before holding the shares three years, include them here after all – enter the amount of the dividend originally reinvested.

A company can make other distributions as well as dividends – for example, if it sells you an asset at less than the open-market price. Some distributions are defined as non-qualifying and are entered in boxes 10.24 to 10.26 (see next page). All other distributions are qualifying and entered here in boxes 10.15 to 10.17. Explain how you got the distribution in the Additional information box on page 9.

In the past, you may have had a bonus issue of redeemable shares. If they are now redeemed, the amount you receive counts as a qualifying distribution and should be entered in boxes 10.15 to 10.17. If, when you originally got the shares, you paid higher rate tax on them, you can now claim some tax relief in box 15.12 on page 5 of the return (see p. 194).

IR35 companies

Do not include dividends you have received from your own personal service company if the company's tax office has agreed that the dividends are not taxable in your hands. This may be the case if, under the 'IR35 rules', you are treated as if you were an employee of your client(s) and your company has been deemed to pay you a salary (whether or not it actually did) on which income tax and national insurance contributions have been charged. If, in fact, you take money out of the company in the form of dividends rather than salary, you would be taxed twice on the same income if the dividends were taxed as well. Your company rather than you must claim relief for the dividends. Once the Inland Revenue has agreed the claim, you do not include the dividends on your tax return at all.

Unit trusts and open-ended investment companies

Distributions from most authorised unit trusts and open-ended investment companies (oeics) are treated in the same way as dividends (see p. 65). If you have invested in an accumulation unit trust or oeic, you don't receive the income but the unit trust or oeic managers reinvest it for you in more units or oeic shares. However, for tax purposes this is treated in exactly the same way as if you received the cash. You will receive a tax voucher with a tax credit.

	Dividend/distribution	Tax credit	Dividend/distribution plus credit
• Dividend distributions from UK authorised unit trusts and open-ended investment companies	10.18 £	10.19 £	10.20 £

Your dividend vouchers show the amount of the dividend and the tax credit. If you own units in more than one unit trust, add up the distributions and tax credits and enter the totals for each in boxes 10.18 and 10.19. Add them together to get the entry for box 10.20. Don't enter any equalisation payments (see p. 124).

Scrip dividends

	Dividend	Notional tax	Dividend plus notional tax
• Scrip dividends from UK companies	10.21 £	10.22 £	10.23 £

If you received new shares instead of cash as a dividend, this is known as a scrip dividend. The value of the scrip dividend is its cash equivalent and is the amount of cash dividend forgone. It should be shown on your dividend statement as 'the appropriate amount in cash'. This is what you enter in the dividend box. For the tax year ending 5 April 2003, you are treated as having received the cash equivalent grossed up at 10 per cent (see Appendix B).

Enter in box 10.21 the appropriate amount of cash. In box 10.22 enter the notional tax (11.11 per cent of the cash equivalent). Add together boxes 10.21 and box 10.22, and enter the sum in box 10.23.

Non-qualifying distributions

	Distribution/Loan	Notional tax	Taxable amount
• Non-qualifying distributions and loans written off	10.24 £	10.25 £	10.26 £

A non-qualifying distribution is broadly one which gives a future rather than a current claim on the company's assets, such as a bonus issue of redeemable shares. The amount of the distribution is the nominal value of the securities you received less any consideration (for example, cash) you paid.

Enter the amount of the distribution in box 10.26. Multiply box 10.26 by 10 per cent to get the amount of notional tax to enter in box 10.25. Leave box 10.24 blank. If you are a higher rate taxpayer, you'll have extra tax to pay on this distribution. When the shares are eventually redeemed, there could be further higher rate tax to pay (see p. 165) but you will then be able to claim relief to prevent your having been taxed twice on the same income (see p. 194).

For loans written off, contact your tax adviser or tax office.

PENSIONS AND SOCIAL SECURITY BENEFITS

***INCOME** for the year ended 5 April 2003, continued*

Q11 **Did you receive a taxable UK pension, retirement annuity or Social Security benefit?**
Read the notes on pages 13 to 15 of the Tax Return Guide.

YES

If yes, tick this box and then fill in boxes 11.1 to 11.14 as appropriate.
If not applicable, go to Question 12.

If you received none of these, go straight to Q12. But if you received one or more of these, you will need to find out whether what you received should be entered here in your tax return. Some pensions and benefits are not taxable.

Pensions and benefits that should not be included in your tax return
If you received any of the following, you do not need to give details here in the tax return because they are tax-free:

- additions to your state pension or social security benefits which you get because you have a dependent child
- attendance allowance
- bereavement payment
- child benefit
- child's special allowance (only payable to those already claiming before 6 April 1987)
- Christmas bonus for pensioners and winter fuel payment
- council tax benefit
- disability living allowance
- disabled person's tax credit
- educational maintenance allowance
- Employment Zone payments
- guardian's allowance
- home renovation and repair grants
- housing benefit (rent rebates and allowances)
- incapacity benefit for the first 28 weeks (and not taxable after that time if you were receiving invalidity benefit before 13 April 1995 unless there is a break in your claim; incapacity benefit replaced invalidity benefit)
- income support (if you're not required to be available for work)
- industrial disablement pension

- jobfinder's grant, employment training allowances, employment rehabilitation and New Deal training allowances
- maternity allowance
- pensions and benefits for wounds or disability in military service or for other war injuries
- school uniform grants and fares to school
- severe disablement allowance, including age-related addition
- social fund payments
- student grants, scholarships and loans
- vaccine damage payments
- war widow's pension and some pensions paid to other dependants of deceased Forces and Merchant Navy personnel. Ask the Orderline for Help Sheet *IR310 War widow's and dependant's pensions*
- winter fuel payments and cold weather payments
- working families' tax credit
- similar benefits to those above paid by foreign governments.

Pensions and benefits that should be entered in your tax return
Details of the following should be entered here:

- income withdrawals from a personal pension plan where the purchase of an annuity has been deferred
- industrial death benefit pension (but not child allowance)
- invalid care allowance
- jobseeker's allowance (up to the taxable amount)
- old person's pension for people aged 80 or over
- pension for injuries at work or for work-related illnesses
- pension from a former employer or a pension from your late husband or wife's employer
- pension from a free-standing additional voluntary contribution
- pension from a personal pension scheme or retirement annuity contract or trust scheme
- pension from service in the armed forces
- state retirement pension, the basic pension, state earnings related pension and graduated pension
- statutory sick pay, statutory maternity pay and statutory paternity pay paid by the Inland Revenue
- taxable incapacity benefit
- widowed mother's allowance and widowed parent's allowance
- widow's pension and bereavement pension.

If you receive any of the above pensions or benefits, tick the YES box in answer to Q11.

Refunds of surplus additional voluntary contributions are not entered here. Details should be put in boxes 12.10 to 12.12. Overseas pensions and taxable benefits paid under the rules of another country should be entered in the Foreign supplementary pages (covered in Chapter 21).

The documents you need

Gather details of any state retirement pension and bereavement benefits – you can ask your social security office to give you a form BR735 showing how much you have received during the tax year. The Department for Work and Pensions (DWP) should send you details of the taxable amount of other social security benefits that you have had, for example on form P60U or P45U for jobseeker's allowance. For non-state pensions, you need the P60 the pension payer gives you or any other certificate of pension paid and tax deducted.

State pensions and benefits

■ *State pensions and benefits*

Enter the amount of pension or benefit you were entitled to for the tax year ending 5 April 2003, whether or not you actually received that amount in the year. You should enter the total of all the weekly amounts which you were entitled to in the year, even if you chose to receive your pension or benefit monthly or quarterly.

State retirement pension

The state retirement pension is taxable but paid without tax deducted. So if you have other income you will find that tax on your state retirement pension might be collected from your other income.

	Taxable amount for 2002-03
• State Retirement Pension - *enter the **total** of your entitlements for the year*	11.1 £

In box 11.1, you should enter the amount you were entitled to receive in the tax year ending 5 April 2003, but excluding any amount paid for a dependent child, the Christmas bonus and winter fuel payment.

A married woman might receive a pension which is based on her husband's contributions and not her own (but not any dependency allowance which he receives for her before her 60th birthday). She can claim a personal allowance to deduct from her income, so the pension should be entered in her tax return, not her husband's.

Widow's pension or bereavement allowance

From 6 April 2001, widow's pension was replaced by bereavement allowance for new claimants. If you first claimed before that date, you continue to receive widow's pension. Bereavement allowance is available to widowers as well as widows.

• Widow's Pension or Bereavement Allowance	11.2	£

Enter the full amount you were entitled to receive in the tax year ending 5 April 2003, including any earnings-related additional pension, in box 11.2.

For more information on the benefits available to widows and widowers, ask for leaflet GL14 *Widowed?* from your local social security office or the DWP website.

Widowed mother's allowance or widowed parent's allowance

• Widowed Mother's Allowance or Widowed Parent's Allowance	11.3	£

From 6 April 2001, widowed mother's allowance was replaced by widowed parent's allowance for new claimants. If you first claimed before that date, you continue to receive widowed mother's allowance. Widowed parent's allowance is available to widowers as well as widows.

You should include in box 11.3 the flat rate basic allowance which you were entitled to and any earnings-related increase. But don't include any child dependency increase.

Industrial death benefit pension

• Industrial Death Benefit Pension	11.4	£

In box 11.4 you should enter the yearly pension you are entitled to receive under the industrial death benefit scheme. But do not include industrial death benefit child allowance which is tax-free.

Jobseeker's allowance

• Jobseeker's Allowance	11.5	£

Jobseeker's allowance is taxable but paid without any tax deducted.There are two kinds of allowance, one based on your National Insurance contribution record and one means-tested. There is a limit on the overall amount that is treated as taxable.

The DWP will usually have given you a statement of the total jobseeker's allowance paid and the taxable portion (either Form P60U or Form P45U). You should enter the taxable amount in box 11.5. If you haven't received a P60U, contact your social security office; if you haven't received a P45U, tell your tax office.

Invalid care allowance

• Invalid Care Allowance	11.6	£

Enter the amount you were entitled to receive in the tax year ending 5 April 2003. Include any addition for a dependent adult, but exclude any additional amount for a dependent child, because this is tax-free.

Statutory sick pay, statutory maternity pay and statutory paternity pay

• Statutory Sick Pay, Statutory Maternity Pay and Statutory Paternity Pay paid by the Inland Revenue	11.7	£

Generally, these are paid by your employer and taxed under the PAYE system (see Chapter 25). They will be included in your P60 or P45. Details should be entered in the Employment supplementary pages.

But if your employer didn't pay you, and the Inland Revenue did so instead, enter the total received here in box 11.7.

Taxable incapacity benefit

	Tax deducted		Gross amount **before** tax	
• Taxable Incapacity Benefit	11.8	£	11.9	£

Some incapacity benefit is tax-free. You will not pay tax on it when you receive it during your first 28 weeks of incapacity or you are receiving it for a period of incapacity which began before 13 April 1995, and for which invalidity benefit used to be payable.

The DWP will give you a form showing you whether your incapacity benefit is taxable or not. If it is taxable, enter the amount of the benefit in box 11.9 and any tax that has been deducted in box 11.8.

Other pensions

Apart from the state pension, you can get a pension from your employer, from what you have paid into a personal pension scheme or a retirement annuity contract.

■ *Other pensions and retirement annuities*

You should enter here details of pensions paid to you by someone in the UK unless they are paying you on behalf of someone outside the UK. Pensions received from abroad will be entered in the Foreign pages (see p. 298).

• Pensions (other than State pensions) and retirement annuities - *if you have more than one pension or annuity, please add together and complete boxes 11.10 to 11.12. Provide details of each one in box 11.14*	Amount after tax deducted 11.10 £	Tax deducted 11.11 £	Gross amount before tax 11.12 £

You should total the amount you receive from all your pensions (excluding state pension) and put it in box 11.10. You should include in the total:

- annuity payments from a personal pension scheme
- if you have taken advantage of the ability to defer buying the annuity, the income withdrawals which you receive during the deferred period
- any annual payments from a retirement contract or trust scheme.

Put the amount of tax deducted in box 11.11. The information about an employer's pension or personal pension should be on your P60 and for other pensions from a certificate given to you by the pension payer. Adding up boxes 11.10 and 11.11 should give you the total for box 11.12, unless you have received some non-cash benefit. If you have, you'll need to ask your tax office what to do.

If the amounts you have entered include pensions or annuities from more than one source, give details in box 11.14. If there is not enough space here, use the Additional information box 23.5 on page 9 of the return.

There are some special pensions which can be partially free of UK tax:

Tax-free pensions
Part of your pension may be tax-free if you receive it as a former employee who was awarded a pension on retirement because you were disabled by injury on duty or a work-related illness. If that pension is more than the amount you would receive if you had retired at the same time on the grounds of ordinary ill-health, the extra amount is free of tax. You should not enter any tax-free amounts in the tax return.

10 per cent deduction
This applies to some UK pensions for service for certain overseas governments. Only 90 per cent of the pension is taxed.

- Deduction - *see the note for box 11.13 on page 15 of your Tax Return Guide*

	Amount of deduction	
	11.13 £	11.14

Enter the full pension received in box 11.12 and the 10 per cent deduction in box 11.13.

OTHER INCOME TO BE ENTERED HERE

Q12	**Did you make any gains on UK life insurance policies, life annuities or capital redemption policies or receive refunds of surplus funds from additional voluntary contributions?**	YES	If yes, tick this box and then fill in boxes 12.1 to 12.12 as appropriate. If not applicable, go to Question 13.

Question 12 asks about payments from life insurance policies and certain other investments and pension schemes that are treated as income.

Life insurance policies

Gains on life insurance policies, contract for life annuities and capital redemption policies are treated as investment income and may be taxable.

With most policies, the life insurance company will have paid tax on the income and gains which its life fund makes as they arise. This is deemed to be equivalent to income tax at the basic rate. So if you pay tax at the basic rate or less, there is no tax for you personally to pay. But you cannot reclaim any of the tax already paid even if you personally would not be liable for tax on income or gains or would be liable only at the starting rate.

The further tax treatment of a life insurance gain depends on whether the policy is qualifying or non-qualifying. Most policies where you pay regular premiums are qualifying. If you pay just a single premium, the policy will almost certainly be non-qualifying and have less favourable tax treatment.

Taxation of qualifying policies

Tax at the basic rate is treated as already paid. There is usually no higher-rate tax when the policy matures – that is, comes to the end of its term or the person insured by the policy dies. You do not enter details in your tax return.

The exception is if you cash in the policy or make it paid up before the end of its term. If this happens before it has run for ten years, or three-quarters of its term if this is less, the policy is treated as a non-qualifying policy (see below).

Taxation of non-qualifying policies
Higher-rate income tax may be due when you receive proceeds from a non-qualifying policy. A gain from this type of policy can cause you to lose age allowance (see p. 11) or tax credits (see pp. 12 and 202).

A chargeable event may occur when a policy matures, the holder dies, the policy is assigned or surrendered, or a partial withdrawal is made. Each time there is an event, the gain (if any) is calculated. The gain is usually the total you have received from the policy since it started less any earlier gains that have already been taxed and less whatever you have paid into the policy. Where the person insured dies, the calculation uses the cash-in value just before death, which may be less than the death benefit actually paid out.

Many qualifying policies let you draw an income by cashing in part of the policy. There is no tax to pay at the time you make such withdrawals provided they come to no more than 5 per cent a year of the amount you have paid into the policy. If you don't cash in the full 5 per cent each year, you can carry forward the unused amount, meaning you may be able to cash in more than 5 per cent in a later year. You can make 5 per cent withdrawals for up to 20 years. When the policy comes to an end, the amounts you have withdrawn are added to your final gain or loss to work out the tax due.

If in any year, you withdraw more than the cumulative 5 per cent a year limit, there may be an immediate tax bill on the excess. If, on maturity, you make a loss, you can claim corresponding deficiency relief in box 12.9 (see p. 176) up to the amount of the earlier withdrawals on which tax was paid.

Whenever there is a chargeable event producing a gain, the insurance company must send you a 'chargeable event certificate'. This tells you the amount of the gain, whether basic rate tax is treated as already paid and, if so, the amount. There will be higher-rate tax to pay if your taxable income plus the gain come to more than the threshold at which higher-rate tax starts to be paid. For the tax year ending 5 April 2003, this is usually £29,900 but will be higher if you have paid pension contributions or made Gift Aid donations.

Tax is due at the difference between the higher and basic rates: 40–22 = 18 per cent for the tax year ending 5 April 2003. But you may be able to claim top-slicing relief: divide the gain by the number of full years you held the policy to find the average gain. Work out the tax due if the average gain was added to your income and multiply this by the number of years the policy was held.

Although most UK life insurance gains are treated as having had basic rate tax deducted, some are not. The chargeable event certificate should make clear where this is the case.

Taxation of personal portfolio bonds
A personal portfolio bond is an investment-type life insurance policy where the return is linked to a fund of investments usually chosen by or on behalf of the policyholder. No other policyholders have policies linked to the fund, so the bond is personal to a single investor. By placing the investments within a life insurance policy, instead of holding them direct, the return on the investments is taxed as that of the insurance company rather than the policyholder. If, as is typical, an offshore insurer issues the policy, the investments roll up within the fund free of UK taxes. The government treats this as tax avoidance, and from 6 April 1999 onwards there is an extra tax charge for holders of these bonds (though some pre-1999 bonds are not affected). As well as the normal rules applying to non-qualifying policies (see above), there is an annual tax charge on personal portfolio bonds. The annual charge is levied on a deemed gain equal to 15 per cent of the premiums paid up to the end of each policy year plus the total of deemed gains for earlier years. For more information, see *Personal portfolio bonds – guidance notes for insurers and practitioners* and Help Sheet *IR321 Gains on foreign life insurance policies*, both available from the Orderline (see p. 147).

	Number of years	Amount of gain(s)
• Gains on UK annuities and friendly societies' life insurance policies where no tax is treated as paid	12.1	12.2 £

If you have made a single gain and it is not treated as having had basic rate tax deducted, put the amount of the gain in box 12.2 and the number of complete years since the insurance was made in box 12.1. These figures are shown on the chargeable event certificate.

	Number of years	Tax treated as paid	Amount of gain(s)
• Gains on UK life insurance policies etc. on which tax is treated as paid - *read pages 15 to 18 of your Tax Return Guide*	12.3	12.4 £	12.5 £

If you have made a single gain and it is treated as having had basic rate tax deducted, put the amount of the gain in box 12.5 and the notional tax in box 12.4 (22 per cent of the amount in box 12.5). Enter the number of complete years in box 12.3. Copy these figures from the chargeable event certificate.

Where you have made more than one sort of gain, or you hold a cluster of policies, things become complex. You will probably need to put additional information in the section on page 9 of the tax return. Ask the Orderline (see p. 147) for a copy of Help Sheet *IR320 Gains on UK life insurance policies.* Consult your tax office or tax adviser for more guidance.

	Number of years	Tax deducted	Amount of gain(s)
• Gains on life insurance policies in ISAs that have been made void	12.6	12.7 £	12.8 £

Normally, gains on life insurance policies held within an ISA are tax-free and you do not include them in your tax return. But there are strict rules on the types of policy which qualify to be held through an ISA. If it's found that the life policy you hold does not qualify or has ceased to qualify, the policy may come to an end and there may be tax to pay on any gain. Tax is worked out as for a non-qualifying policy – see p. 174. Your ISA manager will give you the information you need. Enter the amount of gain in box 12.8, the number of complete years the policy ran in box 12.6 and tax already paid by the ISA manager in box 12.7.

Corresponding deficiency relief

	Amount
• Corresponding deficiency relief	12.9 £

If you had a life insurance policy on which you made a loss on final surrender, you may be able to claim a relief to ensure that the amount treated as income is not more than the total gain made under the policy (see p. 174). Ask for Help Sheet *IR320 Gains on UK life insurance policies.*

Refund of surplus funds from additional voluntary contributions

	Amount received	Notional tax	Amount plus notional tax
• Refunds of surplus funds from additional voluntary contributions	12.10 £	12.11 £	12.12 £

Additional voluntary contributions are extra payments you can make to your employer's or your own free-standing additional voluntary contribution scheme (see p. 71). A condition of the contributions is that they cannot buy you pension benefits greater than the maximum limits set by the Inland Revenue for approved schemes. If you inadvertently contribute so much in additional voluntary contributions that the benefits would exceed the limits, the excess will be paid back to you at retirement, with a deduction to cover the tax relief the contributions have enjoyed.

Your certificate from your pension scheme provider should show you the amount of surplus contributions and the tax refunded to you. Enter the total amount in box 12.12, the amount actually repaid to you in box 12.10 and the tax deducted in box 12.11. (But don't include any refund of contributions because you have left a scheme after less than two years.)

Any other income

Q13 **Did you receive any other taxable income which you have not already entered elsewhere in your Tax Return?** *Fill in any supplementary Pages before answering Question 13. (Supplementary Pages follow page 10, or are available from the Orderline.)*	YES	If yes, tick this box and then fill in boxes 13.1 to 13.6 as appropriate. If not applicable, go to Question 14.

You should already have filled in the appropriate supplementary pages for income from employment, share schemes, trusts and abroad. Similarly, business income should already be entered in the supplement for self-employment, partnership or land and property, as appropriate. This section of the tax return is for odd bits of income you have not entered elsewhere. The income can be divided into two lists:

A: Income against which you can set losses

- freelance or casual income
- profits from the odd literary or artistic activity
- income received after you close a business (post-cessation receipts). This could include money which you have recovered from a bad debt or royalties arising after the business ceased from contracts made before it ceased. You can claim to have this treated as income for the year in which the business ceased (tick box 23.4 on page 9 of the tax return). Or you can enter the total here
- any recovery of expenses or debts for which you claimed relief as post-cessation expenses
- sale of patent rights if you received a capital sum
- rental from leasing equipment you own
- income from guaranteeing loans, dealing in futures and some income from underwriting
- other miscellaneous sources.

B. Income you can't set losses against

- receipts from covenants entered into for genuine commercial reasons in connection with the payer's trade, profession or vocation
- annual payments received in the year, including those from UK authorised unit trusts and annual payments paid by a former employer that do not count as a pension
- benefits of certain insurance policies relating to sickness or disability (see below)
- a taxable lump sum from an unapproved retirement benefits scheme (see below).

If you have more than one source of other income, you should ask for Help Sheet *IR325 Other taxable income* which contains a Worksheet to help you keep track of your different sources of other income and the losses you can claim.

From any type of income in list A above (but not list B), you can deduct expenses that you had to incur wholly in order to earn the income. You can't deduct expenses incurred partly or wholly for private reasons. And, if you had to buy capital items, you should instead deduct capital allowances (see p. 257).

If your expenses come to more than the income from a particular source, you have made a loss. You can set the loss against any of the types of income in list A above, but not against any of the income in list B. If you can't use up all your losses in the year ending 5 April 2003, you can carry them forward to set against any of the list-A types of income in future years. Similarly, if you have made losses in previous years, you may have elected to carry them forward and can now set part or all of them against any list-A income you have in the year ending 5 April 2003.

- Other taxable income – also provide details in box 23.5 - *read the notes on pages 18 to 20 of your Tax Return Guide*
- Tick box 13.1A if box 13.1 includes enhanced capital allowances for environmentally friendly expenditure

Amount after tax deducted	Tax deducted	Amount before tax
13.1 £	13.2 £	13.3 £
	Losses brought forward	Earlier years' losses used in 2002-03
13.1A	13.4 £	13.5 £
	2002-03 losses carried forward	
	13.6 £	

In box 13.1, put the total of your other income from all the sources after any tax deducted and after subtracting any allowable expenses and capital allowances. If you have deducted any first-year capital allowances for environmentally friendly expenditure (see p. 259) in arriving at the figure in box 13.1, tick box 13.1A. If overall you have made a loss, enter zero. In box 13.2, put the amount of tax deducted from any of the payments you received. Add together boxes 13.1 and 13.2 and, if applicable, deduct any losses made on list-A income in the year ending 5 April 2003 from other list-A income for the year. Enter the result in box 13.3.

If, in box 13.3, you cannot use up all your losses made in the year ending 5 April 2003, put the remainder in box 13.6 so that you can carry them forward to a future tax year.

In box 13.4, enter the amount of losses you are bringing forward from earlier years. If you are setting any of these losses against list-A income for the year ending 5 April 2003, enter the amount in box 13.5.

The total losses you can carry forward to future years equal box 13.4 less box 13.5 plus box 13.6.

Cashbacks and incentives
You should enter as other income any cashbacks or other incentives which you received to take out a mortgage or purchase something (such as a car) if there is tax to pay. Ask the person who gave you the incentive or check with your tax office to find out if it is taxable. Include it in box 13.3. If you're not sure whether there is tax to pay, enter the amount you received in box 13.3, but also tick box 23.2 on page 9 and give details under Additional information.

Insurance policies relating to sickness and disability
Some part of income received under an income protection (also called 'permanent health') insurance policy may be taxable and should be entered as other income. This does not include income from a policy which you paid for yourself, as that is tax-free. Income from your employer for sickness and disability should go on the Employment pages. But if you have left your employer and you are still receiving benefits because you are covered by your former employer's scheme, you should enter that amount here (part might be tax-free if you contributed to the cost of the scheme). Check with your tax office if you are not sure how much is taxable, and ask for leaflet *IR153 Tax exemption for sickness or unemployment insurance payments*.

Unapproved retirement benefit schemes
Most, but not all, pension schemes set up by employers are approved and so qualify for special tax treatment. If you belong to an unapproved scheme, any lump sum you receive from it is treated as taxable income unless you can show that the lump sum had built up from contributions you paid yourself or contributions paid by your employer but on which you paid tax, or the payment was made because of accidental death or disablement. If the lump sum is the only retirement benefit you get from that employment and you do not also belong to an approved pension scheme, the lump sum might be tax-free – contact your tax office. If you have filled in the Employment supplement, you should have entered this income in boxes 1.26 and 1.28 and do not need to give details again here.

RELIEFS

CHAPTER 14

You can pay less tax by spending more money on things the government wants to encourage – and thus gives tax relief on – such as pensions and gifts to charity. In some instances you can get tax relief at your highest rate of tax, which could be 40 per cent. Assuming that you want to spend the money, buying any of these things could be highly advantageous. You claim for them on pages 5 and 6 of the basic tax return.

You get your tax relief in different ways. Frequently you get basic rate tax relief by deducting it from what you spend. Any higher rate tax relief that is due you will claim here in the tax return and give yourself the relief when you are working out your tax bill. Or you could get higher rate relief through your PAYE code. Non-taxpayers will not have to repay the tax deducted, except in the case of Gift Aid.

If you don't get basic rate relief by deducting it from what you pay, you will claim the relief here in the tax return and get it through your tax bill or your PAYE code.

TAX-SAVING IDEA

You can go back nearly six years to claim deductions which you forgot to claim at the time or didn't know you were able to. You will get tax relief at the rate you should have got it if you had claimed the deduction at the right time. Provided you claim by 31 January 2004, you can go back as far as the year ending 5 April 1998.

The documents you need

You must gather together all the supporting documents you need to be able to prove to your tax inspector that you are entitled to the relief you are claiming (but keep the documents safe, don't send them with your tax return). These could include:

- certificates of premiums paid from your pension provider
- certificates of interest paid on loans
- maintenance agreements, court order, Child Support Agency assessments
- share certificate in a venture capital trust

- Forms EIS3 or EIS5 (for Enterprise Investment Scheme)
- certificates from community development finance institutions
- details of donations to charity by Gift Aid
- certificates from charities accepting gifts of land or buildings.

What deductions can you claim?

***RELIEFS** for the year ended 5 April 2003*

You can claim here for:

- pension contributions
- additional voluntary contributions to a pension scheme
- interest paid on qualifying loans
- maintenance payments
- investments in growing business (venture capital trusts or enterprise investment scheme)
- investments in certain community development schemes
- post-cessation expenses for a business and losses on relevant discounted securities
- payments under annuities made in connection with your business
- certain payments to a trade union or friendly society
- certain contributions to a compulsory employer's scheme to provide benefits for your husband, wife or children in the event of your death
- relief for higher rate tax paid on the issue of bonus shares where they are subsequently redeemed
- payments to charities (through Gift Aid)
- gifts of shares, unit trusts or property to charities.

> **EXAMPLE**
>
> Tony Jabot is saving for his retirement through a stakeholder pension scheme. He pays in £1,000 in the tax year ending 5 April 2003, but this costs him just £780 because he is a basic rate taxpayer and gets 22 per cent tax relief.

PENSIONS

For the tax year ending 5 April 2003, you can get tax relief at your highest rate of tax on contributions to a pension scheme. If you are an employee, your employer can also make contributions to an approved pension scheme for you, and these do not count as a taxable fringe benefit for you. There are more details about saving for your pension in Chapter 8.

If you are an employee, you might belong to an occupational pension scheme through work and could be topping this up through payments to a free-standing additional voluntary contribution (FSAVC) scheme. From 6 April 2001 onwards, most employees can also save for retirement through personal pension plans, including those that qualify as stakeholder pension schemes. Only occupational scheme members who are 'controlling directors' or earn more than £30,000 a year cannot save in this way. Everyone else – for example, the self-employed, people who are not working, even children – can have a personal pension or stakeholder scheme. If you started to save before 1 July 1988, you might be making contributions to a retirement annuity contract. See Chapter 8 for more details.

> **TAX-SAVING IDEA**
>
> Make the most of the amount you are allowed to save in pension schemes if you are an employee. In many cases you can pay up to 15 per cent of your earnings (including fringe benefits) each year into your employer's scheme and additional voluntary contribution schemes plus up to £3,600 a year into personal pension plans, including stakeholder schemes (see p. 73).

Q14 Do you want to claim relief for your pension contributions? YES ☐

Do not include contributions deducted from your pay by your employer to their pension scheme or associated AVC scheme, because tax relief is given automatically. But ***do include*** *your contributions to personal pension schemes and Free-Standing AVC schemes.*

If yes, tick this box and then fill in boxes 14.1 to 14.11 as appropriate.
If not appliable, go to Question 15

With an occupational pension scheme, you are likely to get tax relief on your contributions deducted at source (they will be deducted from your salary before your employer works out your income tax through the PAYE system). If this is the only way you are saving for a pension, or if you are not saving at all for a pension, you can skip Q14 and go on to Q15.

What you should claim for

In the tax return you can claim tax relief for payments into two main types of pension scheme:

- retirement annuity contracts. If you started saving before 1 July 1988, the scheme will be one of these contracts, unless you have since converted it into a personal pension
- personal pensions. If you started saving on or after 1 July 1988, the scheme will be a personal pension. A personal pension started on or after 6 April 2001 may be a stakeholder scheme.

It is possible for you to have both a retirement annuity contract and a personal pension scheme, but you cannot get double the tax relief. The tax relief for the retirement annuity contract is always given before the relief for the personal pension plan. Relief for a retirement annuity contract reduces the available relief for personal pensions. In addition, where you contribute to both retirement annuity contracts and personal pensions in the same year, the sum of the contributions must not normally come to more than the contribution limit for personal pensions. However you may be able to make larger payments to a retirement annuity contract if you can carry forward relief from earlier years (see p. 78). The Inland Revenue has produced Help Sheet *IR330 Pension payments* which has an explanation and working sheets.

Retirement annuity contracts

First give information about any payments in the tax year ending 5 April 2003 to retirement annuity contracts, including whether you wish to carry payments back to an earlier year, and about any payments you have made since 5 April 2003 which you want to bring back to get tax relief in this tax return.

■ ***Payments to your retirement annuity contracts - only fill in boxes 14.1 to 14.5 for policies taken out before 1 July 1988.***
See the notes on page 20 of your Tax Return Guide.

Qualifying payments made in 2002-03	**14.1** £	2002-03 payments used in an earlier year	**14.2** £	Relief claimed box 14.1 *minus* (boxes 14.2 and 14.3, but not 14.4)
2002-03 payments now to be carried back	**14.3** £	Payments brought back from 2003-04	**14.4** £	**14.5** £

In Box 14.1, enter the amount of payments which you have made to a retirement annuity in the year ending 5 April 2003. You will be entering gross figures because these payments are made without deducting any tax.

You are allowed to carry back pension payments made in one tax year to the

EXAMPLE

Paul Taylor has a retirement annuity contract. For the year ended 5 April 2003, he earned £20,000 and is aged 37. He can save £3,500 within the limits of 17.5 per cent of his net relevant earnings. He made payments of £3,000 and enters this figure in box 14.1. However, £1,000 of his pension contributions were made before he returned his tax return for the last tax year and he had asked for them to be carried back to the year ending 5 April 2002. He enters that amount in box 14.2. He chooses now to carry back a further £1,000 to the last tax year as he was a higher rate taxpayer and this would mean he would get more tax relief. The figure of £1,000 is entered in box 14.3.

The amount of contributions on which he is now claiming tax relief in the year ended 5 April 2003 is box 14.1 minus box 14.2 minus box 14.3, that is £3,000 minus £1,000 minus £1,000. He is claiming relief on pension contributions of £1,000 for the year ended 5 April 2003.

previous year (or possibly the year before that) – see p. 79. You get tax relief at the rate of tax you paid in the earlier year. The tax return asks you whether you are using the carry back option. There are several possibilities.

First, you may already have claimed tax relief on some of the amount in box 14.1 that you have already carried back to, say, the year ending 5 April 2002. If so, enter the amount carried back in box 14.2.

You may want to claim now to carry back part or all of what you have paid in the year ending 5 April 2003 to the previous year (or the one before). If so, put the amount to be carried back in box 14.3. If you are working out your own tax bill, put the amount of tax relief you are claiming in box 18.5 (see p. 153).

You can carry back part or all of a payment made in the tax year ending 5 April 2004 to the tax year ending 5 April 2003. You have until 31 January 2005 to decide whether to do this. But, if you have already made the payment, you can claim now to carry it back by putting the amount in box 14.4. If you are working out your own tax bill, put the tax relief you are claiming in box 18.8 (see p. 153). If you make the payment after you have filed your tax return, you do not have to wait until your next return. You can get the tax relief earlier by claiming on forms PP43 and PP120 from your tax office.

The amount of relief you are claiming for your retirement annuity contract payment for the tax year ending 5 April 2003 will be worked out in box 14.5 (box 14.1 minus box 14.2 minus box 14.3). If the amount you are claiming for this year is greater than the percentage limit (see p. 78), you may have unused relief from the previous six years to set against the excess. There is no place on the tax return to claim unused relief carried forward from earlier years. Simply enter the pension contributions actually made, but keep your workings in case the Inland Revenue queries your payments. Use the working sheets which come with Help Sheet *IR330 Pension payments*.

> **TAX-SAVING IDEA**
>
> If you have a retirement annuity contract, keep a tally over the years of the maximum you can pay into the scheme. You may find later you can afford to go back up to six years (seven years if you also opt to carry back a contribution to the previous year) and use up any tax relief you didn't claim at the time.

Personal pensions including stakeholder pension schemes

Give information about your payments in the tax year ending 5 April 2003, about any you wish to carry back to an earlier year, and about any payments you have made since 5 April 2003 which you want to bring back to get tax relief in this tax return.

■ ***Payments to your personal pension (including stakeholder pension) contracts** - enter the amount of the payment you made with the basic rate tax added (the **gross** payment). See the note for box 14.6 on page 22 of your Tax Return Guide.*

Gross qualifying payments made in 2002-03	14.6 £	
2002-03 gross payments carried back to 2001-02	14.7 £	Relief claimed box 14.6 *minus* box 14.7 (but not 14.8)
Gross qualifying payments made between 6 April 2003 and 31 January 2004 brought back to 2002-03 - *see page 22 of your Tax Return Guide*	14.8 £	14.9 £

In Box 14.6, enter the amount of payments which you have made to a personal pension in the year ending 5 April 2003.

You make contributions to a personal pension after deducting basic rate tax relief. The tax return asks for the gross amount, so you will need to adjust the payment you made. This should be shown on your payment certificate. Alternatively, for the tax year ending 5 April 2003, divide the amount you paid by 0.78.

> **TAX-SAVING IDEA**
> Even if the tax year has ended, you have not necessarily lost your pension contribution relief. Provided you pay into a personal pension or stakeholder scheme by 31 January 2004, you can elect to have the contribution treated as if paid in the tax year ending 5 April 2003. You must elect to carry back the contribution either before or at the time you pay it.

You are allowed to carry back pension payments made between 6 April 2002 and 31 January 2003 to the tax year ending 5 April 2002. You had to make the carry back election using form PP43 either before or at the time you made the contribution. Enter the gross amount, if any, carried back to the year ending 5 April 2002 in box 14.7.

Similarly, you may have paid a contribution between 6 April 2003 and the date you are filing your tax return which you have elected to carry back to the tax year ending 5 April 2003. Enter the gross amount, if any, that you are now carrying back to the year ending 5 April 2003 in box 14.8. If higher rate tax relief is due, it will be given as a tax credit to set against tax now due to be paid or, if necessary, paid out to you as a refund. If you are working out your own tax bill, put the tax relief you are claiming in box 18.8 (see p. 153).

Any payments you make after sending in your tax return but on or before 31 January 2004 can also be carried back to the tax year ending 5 April 2003. You must notify the pension provider on form PP43 either before or at the time you make the payment that you wish to carry it back in this way. To claim higher rate tax relief, send your tax office forms PP43 and PP120.

> **TAX-SAVING IDEA**
> Nearly everyone can pay up to £3,600 a year into personal pensions and stakeholder schemes. This works out at £2,808 a year after deducting basic rate tax relief. You get the relief even if you are a non-taxpayer or pay tax only at the starting rate.

The amount of relief you are claiming for your personal pension plan will be worked out in box 14.9 (box 14.6 minus box 14.7). You have already had basic rate tax relief on these contributions. You keep the basic rate relief even if you are a non-taxpayer or your highest rate of tax is only the starting rate. Claiming here, will ensure you get any higher rate relief.

Contributions to an employer's scheme

■ *Contributions to other pension schemes and Free-Standing AVC schemes*

• Amount of contributions to employer's schemes **not deducted** at source from pay **14.10** £

Contributions to your occupational scheme are usually deducted from your salary by your employer and these are not included here. Put here (box 14.10) any contributions which have not been deducted from your salary before tax, for example, additional voluntary contributions paid late in the tax year.

Free-standing additional voluntary contributions

• Gross amount of Free-Standing Additional Voluntary Contributions paid in 2002-03 **14.11** £

If you are paying in less than the maximum permitted amount to an occupational pension and want to improve the benefits you will get, you can get tax relief on additional voluntary contributions (see p. 72).

> **TAX-SAVING IDEA**
> If you belong to an occupational pension scheme, there are several ways you can top up the pension you will get. Paying into a stakeholder pension scheme will usually be a better choice than making additional contributions to an FSAVC scheme because you can take part of the proceeds of a stakeholder scheme as a tax-free lump sum at retirement. You can't take a lump sum from an FSAVC scheme. But the stakeholder route is not open to you if you are a controlling director or earn more than £30,000 a year – see Chapter 8.

Where these are made to a free-standing AVC scheme, you make the contributions after deducting basic rate tax. You get this relief even if you are a non-taxpayer or starting rate taxpayer. If you are a higher-rate taxpayer, you get extra relief. Box 14.11 asks for the gross amount you paid. This may be shown on your annual statement. Alternatively, divide the amount you paid by 0.78 to find the gross figure.

OTHER RELIEFS YOU CAN CLAIM

Q15 Do you want to claim any of the following reliefs? *If you have made any annual payments, after basic rate tax, answer 'Yes' to Question 15 and fill in box 15.9. If you have made any gifts to charity go to Question 15A*	YES	If yes, tick this box and then fill in boxes 15.1 to 15.12, as appropriate. If not applicable, go to Question 15A

Your tax return on page 5 lists a variety of reliefs you might be able to claim. If you are not entitled to any of these deductions from your income, go to Q15A.

Loan interest

• Interest eligible for relief on qualifying loans	15.1 £

Claim here for tax relief on the interest for a variety of loans, including loans to buy:

- a share in or putting capital into a co-operative or a partnership (but not if you are a limited partner)
- plant or machinery (but not a car – see p. 232) for use in your job if you are an employee or partner (if you are self-employed you claim in the Self-employment supplementary pages)
- shares in or putting capital into a close company (see below). To be eligible you should own more than 5 per cent of the company or be a shareholder and work for most of your time in the business.

A close company is one which is controlled by a small number of people. Broadly, it should be controlled by five or fewer 'participators', such as shareholders, or any number of shareholder directors.

You may also be able to claim relief here if you are an employee and get a low-interest or interest-free loan from your employer which counts as a taxable benefit (see p. 102).

Don't enter here to claim tax relief on the interest on a loan for a self-employed business (use box 3.60) or to buy a property you let (use box 5.26) or a mortgage that is part of a home income plan (see p. 55). Nor should you enter interest on a loan to purchase your home, an overdraft or credit cards – they do not qualify for tax relief.

Maintenance payments

- Maintenance or alimony payments you have made under a court order, Child Support Agency assessment or legally binding order or agreement

Amount claimed up to £2,110

15.2 £

In general, from 6 April 2000 onwards, you can no longer get tax relief on maintenance payments you make to your former (or separated) wife or husband. However, if either of you were born before 6 April 1935, you can still qualify for some relief. If you can claim because of your spouse's age, put their date of birth in box 15.2A.

Provided you or your former (or separated) wife or husband were aged 68 or over on 5 April 2003, you can claim relief for payments made under a legally binding agreement, such as a court order, a Child Support Agency assessment, or a written agreement.

No relief is available for voluntary payments. Although maintenance paid to your former wife or husband to maintain your children under the age of 21 is allowed, payments made *to* your children do not qualify for relief.

Payments cease to qualify for relief from the date on which your former wife or husband remarries.

EXAMPLE

Peter Smith, aged 65, pays maintenance to his ex-wife, Pat, who is three years older than him. Since Pat was born before 6 April 1935, Peter's maintenance payments qualify for tax relief. In the year ending 5 April 2003, Peter paid Pat £400 on the first day of each month (£4,800 over the whole year). However, Pat remarried on 20 October 2002, and although Peter carried on paying maintenance, the payments from that date onwards do not qualify for relief. Peter's qualifying payments (May to October) come to £2,400. This is more than the maximum relief of £2,110, so he puts £2,110 in box 15.2.

Only payments up to a set limit qualify for relief. The limit is £2,110 in the year ending 5 April 2003. The £2,110 limit applies even if you are making payments to more than one former wife or husband. You do not get tax relief at the rate of tax you pay. Relief is given at a fixed rate of 10 per cent in the year ending 5 April 2003.

In box 15.2, enter the amount of qualifying maintenance you paid during the year to 5 April 2003 or £2,110, whichever is lower. Give details of the relevant court order or agreement under Additional information on page 9.

Investing in growing businesses

There are some schemes which encourage investment into growing businesses which require risk capital. These types of investments can carry a high degree of risk and to compensate for this investors are offered tax incentives. For more details, see Chapter 8.

Venture capital trusts

	Amount on which relief is claimed
• Subscriptions for Venture Capital Trust shares (up to £100,000)	15.3 £

If you invest in a venture capital trust (VCT), you are not investing directly in these companies but in a fund like an investment trust which is quoted on the Stock Exchange.

When you buy new ordinary shares in a venture capital trust, you can get income tax relief at 20 per cent on your investment up to £100,000 for the year ending 5 April 2003, as long as you hold your shares for three years. (If 20 per cent tax relief would come to more, relief is restricted to your tax bill for the year in which you make the investment. In working this out, the effect of most other reliefs – such as some allowances, enterprise investment scheme relief, Gift Aid relief, and so on – is ignored.)

Provided you are given at least some income tax relief on your venture capital trust investment, you can also claim capital gains tax deferral relief where the venture capital trust investment was funded out of the proceeds of the disposal of another asset on which you made a capital gain – see p. 132.

Any dividends paid out by the venture capital trust and gains you make on the shares in the trust are all free of tax.

In box 15.3, put the amount you have invested in venture capital trusts, up to a maximum of £100,000. Keep in a safe place any certificates you get from venture capital trusts as your tax office may ask to see them.

Enterprise Investment Scheme

• Subscriptions under the Enterprise Investment Scheme (up to £150,000) - *also provide details in box 23.5, see page 24 of your Tax Return Guide*	Amount on which relief is claimed **15.4** £

You can get tax relief of 20 per cent on investments (not more than £150,000 in the tax year ending 5 April 2003) made in the shares of unquoted trading companies. (If 20 per cent tax relief would come to more, relief is restricted to your tax bill for the year in which you make the investment. In working this out, the effect of most other reliefs – such as some allowances, Gift Aid relief, and so on – is ignored.)

Any gain you make on the shares may be free of capital gains tax.

You can also claim capital gains tax deferral relief where the enterprise investment scheme investment was funded out of the proceeds of the disposal of another asset on which you made a capital gain – see p. 86. (Deferral relief is available regardless of whether you get any income tax relief.) There are a lot of detailed rules about which companies are eligible and whether you yourself are eligible.

If you have invested in shares eligible for the enterprise investment scheme after 5 April, but before 6 October 2003, you can ask for half the investment up to a maximum of £25,000 to be deducted from your income for the year ending 5 April 2003.

You can claim here in this tax return for an investment only if you have received Form EIS3 from the company in which you invested (Form EIS5 for an investment made through a fund). This form certifies that the company qualifies for the scheme.

Enter in box 15.4 the total investments (up to £150,000) for which you are claiming relief in the tax year ending 5 April 2003. If you have made an investment for which you have not yet received Form EIS3, or form EIS5, don't enter it here. You can either claim before 31 January 2004 by asking your tax office to amend this tax return or you can claim using the form in EIS3 after 31 January 2004.

Enter details of each investment for which you are claiming relief in the section headed Additional information on page 9 of the tax return.

Community investment tax relief

• Community Investment Tax relief - invested amount relating to previous tax year(s) and on which relief is due	15.5 £		Total amount on which relief is claimed
• Community Investment Tax relief - invested amount for current tax year	15.6 £	box 15.5 + box 15.6	15.7 £

You can claim tax relief on loans you make to, or shares you buy in, a community development finance institution. These institutions have been set up to finance small businesses and social enterprise projects in disadvantaged communities. The institutions must be accredited by the Inland Revenue and, to get tax relief, you must have a certificate from the institution.

You get income tax relief of up to 5 per cent a year of the amount you lend or invest for a maximum of five years. If the 5 per cent relief would come to more, relief is restricted to your tax bill for the year. In working this out, the effect of most other reliefs – such as some allowances, Gift Aid relief, and so on – is ignored. See Inland Revenue guide *Community Investment Tax Relief (CITR) Scheme. A brief guide for investors.*

The scheme started on 23 January 2003, so for the tax year ending 5 April 2003, you fill in only boxes 15.6 and 15.7 with the amount you have lent or invested. Leave box 15.5 blank.

Closing a business

• Post-cessation expenses, pre-incorporation losses brought forward and losses on relevant discounted securities, etc. - *see page 24 of your Tax Return Guide*	Amount of payment 15.8 £

Even after you have closed a business, you may find that there are certain obligations and expenses which you have to meet. For example, you may need to put right some defect in work which you carried out.

You can deduct some expenses from any other income and gains you have in the year in which the business expense arises, if you have no income from your closed business. The relief is available for expenses incurred within seven years after the business closure. You must claim for the relief by 31 January in the second year after the tax year in which you incurred the expense. So for an expense which you met in the tax year ending 5 April 2003, you must claim by 31 January 2005.

The expenses which qualify for this special relief are:

- costs of putting right defective work you did or faulty goods or services

which you supplied and the cost of paying any damages as a result
- premiums for insurance against claims due to defective work or faulty goods and services
- legal and other professional expenses you incur in defending yourself against accusations of defective work or providing faulty goods or services
- debts owed to the business which you included in your accounts but which have subsequently turned out to be bad debts
- cost of collecting debts owed to the business and included in its accounts.

Expenses which don't qualify for post-cessation relief can only be set against future income which comes from the closed business. There are some special rules about unpaid expenses. Ask your tax adviser or tax office for help.

Enter in box 15.8 the amount of expenses which you want to deduct from your income in the tax year ending 5 April 2003 (and in box 8.5 of the Capital gains pages the amount you want to deduct from your capital gains). If you are later reimbursed for any expenses or bad debts entered in this section, remember to enter the amount recovered under *Other taxable income* (box 13.3 of the tax return – see p. 178).

If you used to run a business on a self-employed basis but have converted the business to a company, you may be able to claim relief for losses made while you were self-employed against your income from the company. You must previously have opted to carry forward the losses to set against future profits (see p. 277), you must have transferred the self-employed business solely or mainly in exchange for shares in the new company and you must meet certain other conditions. Enter the loss you are claiming in box 15.8.

You also claim in box 15.8 for losses on the disposal of relevant discounted securities (formerly deep discount bonds and deep gain securities), including gilt strips (see p. 163). A loss incurred in the tax year ending 5 April 2003 can be deducted only from the income in the same tax year.

Annuities

		Payments made
• Annuities and annual payments	15.9	£

Annuities and covenants entered into for full value, for genuine commercial reasons, that you pay in connection with your trade or profession are eligible for tax relief at your highest rate. (But covenants paid to individuals in other circumstances do not qualify for any relief.)

Your payments are treated as if basic rate tax relief has already been deducted. If you're a higher rate taxpayer, extra relief is given through your self-assessment tax bill.

In box 15.9, enter the total you actually paid during the year ending 5 April 2003.

Payments to a trade union or friendly society

		Half amount of payment
• Payments to a trade union or friendly society for death benefits	15.10	£

Friendly societies supported their members before the arrival of the welfare state by paying sickness benefit, unemployment benefit and widow's pensions. Although rare, some continue in existence and you can get tax relief on premiums you pay on certain combined sickness and life insurance policies they offer. The tax relief is on one half of the premium; you can also get the same tax relief on part of your trade union subscription if it includes pension, funeral or life insurance benefits. With the friendly society policy, to be eligible for tax relief the premiums must be £25 or less a month and 40 per cent or less of the premium should be for the death benefit.

Ask your friendly society or trade union to tell you how much of the premium was for pension, life insurance, funeral or death benefit. Enter in box 15.10 half that amount.

Payment to employer's compulsory scheme for dependants' benefits

		Relief claimed
• Payment to your employer's compulsory widow's, widower's or orphan's benefit scheme *- available in some circumstances – **first** read the notes on page 25 of your Tax Return Guide*	15.11	£

Some employer's require you to join a scheme (separate from any occupational pension scheme) to provide a pension for your widow, widower or children in the event of your death. Contributions you make may qualify for tax relief that is normally given through PAYE, in which case you should leave box 15.11 blank.

Exceptionally (for example, where you have to make a lump sum contribution at retirement), you might not get all the relief you are entitled to through PAYE. You can claim relief at the basic rate on up to £100 of an otherwise unrelieved payment. In box 15.11 enter the amount of relief you are claiming (not the payment on which you are claiming relief). To work out the relief, take the lower of £100 or the payment on which you have not received relief through PAYE and multiply by 22 per cent. For example, if the payment was £50, enter 22% × £50 = £11 in box 15.11.

Relief on qualifying distributions on the redemption of bonus securities or shares

If you receive bonus shares or securities, when they are subsequently redeemed the amount you receive will count as a distribution for tax purposes. You will then receive a tax credit and, if you're a higher rate taxpayer, will have extra tax to pay.

		Relief claimed
• Relief claimed on a qualifying distribution on the **redemption** of bonus shares or securities.	**15.12**	£

This means that you could pay tax twice on the same income, because higher rate taxpayers are also liable for extra tax when such shares are issued. To prevent this, you can claim an allowance equal to the extra tax paid on the issue of the shares. The allowance is given as a reduction in your tax bill.

If you are liable to higher rate tax on dividends during the year ending 5 April 2003 and have entered income from a redemption of the shares in box 10.17 (see p. 165), in box 15.12 enter the amount of relief you are claiming.

The amount of relief is the value of the shares when you first received them (box 10.26 on the relevant year's tax return) multiplied by the difference between the higher rate of tax charged on dividends and the rate treated as already paid. This is:

- for the period 6 April 1999 to 5 April 2003, 32.5% − 10% = 22.5%
- for the period 6 April 1993 to 5 April 1999, 40% − 20% = 20%
- for periods before 6 April 1993, 40% – basic rate tax.

Giving to charity

Q15A **Do you want to claim relief on gifts to charity?** *If you have made any Gift Aid payments answer 'Yes' to Question 15A. You should include Gift Aid payments to Community Amateur Sports Clubs here. You can elect to include in this Return Gift Aid payments made between 6 April 2003 and the date you send in this Return. See page 26 in the Tax Return Guide and the leaflet enclosed.*	**YES**	If yes, tick this box and then read page 26 of your Tax Return Guide. Fill in boxes 15A.1 to 15A.5 as appropriate. If not applicable, go to Question 16.

As well as making donations in the street, you can make more formal donations and use the tax system to reduce what it costs you to make the donation. You can get tax relief up to your highest rate on donations made using the Gift Aid scheme, which now also includes any charitable donations you make by deed of covenant. You can also claim income tax relief on shares, similar investments and property that you give to charity or sell to a charity for less than their market value.

> **TAX-SAVING IDEAS**
>
> If you are giving to charity, try to arrange to do so through the Gift Aid scheme. The charity you support can receive more by reclaiming basic rate tax relief on what you give.
>
> If you are a couple, make sure the donation is made by whichever of you has the highest rate of tax.

Gift Aid

In the tax year ending 5 April 2003, you get tax relief at your highest rate on any cash gifts made to charity under the Gift Aid scheme. There is no minimum or maximum on the amount of donations that can qualify. From 6 April 2002 onwards, you can also use Gift Aid to make cash gifts to community amateur sports clubs registered with the Inland Revenue. (Membership fees do not count as gifts.) For a list of registered clubs, see www.inlandrevenue.gov.uk/cascs.

The amount you give is treated as a payment from which tax relief at the basic rate has already been deducted. The charity claims back the relief, so increasing the amount of your gift. If you are a higher rate taxpayer, you get extra relief deducted from your self-assessment tax bill or through PAYE.

> **EXAMPLE**
>
> An envelope is pushed through Julia West's door requesting a donation to the charity, Christian Aid. Julia gives £20 and completes the Gift Aid declaration on the back of the envelope. This is treated as if it is a gift from which basic rate tax relief of £5.64 has already been deducted. The charity claims £5.64 from the Inland Revenue, bringing the total value of Julia's gift to £25.64. (£5.64 is 22 per cent of the grossed up gift of £25.64).
>
> Because she is a higher rate taxpayer, Julia is entitled to more tax relief and claims it through her tax return. In box 15.5, she enters the amount she actually gave, £20 (not the grossed up amount of £25.64). She gets her higher rate tax relief as a deduction from her tax bill due on 31 January 2004.

If you don't pay enough income tax and/or capital gains tax to cover the relief you have deducted from your donation, you will have to hand money back to the Inland Revenue. This may affect you if you pay tax at the starting rate for the year ending 5

> **TAX-SAVING IDEA**
>
> If you're aged 65 or over and losing age allowance (see pp. 11 and 50), gifts to charity can be especially tax-efficient. This is because the grossed-up value of donations made under the Gift Aid scheme are deducted from your total income when working out how much age allowance you qualify for.

April 2003 or you are a non-taxpayer. For example, if you made a donation of £78, the charity would claim back £22 bringing the gross amount of your donation to £100. If your tax bill for the year came to only £10, you would have to repay £22 – £10 = £12 to the Inland Revenue (this is taken into account when working out your overall tax bill).

> **TAX-SAVING IDEA**
> It is worth carrying back a Gift Aid donation to the previous year if the tax you would save through higher-rate tax relief on the donation, an increase in age allowance (see p. 11 and 50) or an increase in the children's tax credit (see p. 202) in the earlier year would exceed the tax you could save in the year the donation was made.

To qualify for tax relief, you must give the charity concerned a Gift Aid declaration, stating that you are a UK taxpayer and giving your name and address. If you do this over the phone, the charity must send you a written record of the declaration. Keep a copy of any declarations.

- Gift Aid and payments under charitable covenants made between 6 April 2002 and 5 April 2003 — **15A.1** £
- Enter in box 15A.2 the total of any 'one off' payments included in box 15A.1 — **15A.2** £
- Enter in box 15A.3 the amount of Gift Aid payments made after 5 April 2003 but treated as if made in the tax year 2002-03 — **15A.3** £

You may be making regular donations to a charity using Gift Aid (for example, by deed of covenant – see below). However, some or all of your gifts might be one-off payments that you will not necessarily repeat in another year. Enter the amount of such one-off payments in box 15.6 so that your tax office knows not to include them as regular items when working out your PAYE code if you have one.

You can elect for a Gift Aid donation made in the year ending 5 April 2004 to be carried back and treated as if you had paid it in the year ending 5 April 2003. You must have taxable income or gains in the earlier year at least equal to the amount carried back plus the basic rate tax relief on it. The election must be in writing and must be made by the earlier of the date you file your tax return or 31 January 2004. Put the amount of any donation you want to carry back in this way in box 15A.3.

> **TAX-SAVING IDEA**
> If you're aged 65 or over and losing age allowance (see pp. 11 and 50), gifts of shares, unit trusts, oeics (open-ended investment companies) or property to charity can be especially tax-efficient. This is because the value of such gifts is deducted from your total income when working out how much age allowance you qualify for.

> **TAX-SAVING IDEA**
>
> If you want to make a substantial gift to charity and you own shares or property which are standing at a substantial profit, it will usually be more tax-efficient to give the shares or property direct to the charity rather than selling them first and making a Gift Aid donation of the cash raised. The charity will generally receive more and you may benefit from greater tax relief. But note that the tax relief from giving shares or property can only be set against your income – not against any capital gains, for example, from the sale of other assets.

Covenants

A covenant is a legally binding agreement to make a series of payments. For covenanted payments made on or after 6 April 2000, the Gift Aid rules apply (see above).

Payments under covenants started before 6 April 2000 automatically come into the Gift Aid scheme and there is no need to supply a Gift Aid declaration. Where you have entered into a covenant from 6 April 2000 onwards, to qualify for tax relief you must give the charity concerned a Gift Aid declaration.

Gifts of shares, unit trusts and property to charities

• Gifts of qualifying investments to charities – shares and securities	15A.4	£
• Gifts of qualifying investments to charities – real property	15A.5	£

You can get income tax relief at your highest rate on gifts to charities of shares, units in unit trusts and shares in open-ended investment companies (oeics). Shares must be quoted on a recognised stock exchange either in the UK (including the Alternative Investment Market) or in another country. Unit trusts and oeics must be UK-authorised or equivalent foreign investment schemes.

Similarly, from 6 April 2002 onwards, you can get income tax relief at your highest rate on a gift to a charity of a freehold or leasehold interest in UK land or buildings. You must have a certificate from the charity showing that it has accepted the gift.

If you own the property jointly, all the owners must agree to give the whole property to the charity and you get relief in proportion to your share.

If you or someone connected to you gets an interest or right in the property within five years of 31 January following the tax year in which you made the gift, the tax relief will be clawed back.

Relief is given by deducting the value of your gift from your total income for the year ending 5 April 2003. (There is also no capital gains tax on gains made on shares or property given to charity – see p. 106.)

Enter the value of your gift in box 15.7. This is the market value of the shares, units or property at the time of the gift less any sum you receive (for example, if you are selling the shares or property to the charity at a knock-down price) and less the value of any benefits you receive from the charity as a result of the gift. Add any disposal costs, such as brokers' fees or legal fees, to the value.

For more information, ask the Orderline (see p. 147) for Help Sheet *IR342 Charitable giving* and leaflet *IR178 Giving shares and securities to charity.*

ALLOWANCES

CHAPTER 15

Another way of reducing the amount of income tax you have to pay is to claim any allowances to which you are entitled. These are deducted from your income, along with reliefs (deductions), to make your taxable income smaller – and so also your tax bill.

Personal allowances

Everyone gets a personal allowance. It comes automatically; you don't have to claim it in the tax return.

> **TAX-SAVING IDEA**
>
> You can go back nearly six years to claim an allowance which you forgot at the time or didn't know you were entitled to. You get tax relief at the rate of tax which would have applied if you claimed the deduction at the right time. Provided you claim by 31 January 2004, you can go back as far as the year ending 5 April 1998.

Age-related personal allowances

However, people aged 65 or over during the tax year ending 5 April 2003, can claim a higher allowance. There is one level of age-related allowance if you were 65 or over during the tax year ending 5 April 2003 and a still higher rate if you were 75 or over. On the tax return it says if you were born before 6 April 1938, enter your date of birth in box 22.6 to claim the age-related allowance. Box 22.6 is in the middle of page 9 of the return.

***ALLOWANCES** for the year ended 5 April 2003*

Q16 **Do you want to claim blind person's allowance, married couple's allowance or the Children's Tax Credit?** **YES** ☐

If yes, tick this box and then read pages 26 to 31 of your Tax Return Guide. Fill in boxes 16.1 to 16.33 as appropriate. If not applicable, go to Question 17.

You get your personal allowance of £4,615 automatically. ***If you were born before 6 April 1938, enter your date of birth in box 22.6*** *- you may get a higher age-related personal allowance.*

Blind person's allowance

Anyone registered as blind with a local authority can claim blind person's allowance. The amount of the allowance for the tax year ending 5 April 2003 is £1,480.

■ *Blind person's allowance*	16.1 / /	16.2

In box 16.1, enter the date you were registered blind if this is the first year you are claiming, and enter the name of the local authority in box 16.2.

If you are not registered until after 5 April 2003 but before 6 April 2004, you can still get the allowance for the tax year ending 5 April 2003 if you can show that you were blind at that date, for example, with an ophthalmologist's certificate.

The requirement for Scotland and Northern Ireland is different. You don't need to be registered. You can claim blind person's allowance if you are not able to perform any work for which eyesight was essential. To claim, write Scotland claim or Northern Ireland claim in box 16.2.

If your income is less than your allowances, including blind person's, and you are married and living with your husband or wife, you can transfer the unused part of this allowance to your partner (see pp. 50 and 207). If both of you are blind, you can claim two allowances.

Married couple's allowance

Where husband or wife was born before 6 April 1935, a couple can claim the married couple's allowance. For other couples, the allowance was abolished from 6 April 2000 onwards. If you were both born on or after 6 April 1935, do not complete boxes 16.3 to 16.13.

The maximum allowance where either husband or wife reaches age 68 or more in the tax year ending 5 April 2003 is £5,465. Where either of you was aged 74 or over on 6 April 2002, the maximum allowance is £5,535. If the husband's total income exceeds £17,900, the allowance is reduced but never to less than a basic amount of £2,110 (see p. 50). The allowance gives tax relief at 10 per cent as a reduction in your tax bill.

If you are eligible for married couple's allowance but you have a child under 16 living with you, you could claim children's tax credit (see p. 202) instead. You cannot have both married couple's allowance and the credit. Check how much of each you would get and claim the larger amount.

A married man can claim married couple's allowance if he was married and living with his wife for at least part of the tax year. He can also claim the allowance if he was living apart from his wife but neither husband nor wife intended the separation to be permanent.

Married couple's allowance is automatically given to the husband unless:

- either of you has asked for half the basic amount to be given to the wife (in other words, £1,055 is transferred), or
- both of you have asked for the whole basic amount of £2,110 to be given to the wife.

Any married couple's allowance in excess of £2,110 always goes to the husband.

Normally, you must elect to transfer half or all of the basic allowance to the wife before the start of the tax year. But if you marry during the tax year, you have until the end of the year (in other words, 5 April following your marriage) to elect for the transfer. This means it is too late to alter the way the allowance is given for the tax year ending 5 April 2003. It is also too late to alter the way the allowance is given for the tax year ending 5 April 2004, unless you marry on or after 6 April 2003. You have until 5 April 2004 to elect how the allowance is given for the tax year ending 5 April 2005. Make the election by writing to your tax office.

• Enter your date of birth (if born before 6 April 1935)	16.3	/ /
• Enter your spouse's date of birth (**if** born before 6 April 1935 **and** if older than you)	16.4	/ /

If you are a married woman claiming any of the basic allowance for the tax year ending 5 April 2003 or you are a married man, put your date of birth in box 16.3. If your husband or wife is older than you and was born before 6 April 1935, put their date of birth in box 16.4, otherwise leave 16.4 blank.

Then, if you are a married man fill in boxes 16.5 to 16.9. If you are a married woman fill in boxes 16.10 to 16.13.

• Wife's full name	16.5		• Date of marriage (if after 5 April 2002)	16.6	/ /
• Tick box 16.7, or box 16.8, if you or your wife have allocated half, or all, of the minimum amount of the allowance to her			Half	16.7	All 16.8
• Enter in box 16.9 the date of birth of any previous wife with whom you lived at any time during 2002-03. *Read 'Special rules if you are a man who married in the year ended 5 April 2003' on page 27 before completing box 16.9.*				16.9	/ /

If you are a married woman, leave boxes 16.5 to 16.9 blank and go to box 16.10.

If you are a married man, give your wife's name in box 16.5. If your marriage took place before 6 April 2002 and you are receiving the whole married couple's allowance, leave boxes 16.6 to 16.9 blank.

If half or all of the basic allowance has been transferred to your wife, tick box 16.7 or 16.8 as appropriate.

If you were married on or after 6 April 2002, put the date of your marriage in box 16.6. You can claim one-twelfth of the full allowance for each month of your marriage (see p. 51). If prior to your marriage you were living with a previous wife and either of you were born before 6 April 1935, you can instead claim the full married couple's allowance for the year ending 5 April 2003 and you should put your former wife's date of birth in box 16.9.

• Tick box 16.10, or box 16.11, if you or your husband have allocated half, or all, of the minimum amount of the allowance to you	Half 16.10	All 16.11
• Husband's full name 16.12	• Date of marriage (if after 5 April 2002)	16.13 / /

If you are a married man, leave boxes 16.10 to 16.13 blank. If you are a married woman, your marriage took place before 6 April 2002 and you are not receiving any of the married couple's allowance, leave boxes 16.10 and 16.11 blank. Otherwise, tick either box 16.10 or box 16.11 as appropriate. (But if your husband died during the year ending 5 April 2003, leave boxes 16.10 and 16.11 blank and tick box 16.28 – see below.)

Put your husband's name in box 16.12. If your marriage took place on or after 6 April 2002, give the date of the marriage in box 16.13 unless you continue to qualify for part or all of the married couple's allowance for the year ending 5 April 2003 from a previous marriage, in which case leave 16.13 blank.

EXAMPLE

George, 67, was born on 7 June 1935 and would not qualify for married couple's allowance except that his wife, Hannah, who is older than him, was born on 23 February 1935. As a result George qualifies for an allowance of £5,465 in the year to 5 April 2003. George and Hannah are both taxpayers. Before 6 April 2002, the couple wrote to their tax office electing to have the full basic allowance transferred to Hannah. This means Hannah gets £2,110 of the married couple's allowance, reducing her tax bill by 10% × £2,110 = £211. George keeps the other £3,355, reducing his tax bill by 10% × £3,355 = £335.50.

Children's tax credit

This is an allowance for people looking after children.

The maximum credit in the year ending 5 April 2003 is usually £5,290. It gives you tax relief at 10 per cent as a reduction in your tax bill. Therefore, the maximum tax saving is 10% × £5,290 = £529.

TAX-SAVING IDEA

Widow's bereavement allowance used to be available to widows whose husbands died before 6 April 2000. The allowance was available in the year of death and in the following year. The allowance was not available to widowers. The UK High Court has declared this to be incompatible with the European Convention on Human Rights. However, it ruled that, although the Inland Revenue had the power to make extra-statutory payment of the allowance to widowers, it did not have the duty to do so, and the widower concerned lost his case. The case has gone to appeal and, at the time of writing, the outcome was awaited. In the meantime, two cases taken to the European Court of Human Rights have been successful. But the Inland Revenue has compensated only the widowers who brought those cases, not any others. If the UK appeal is lost, it seems the only way to claim the allowance will be through the European Court.

You cannot be eligible unless you have first made a claim through your tax office. Because of the time limit on back claims (see p. 23), if you claim by 31 January 2004, you can go back as far as the year ending 5 April 1998 to claim the allowance. So you would be affected if your wife died between 6 April 1996 and 5 April 2000. (Men who claimed earlier have been able to go back further.) For more information, see www.taxaid.org.uk and www.liberty-human-rights.org.uk.

The maximum credit in the year ending 5 April 2003 is increased to £10,490 if you are looking after a baby born in that tax year. In that case, the maximum tax saving is 10% × £10,490 = £1,049.

The standard amount of the credit is reduced if you are a higher rate taxpayer. The credit is reduced by £2 for every £3 of income on which you pay higher rate tax. For example, if you pay higher rate tax on £900 of your income, the credit is reduced by ⅔ × £900 = £600 to £5,290 − £600 = £4,690. This would give you a tax saving of 10% × £4,690 = £469. Your tax office will work out whether any reduction applies, unless you have opted to calculate your own tax bill.

For the year ending 5 April 2003, you can claim children's tax credit if you are a single parent, married couple or unmarried couple looking after:

- your own child, a stepchild, adopted child, or any other child for whom you meet at least half of the maintenance costs

TAX-SAVING IDEA

If you look after a child under the age of 16 and you or your wife were born before 6 April 1935, you can claim either married couple's allowance or children's tax credit. Claim whichever is higher.

- the child was under the age of 16 on 6 April 2001, and
- the child lived with you for at least part of the year.

• Enter in box 16.14 the date of birth of a child living with you who was born on or after 6 April 1986. *If you have a child living with you who was born on or after 6 April 2002 make sure you enter their date of birth in this box in preference to claiming for an older child.*	16.14 / /
• Tick box 16.15 if the child was your own child or one you looked after at your own expense. If not, you cannot claim CTC – go to box 16.27, if appropriate, or Question 17.	16.15
• Tick box 16.16 if the child lived with you **throughout** the year to 5 April 2003. If you ticked box 16.16 and - you were a lone or single claimant, you have finished this question; go to Question 17,	16.16

The maximum children's tax credit you can have in the year ending 5 April 2003 is £5,290 (or £10,490) regardless of the number of children you look after. If you have more than one child, you should claim for your youngest child.

You may have to share the credit if your child lives part of the year with someone else. If you do not share the credit and you are a single parent, you only complete boxes 16.14 to 16.16 and then go on to question 17. Other claimants need to complete more of the boxes in question 16.

• If the child lived with you for only **part of the year** you may only be entitled to a proportion of the CTC. Enter in box 16.17 your share in £s that **you have agreed** with any other claimants that you may claim for this child. But leave boxes 16.17 to 16.25 blank if you separated from, or started living with, your partner during the year to 5 April 2003. Special rules apply to work out your entitlement; ask the Orderline for *Help Sheet IR343: Claiming Children's Tax Credit when your circumstances change* which explains how to complete box 16.26.	16.17 £

If the child you are claiming for lives with someone else for part of the year – for example a former partner or a grandparent – you may have to share the credit with that person. You should decide between you how to split the credit and you can choose any proportions. Multiply the share that you have agreed and the maximum credit to find your share in £s. Put that amount in box 16.17. For example, if you and the other person have agreed that you will get three-quarters of the credit, work out 75% × £5,290 = £3,968 and put that amount in the box.

If you can't reach a decision, the general commissioners (see p. 26) will decide the split for you. In box 16.17, put your share of the credit based either on the commissioners decision or, if that is not yet available,

TAX-SAVING IDEA

If you are separated and have two (or more) children under 16, both of whom spend part of the year with you and part with your former partner, you and your former partner should each claim children's tax credit for a different child. That way, you will each be eligible for the full credit (£5,290 in the year ending 5 April 2003).

your own estimate of what the share is likely to be. If you have put an estimated figure in box 16.17, also tick box 23.2 on page 9 of the return and, in the Additional information box, give details of the child and all the claimants.

Do not put anything in box 16.17, if you and the other claimant split up during the course of the year ending 5 April 2003. Instead complete box 16.26 (see below).

- Enter in box 16.18 your partner's surname **16.18** [ ]
- Enter in box 16.19 your partner's National Insurance number **16.19** [ ]
- Tick
  - box 16.20 if **you** had the higher income in the year to 5 April 2003, **16.20** [ ]

  or
  - box 16.21 if **your partner** had the higher income in that year **16.21** [ ]
- Tick box 16.22 if either of you were chargeable to tax above the basic rate limit in the year to 5 April 2003. **16.22** [ ]

If you live with your husband, wife or unmarried partner, there are special rules about which of you can claim the credit. If either or both of you pay tax at the higher rate, the credit will automatically be given to whichever of you has the highest 'total income' (see p. 4). This is the case even if the person with the highest income is not the child's parent.

Enter your partner's surname and National Insurance number in boxes 16.18 and 16.19. Tick either box 16.20 or 16.21 to show which of you had the highest total income in the year ending 5 April 2003. If either of you paid tax at the higher rate, tick box 16.22.

TAX-SAVING IDEA

Where a couple look after a child, children's tax credit automatically goes to the person with the highest 'total income' if either or both pay tax at the higher rate. This rule is designed to reduce the amount of credit available to high-earning families. However, 'total income' broadly means all your taxable income less reliefs that can be set off against income. These reliefs do not include personal pension contributions (because tax relief is given in a different way), but pension contributions can reduce the amount of income taxed at the higher rate. So making pension contributions can increase the amount of children's tax credit you get. See example.

EXAMPLE

Sanjay Patel is married with two young children. He has an income of £38,000 in the year ending 5 April 2003, while his wife Rita has just £10,000. As Sanjay is a higher-rate taxpayer and has the higher income, children's tax credit is automatically awarded to him.

After allowing for his personal allowance (£4,615) and income taxed at the starting and basic rates (£29,900), Sanjay pays higher rate tax on £3,485 of his income. This means the children's tax credit is reduced by ⅔ × £3,485 = £2,323 to £5,290 − £2,323 = £2,967.

But suppose Sanjay paid £2,718 (after deducting basic rate tax relief) into a stakeholder pension scheme. Including the tax relief, this is a gross contribution of £3,485. To give him higher rate relief on the contribution, the top of his basic rate band is increased to £29,900 + £3,485 = £33,385. Now none of Sanjay's income is taxed at the higher rate and so he gets the full children's tax credit of £5,290.

- I had the higher income and I am claiming all of our entitlement to CTC **16.23**
- We are both making separate claims for half of our entitlement to CTC **16.24**
- We elected before 6 April 2002, or because of our special circumstances, during the year to 5 April 2003 (see page 31 of your Tax Return Guide), for the partner with the lower income to claim all of our entitlement to CTC **16.25**

If neither of you paid tax at the higher rate in the year ending 5 April 2003, children's tax credit normally goes to whichever of you has the highest total income, but you can choose to share the credit equally. Alternatively, provided you made an election before 6 April 2002, you can opt for the whole credit to be given to the person with the lower income. If you have the lower income and your partner is claiming the whole credit, you do not need to enter anything here. Otherwise, tick one of the boxes 16.23 to 16.25 to indicate your choice.

- If you separated from, or starting living with, your partner in the year to 5 April 2003, enter in box 16.26 the amount of CTC you are claiming *(following the guidance in Help Sheet IR343: Claiming* **16.26** £

If you married, started living with someone or split up from a partner during the year ending 5 April 2003, this may affect whether you can claim children's tax credit and whether you have to share it with someone else. To work out the position, you divide the year into sections. The credit is then apportioned to each section of the year on the basis of 1/365 of the credit for each day. The credit for each section is then given to the person with the higher income (for the year not just a section of the year), split with other claimants, and so on, according to the normal rules. Sum the credit you get from each section of the year and enter the total in box 16.26.

For example, if you split up on 8 August, you would divide the year into one section running from 6 April 2002 to 7 August 2002 and a second section running from 8 August 2002 to 5 April 2003. There are 124 days in the first section of the year, so credit of $^{124}/_{365} \times £5,290 = £1,797$ would be available for the first section of the year. Say your partner paid tax at the higher rate so you get no credit for the first section of the year. There are 241 days in the second section of the year, so credit of $^{241}/_{365} \times £5,290 = £3,493$ would be available. You and your former partner agree to share the credit equally, so you get $50\% \times £3,493 = £1,747$. Sum the credit for each section of the year, $£0 + £1,747 = £1,747$ and put the answer in box 16.26.

If your circumstances change more than once during the year, you need to split the year and the credit into more than two sections. For more information see Inland Revenue Helpsheet *IR343 Claiming children's tax credit when your circumstances change.*

Children's tax credit is being abolished from 6 April 2003 onwards. You may instead be able to claim a new state benefit called child tax credit (see p. 12).

Transfer of surplus allowances

You can transfer any unused amount of married couple's or blind person's allowance to your wife or your husband if you did not have enough income in the year to use up the allowance and you lived with your wife or husband for at least part of that year.

■ ***Transfer of surplus allowances*** - *see page 31 of your Tax Return Guide before you fill in boxes 16.27 to 16.33.*

• Tick box 16.27 if you want your spouse to have your unused allowances	16.27
• Tick box 16.28 if you want to have your spouse's unused allowances	16.28
• Tick box 16.29 if you want to have your partner's unused CTC	16.29
• Tick box 16.30 if your surplus CTC should be transferred to your partner	16.30

Please give details in the 'Additional information' box, box 23.5, on page 9 - *see page 31 of your Tax Return Guide for what is needed.*

If you want to calculate your tax, enter the amount of the surplus allowance you can have.

• Blind person's surplus allowance	16.31 £
• Married couple's surplus allowance	16.32 £
• Surplus CTC	16.33 £

If you want your wife or husband to have the surplus of married couple's or blind person's allowances, tick box 16.27. In the Additional information box on page 9 of your tax return, give your spouse's name, address, tax reference, National Insurance number and tax office.

Similarly, you can transfer any unused children's tax credit to your partner (whether you are married or not) if you did not have enough income to use up your full credit and you lived with that person for at least part of the year. To make this transfer, tick box 16.30 and give your partner's name, address, tax reference, National Insurance number and tax office in the Additional information box on page 9.

If you want to claim and use your spouse's unused allowances, tick box 16.28. Give your spouse's name, address, tax reference, National Insurance number and tax office in the Additional information box on page 9.

If you want to claim your partner's (married or not) unused children's tax credit, tick box 16.29 and give your partner's details in the Additional information box on page 9.

If you are working out your own tax bill, enter in boxes 16.31 and 16.33 the amount of the surplus allowances and/or credit you are claiming. You can ask your tax office for help if you are not sure of the amount.

EMPLOYMENT

Q1 Were you an employee, or office holder, or director, or agency worker or did you receive payments or benefits from a former employer (excluding a pension) in the year ended 5 April 2003?
If you were a non-resident director of a UK company but received no remuneration, see the notes to the Employment Pages, page EN3, box 1.6.

YES | EMPLOYMENT

It is usually easy to tell whether or not you are an employee. There are some grey areas, however, where the Inland Revenue will seek to tax you as an employee even if you think of yourself as self-employed:

- if you are a company director (even if you own the company). Note that, from 6 April 2000, if you are a director of your own personal services company, special tax rules may apply (see p. 211)
- if you work on a freelance or consultancy basis, but have to work closely under the control of your boss, working a set number of hours at an hourly rate, say, and at a particular location
- if you work on a casual, part-time basis
- if you work as a temp through an agency. This includes, for example, locum doctors; but it does not apply to entertainers or models working through an agency, or to people who work solely from home
- you have more than one job: you may be classed as an employee for one job, even if you are clearly self-employed in another.

The key significance of being an employee is that in most cases your employer will have to operate PAYE (see Chapter 3) on your earnings from that job and deduct tax and National Insurance before paying you. Exceptionally, the Inland Revenue has agreed that most actors can count as employees for National Insurance purposes but as self-employed for income tax.

For many employees, the advantage of being paid under PAYE is that the right amount of tax on all their income should be deducted from their earnings and so they do not have to worry about paying a separate tax bill. If their income from their job is their only income many also do not need to fill in a tax return. But you may still have to fill one in if:

- you are a higher rate taxpayer and get taxable perks such as a company car or receive investment income
- you have other income which is paid out before tax is deducted, such as some types of investment income
- your tax affairs are complex for any other reason.

If you are an employee and are sent a tax return, you need to tick the box at Q1 of the basic tax return and fill in a separate Employment page for each job you have. If you are not sure of your status, check with your tax office.

Your employer

Details of employer

Employer's PAYE reference - may be shown under 'Inland Revenue office number and reference' on your P60 or 'PAYE reference' on your P45

1.1

Employer's name

1.2

Date employment started
(only if between 6 April 2002 and 5 April 2003)

1.3 / /

Date employment finished
(only if between 6 April 2002 and 5 April 2003)

1.4 / /

Tick box 1.6 if you were a director of the company

1.6

and, if so, tick box 1.7 if it was a close company

1.7

Employer's address

1.5

Postcode

> **TAX-SAVING IDEA**
>
> A disadvantage of being an employee is that you cannot deduct as many expenses from your taxable income as you could if you were self-employed. So if you are setting up on your own, check that you will meet the Inland Revenue's conditions for self-employment.

So that your tax office can tie up the information on your tax return with that provided by your employer, give your employer's name, address and PAYE reference (shown on the P60 or P45). If the employment started or ended during the tax year ending 5 April 2003, you also need to give the start or end dates of the job, the length of time you worked there, whether or not you are a director (box 1.6) and if it is a close company (box 1.7). This may affect how your perks and benefits are taxed.

What is taxed

Broadly speaking, the Inland Revenue seeks to tax any benefit you get from being employed, even if you get it from someone other than your employer. The tax return organises your remuneration into the following categories:

- money (including earnings from working abroad)
- benefits (taxable perks given by your employer) and expenses payments (either flat-rate allowances or reimbursement for expenses you have incurred)
- lump sums received on retirement, redundancy or death.

Not all of these will actually be taxable. But in general, you have to put it all down first, and the tax return then guides you to enter the various tax reliefs which you can deduct, for example, tax relief for expenses incurred in doing your job.

One thing you do not have to enter anywhere on your tax return is details of your National Insurance contributions as an employee. These should all be sorted out for you by your employer.

The date income is taxable

As a general rule, you are counted as receiving income from employment from the earlier of:

- the date you get it
- the date you are entitled to it, even if you do not actually get it till later on.

So if, for example, you are entitled to payment on 15 March 2003, but do not actually receive it until 15 April, you must still include it in your tax return for the tax year ending 5 April 2003. If you receive payment early – on 15 March 2003, for work not completed until 15 April, for example – it is taxable from the date you received it, that is 15 March.

If you are a director, your earnings for a particular period may be decided on one date, credited to you in the company accounts on another date, but not paid out till much later. It is the earliest date that counts, unless the earnings for a particular period were decided before that period ended. In this case, you are treated as receiving them on the last day of the period to which the earnings relate.

IR35: special rules for personal service companies

Special rules may apply if you are a director of a company which hires out your services to clients and:

- you or your family (including an unmarried partner) control more than

> **TAX-SAVING IDEA**
>
> You must pay income tax and National Insurance on any deemed payment for the tax year in which the money is earned by your personal service company. If that money is paid out to you as salary in a later year, tax and National Insurance will again be due – in other words, the same income will be taxed twice. To avoid this, make sure any deemed payment retained within the company is eventually paid out as dividends, not salary. IR35 rules allow dividends up to the amount of any deemed payments to be paid without further tax being due (see p. 165) and dividends are not in any case subject to National Insurance.

5 per cent of the ordinary share capital of the company, or

- you or your family are entitled to more than 5 per cent of any dividends paid out by the company, or
- the company can or does make payments to you other than salary but they are basically payment for the services you provide to clients.

These so-called 'personal service companies' have been popular with people working as contractors or consultants, for example in the information technology and engineering industries. If you were employed direct by a client, you would pay tax and National Insurance on your salary and the client would pay employer's National Insurance. But if the client contracts with your personal service company to hire your services, the client pays a fee to your company on which there is no employer's National Insurance. And if your company pays you dividends instead of salary, you also escape paying National Insurance. The Inland Revenue views this as tax avoidance.

For income earned by your company on or after 6 April 2000, the Inland Revenue has closed this loophole. If in the absence of your company your work for a client would essentially be the same as that of an employee (rather than a self-employed person), you may be caught by the IR35 rules (named after the number of the press release which introduced them) and have to pay extra tax and National Insurance. The Inland Revenue uses the normal tests for deciding whether you count as an employee or self-employed (see p. 250).

If the IR35 rules do apply, you will be treated for income tax and National Insurance purposes as if you had received a salary (called a 'deemed payment') equal to:

- the fees received by your company, less

EXAMPLE

Bill Brown is a software designer. He is owner-director of a company, BB-IT Ltd, which hires Bill out to clients. For the whole year ending 5 April 2003, Bill is contracted to Gigasoft plc, working full-time in their offices for a monthly fee of £6,000. The contract is caught by the IR35 rules. BB-IT Ltd paid Bill a salary of £24,000, £2,500 for an annual season ticket to cover travel to Gigasoft's offices and £4,000 to Bill's pension scheme. At the end of the year, BB-IT Ltd must work out whether there is any deemed payment under the IR35 rules on which income tax and National Insurance contributions are due:

Income caught by IR35 (12 × £6,000)	£72,000
Less	
Salary actually paid	£24,000
Employer's National Insurance already paid ([£24,000 – £4,615] × 11.8%)	£2,287
Less employee-related expenses (ie season ticket) which would be allowed under normal rules	£2,500
Less pension scheme contribution	£4,000
Expense allowance to cover costs of running personal service company (5% of £72,000)	£3,600
Deemed payment before deducting employer's National Insurance	£35,613
Employer's National Insurance on deemed payment (£31,854 × 11.8%)	£3,759
Deemed payment	£31,854

Bill is deemed to receive extra salary of £31,854 on 5 April 2003. The company is responsible via PAYE for paying Bill's income tax and employee's National Insurance on this amount as well as employer's National Insurance of £3,759.

- any salary paid by the company on which you have paid tax and National insurance in the normal way, less
- a 5 per cent expense allowance designed to cover the costs of running your personal service company.

The deemed payment is treated as paid on the last day of the tax year – in other words, 5 April 2003 in the case of the tax year covered by the current tax return. Tax and National Insurance were due to be paid through the PAYE system by 19 April 2003.

The deemed payment, just like salaries that are actually paid out, is deducted from the company's profits when working out corporation tax.

Your company does not actually have to pay you the deemed payment – it could be retained within the company or paid to you as dividends. IR35 includes rules to allow special distributions (dividends) to be made during the tax year or later up to the amount of any deemed payment without further tax being due – see p. 165.

The IR35 rules affect only the income tax and National Insurance position. They do not affect the legal status of your company's contract with the client.

The rules apply on a contract-by-contract basis. Some of the work you do through your personal service company may count as equivalent to self-employment and so fall outside the rules; other contracts may be deemed equivalent to employment and so fall within the rules. You can ask your tax office to advise on the status of existing contracts (but not draft contracts).

For more information, ask the Orderline (see p. 147) for booklets *IR175 Supplying services through a limited company or partnership* and *IR2003 Supplying services*. If you have internet access, see www.inlandrevenue.gov.uk/ir35.

Include any deemed payment in box 1.8. Income tax on the deemed payment paid through PAYE should be included in box 1.11.

The documents you need

Most of the information you need will be on Forms P60, P11D or P9D.

Your P60 is a form your employer must give you by 31 May after the end of the tax year (that is, by 31 May 2003 for the tax year ending 5 April 2003). The P60 is a summary of how much you have been paid, and how much tax has been deducted. If you haven't got a P60, you should be able to find the information from your pay slips. If you left a job during a tax year, the information will be on your P45.

If you work through your own personal services company, your company must provide you with a P60 in the normal way. The P60 (and any P45) will show any deemed payment under the IR35 rules and tax on it in the same way as ordinary pay.

Your employer has to declare to the Revenue any taxable benefits or expenses you receive and the cash equivalent on form P11D or form P9D. Which form you get depends on how much you earn. You should get a copy from your employer by 6 July after the end of the tax year, that is by 6 July 2003 for the tax year ending 5 April 2003.

Note that if you leave a job, you will not automatically be given a form P11D or P9D, but your ex-employer must give you one if you ask for it within three years after the end of the tax year in which you left. Your employer has 30 days from receiving your request in which to supply the form (if this is after the normal 6 July deadline).

Your P11D or P9D should be the starting point of all the expenses payments you have received. But you also need to keep receipts or documentation to back up your claim to deduct allowable expenses, particularly if they were not reimbursed by your employer and so did not appear on your P11D or P9D.

If you receive a lump sum from your employer, for example, when you left your job, it may be included on your P60, your P11D, or your P45, or you may just have a letter from your employer. Your employer should be able to help you decide which category a payment falls within. If there is any doubt, employers can get advance decisions from their tax office, so it is worth talking about the tax consequences with your employer before any payment is made.

MONEY FROM EMPLOYMENT

Income from employment		
■ *Money - see Notes, page EN3*		Before tax
• Payments from P60 (or P45)	1.8	£

You should enter as money:

- ◆ salaries, deemed payments under IR35 rules, wages, fees, overtime, bonuses, commission and honoraria (after deducting money you have donated to a payroll giving scheme, or contributed to your employer's pension scheme, see below)
- ◆ amounts voted to you as a director and credited to an account with the company, even if you cannot draw the money straight away
- ◆ voluntary payments and gifts, whether from your employer or anyone else, such as tips and Christmas boxes (excluding some small gifts and personal gifts such as long-service awards, see Tax-free fringe benefits on p. 89)
- ◆ incentive awards (but see below)
- ◆ the taxable value of shares withdrawn early from an approved profit-sharing scheme
- ◆ sick pay, including statutory sick pay and statutory maternity pay and statutory paternity pay (see overleaf)

- holiday pay
- various payments to do with your employment which are not strictly pay. Examples are golden hellos paid to entice you to join the company; a loan written off because you satisfied or completed an employment condition; payments made to recognise changes in your conditions of service or employment; payments made if you leave a job and agree, in return for a lump sum, not to compete with your employer.

P60 forms vary slightly in design. The figure to look for is your pay 'for tax purposes' or 'this employment pay'. Enter the figure from Form P60 in box 1.8, but check that it does not include employer's contributions to a pension scheme or what you give under a payroll giving scheme (see below). If you were unemployed during the year, your P60 may give details of any jobseeker's allowance you received. Do not enter this in your Employment page – enter it instead in box 11.5 in the basic tax return.

Contributions to an occupational pension scheme

You can get tax relief on contributions you make to your employer's occupational pension scheme, up to a maximum of 15 per cent of your taxable income from the job in the year ending 5 April 2003. This tax relief is given by deducting your contributions from your pay before tax is worked out on it, so giving you relief at your top rate of tax. The figure you enter as taxable pay in box 1.8 should be the figure after deducting pension contributions.

Details of contributions to other types of pension plan or scheme do not go here, even if your employer arranges for them to be paid direct from your salary. Instead they go in boxes 14.6 to 14.10 in the basic tax return.

Payroll giving schemes

You can get tax relief on charitable donations of any amount (was up to £1,200 a year before 6 April 2000) through a payroll giving scheme offered by your employer. The biggest scheme run by the Charities Aid Foundation is called Give As You Earn, or GAYE. The money is deducted from your pay each week or month and passed straight to the charity by your employer. The donations are deducted from your pay before your tax is worked out on it, in the same way as contributions to an occupational pension scheme, so remember to check that what you enter in box 1.8. is your pay after deduction of payroll giving donations. Where you make a donation to charity through payoll giving on or after 6 April 2000 up to 5 April 2004, the government adds a supplement equal to 10 per cent of the amount you give, so boosting the amount received by the charity.

Incentive awards

Broadly speaking, these are taxable whether you receive them from your employer or from someone else in connection with your job; for example, a car sales representative may receive prizes from the car manufacturer. However, the person paying the award may pay the tax for you, through a taxed award scheme. In this case, the award still counts as part of your income, but the tax paid on your behalf will reduce your tax bill. Whoever makes the award should give you a Form P443 stating the value of the award and how much tax has been paid on it, unless the figures have been included on your P60. You should include the amount of the award in box 1.10 and the tax already paid in box 1.11.

Suggestion scheme awards are tax-free and need not be entered, provided that there is a formal scheme open to all employees, and the suggestion concerned is outside your normal job. If the suggestion is not taken up, the maximum award is £25; if it is implemented, the maximum award is 50 per cent of the first year's expected net benefit, or 10 per cent of the benefit over five years, with an overall maximum of £5,000.

Sick pay, maternity pay and paternity pay

If you are off work through illness or on maternity or paternity leave, any payment made to you by your employer, including statutory sick pay (SSP), statutory maternity pay (SMP) or statutory paternity pay, is taxable. It will be taxed before you get it and shown on your P60 or P45 in the same way as other income, and you enter it with your other taxable pay in box 1.8. There are two exceptions to this rule:

- occasionally, SSP, SMP or SPP may be paid directly to you by the Inland Revenue. In this case, the benefit is still taxable, but tax is not deducted before it is paid to you and rather than enter it under Employment you should enter it in box 11.7 on page 4 of the basic tax return
- if you pay part or all of the premiums for an insurance policy taken out by your employer to meet the cost of employees' sick pay. In this case, the proportion of the sick pay which arises from your contributions is tax-free and need not be entered on the tax return. Any sick pay arising from your employer's contributions is taxable. Put it in box 1.8.

Working families' tax credit and disabled person's tax credit

Although confusingly these items are called 'tax credits', they do not in fact affect your tax bill in any way. Rather, they are means-tested state benefits which, if you are an employee, are paid to you through your pay packet. Details are included on your P60, but these are tax-free benefits that do not need to go anywhere on your tax return. Do not include any working families' tax credit or disabled person's tax credit in the amounts you enter on the Employment pages.

Tips and other payments

• Payments not on P60 etc.	- tips	1.9	£
	- other payments (excluding expenses entered below and lump sums and compensation payments or benefits entered overleaf)	1.10	£

Boxes 1.9 and 1.10 are there to catch any income which does not appear on your P60 (for example, because it is paid by people other than your employer or it comprises earnings from a foreign source earned in an earlier year but only remitted in the year ending 5 April 2003) and for which there is no other place on the Employment page.

Tax deducted

		Tax deducted
• UK tax deducted from payments in boxes 1.8 to 1.10	1.11	£

The tax your employer has deducted under PAYE is set against your tax bill. Enter it in box 1.11, together with any other tax deducted (for example, under a taxed incentive scheme). Occasionally, your employer may have given you more tax back as a refund than was actually deducted. If so, remember to enter the amount in brackets.

If you left a job and later received a tax refund from the Inland Revenue or the Department for Work and Pensions, enter in box 1.11 the tax shown on your P45. Put the subsequent repayment in box 20.1 on the basic tax return (see p. 153).

FRINGE BENEFITS AND EXPENSES

■ *Benefits and expenses - see Notes, pages EN3 to EN6. If any benefits connected with termination of employment were received, or enjoyed, after that termination and were from a* ***former*** *employer you need to complete Help Sheet IR204, available from the Orderline. Do not enter such benefits here.*

Many employers give their employees non-cash fringe benefits, such as a company car or free medical insurance (see Chapter 9). Generally, you are taxed on the cash equivalent of these benefits (and the same applies, as for pay, if the benefit or expense is paid to you by someone other than your employer). Benefits for your family or household are regarded as a payment to you. However, some types of benefits are tax-free, and others are taxable only for higher-paid employees.

Expense payments you receive are yoked together with benefits in this section and sometimes the dividing line between them can be a fine one; for example, a company car may be a way of covering your travelling costs for work, as well as a perk of the job.

Payments you do not need to enter

There are three sorts of payments which you can ignore when filling out the benefits and expenses section of the Employment supplementary page.

Dispensations

You do not need to enter in your tax return expenses payments which are covered by a dispensation. A dispensation is a special permission from the Revenue which means that your employer does not have to include on your P11D or P9D expenses which would be tax-free anyway. Dispensations are usually given for things like travelling and subsistence expenses on an approved scale: they do not generally cover fringe benefits.

PAYE Settlement Agreements

The tax on some of your expenses and benefits may already have been paid by your employer under a PAYE Settlement Agreement (PSA). This is a voluntary agreement between an employer and the Inland Revenue under which the employer undertakes to pay the tax otherwise due from you on some types of benefits and expenses. The advantage for your employer is the saving of paperwork; the advantage for you is that you do not need to enter the payments on your return and they are tax-free in your hands. Only some types of benefits and expenses can be covered by this sort of agreement, for example, minor expenses such as taxi fares and benefits such as parties shared by many employees.

> **TAX-SAVING IDEA**
> Remember – you do not need to enter items covered by a dispensation or PAYE Settlement Agreement.

Tax-free fringe benefits

You do not need to enter the details of any fringe benefits which are tax-free (see p. 89 for a list). Note that there are conditions to be met before most of these benefits can be tax-free. Fuller information is given in Help Sheet *IR207 Non-taxable payments or benefits for employees.*

Payments you need to enter

There are some benefits which are always taxable and need to be entered on the tax return. They are assets which are transferred to you (including payments in kind), vouchers (except, from 6 April 2002 onwards, vouchers for minor benefits that are exempt from tax, such as a travel card for free travel on a works bus) and goods paid for by credit cards, living accommodation (with a few exceptions) and mileage allowance in excess of the Inland Revenue authorised mileage allowance payments.

You may receive other benefits. But if you earn at a rate of less than £8,500 a year and are not a director they will be tax-free and you do not need to enter them on the tax return. Chapter 9 gives much more detail. It helps you work out whether you are paid at the rate of £8,500 a year or not and helps you work out the taxable value of benefits which you need to enter here.

Assets transferred to you and payments made for you

		Amount
• Assets transferred/ payments made for you	1.12	£

Payments in kind may be taxed in a number of ways, depending on how much you earn and whether you have the alternative of cash instead (see p. 93 to find out the taxable value). You should be able to get the amount to enter in box 1.12 from your P11D. If you earn less than £8,500, the taxable value is the second-hand value. But if you earn £8,500 or more, the taxable value is the larger of the second-hand value or the cost to the employer of providing the asset.

Payments your employer makes for you, like your phone bill, should also be entered in box 1.12. But don't put assets which remain the property of your employer and which you merely have the use of, or services supplied by your employer – these go in box 1.22, unless there is a more specific box.

Vouchers and credit cards

		Amount
• Vouchers, credit cards and tokens	1.13	£

You may be given a voucher for a particular service (for example, a season ticket), a credit token or a company credit or charge card. If so, you are taxed on their cash equivalent unless they appear in the list of tax-free fringe benefits on p. 90 (for example, luncheon vouchers, gift vouchers which count as a small gift, vouchers for minor benefits that are tax free). Cash vouchers worth a specified amount of cash should already have been taxed under PAYE, so you will not usually have to enter them here as a benefit. If you used vouchers or your company credit card to settle expenses of your job (such as train fares), include the full value of the vouchers or card bill here, but claim a deduction for 'Expenses you incurred in doing your job' on the back of the Employment page.

For vouchers and cards which count as a taxable fringe benefit, broadly speaking you pay tax on the expense incurred by the person who provided them, less any amount that you have paid yourself. You will not have to pay tax on any annual card fee or interest paid by your employer.

Company credit cards and charge cards are often provided as a convenient way of paying business expenses. If so, you still have to enter the value of any vouchers or goods or services obtained with a credit card or credit token in box 1.13. You can claim any allowable business expenses back in boxes 1.32 to 1.35. For more information see Help Sheet *IR201 Vouchers, credit cards and tokens.*

Living accommodation

		Amount
• Living accommodation	1.14	£

The basic taxable charge for any living accommodation (unless it counts as a tax-free fringe benefit, see p. 90), and the extra charge if applicable, should be entered in box 1.14. However, if you have the alternative of getting cash instead of accommodation, and the cash alternative comes to more than the taxable value of the accommodation, you should enter the surplus cash (ie in excess of the taxable value) in box 1.12 and the taxable value in box 1.14. This applies even if you have decided to live in the accommodation.

Help Sheet *IR202 Living Accommodation* explains how to work out the taxable value for various types of accommodation.

Mileage allowances

		Amount
• Excess mileage allowances and passenger payments	1.15	£

If you use your own car, motorbike or bicycle for work, you may be paid a mileage allowance for the business mileage you do. From 6 April 2002 onwards, any allowance up to the Inland Revenue approved mileage allowance payment (see p. 92) is tax-free and you do not enter it on your tax return. But anything in excess of the approved payment is taxable and should be entered in box 1.15. This is the case even if your actual costs are higher than the authorised rate, so that you are not making any profit out of the excess allowance. The amount of any excess should be shown on the P11D.

Similarly, your employer can pay you a tax-free passenger allowance up to the approved payment if you carry a colleague in your vehicle on business trips (see p. 91). Any excess over the approved amount is taxable and must be entered in box 1.15.

If your employer does not pay you any mileage allowance or pays you less than the approved payment, you can claim a deduction up to the approved amount (regardless of your actual costs) in box 1.32 (see p. 229). This does not apply to passenger allowances.

For more information, see Inland Revenue Help Sheet *IR124 Using your own vehicle for work*.

Company cars

		Amount
• Company cars	1.16	

A company car is taxable only if you earn at the rate of £8,500 a year or more (see p. 97). Put in box 1.16 the cash equivalent of cars made available to you (or to members of your family or household) for private use. Check the figure with your employer or on your form P11D. Chapter 9 and Help Sheet *IR203 Car benefits and car fuel benefits* will be useful.

Fuel for company cars

		Amount
• Fuel for company cars	1.17	£

If you have a company car, you may get free fuel for private use as well. In the

TAX-SAVING IDEA

From 6 April 2002, the taxable value of a company car is based on its carbon dioxide emissions. This makes larger company cars an expensive fringe benefit. By contrast, the taxable value of a van is low. If you are in a position to choose, you could save tax by opting for a van rather than a car. For a vehicle to count as van it must be *'of a construction primarily suited for the conveyance of goods...and of a design weight not exceeding 3,500 kilograms'*.

tax year ending 5 April 2003, this is taxed according to a fixed scale of charges added to your taxable income (see p. 100) and only taxable if you earn at the rate of £8,500 a year or more. Enter the amount in box 1.17.

From 6 April 2003 onwards, fuel is taxed in a similar way to company cars with the tax charge based on the car's carbon dioxide emissions (see p. 101).

Vans

		Amount
• Vans	1.18	£

A van is only taxable if you earn at the rate of £8,500 a year or more (see p. 97). The basic taxable value of a van is £500, but there may be reductions (see p. 101). Enter the adjusted taxable amount in box 1.18.

Interest-free and low-interest loans

		Amount
• Interest-free and low-interest loans *see Note for box 1.19, page EN5*	1.19	£

Free or cheap loans are only taxable if you earn at the rate of £8,500 a year or more. The basic rule is that you have to pay tax on the difference between the interest you pay and the interest worked out at an official rate set by the Inland Revenue. But there can be exceptions (see p. 102).

In box 1.19, you should put the cash equivalent (your employer should tell you what this is).

If the loan is for a qualifying purpose (for example, to buy an interest in a partnership) and you are paying interest on the loan, you should claim tax relief in box 15.1 of the basic tax return.

If the loan is eventually written off, you pay tax on the amount written off. Include the amount with the taxable value of any other loans in box 1.19. There is no box 1.20.

Private medical or dental insurance

		Amount
• Private medical or dental insurance	1.21	£

This is taxable only if you earn at the rate of £8,500 a year or more. Enter the taxable amount, which you should find on Form P11D, in box 1.21. For more explanation, see p. 103.

Other benefits

		Amount
• Other benefits	1.22	£

This is a box to sweep up any other taxable perks which you have not already entered elsewhere. Remember, though, that it applies only if you earn at a rate of £8,500 or more. The figures should be shown on your P11D. The main types of benefits you may have to enter here are listed on p. 103.

Expenses payments and balancing charges

		Amount
• Expenses payments received and balancing charges	1.23	£

You should enter here the total expenses payments and expense allowances you received. You can deduct tax-free expense payments later on in boxes 1.32 to 1.35. The only expenses which you should not enter either here or later on are those for which your employer has a dispensation.

Your expenses payments should be shown in your P11D or P9D. In your P11D they will be broken down into the gross amount received, any contributions you made or amounts on which tax has already been deducted, and the taxable amount. Enter the taxable amount in box 1.23.

Balancing charges are not something you will see on your P11D or P9D. They apply only if you claimed capital allowances on something that you bought for your work and that you have now disposed of (see p. 257). You can find further information in Help Sheet *IR206 Capital allowances for employees and office holders*.

LUMP SUMS AND COMPENSATION

Income from employment continued

■ ***Lump sums and compensation payments or benefits including such payments and benefits from a former employer***
Note that 'lump sums' here includes any contributions which your employer made to an unapproved retirement benefits scheme

*You must read page EN6 of the Notes **before** filling in boxes 1.24 to 1.30*

You may have something to enter here if:

- you received a lump sum when you left a job, such as redundancy pay
- you retired and received a lump sum from a non-approved retirement scheme (that is, anything other than an Inland-Revenue approved, foreign government or other statutory pension scheme)
- your employer (or ex-employer) paid you a lump sum which you have not already entered as pay (for example, in box 1.8 or box 1.10).

You will need Help Sheet *IR204 Lump sums and compensation payments* in order to work out what to enter in each of the boxes. It is important to enter the right bit in the right category because each is taxed under different parts of tax legislation. You can get various types of tax relief on some categories, but not on others. One payment might be made up of several different types. They may also affect your overall tax calculation.

• Tax deducted from payments in boxes 1.27 to 1.29 - *leave blank if this tax is included in the box 1.11 figure.*	1.30	Tax deducted £

Your employer may deduct tax from any taxable sums you get before paying you. If so, make sure you enter it in box 1.30, so that it is taken into account when working out your tax bill. But do not put in this box any tax which you have already included in box 1.11.

Payment expected under the terms of your employment

Taxable lump sums		
• From box B of *Help Sheet IR204*	1.27	£

Lump sums that you should enter here include:

- any payment that you receive under the terms and conditions of your contract, or where the expectation that you would get it is firm enough for it to be regarded as part of your contract – for example, a payment based on length of service which it is your employer's established policy to make when a job ends
- payments received in return for your undertaking not to carry out certain actions, sometimes called a restrictive covenant (if not already entered with other pay in box 1.8 or 1.10)
- bonuses on leaving a job (for example, for doing extra work in the period leading up to redundancy). Do not enter redundancy payments themselves in this category – they go in box 1.29, after deducting various reliefs.

All these payments are taxable in full. For tax purposes, they are treated just like the rest of your pay.

Payments from non-approved retirement schemes

• Retirement and death lump sums	**1.26** £

• From box K of *Help Sheet IR204*	**1.28** £

Most pension schemes are approved by the Inland Revenue or statutory schemes, and the lump sums you receive from them are tax-free (within limits). Payments from a non-approved scheme are also tax-free if they:

- arose because of an accident you suffered at work, or
- were funded by a contribution from your employer on which you have already paid tax, or
- arose from your own contributions, or
- came from an overseas scheme, provided further conditions are met. (Ask your tax office about extra-statutory concession *A10 Lump sums paid under overseas pension schemes*.

If you have any tax-free payments, the total should go in box 1.26. Any taxable payments you receive should be entered in box 1.28.

Other payments
Some payments are tax-free altogether if:

- you get them as a result of accident or chronic illness which meant that you couldn't do your job
- 75 per cent of your service in the job was foreign service, or if you worked abroad for least ten out of the last 20 years (and 50 per cent of your time in the job, if longer than 20 years). If you can't meet these conditions, you may still get some relief – see Help Sheet *IR204 Lump sums and compensation payments*.

Enter these payments under reliefs in box 1.25.

• £30,000 exemption	**1.24** £
• Foreign service and disability	**1.25** £

• From box L of *Help Sheet IR204*	**1.29** £

The first £30,000 of the following payments are also tax-free:

- redundancy pay (either statutory or at the employer's discretion)
- pay in lieu of notice which is not included in your terms and conditions of employment
- any other payments on leaving a job which were not part of your terms and conditions, and not 'expected' or received as payment for work done.

Enter the first £30,000 (or total received) under reliefs in box 1.24. Anything over £30,000 is taxable and should be entered in box 1.29. Use *Help Sheet IR204* to help you calculate the exact figure.

FOREIGN EARNINGS

The broad principle of the UK tax system is that you are taxed on foreign earnings if you are resident or ordinarily resident in this country, even if your permanent home (your domicile) is elsewhere. A full explanation of all these terms is included in Chapter 24. If you think you may be able to claim non-residence you should read that chapter first.

You should include foreign earnings in boxes 1.8 to 1.10 (your employer may already have included foreign earnings in your P60). But if you are a UK resident, or a British citizen, a Crown employee or a citizen of some other countries you can claim personal allowances to set against your income. You may also be able to claim deductions in boxes 1.31, 1.37 and 1.38 which make the possibility of tax on foreign earnings a less fearsome prospect.

Foreign earnings not taxable in the UK

■ ***Foreign earnings not taxable in the UK in the year ended 5 April 2003*** *- see Notes, page EN6*	**1.31** £

Depending on your residence status and the place where your duties of employment were carried out, you might not have to pay UK income tax on all your foreign earnings for the year ending 5 April 2003. For example, this might apply if you have included in the Employment Pages earnings which you are prevented from bringing back to the UK by law, because of government action or a shortage of foreign currency in the country concerned. The various situations in which your foreign earnings might be tax-free are complex and you should use the worksheet contained in *Help Sheet IR211 Employment – residence and domicile issues.*

Foreign earnings deduction

■ *Foreign Earnings Deduction* (seafarers only) **1.37** £

The foreign earnings deduction can only be claimed for the tax year ending 5 April 2003 by seafarers. You can get information on this from Help Sheet *IR205 Foreign Earnings Deduction: Seafarers.*

Foreign tax

■ *Foreign tax for which tax credit relief not claimed* **1.38** £

If you work abroad, you may be liable to two lots of tax: tax charged by the country in which you earn the money and UK tax. You have two options for avoiding this double taxation:

- claiming tax credit relief (if you are a UK resident)
- deducting the foreign tax from your foreign earnings.

Because tax credit relief can wipe out all or part of the foreign tax, it is usually the best option, but it is not always available. There are various Inland Revenue working sheets which may help you decide which is the best option for you (see Chapter 21 for more details). If you decide to claim tax credit relief, leave box 1.38 blank and complete the Foreign supplementary page. Otherwise, enter the amount of foreign tax in box 1.38.

EXPENSES INCURRED IN DOING YOUR JOB

■ *Expenses you incurred in doing your job* - *see Notes, pages EN7 to EN8*

You should already have entered all the expenses payments and allowances you received in box 1.23. However, not all these payments will be taxable, and there may be expenses for which you were not reimbursed and on which you can claim tax relief. So you should enter all your tax-allowable expenses, whether or not you were reimbursed, in boxes 1.32 to 1.36.

The only exception is expenses for which your employer has a dispensation (see p. 219). These should not be entered anywhere on your tax return, unless your allowable expenses came to more than the amount covered by the dispensation (in which case you should enter the extra). Your employer should be able to tell you what dispensations exist.

The overall rule is that only those expenses which are expended wholly, exclusively and necessarily in doing your job are allowable, except for travel and related meal and accommodation expenses, which must be necessarily incurred. In both cases, necessarily means that it would be necessary for anybody doing the job, not just necessary for you.

There is no neat list of definitions in tax law, and much depends on previous court judgements. In practice, a lot comes down to agreement with your tax inspector and you should keep all the evidence you have (receipts, mileage details and so on) to back up your claims. However, the main tax-allowable expenses are listed below.

Travel and subsistence costs

• Travel and subsistence costs	**1.32**	£

You can claim tax relief for travel costs, for example fares, you incur making business journeys. If you use your own car, motorcycle or bicycle for work, from 6 April 2002 onwards, any tax and tax relief are based on the Inland Revenue approved payments (see p. 92) not your actual costs. Mileage allowance up to the Inland Revenue approved payment is tax-free and not entered on your tax return. Any excess is taxable and should already have been entered in box 1.15 (see p. 221), but you cannot claim any tax relief on the excess even if your actual costs exceeded the statutory payment. And you cannot claim capital allowances or interest on a loan to buy a vehicle. If you did not get any mileage allowance, or you received less than the approved payment, use box 1.32 to claim the shortfall up to the approved payment (regardless of the actual expenses you incurred). You will need to have kept a record of your business mileage during the year ending 5 April 2003 and any allowance you had from your employer.

A business journey is either:

- travel between one place of work and another required in the performance of your duties (travel 'on the job'), or
- travel to and from a workplace, provided it does not count as ordinary commuting or private travel and attendance at the workplace is a requirement of your duties, not just a matter of personal convenience.

You can't claim for journeys that count as ordinary commuting, defined as travel between your home and your *permanent* workplace – even if the journeys take place at abnormal hours. However, the cost of travelling from home to work following an emergency call-out may be allowed in limited circumstances (eg for NHS employees whose duties of employment commence before starting on the journey).

You can claim for journeys between home and a *temporary* workplace. A workplace counts as temporary if you go there for a limited duration or for a temporary purpose. But it loses its temporary status if you spend at least 40 per cent of your working time there over a period which lasts (or is likely to last) for more than 24 months.

If you have a permanent place of work, you might sometimes travel direct from home to another place where you are required to perform your duties, or travel from that place direct to home. In this situation, you can claim the actual travel expenses you incur unless the journey is not significantly different from the ordinary commuting journey.

If travelling is your job – for example, you are a travelling salesperson or a lorry driver – you might not have any permanent place of work. In that case, journeys from home to the places you visit on business may count as business travel. But if you work in a defined geographical area, any travel from home to the edge of that area, and back again, is ordinary commuting and you cannot claim the costs of that part of your journeys.

If a journey counts as business travel, you can also claim relief for:

- meals and accommodation costs (subsistence) incurred in making the business journey
- other business expenses arising because of the journey, for example telephone costs. You cannot deduct personal expenses, such as phone calls home, daily newspapers and personal laundry – but in practice, you may not have had to include these in box 1.23 in any case, since small amounts of personal expenses are tax-free (see p. 92).

You should ask for and keep receipts for the subsistence and other business expenses you incur to back up your claim.

The rules can be interpreted in a number of different ways depending on the facts of the case. If you are unsure what you can claim, the Inland Revenue guide *490: Employee Travel – a Tax and NICs Guide for Employers* (to which your employer should have access and available from the Inland Revenue website www.inlandrevenue.gov.uk) gives the full rules and useful examples.

Add together all the allowable travel costs incurred, including accommodation and meal costs on business journeys and any other expenses of business journeys (such as business phone calls, but not personal items like phone calls home). Enter the total in box 1.32. If this box includes expenses of travelling between home and a permanent workplace, tick box 1.36.

> **TAX-SAVING IDEA**
>
> If your journey counts as business travel, don't forget to include the cost of any meals and accommodation which are attributable to the journey (other than the usual expenses you incur when at your normal place of work).

Fixed deductions for expenses

• Fixed deductions for expenses	1.33	£

The Inland Revenue has agreed flat-rate expenses with various trade unions and other bodies to cover the costs of providing equipment and special clothing which is not provided by employers. For example, carpenters and joiners in the building trade can claim a flat-rate £105, uniformed bank employees can claim £40. Ask your union or other staff body if you are covered. You do not have to claim the flat-rate deduction – if you spend more, you can claim more, but if so, you should enter the amount in box 1.35, under other expenses, not here.

Professional fees and subscriptions

• Professional fees and subscriptions	1.34	£

You may pay for membership of a particular body or society which is relevant to your work. You can claim it in box 1.34 as an allowable expense provided that:

- membership of the organisation, or registration with it, is a condition of your job, for example, as a dentist, optician or solicitor, or
- the organisation is approved by the Revenue as being a non-profit body which exists for a worthy purpose such as to maintain professional standards, and membership is relevant to your work.

Any such organisation should be able to tell you whether it is on the Revenue's list of approved bodies.

Other expenses and capital allowances

• Other expenses and capital allowances	1.35	£

Other expenses must be wholly, exclusively and necessarily incurred in the performance of your duties. This means that you cannot claim expenses which merely put you in a position to do your job – for example, a journalist's expenditure on newspapers, employment agency fees, childcare. There are special rules for business entertaining – check with your employer whether these affect you. The expenses you should be allowed are:

- the costs of providing and maintaining tools and special clothing which you have not already claimed a fixed deduction for in box 1.33. Special clothing does not cover clothes which you could wear outside work, even if you would never choose to do so
- the cost of special security needed because of your job – you can claim this only if your employer paid for the security or reimbursed you, and you have already entered the appropriate amount as a benefit
- costs and expenses if you are held liable for some wrongful act as an employee, or insurance premiums to cover you against such costs
- training expenses for which you are not reimbursed, providing that your employer requires or encourages you to attend the course and gives you paid time off to do so, it is full-time (or virtually so) and lasts for at least four weeks. The expenses allowed are fees (unless you have already had tax relief on these), the cost of essential books and the full cost of daily travel to and from the course. You can claim any additional costs incurred if you have to stay away from home, provided you still have to meet the costs of maintaining or renting your own home
- if you carry out some or all of the central duties of your job from home and the nature of the job itself requires that such work be done from home, a proportion of the heating and lighting costs, and, for a room used exclusively for work, council tax. You're not allowed to claim these expenses if you simply work from home from choice. Moreover, even if your contract of employment requires you to work from home, these expenses are not allowable if the work could in fact be done elsewhere.

You may also be able to claim capital allowances in this section if you buy equipment such as a computer which is necessary (as defined on p. 229) for your job. You cannot claim an allowance if your employer would have provided the equipment had you not chosen to do so. You used to be able to claim capital allowances on a car or other vehicle you bought to use in your job. But from 6 April 2002 onwards, capital allowances and interest on a loan to buy such a vehicle are already taken into account in the Inland

Revenue approved payments that can be either paid to you by your employer (see p. 221) or claimed by you as an allowable expense (see p. 229).

> **TAX-SAVING IDEA**
>
> For an employee to claim tax relief on expenses related to working from home, the work must be such that any employee doing the job would of necessity have to carry out some or all of the central duties from home. The Inland Revenue has identified some types of employment where that condition is normally met. They are: insurance agent, university lecturer, councillor, examiner, midwife and minister of religion. If your tax office accepts your home as a workplace, you will also be able to claim the cost of travel to and from home on business.

When you finally dispose of an asset on which you claimed capital allowances there may be a balancing charge to add to your taxable income. (See Chapter 18 for how to work these out.)

Student loans

■ *Student Loans repaid by deduction by employer - see Notes, page EN8* **1.39** £

If your income for the year ending 5 April 2003 exceeds £10,000, you are required to start or continue repaying any income contingent student loans (see p. 152). The Inland Revenue will have notified your employer to deduct repayments through PAYE. In some circumstances, the amount deducted might not be the full repayment due for the year. This will be the case where, for example:

- you have more than one job. Each employer will ignore the first £10,000 of your earnings from the job concerned
- you have unearned income of more than £2,000.

Any repayments due but not made through PAYE will now be collected through the self-assessment system. A person who has not received a tax return is not required to pay any more than has already been deducted through PAYE, but can voluntarily pay extra.

For each set of Employment pages you complete, in box 1.39 enter the amount of student loan repayments deducted by your employer as shown on your P60 or pay slips.

SHARE SCHEMES

CHAPTER 17

Q2 Did you have any taxable income from share options, shares or share related benefits in the year? (This does not include
- dividends, or
- dividend shares ceasing to be subject to an Inland Revenue approved share incentive plan within three years of acquisition they go in Question 10.) YES SHARE SCHEMES

Part of your payment from a job may come in the form of shares (or share options – the right to buy shares at a set price at some point in the future) in your employer's company. However, there are special approved schemes under which you can get your shares or options tax-free. You only have to tick the YES box and complete these supplementary pages if your shares or share options are not received through an approved scheme, or if you are in a scheme but breach its rules in some respect. You have to complete pages 2 and 3 of the supplementary pages before page 1, and you need to fill in a separate page 2 and/or page 3 (or a photocopy) for each taxable event arising from a share scheme.

The benefit you get from share schemes may come in the following forms:

- a gift of the shares themselves, or a discount on the purchase price
- an option to buy a set number of shares, at a set price, at a particular time in the future
- dividends from the shares once they become your property
- a capital gain (or loss) arising from movements in the share price once the shares become your property.

The share dividends are taxed like the dividends from any share you own and you enter them at Q10 of the basic tax return (see Chapter 13). Similarly, the shares are generally subject to the normal capital gains tax rules (see Chapter 10). However, recent changes to the rules mean that most employee shares benefit from a high level of tax relief even if you hold them for only a couple a years. This makes shares schemes a particularly attractive way of acquiring shares. You give details of capital gains on the Capital gains supplementary pages. The Share scheme supplementary pages apply only on the gift (or discounted purchase) of the shares themselves, or an option to buy them, and to any associated advantages. Occasionally, with some unapproved schemes, they may also apply when you sell the shares themselves.

DIFFERENT TYPES OF SHARE SCHEMES

For tax purposes, share schemes fall within four broad categories:

- approved profit-sharing schemes
- share option schemes – either approved savings-related schemes or discretionary share option schemes (that is, company share option plans and executive share option schemes), enterprise management incentive options or unapproved schemes
- approved share incentive plan (formerly called the all-employee share ownership plan)
- cheap or free gifts of shares through an unapproved scheme (sometimes called share incentive schemes).

You may have come across Employee Share Ownership Trusts (ESOTs) – these are a special type of trust set up to acquire shares in the company and distribute them to employees. For the employee, the shares are taxable in the same way as shares received through an unapproved scheme (see p. 247).

If you received shares or share options which are taxable in the tax year ending 5 April 2003, you will need to declare them on the Share schemes supplementary pages, unless they have already been taxed under PAYE or have been included on Form P11D. If under PAYE, you should put the taxable value of the benefit in box 1.8 of the Employment page, and the tax in box 1.11. If on Form P11D, the taxable value goes in box 1.22.

> **TAX-SAVING IDEA**
>
> As an employee, you do not often have a choice of scheme, since employers are likely either to have just one scheme, or to have one scheme that is open to all employees and another which is open to a select few. But if you know that your employer is considering a scheme, try to make your voice heard so that the scheme which is chosen is one which suits you.

The documents you need

You should have some correspondence from your employer concerning your scheme, including (where relevant) a share option certificate and a copy of the exercise note. You will also need to know the market price of the shares at various dates – if your employer cannot help, ask your local reference library.

If the company is not quoted on a recognised stock exchange, the market value has to be agreed with the Inland Revenue.

Approved profit-sharing schemes

These are a way of transferring free shares in a company to its employees via a special trust. As long as you stick to the rules, shares you receive under an approved profit-sharing scheme will be tax-free and you will not need to enter them on the Share scheme pages.

The shares will be taxable only if you sell them within three years of being allocated them. However, there is an exception if the shares are sold before the three years are up and the job ended because of an injury, disability, redundancy or death or reaching a specified age (between 60 and 75). In this case, tax is due on only 50 per cent of the market value of the shares when allocated.

Approved profit-sharing schemes are being phased out. No new shares could be allocated after 31 December 2002. If during the year ending 5 April 2003, you were allocated free shares from a share incentive plan (see p. 244) – or would have been if you had met any performance target conditions – and later received shares from an approved profit-sharing scheme run by the same employer, the profit-sharing scheme loses its approval and the shares are taxed according to the rules for an unapproved share scheme (see p. 247).

Working out the tax

If tax is due, the taxable value is the lesser of:

- the initial market value of the shares at the date when they were allocated to you (occasionally, an earlier date may be used), or
- the actual proceeds of selling them, minus your expenses of selling, for example, stockbrokers' commission. If you give them away, the market value at the time of the gift will be used.

Your employer should work out the taxable value for you and deduct the right amount of tax before passing on the proceeds. If you have left the company, the trustees will work out

> **TAX-SAVING IDEA**
>
> When you take your shares out of an approved profit-sharing scheme, savings-related share option scheme or approved share incentive plan, you can transfer them into an ISA (see p. 81), providing you do so within 90 days. From 6 April 2001 onwards, shares from any of these schemes may also be transferred within 90 days to a personal pension, including a stakeholder scheme (see p. 73). Both personal pensions and ISAs ensure that future growth in the value of your shares is free of capital gains tax and that part or all of any income from them is free of income tax.

the taxable value and deduct basic-rate tax: enter the taxable amount at box 1.8 and the amount deducted at box 1.11 in the Employment supplementary page. For more information, see Inland Revenue leaflet *IR95 Approved profit sharing schemes – an outline for employees.*

Share option schemes

For tax purposes, there are three key events in the life of an option:

- when you are first granted the option. If you receive the option through an approved scheme, there is never any tax to pay on the grant of the option. But there could be a tax bill in the case of an unapproved scheme
- when you exercise your right to buy the shares. You have to pay tax on the exercise only if you fail to meet various conditions. You don't have to exercise the option and there is no tax if you just let it lapse
- if you cancel the option in return for some benefit. There is always tax to pay in this event.

To work out the taxable amount (if any), you need to keep records of:

- the date on which each key event takes place
- the number of shares involved
- the share price – both the price you actually have to pay, and the market value at the time of each event
- any cash you contributed for the option, or any cash (or other benefit) you received for cancelling it.

You have to give this information on page 2 of the Share schemes supplementary pages for each occasion on which your options are taxable (photocopy the form if necessary or ask the Orderline – see p. 147 – for extra copies).

Approved savings-related share options

Share options

*Read the Notes on pages SN1 to SN8 **before** filling in the boxes*

■ ***Approved savings-related share options***

	Name of company and share scheme	Tick if shares unlisted	Taxable amount
• Exercise	2.1	2.2	2.3 £
• Cancellation or release	2.4	2.5	2.6 £

These schemes give you the right (or 'option') to buy a set number of ordinary shares in your employer's company at some point in the future, at a price fixed now, but you must do so using savings you build up in a Save-As-You-Earn (SAYE) plan. If you meet the various conditions laid down by the

Revenue, you will get your shares tax-free (see Inland Revenue leaflet *IR97 Approved SAYE share option schemes – an outline for employees*).

Among other conditions you must agree to:

- save a set amount each month, with a minimum of £5 a month and a maximum of £250
- save for a set period – three or five years. Five-year contracts may give you the option of leaving your money invested until the seventh anniversary.

> **TAX-SAVING IDEA**
>
> Whether or not you will benefit from a savings-related share option scheme depends on the option price and the share price when you exercise your option.
>
> You do not have to exercise your option if you would make a loss and the return on SAYE schemes is tax-free. So if you are a higher rate tax-payer, or are optimistic that you will make some profit on the shares, joining the scheme is worthwhile.

The price of the shares (the subscription price) is fixed when you are granted the option, but cannot normally be less than 80 per cent of their market value at that time (or up to 30 days before). So if, for example, shares in Horridges' plc stand at 400 pence, the lowest subscription price is 320 pence. You have no tax to pay when the option is granted to you. You will not have tax to pay when the option is exercised unless:

- you exercise your option when your company is taken over or sold, and you have not yet held it for three years. In this case, fill in the Options exercised column on page 2 of the Share schemes supplementary page (boxes 2.45 to 2.49 and 2.51) and carry the taxable amount to box 2.3 on page 1 (see opposite for the calculation)
- you benefit from the option in any way other than using it to buy shares – for example, if you receive compensation for not using or agreeing not to use your option. Fill in the Options cancelled/released column on page 2 (boxes 2.45, 2.49 and 2.52) and then carry the taxable amount to box 2.6 on page 1.

Approved discretionary share options

Discretionary schemes may be restricted to groups of employees. Their original name was executive share option schemes, replaced in 1995 by company share option schemes. Broadly, options received under both these schemes are tax-free as long as you exercise them within strict time limits (see below).

■ ***Approved discretionary share options***

	Name of company and share scheme		
• Exercise	2.7	2.8	2.9 £
• Cancellation or release	2.10	2.11	2.12 £

Unlike savings-related share option schemes, the price at which you can buy the shares under your option must not be less than the market value of the shares when the option is granted (or up to 30 days before). However, you may have been granted a discount of up to 15 per cent of the market value if you:

- were granted options in an executive share option scheme after 1 January 1992 and before 17 July 1995, and
- your company already had an approved savings-related share option scheme or approved profit-sharing scheme.

If you did receive a discounted option after those dates, this becomes an unapproved share option (see p. 243).

TAX ON THE EXERCISE OF AN OPTION

Step 1: take the market value of the share at the date the option was exercised (which you should have entered in box 2.51) and multiply by the number of shares you actually bought (entered at box 2.47). This gives you the market value of all the shares you have bought.

Step 2: take the price at which you exercised the option (in box 2.48) and multiply by the number of shares you bought (at box 2.47). This is the actual price.

Step 3: deduct the actual price (at Step 2) from the market value (at Step 1). If you paid anything for the option (box 2.49), you can deduct that too. The result is the taxable amount to enter on page 1 of the Share schemes supplementary page in box 2.3, 2.9, 2.15 or 2.24 as appropriate.

The grant of an option

This is taxable only for an unapproved share option which can be exercised more than ten years after it was granted. The method is the same as if you were exercising the option, except that you start with the market value at the time the option is granted. Fill in the Options granted column on page 2 of the Share schemes supplementary page and carry the taxable amount to box 2.21 on page 1.

The cancellation of an option

If you get anything in return for not exercising your option, the taxable amount is what you received, less anything you paid for your option. Fill in the Options cancelled/released column on page 2, and box 2.6, 2.12, 2.18 or 2.27.

You only have to pay tax on other options if:

- you give up the right to exercise the option in return for some benefit, or
- the scheme had ceased to be approved by the time you exercised your options, or
- you exercise the option within three years of being granted it, or
- you exercise the option more than 10 years after being granted it, or
- it is less than three years since you last exercised an option under *any* executive share option scheme or company share option scheme (other than SAYE).

TAX-SAVING IDEA

If you are granted options in an approved share option scheme, keep records of when you exercise them, and the dates by which you can next do so. For example, if you are granted options in 1993, you must exercise them by 2003 to avoid tax; if you exercised part of your options in 2000, you cannot exercise any more until 2003 without paying tax.

If the first point applies, fill in the Options cancelled/released column on page 2 of the Share schemes supplementary page (boxes 2.45, 2.49 and 2.52) and then fill in boxes 2.10 to 2.12 on page 1. If any of the other conditions apply, fill in the Options exercised column on page 2 (boxes 2.45 to 2.51) and then fill in boxes 2.7 to 2.9 on page 1.

WARNING

If there is a tax charge to pay when you exercise an option, it is based on the market value of the shares at that time. The tax charge will not be reduced if the value of the shares subsequently falls. Make sure you set aside enough money to pay the tax bill. This may mean selling some of the shares as soon as you get them. If you plan to sell shares later to meet the tax bill, you are gambling that the share price will not fall in the meantime.

Enterprise management incentive options

This scheme, available since 28 July 2000, is designed to help small high-risk firms recruit and retain key employees. In the year ending 5 April 2003, independent trading companies with assets of no more than £30 million (£15 million before 1 January 2002) that qualify for the scheme can offer share options to any number of employees. The maximum value of shares subject to unexercised options outstanding at any time is £3 million. The shares may be quoted or unquoted. The option must be capable of being exercised within 10 years. Each employee can hold a maximum of £100,000 of unexercised options in total. (In the case of several different options, the value of each one is based on the share price on the date it was granted.)

■ ***Enterprise Management Incentive options***

	Name of company and unique option reference		
• Exercise	2.13	2.14	2.15 £
• Cancellation or release	2.16	2.17	2.18 £

To be an eligible employee, you must work for the company at least 25 hours a week or, if less, at least 75 per cent of your total work time, and you must control no more than 30 per cent of the company's ordinary share capital.

There is no income tax to pay when an option is granted. There is also no income tax to pay when you exercise an option unless:

> **TAX-SAVING IDEA**
>
> If you acquire shares on or after 6 April 2002 on the same day from more than one share scheme, if you later dispose of some of them, you can elect to have the shares from each scheme treated separately and the disposal matched to the shares that show the smallest capital gain (see p. 127).

- it was a discounted option – in other words, the price you paid for the shares was less than the market value of the shares at the time the option was granted; or
- a disqualifying event took place and you failed to exercise the option within the 40 days following the event.

If neither of these situations applies, you do not need to give any information on the Share scheme pages about your options under the scheme.

For a discounted option, complete boxes 2.55, 2.57 to 2.60 and 2.62 in the Options exercised column on page 2 and also boxes 2.13 to 2.15 on page 1.

If a disqualifying event occurred more than 40 days before you exercised the option, complete boxes 2.55 to 2.59, 2.61 and 2.62 in the Options exercised column on page 2 as well as boxes 2.13 to 2.15 on page 1.

If the option was both discounted and affected by a disqualifying event more than 40 days before exercise, complete all the boxes 2.55 to 2.62 in the Options exercised column on page 2 as well as boxes 2.13 to 2.15 on page 1.

Your employer should be able to tell you if a disqualifying event has taken place. Disqualifying events are:

- the company becomes a 51 per cent subsidiary of another company or, in some other way, comes under the control of another company. This is not a disqualifying event if, within six months of the takeover, your original

EXAMPLE

In August 2002, under an enterprise management incentive scheme, Sam Wright is granted an option over 50,000 shares priced at £1 each at the time the option is granted. It gives him the right to buy the shares at 75p each when he exercises the option at any time up to July 2012. There is no tax to pay when the option is granted.

In December 2002, when the shares are priced at £1.50 each, the company ceases to qualify as a trading company, having moved into insurance business. Sam exercises his option in March 2003, when the share price has reached £2. Income tax is due when the option is exercised because it is a discounted option and because a 'disqualifying event' took place more than 40 days earlier. The taxable amount is worked out in two stages.

First, Sam must calculate the taxable amount resulting from the discount. The market value of the shares in August 2002 when the option was granted was 50,000 × £1 = £50,000. The price he paid for the shares in March 2003 was 50,000 × 75p = £37,500. Therefore gain from the discount is £50,000 − £37,500 = £12,500. But Sam has agreed to pay the employer's National Insurance of 11.8% × £12,500 = £1,475 in respect of this gain, so the net amount on which income tax is due is £12,500 − £1,475 = £11,025.

Next, Sam must work out the taxable amount triggered by the disqualifying event. The market value of the shares in March 2003 when Sam exercise the option is 50,000 × £2 = £100,000. From this, Sam deducts the market value of the shares in December 2002 when the company was taken over (50,000 × £1.50 = £75,000). This gives a gain since the disqualifying event of £100,000 × £75,000 = £25,000. Sam can deduct the employer's National Insurance he has paid in respect of this amount (11.8% × £25,000 = £2,950) leaving a net amount on which tax is due of £25,000 − £2,950 = £22,050.

The total taxable amount that Sam enters in box 2.15 is £11,025 + £22,050 = £33,075. Sam is a higher rate taxpayer, so pays income tax of 40% × £33,075 = £13,230 as a result of exercising his option. In addition he has paid £1,475 + £2,950 = £4,425 in employer's National Insurance contributions. (Sam's income was already above the threshold at which employee's National Insurance contributions cease.)

option is replaced by an equivalent option over shares in the new company

- the company ceases to count as a trading company under the scheme rules (Some 'low risk' trades are in any case excluded – for example, dealing in land or shares, banking, insurance, farming, market gardening, managing woodlands, running hotels, nursing homes or residential care homes, and so on)
- the company had been preparing to become a trading company but this failed to materialise within two years of the option being granted
- you stop working for the company

- you no longer work 25 hours or more (or 75 per cent or more of your time) for the company
- the option is altered so that the market value of the option shares increases or the option ceases to meet the rules for the scheme
- the share capital of the company is altered without prior approval from the Inland Revenue
- shares to which the option relates are converted to shares of a different class, unless all the shares of one class are converted to shares of one other class and certain other conditions are met
- relating to your employment with the same company, you are granted an option under an approved company share option plan (see p. 238) and together with your enterprise management incentive options this takes your holding of unexercised options above £100,000.

Unapproved share options

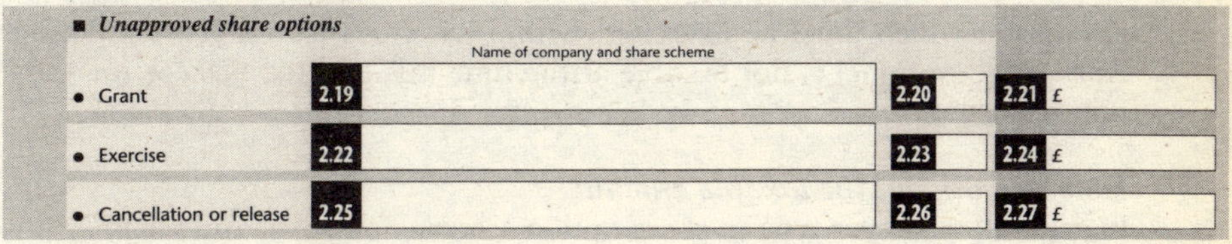

■ *Unapproved share options*

	Name of company and share scheme		
• Grant	2.19	2.20	2.21 £
• Exercise	2.22	2.23	2.24 £
• Cancellation or release	2.25	2.26	2.27 £

> **TAX-SAVING IDEA**
> Beware of accepting a long option at a discounted price if you think there is a strong risk that the share price will fall. You will have tax to pay now, even though you are unlikely to benefit from the option.

With unapproved schemes, income tax may be payable on both the grant and exercise of an option, or if it is given up in return for some benefit. However, there is no income tax to pay if the option is exercised by your legal representatives after your death, or if the option is not a long option.

A long option is one which can be exercised more than 10 years (seven years if you got the options before 6 April 1998) after the date on which it was granted. You pay tax at the time it is granted on the market value of the shares at that time, less the price at which you can exercise the option, less anything you pay for the option. So there will be no tax to pay if the option is to buy shares at the market value at the time the option was granted. You may have further tax to pay when you finally exercise the option, but you can set against the tax due then any income tax you paid when the option was granted. You can also deduct any employer's National Insurance on the gain that you've voluntarily agreed to pay (see next page).

> **EXAMPLE**
>
> In 1994 Edward Brough was granted an option which can be exercised at any time between 1 January 1999 and 1 January 2004. This counts as a long option, so he had to pay tax when it was granted. The market value of the shares in 1994 was £3. Edward has the option to buy 1,000 shares at £2. The market value of the shares over which he has the option was £3 × 1,000 = £3,000: he has the option to buy them at £2 × 1,000 = £2,000. The taxable amount was £3,000 – £2,000 = £1,000. As a higher-rate taxpayer, Edward paid £1,000 × 40 per cent = £400 tax on this.
>
> In October 2002 Edward exercised his option. This cost him £2 × 1,000 = £2,000. Since the market price had risen to £3.50, the market value of the shares was £3.50 × 1,000 = £3,500. The taxable amount is £3,500 – £2,000 = £1,500, incurring tax at £1,500 × 40 per cent = £600. However, Edward can set against this the tax he has already paid, so he only actually has to pay £600 – £400 = £200.

An option which must be exercised within ten years (seven years for pre-6 April 1998 options) is not taxable at the time it is granted (except for some non-residents).

How to work out the taxable amount

In general, whatever type of share option scheme you have, and whether it is approved or unapproved, if the event (the grant, exercise or cancellation) is taxable, the amount is worked out as in the box on p. 239. You enter the amounts in the right-hand column of page 1 headed Taxable amount.

Slightly different rules apply if you have voluntarily agreed to pay any employer's National Insurance contributions on the gain. When you exercise the option, your employer (and you) could be liable for National Insurance contributions. The amount due will depend on the share price at the time of exercise which can't be predicted in advance. To save a company facing a large and unpredictable tax bill at some unknown future date, the company is allowed to make an agreement with you so that you pay the employer's National Insurance contributions (as well as any employee's National Insurance due) when you exercise the option. You can deduct any employer's (but not employee's) National Insurance you pay in this way when working out the amount of income tax due.

Approved share incentive plans

Approved share incentive plans (formerly called all-employee share ownership plans) have been available since 28 July 2000. Their aim is to give you a continuing stake in the company you work for. You can acquire shares in up to four different ways:

Approved Share Incentive Plans

Read the Notes on page SN2 ***before*** *filling in the boxes*

column, as appropriate, and make sure you fill in boxes 2.40 and 2.42

	Name of company and share plan		
• Shares ceasing to be subject to the plan	2.28	2.29	2.30 £

- **free shares** – you can be awarded up to £3,000 of free shares each tax year. The award can be conditional on performance, length of service, and so on. You must normally keep the shares within the plan for a minimum holding period which can be no less than three years and no more than five years
- **partnership shares** – you can ask your employer to deduct regular sums from your pay with which to buy shares in the company. The maximum deduction is £125 a month (or its equivalent) and total deductions must come to no more than 10 per cent of your pay. The plan can set a minimum deduction but this must be no more than £10 a month. You can withdraw these shares from the plan at any time but this may trigger a tax charge (see below)
- **matching shares** – your employer can decide to award you up to two matching shares for every partnership share you buy. You must normally keep the matching shares within the plan for a minimum holding period which can be no less than three years and no more than five years
- **dividend shares** – you can opt to have cash dividends paid on any of the above shares reinvested to buy more shares. The maximum value of dividend shares you can buy in any year is £1,500. You must leave dividend shares within the plan for at least three years.

There is no tax to pay when any of these shares are acquired. You get tax relief through PAYE on any amount used to buy partnership shares. There is

EXAMPLE

In December 2002, Lynne Harper was awarded 100 free shares in her employer's company, Treats plc, through its share incentive plan. Over the period September 2002 to February 2003, Lynne has also had £20 a month deducted from her pay to buy partnership shares in Treats plc. By February, 6 × £20 = £120 has been deducted and she has bought 24 partnership shares. As Lynne is a basic rate taxpayer, she gets tax relief of £4.40 on each £20 deduction, reducing the cost to her of £120-worth of shares to just £120 − (6 × £4.40) = £93.60.

In February 2003, Lynne takes a better job with another company. As she is leaving Treats plc, her shares cease to be subject to the share incentive plan and tax may now be due. Including the free shares, she has 124 shares in all. The share price stands at £5.50. The taxable value of the shares is 124 × £5.50 = £682. Basic rate tax on this comes to 22% × £682 = £150.04.

also no income tax due if you leave shares within the plan for at least five years (three years in the case of dividend shares).

An income tax bill will only arise and you only need to give details on the Share scheme pages if any free shares, partnership shares or matching shares cease to be subject to the plan (for example, on your changing job) within five years of them being awarded to you or bought by you, and the reason they ceased was **not** due to your leaving employment because of:

- injury or disability
- redundancy
- a job transfer covered by the Transfer of Undertakings (Protection of Employment) Regulations 1981
- transfer or sale of the company out of a group running the plan
- retirement on or after an age specified in the plan (50 or above)
- death.

If the situation above has occurred and none of the exemptions listed apply, give details in boxes 2.64 to 2.68 on page 3 and boxes 2.28 to 2.30 on page 1.

There may also be income tax to pay if any dividend shares cease to be subject to the plan within three years of the date you bought them and none of the reasons listed above applies. In this case, you should enter the amount of cash dividend used to buy the shares in boxes 10.15 to 10.17 of the main tax return (see p. 165).

If you have already paid through PAYE any tax due on free shares, partnership shares, matching shares or dividend shares ceasing to be subject to the plan, enter the amount in box 2.41 on page 1 of the Share scheme supplement.

For more information, ask the Orderline (see p. 147) for Help Sheet *IR2002 Share incentive plans: a guide for employees*.

How to work out the taxable amount

Where free shares, partnership shares or matching shares cease to be subject to the plan within three years of being granted or bought, the taxable amount is the market value of the shares at the time they leave the plan.

Where free or matching shares cease to be subject to the plan after three years but within five years of being granted or bought, the taxable amount is the lower of the market value at the time they leave the plan and their market value at the time they were awarded to you.

Where partnership shares cease to be subject to the plan after three years but within five years of being granted or bought, the taxable amount is the lower of the market value at the time they leave the plan and the total deductions in pay used to buy them.

Free or cheap shares through an unapproved scheme

Employers have many reasons for offering cheap or free shares. These count as part of your payment from the job. The exact tax treatment depends on whether the shares are counted as your earnings (and entered under Shares acquired from your employment in boxes 2.31 to 2.33), or treated as a fringe benefit (and entered under Shares as benefits in boxes 2.34 to 2.36), unless these have already been shown under Earnings from employment.

The distinction is fine, but significant: whereas with shares which count as earnings you are taxed on the difference between the market value of the shares and the price at which you acquired them, with shares which count as benefits you are taxed as if you received an interest-free loan from your employer (see p. 102). In some circumstances, this may mean no tax to pay.

You should enter under Shares as benefits (see opposite):

- shares you are allowed to pay for in instalments (partly-paid shares)
- shares which you buy but where part of the purchase price is deferred, for example, when a particular profit target is met
- any other exceptional cases in which cheap or free shares do not count as earnings.

All other free or cheap shares should go under Shares acquired from your employment (see below). Even after you have acquired the shares, you may be considered to receive further taxable benefits from them, for example, an increase in their value when a restriction is lifted. You should enter these under Post-acquisition charges in boxes 2.37 to 2.39.

Shares acquired from your employment

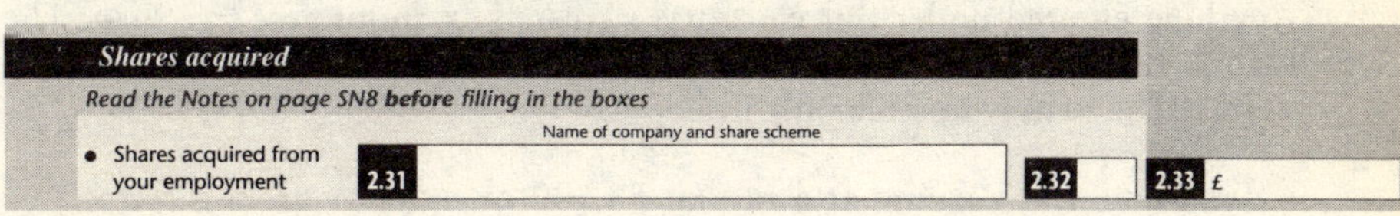
Shares acquired

Read the Notes on page SN8 ***before*** *filling in the boxes*

Name of company and share scheme

- Shares acquired from your employment 2.31 | 2.32 | 2.33 £

You may get some benefit tax-free if the company for which you work decides to sell shares to the public and offers shares on special terms to its employees. You have to distinguish between:

- a discounted price offered to employees
- a priority allocation of the shares.

The discounted price is taxable: you pay tax on the difference between the price you pay and that paid by the general public. Enter the taxable amount under Shares acquired from your employment.

The calculation is very straightforward. Take the market value of the shares at the time you acquired them. Deduct anything you paid for them. The result is the taxable amount. The benefit of the priority allocation itself is tax-free and need not be entered unless:

- it is reserved for directors or higher-paid employees, or those who are entitled to it do not all get it on similar terms, and
- the shares reserved for employees in their priority allocation are more than a certain percentage of the overall shares on offer – normally, more than 10 per cent of the total shares on offer.

EXAMPLE

Linden works for Good Holdings, which has just been offered for sale to the public. Using the priority allocation for employees, Linden bought 500 £1 shares, at the discounted staff price of 80p. Linden is not taxed on the benefit of the priority allocation. However, the discounted price is taxable. The market value of the 500 shares was £1 × 500 = £500, but Linden only paid 80p × 500 = £400. She is taxed on £500 – £400 = £100.

Shares as benefits

• Shares as benefits	2.34	2.35	2.36 £

Anything entered under this category is treated as an interest-free loan. The loan is the difference between what you paid and the market value of the shares. The loan is taxable only if:

- you count as earning at a rate of £8,500 or more or are a director (see p. 94 for how this is worked out)
- the total amount of all the cheap or interest-free loans from your employer outstanding in the tax year comes to more than £5,000 (see p. 102).

If tax is payable, it will be spread out over the whole life of the deemed loan.

The taxable value of the loan is the theoretical interest you would have paid had you been charged interest at an official rate set down by the government.

Post-acquisition charges or lifting of risk of forfeiture

• Post-acquisition charges or lifting of risk of forfeiture	2.37	2.38	2.39 £

You are charged tax on any further benefit from cheap or free shares. This applies even if you have since left the company. There is no charge if the shares were on offer to the public generally (and you did not buy them through a special offer for employees). Otherwise, you may have further tax to pay on:

- an increase in value when rights or restrictions attached to the shares are changed – for example, if you gain the right to dividends
- an increase in value if the shares are in a dependent subsidiary company
- other benefits reserved only for insiders (that is, which are not available to at least 90 per cent of all the shareholders), such as bonus or rights issues of shares, cash, vouchers or tokens
- gains on conversion of shares.

You need to enter these in boxes 2.37 to 2.39 on page 1 of the Share schemes supplementary page, giving the details on page 3.

There are also certain circumstances when you may be taxed if you receive shares which can become forfeit if certain conditions are not met. Ask the Orderline for Help Sheet *IR217 Shares acquired: post-acquisition charges*.

BUDGET 2003

In Budget 2003, several changes to employee shares schemes were announced to take effect from Budget Day, 9 April 2003. See p. 33 for details.

SELF-EMPLOYMENT

CHAPTER 18

Q3	Were you self-employed (but not in partnership)? (You should also tick 'Yes' if you were a Name at Lloyd's.)	YES	SELF-EMPLOYMENT

If any of your income for the tax year ending 5 April 2003 came from running your own business as a self-employed person, answer YES to Q3 on the basic tax return. You'll need to fill in a separate set of Self-employment supplementary pages for each business you have.

Self-employed people are able to claim more income tax reliefs than employed people and they usually pay less in National Insurance, so you might need to prove to your tax office that you really are self-employed. In general, you'll count as self-employed provided you can answer yes to all of the following questions:

- do you control how your business is run? For example, do you decide what work you take on, where you do the work, what hours you keep?
- is your own money at risk in the business? For example, have you had to pay for your own premises, do you have to finance the lag between incurring costs and receiving payments?
- do you have to meet any losses as well as keeping any profits?
- do you provide the major equipment necessary for your work – for example computer and photocopier for office-based work or machinery for an engineering business? It's not enough that you provide your own small tools – many employees do this too
- are you free to employ other people to help you fulfil the contracts you take on? Do you pay your employees yourself?
- if a job doesn't come up to scratch, do you have to redo it or correct it in your own time and at your expense?

Usually, it will be obvious whether you are an employee or self-employed. But sometimes it's not so clear – for example, if you are newly in business doing work for just one client, perhaps working at a former employer's premises on a freelance basis. Beware if you work through an agency – for example as an agency carer or temporary secretary. Even if you choose whether or not to take on a particular job, you will almost certainly count as an employee rather than self-employed.

> **TAX-SAVING IDEA**
> As a self-employed person, you can claim more tax reliefs than an employee. However, you may be able to save even more tax by running your business as a company rather than as a self-employed person – see p. 280.

If you pay tax and National Insurance as if you are self-employed, but later your tax office decides you are really an employee, you could face a large bill for back taxes, so it is important to get your status straight right from the start. If you're in any doubt, you can ask your tax office for a written decision about your employment status. If you don't agree with the decision, you can appeal.

BUSINESS DETAILS

Business details

Name of business
3.1

Description of business
3.2

Address of business
3.3

- Tick box 3.6 if details in boxes 3.1 or 3.3 have changed since your last Tax Return
3.6

The first part of the supplement simply deals with basic details – the name and nature of your business and the address from which you trade.

Your accounting year

Accounting period - *read the Notes, page SEN2 before filling in these boxes*

Start
3.4 / /

End
3.5 / /

You also need to give the start and finish dates of the accounting period for which you are giving details. Normally, an accounting period is a year long, with the new accounting year starting immediately the previous year ends. But in the first and last year or two of your business, or if you change your accounting date, your accounting year might be longer or shorter (see below).

If you are a foster carer or adult carer, you may have an arrangement with the

Inland Revenue for working out your taxable profits in a special way. If so, you need only complete boxes 3.1 to 3.13, 3.92 and 3.94 to 3.96. You leave the other boxes blank, unless your tax office advises otherwise. Similarly, if you carry on your business completely overseas and think you should be taxed only on the remittance basis because of your residence status, fill in only boxes 3.1 to 3.13, 3.74, 3.75, 3.92, 3.93 and tick box 3.94. You also need to complete the Non-residence supplement (see p. 329). In either case, tick box 3.9, so the Inland Revenue knows why boxes have been left blank.

You may already have given information about your latest set of accounts in last year's return (for example, if your accounting periods overlap). If so, you do not need to give all the information again: you can leave boxes 3.14 to 3.73 and 3.99 to 3.115 blank, but tick box 3.10 (see below). Similarly, if your accounts do not run from the last accounting date, explain why in the Additional information box and tick box 3.11 (see below).

- Tick box 3.6 if details in boxes 3.1 or 3.3 have changed since your last Tax Return **3.6**
- Date of commencement if after 5 April 2000 **3.7** / /
- Date of cessation if before 6 April 2003 **3.8** / /
- Tick box 3.9 if the special arrangements for certain trades apply - *read the Notes, pages SEN11 and SEN12* **3.9**
- Tick box 3.10 if you entered details for all relevant accounting periods on last year's Tax Return and boxes 3.14 to 3.73 and 3.99 to 3.115 will be blank *(read Step 3 on page SEN2)* **3.10**
- Tick box 3.11 if your accounts do not cover the period from the last accounting date (explain why in the 'Additional information' box, box 3.116) **3.11**
- Tick box 3.12 if your accounting date has changed (only if this is a permanent change and you want it to count for tax) **3.12**
- Tick box 3.13 if this is the second or further change (explain in box 3.116 on Page SE4 why you have not used the same date as last year) **3.13**

What profits are taxed

This first section of the Self-employment pages establishes which profits form the basis of your tax bill for the year ending 5 April 2003, and what information you need to give the Revenue about them. In most cases, your tax bill for the year ending 5 April 2003 will be based on the profits you make during the accounting period which ended during that tax year (the current year basis). However, there are special rules if you are in the opening or closing years of the business or, have changed your accounting date.

STARTING OR CLOSING A BUSINESS

If you become self-employed and liable to pay Class 2 National Insurance contributions on or after 31 January 2002, you must register with the Inland Revenue within three months of the end of the month you started in business. There is a £100 penalty for failing to do so. You can register by calling a helpline for the newly self-employed on 08459 154515 or by completing form CWF1 in the back of Inland Revenue leaflet *P/SE/1: Thinking of working for yourself?*. Registration ensures that arrangements are made for you to pay the National Insurance contributions (see p. 278) and that you will be sent a tax return at the appropriate time. You can also register for VAT (see p. 264).

The penalty is waived if you can show that your profits are less than £4,095 a year or the pro-rata equivalent in the year ending 5 April 2004 (£4,025 in the year ending 5 April 2003).

You must register – and incur the penalty if you don't – even if you are also an employee and pay enough Class 1 contributions not to have to make any Class 2 payments. Ask to defer the Class 2 contributions (see p. 279).

If you do not register, under separate rules you must tell your tax office within six months of the end of the tax year (ie by the following 5 October) if you have any profits on which income tax is due.

When you start a business, special rules say how you will be taxed in the first two or three years.

First tax year during which you're in business
You are taxed on your profits from the date your business started to the end of the tax year (that is the following 5 April). This is worked out by waiting until your first set of accounts is drawn up and then allocating a proportion of those profits to the period up to the end of the tax year. This is usually done on the basis of days, but weeks, months or fractions of a year are also acceptable. For example, suppose you started in business on 1 January 2003 and your first accounting period runs to 31 January 2004. Out of that first 396-day accounting period, 95 days fall between 1 January to 5 April, so your profits for the tax year ending 5 April 2003 are deemed to be $^{95}/_{396}$ths of the profit for the whole accounting period.

Second tax year during which you're in business
In most cases, the end of an accounting period (not necessarily your first) will fall sometime during this second tax year. Provided you have been trading for at least 12 months, your tax bill will be based on profits for the 12 months up to that date. In the example above, there is an end accounting date falling within the tax year ending 5 April 2004. This is 31 January 2004 and, at that date, the business has been running for more than a year. Therefore, tax will be based on profits for the 12 months up to 31 January 2003 – that is $^{365}/_{396}$ths of the profits for the whole accounting period.

If there is an accounting date within the tax year, but you have been trading for less than 12 months, your tax is based on the first 12 months of trading, with a proportion of the profits from your next accounting period being used to make up the full 12 months. For example, suppose you started in business on 1 March 2002 and draw up your accounts to 30 June 2002 and then to each subsequent 30 June. Tax in your second year, the year ending 5 April 2003, would be based on the whole of the profits for the period 1 March to 30 June 2002 (122 days) and $^{243}/_{365}$ths of the profits for the accounting year from 1 July 2002 to 30 June 2003.

If there is no accounting date at all during your second tax year, tax is based on the profits for the tax year itself – that is from 6 April to 5 April. For example, if you started in business on 1 March 2002 but did not draw up your first accounts until 30 June 2003, an accounting period of 487 days, you would be taxed on $^{365}/_{487}$ths of the profits for that whole period.

Third tax year during which you're in business

Normally, an accounting period at least 12 months after you started up finishes during your second tax year. From the third year onwards, you are simply taxed on the profits for the accounting year ending during the tax year – that is normal current year basis.

Where unusually the first accounting period to end at least 12 months after start-up comes to a close in your third tax year of trading, you are taxed on profits for the 12 months to the end of that period. From the fourth year onwards, you are taxed on the normal current year basis.

Overlap profits

As you can see, the opening year rules described above mean that some profits may be taxed twice. For example, for the business which started on 1 January 2003, the profits for the first two years were as follows:

Tax year	*Profits on which your tax bill is based*
Year ending 5 April 2003	$^{95}/_{396}$ths × profit for accounting period from 1 January 2003 to 31 January 2004
Year ending 5 April 2004	$^{365}/_{396}$ths × profit for the period from 1 January 2003 to 31 January 2004

This means that (95 + 365) − 396 = 64 days' worth of profit have been taxed twice. This is called 'overlap profit' and the period over which it arose is called the 'overlap period'. One of the principles of the current year basis tax system

EXAMPLE

Jim Newall started working as a freelance computer consultant on 1 July 2000 and drew up his first accounts on 30 April 2001. 30 April is his normal accounting year end. His profit and tax position for the first few years of business was as follows:

Accounting period	*Profit for the period*
1 July 2000–30 April 2001	£ 4,000
1 May 2001–30 April 2002	£ 8,500
1 May 2002–30 April 2003	£18,500

Tax year	*Tax basis*	*Profits on which tax based*
2000–01	Profits for tax year	279 ÷ 304 × £4,000 = £3,671
2001–02	First 12 months of trading	£4,000 + (61 ÷ 365 × £8,500) = £5,420
2002–03	Profits for 12 months to 30 April 2002	£8,500
2003–04	Profits for accounting year ending on 30 April 2003	£18,500

The profit for the period 1 July 2000 to 5 April 2001 is taxed twice, as is profit for the 61 days from 1 May to 30 June 2001. This gives Jim an overlap profit of £3,671 + (61 ÷ 365 × £8,500) = £3,671 + £1,420 = £5,091.

is that, over the lifetime of your business, all your profits should be taxed, but only taxed once. Therefore, you are given overlap relief to compensate you for having paid tax on some profits twice in your opening year. But there is a snag: overlap relief is usually given only when you finally close the business down (see overleaf) and inflation in the meantime will reduce its value.

Businesses that started before 6 April 1994 also have overlap profit as a result of changes to the basis of taxing accounts from 6 April 1996 onwards. And a change of accounting date (see overleaf) can create overlap profit.

TAX-SAVING IDEAS

Fiscal accounting makes accounting for tax very simple, especially in your opening years, but it has drawbacks too: you don't have long to make up your accounts and there's only a short delay between making your profits and paying tax on them (see overleaf).

If you don't choose fiscal accounting, try to keep your profits as low as possible during the first year or two, so that your overlap profit is small.

Fiscal accounting

You can avoid all the problems of opening year rules and overlap relief, if you opt for fiscal accounting. This means using the tax year as your accounting year. By Inland Revenue concession, this includes having an accounting date of 31 March, rather than exactly on the tax year end of 5 April.

For example, you might have started in business on 1 September 2002, drawing up your first accounts on 31 March 2003 and on each 31 March thereafter. Your tax for the tax year ending 5 April 2003 will be based on your profits from 1 September 2002 to 31 March 2003. Your tax for the next year will be based on profits for 1 April 2003 to 31 March 2004 and so on.

For further information see Help Sheet *IR222 How to calculate your taxable profits.*

Changing your accounting date

For the Inland Revenue to accept a change of accounting date for tax purposes, the following conditions must be met: the transitional accounting period running up to the new accounting date (called the 'relevant period') must not exceed 18 months; you must notify your tax office in your tax return by ticking box 3.12; and either there must have been no previous change of accounting date in the last five years or the Inland Revenue must be satisfied that the current change is for bona fide commercial reasons. If you have changed the date within the last five years, tick box 3.13 and explain your reasons in box 3.116.

If you choose a new accounting date earlier in the tax year, the relevant period will be less than 12 months. Your tax bill will be based on your profits for the 12 months up to the new accounting date. This creates some overlap profit.

If you choose a new date which is later in the tax year, your tax bill will be based on the whole relevant period which will be longer than 12 months, but you are then allowed to use some of your overlap relief (see p. 274).

Closing your business

In the tax years up to the one before closure, you are taxed on the normal current year basis. For the tax year in which you close down, you're taxed on profits from your last accounting date up to the date on which you close down less any overlap profits which you have been carrying forward (see p. 254). (For how to claim relief on these overlap profits, see p. 274.) The position for a business closing down in the tax year ending 5 April 2003 is summarised below.

Tax year ending	*Profits on which your tax bill is based*
5 April 2002	Profits for accounting year ending in 2001–02
5 April 2003	Profits from day after end of accounting year ending 2001–02 up to date of closure less overlap profits

If your normal accounting date is early in the year, your final tax bill may be based on a long period – for example, if you closed in December 2002 and your normal accounting date was 30 April, your final tax bill will be based on the 20 months from May 2001 to December 2002. This can mean a large tax bill if the business is profitable even after using overlap relief.

CAPITAL ALLOWANCES

Capital allowances - summary

	Capital allowances	Balancing charges
• Cars costing more than £12,000 (a separate calculation must be made for each car.)	3.14 £	3.15 £
• Other business plant and machinery	3.16 £	3.17 £
• Agricultural or Industrial Buildings Allowance (A separate calculation must be made for each block of expenditure.)	3.18 £	3.19 £
• Other capital allowances claimed (Separate calculations must be made.)	3.20 £	3.21 £
	total of column above	total of column above
Total capital allowances/balancing charges	3.22 £	3.23 £

Your taxable profits are broadly your business income less your business expenses. But when you buy capital items for your business – that is things which will be in use for many years – you are not normally allowed to set the full cost against your business income in the year you buy the item. In your ordinary business accounts, you'll deduct depreciation each year which varies from business to business and is not allowed as an expense when working out your tax. Instead you deduct capital allowances calculated according to standard rules.

To be eligible for capital allowances, the item you have bought must be wholly or partly for business use. You can claim a proportion of the allowance if the item is used partly for business and, in part, privately.

How much you can claim

The basic capital allowance is called a writing-down allowance and it is available for plant and machinery (which covers most of your ordinary business equipment), cars and vans, patents and know-how. In general, capital allowances are not given for what you spend on buying business premises (for example a shop or office), but industrial and agricultural buildings and some hotels with ten or more bedrooms are exceptions. Expenditure which qualifies for allowances is lumped together in one or more pools (see p. 260) and you can claim a certain proportion of the pool at the end of each tax year as a writing down allowance.

The maximum writing-down allowance you can claim is:

- 25 per cent a year for machinery, plant, vans, patents, know-how
- 25 per cent a year for cars, but for any car costing over £12,000, there is also a cash limit of £3,000 a year
- 4 per cent a year for industrial and agricultural buildings and qualifying hotels (or 25 per cent for industrial and commercial buildings in an Enterprise Zone if full first-year allowance – see below – not claimed).

With some types of expenditure, you can claim a higher capital allowance for the year in which you buy the item. Maximum first-year allowances are:

- 40 per cent for spending on machinery, plant, vans and know-how – but excluding cars, items for leasing and long life assets (with an expected life of at least 25 years) – from 2 July 1998 onwards (was 50 per cent for the period 2 July 1997 to 1 July 1998), provided you count as a small or medium-sized enterprise (SME). To be an SME, you must meet two of the following three conditions: your turnover does not exceed £11.2 million a year; your assets do not exceed £5.6 million; you have no more than 250 employees
- 100 per cent for spending on information and communications technology (including computers, Internet capable mobile phones, digital TV, related software and the costs of creating websites) from 1 April 2000 to 31 March 2004, provided you count as a small enterprise. To be a small

> **TAX-SAVING IDEA**
>
> An initial allowance of 40 per cent is available to small and medium-sized businesses buying machinery or plant (excluding cars) for expenditure from 2 July 1998 onwards.

> **TAX-SAVING IDEAS**
>
> Do not claim more capital allowances than needed to reduce your taxable profits to the level of your personal allowances – unless you have other income or gains against which you want to set a loss (see p. 276).
>
> Earmarking a capital item as a short-life asset means you can get full tax relief on the cost of the item in just five years.

enterprise, you must meet two of the following three conditions: your turnover does not exceed £2.8 million a year; your assets do not exceed £1.4 million; you have no more than 50 employees

- 100 per cent for most spending by an SME on machinery, plant, vans and know-how after 11 May 1998 and before 12 May 2002 primarily for use in Northern Ireland
- 100 per cent for industrial or commercial buildings in an Enterprise Zone
- 100 per cent for environmentally friendly spending (see Table)
- 100 per cent for spending on or after 11 May 2001 on renovating or converting residential space above shops or other commercial property into flats for rent, provided various conditions are met (see p. 295).

What counts as environmentally friendly spending?

Date spending incurred	*Item*	*Description*
31 March 2001 onwards	Energy-saving equipment	Items such as boilers, combined heat and power, refrigeration, and so on. A government lists of eligible equipment is available from the Internet (see www.eca.gov.uk) and the Action Energy Helpline 0800 585 794
17 April 2002–31 March 2008	Low-emission cars and refuelling equipment	Low emission cars (emitting no more than 120 gm/km of carbon dioxide or electrically propelled) used in your business or by employees. Equipment for refuelling with natural gas or hydrogen fuel
17 April 2002 onwards	Environmentally friendly spending on items for leasing, letting or hiring	Items as described above. (They are not eligible for the first-year allowance if bought before 17 April 2002 for leasing, letting or hiring.)

You can claim less than the maximum first-year allowance or writing-down allowance. It would be worth restricting your claim if your taxable profits or income were so low that some of the maximum allowance would be wasted. The allowance is not lost. The effect is to carry forward a higher value of assets in your pool of expenditure. This increases the value of the maximum writing-down allowances you can claim in future years. For example, suppose your pool

EXAMPLE

Joe Morris has been running a small dairy since 1979. He makes up his accounts to 31 December each year. For the year to 31 December 2002, he made the following purchases and sales of capital items:

Date	*Capital item*	*Purchase/sale price*
10 March 2002	New van bought	£17,000
5 May 2002	Old van sold (cost £12,000 when new)	£ 5,000
2 November 2002	Second-hand cream separator bought	£38,000

On 31 December 2001, after claiming writing-down allowances, Joe's general pool of capital expenditure stood at £158,000. Joe can claim an initial allowance for the cream separator of 40 per cent × £38,000 = £15,200. The van also qualifies for 40 per cent initial allowance, so he can claim 40 per cent × £17,000 = £6,800. Joe deducts the £5,000 from selling the old van to give a general pool expenditure at 31 December 2002 of £158,000 − £5,000 = £153,000. Joe can claim a maximum writing-down allowance of 25 per cent × £153,000 = £38,250. This gives allowances of £15,200 + £6,800 + £38,250 = £60,250 to set against his taxable income for the year. In fact, he has only enough profits and other income to use up £37,000 of the allowances. His capital pool at 1 January 2003 (including the balance of the expenditure on the van and the cream separator) becomes £158,000 − £5,000 (sale of van) + £17,000 (for van) + £38,000 (for cream separator) − £37,000 of allowances = £171,000.

of expenditure is valued at £10,000. If you claimed the full writing-down allowance of 25 per cent, the allowance would be £2,500 and the value of the pool carried forward would be £7,500, so next year you could claim up to 25 per cent × £7,500 = £1,875. If instead, you claimed only a 10 per cent allowance in the first year, the pool carried forward would be £9,000 and the maximum allowance in the second year would be 25 per cent × £9,000 = £2,250.

Capital pools

Various categories of capital expenditure have to be allocated to their own separate pools. They include:

- any car costing more than £12,000 must usually be hived off to its own pool and the writing-down allowance is limited to the smaller of 25 per cent or £3,000 in each year. The exception is environmentally friendly cars as defined in the table above. Cars costing £12,000 or less used to be grouped together in another separate pool, but this requirement has been

abolished from accounting periods that include 6 April 2000 onwards. The balance from the pool is added to your main pool of expenditure. Vans, lorries and so on do not count as cars
- industrial and agricultural buildings
- an asset used partly for private use must have its own pool and you can claim only a proportion of the allowance reflecting the proportion of business use
- short-life assets. Capital equipment (other than cars) which you expect to have a useful life of no more than five years can be put in a separate pool. The advantage of doing this is that you get tax relief on the full cost of the item more rapidly than if it were in the general pool of expenditure (see Buying and selling capital items below).

You do not get capital allowances on items you lease rather than buy. Instead the leasing charge counts as an allowable expense (see p. 272). If you buy something on hire purchase, the capital element of the charges can qualify for capital allowances but the interest element is treated as an allowable expense (see p. 272).

If you close down your business, in the final accounting period you cannot claim writing-down allowances or first-year allowances. Instead, you may get a balancing allowance on the sale of the business assets (see below).

Buying and selling capital items

When you buy an item of capital, its cost (less any first-year allowance) is added to the appropriate pool of expenditure. This increases the year-end value of the pool in subsequent years on which the writing-down allowance is worked out.

When you first start in business, you might take into the business capital equipment you already own – for example a desk, shelving, a computer. Although no money changes hands, you are treated as having sold the item to your business and you can claim capital allowances (but not first year allowances) in the normal way. Value each item at its second-hand market value given its age, state of repair and so on.

When you sell a capital item, the amount you get for it (up to its original cost) is deducted from the expenditure pool. Occasionally, this may be more than the total value of the pool, in which case, the excess (called a balancing charge) is added to your profits or (taxable income) for the year, increasing your tax bill. It is entered in box 3.15, 3.17, 3.19 or 3.21 as appropriate and added to your profits at box 3.68.

If you sell the item for less than its written-down value – at the extreme, you might scrap it for nothing – the shortfall remains in your pool of expenditure and continues to be written down. So you could be claiming allowances on an item for many years after you have sold it. Only when you finally close down the business can you claim a balancing allowance for any remaining value of the pool. This is where short-life assets come into their own.

If you scrap a short-life asset within five years, you can claim tax relief on the difference between what you get (if anything) for the asset and its written-down value. The relief is given in the tax year in which you scrap it – you don't have to wait until the business closes down. If, having declared an asset as short life, you actually go on using it beyond five years, it is transferred into your general pool of expenditure and treated like any other capital item.

If you are registered for VAT, the amount you put in your expenditure pools should not include VAT (unless you are unable to recover the VAT through your VAT returns or, in some cases, where you are using the VAT flat-rate scheme – see p. 265). If you are not registered for VAT, you claim capital allowances on the cost including VAT.

Claiming capital allowances

Capital allowances are given as a deduction in working out your taxable profits for the year. Enter the capital allowances you are claiming in boxes 3.14, 3.16, 3.18 and 3.20 and the total is deducted from your profits at box 3.70. If you are claiming first-year allowances for any environmentally friendly spending (see p. 259), tick box 3.22A.

INCOME

If your turnover is less than £15,000 a year

Income and expenses - annual turnover below £15,000

*If your annual turnover is £15,000 or more, **ignore** boxes 3.24 to 3.26. Instead fill in Page SE2*

*If your annual turnover is below £15,000, **fill in boxes 3.24 to 3.26 instead of Page SE2**. Read the Notes, page SEN2.*

• Turnover, other business receipts and goods etc. taken for personal use (and balancing charges from box 3.23)	3.24	£
• Expenses allowable for tax (including capital allowances from box 3.22)	3.25	£
		box 3.24 *minus* box 3.25
Net profit (put figure in brackets if a loss)	3.26	£

You must now fill in Page SE3

Complete boxes 3.24 to 3.26. You can get guidance on what expenses are allowable by reading pp. 266–273.

TAX-SAVING IDEA

If your turnover is less than £56,000 in the year from 10 April 2003, you can choose whether or not to register for VAT. Being registered means you can reclaim VAT on things you buy for your business, but you must also charge your customers VAT on your whole turnover (not just the bit in excess of £56,000). Be wary of registering voluntarily if your customers cannot reclaim the VAT you charge them (because, for example, they are private individuals) – you probably won't be able to raise your prices in line with the VAT and unless you can claim back large amounts on things you buy, registration could cause your overall income to fall.

Being VAT-registered means you have the extra administration of keeping VAT accounts and dealing with payments and reclaims. But there are several schemes to reduce the administration for small businesses including, from 2002, a flat-rate scheme. However, you should check that the flat-rate scheme really does save on administration once you take into account preparing your accounts for income tax and that you do not end up paying more VAT as a result.

You do not need to give full details of your accounts. This does not mean that you can get away without preparing proper accounts – you must have these ready, in case your tax inspector asks to see them, together with all the background paperwork (see p. 17).

Note that £15,000 is the annual limit – if your accounts cover a period of under a year, it will be reduced proportionately, and increased if you have a longer accounting period.

Do not complete page 2 of the Self-employed supplement, but go straight to page 3. Turn to p. 274 for guidance on filling in boxes 3.74 and beyond.

If your turnover is £15,000 a year or more

Sales/business income (turnover)

3.29 £

You should complete the details asked for on page 2 of the Self-employed supplementary pages. You don't need to attach a copy of your accounts. If the headings do not tally with the headings you use in your own accounts, don't be tempted to leave any out. Instead, use your judgement to allocate them to boxes on page 2, but make sure that whatever method you adopt is the same as last year and next year's – in other words, be consistent.

If the period over which you are being taxed is covered by two sets of accounts, you need to complete two Self-employment supplements (unless you have already given all the information in last year's tax return).

If you produce a balance sheet, there is space for the entries on page 4 of the supplement. Enter the amounts in boxes 3.99 to 3.115. If you don't have a balance sheet, leave these boxes blank.

Value added tax (VAT)

You must fill in this Page if your annual turnover is £15,000 or more - read the Notes, page SEN2

If you were registered for VAT, do the figures in boxes 3.29 to 3.64, include VAT? **3.27** [ ] or exclude VAT? **3.28** [ ]

If your turnover is £55,000 a year or more from 25 April 2002 (£56,000 from 10 April 2003), you must register for VAT. Below that threshold, you can choose whether or not to register. Registration means that you must normally charge your customers VAT on the goods and services that you sell, but you can usually reclaim VAT on the things that you buy to sell, or use, in your business. You must regularly hand over to the Customs & Excise department of the government the net amount of VAT you have collected (or claim a refund if what you are claiming comes to more than the VAT paid by your customers). This VAT does not form part of your profits and needs to be stripped out before your tax bill is calculated. For this reason, the tax office needs to know whether the figures you report in your tax return include VAT or have already had the VAT element stripped out.

In general, if you are registered for VAT, and have entered VAT-inclusive figures, you will need to tick box 3.27 and enter the net amount of VAT paid over to Customs & Excise as other expenses in box 3.63 or the net refund you received over the year as other income/profits in box 3.50. You may have bought capital equipment on which you claim capital allowances (see p. 257) instead of deducting them as expenses. If you are entering VAT-inclusive figures, there won't be an obvious place to enter the VAT on these capital items. You deal with this by adding the VAT to the amount entered in box 3.63 or (if you received a net refund from Customs & Excise) deducting it from the figure entered in box 3.50. Also write in the amount of VAT on capital items in the Additional information box on page 4.

In general, if you are registered for VAT but your figures exclude VAT, tick box 3.28.

From 25 April 2002, businesses with a taxable turnover before VAT up to

£100,000 (£150,000 from April 2003) can opt to join the VAT flat-rate scheme. Instead of basing your payments to Customs & Excise on full records of VAT on sales and purchases, under the flat-rate scheme they are a single percentage of your VAT-inclusive turnover. The percentage, which varies from 5 to 14.5 per cent, depends on the nature of your business. For full details, see VAT Notice 733 from the Customs & Excise website (www.hmce.gov.uk) or 0845 010 9000.

If you are in the flat-rate scheme and have ticked box 3.27 because you use VAT-inclusive figures in your accounts, put your flat-rate VAT payments in box 3.63. And the amount on which you claim capital allowances (see p. 257) should normally be the cost including VAT.

If you are in the flat-rate scheme and have ticked box 3.28 because you use VAT-exclusive figures, you will have to keep a separate VAT account comparing the amount of VAT you would have paid or reclaimed under the standard system with the amount paid under the flat-rate scheme. Any extra VAT paid under the flat-rate scheme will count as an allowable expense and can be deducted in box 3.63. Any profit you make from using the flat-rate scheme is taxable and should be entered in box 3.50. Given the need to keep a separate VAT account, it seems unlikely the flat-rate scheme will save you administration.

If you are not registered for VAT leave boxes 3.27 and 3.28 blank. You do not charge your customers VAT and the VAT you pay to your suppliers counts as a legitimate business expense. Your figures should include the VAT you have been charged. If you were registered for VAT for part of the year, but not for all, explain why, when the change occurred, and whether your figures are VAT-inclusive or not, in the Additional information box on page 4.

Gross profits

	Disallowable expenses included in boxes 3.46 to 3.63	Total expenses	
• Cost of sales	3.30 £	3.46 £	
• Construction industry subcontractor costs	3.31 £	3.47 £	
• Other direct costs	3.32 £	3.48 £	box 3.29 *minus* (boxes 3.46 + 3.47 + 3.48)
		Gross profit/(loss)	3.49 £
		Other income/profits	3.50 £

Your taxable profits are the income of your business less all the allowable expenses – that is the expenses you are allowed to deduct under the tax rules.

The starting point for working out your taxable profits is your gross profits. If you are in the business of selling something, this will be the income you get from sales less the cost of buying in the items you sell. If you sell your services, this will be the income you receive. For more information on how to take stock and work in progress into account, see Help Sheet *IR222 How to calculate your taxable profits*.

In your accounts, direct costs (for example, marketing, sales discounts) might include a figure for depreciation of equipment or machinery used in producing your goods. This is not an allowable expense (see Capital allowances on p. 257) and should be entered in box 3.32.

Other income or profits (box 3.50) includes things like income from renting out premises, interest on bank and building society accounts, discounts you get, and so on. If you receive any Business Start-up Allowance, put this in box 3.91, not here.

EXPENSES

You don't need to complete page 2 of the Self-employment supplement if your annual turnover is less than £15,000. If it is £15,000 or more, you need to allocate your costs and expenses to boxes 3.30 to 3.63. In the boxes in the right-hand column you should enter total expenses under each heading. In the left-hand column you should enter the amount of any expenses not allowed but which have been included in the right-hand column.

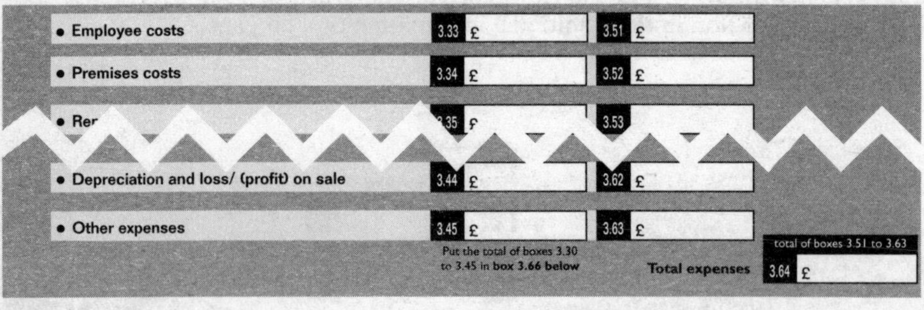

• Employee costs	3.33 £	3.51 £
• Premises costs	3.34 £	3.52 £
• Rer	3.35 £	3.53
• Depreciation and loss/ (profit) on sale	3.44 £	3.62 £
• Other expenses	3.45 £	3.63 £
	Put the total of boxes 3.30 to 3.45 in box 3.66 below	Total expenses — total of boxes 3.51 to 3.63 — 3.64 £

You total the amounts in boxes 3.30 to 3.45 and enter the total in box 3.66.

Deducting an expense from your business income has the effect of giving you tax relief at your top rate(s) of tax, so it is important to claim all the expenses you can. According to tax law, you get tax relief on an expense only if it is incurred wholly and exclusively for business. Strictly speaking, this means you can't get relief at all on expenditure which is partly for your private benefit. In practice, the Inland Revenue does allow you to claim a proportion of some costs where something – for example, your car or home – is used partly for business. However, your tax office may baulk at some expenses which arise because of a joint business and private purpose – for example, combining a trip abroad to see a client with a holiday.

> **TAX-SAVING IDEAS**
>
> Claim all the allowable expenses you can. If you're not sure whether an expense is allowable, deduct it from your taxable profits but ask your tax office to confirm whether this is correct.

It is hard to lay down hard and fast rules which apply to all businesses. Different types of businesses can claim different expenses and to a different extent. It is up to you to show that any claim is justified within the context of your own line of work.

> **EXAMPLE**
>
> Hannah Brown has converted the garage at her home into an office which is used exclusively for her computer software business. She can claim part of her household expenses as allowable expenses for business purposes and, because she uses part of the home exclusively for business, she can also claim part of her mortgage interest. She makes the following calculation:
>
> | | |
> |---|---|
> | add up total household expenses | £1,800 |
> | add up the number of rooms in the house, ignoring separate toilets, halls and landings (unless large enough to be used as rooms) | 8 rooms |
> | divide the expenses by the number of rooms to give a cost per room figure | £1,800 ÷ 8 = £225 per room |
> | multiply the cost per room by the number of rooms used for business (or by the relevant fraction of a room, if a room is used only partly for business) | 1 × £225 = £225 |
>
> She also claims one-eighth of her mortgage interest as a business expense. This comes to ⅛ × £3,600 = £450. However, Hannah may become liable for business rates and, when she sells her home, capital gains tax on the part of the proceeds.

> **TAX-SAVING IDEA**
> Be wary of using part of your home exclusively for business. Although you can claim part of any mortgage interest as an allowable expense, you may also become liable to pay the uniform business rate and there may be capital gains tax on part of the proceeds when you come to sell your home. Ensuring some private use of your work space – for example, for private study, hobbies, civic duties or other voluntary work – means you can't claim any relief for mortgage interest, but you should escape business rates and capital gains tax.

You can claim expenses you incur before you open for business if they would have been allowable anyway. Treat them as expenditure incurred on the first day of business.

Expenses which you incur after you close down can be set against any late income which comes into the closed business. However, if there is no income, tax relief on the expenditure is usually lost. With a few particular types of expense, you can get tax relief by setting the expenses against any other income or gains you have, provided the expense is incurred within seven years of the business ceasing (in box 15.8 of the basic tax return, see p. 191).

Employee costs

• Employee costs	3.33 £	3.51 £

Normally allowed

Salaries, bonuses, overtime, commissions etc paid to your employees, together with the add-on costs, such as National Insurance contributions, pension and insurance benefits. The costs of hiring locums to stand in for you or fees paid to people to whom you subcontract work. Training for employees. Council tax paid on behalf of employees if a genuine part of the pay package, taxed as normal through PAYE. Include the cost of employing your wife, husband or other family member in the business, provided their pay is reasonable for the work done (and bear in mind that the national minimum wage regulations

> **TAX-SAVING IDEA**
> If you employ a family member in your business, there is no income tax or National Insurance on their earnings if you pay them less than the 'primary threshold' (£4,615 in the year ending 5 April 2004). But consider paying them at least the 'lower earnings limit' (£4,004 in the year ending 5 April 2004), so they build up an entitlement to certain state benefits, such as state retirement pension.

may apply). Costs of entertaining staff – for example, a Christmas party.

Not allowed
Your own wages, National Insurance, income tax, pension costs (though you can get personal tax relief for these), your drawings from the business. Wages to employees which remain unpaid nine months after the accounting date (although they can be deducted in the accounting period in which they are eventually paid). Payments to family members if excessive for the work done – be especially careful employing young children which might, in any case, be illegal. Cost of your own training might be allowed but claim in box 3.63 (see p. 273).

Premises costs

• Premises costs	3.34 £	3.52 £

Normally allowed
If you work from dedicated business premises, include any rent, business rates, water rates, cost of lighting, heating, power, insurance, cleaning, security, and so on. If you work from home, you can claim a proportion of your home related expenses – for example, heating, lighting, power, cleaning, maintenance and Council Tax. If part of the home is used exclusively for business, part of your mortgage interest. The proportion you claim must relate to your business use of the home – for example, based on the number of rooms used or floor area. You should explain the basis used in the Additional information box on page 4 of the supplement.

Not allowed
Cost of buying premises (see Capital allowances on p. 257), costs relating to any part of the premises not used for business.

Repairs

• Repairs	3.35 £	3.53 £

Normally allowed
General maintenance and repairs to your business premises and machinery, cost of replacing small tools.

Not allowed
Costs of alterations and improvements (see Capital allowances on p. 257 but also Tax-saving idea on p. 287 which is also relevant to spending by businesses), costs relating to any part of the premises not used for business, general reserve for repairs.

General administrative expenses

• General administrative expenses	3.36 £	3.54 £

Normally allowed
Office expenses, such as postage, telephone, stationery, printing, subscriptions to trade journals, professional fees, accountancy and audit fees and regular expenses not included elsewhere. You can claim the cost of computer software where you pay a regular licence fee to use it or where the software has a limited lifetime (generally taken to be less than two years). In most other cases, software costs count as capital expenditure for which you can claim capital allowances (see p. 257).

Not allowed
Personal expenses, payments to political parties, most donations and fees to clubs, charities and churches. Any non-business part of a cost.

Motor expenses

• Motor expenses	3.37 £	3.55 £

Normally allowed
Costs of running a vehicle used in your business – for example, insurance, servicing, repairs, road tax, breakdown insurance, parking charges, fuel, hiring or leasing charges. A proportion of those costs if you also use the vehicle privately.

TAX-SAVING IDEA

If you use your car on business, you must normally keep a record of your expenses and a log of both business and private mileage so you can claim the business proportion of your total motoring costs. However, if at the time you buy the car, your turnover is no more than the VAT registration threshold (£56,000 from 10 April 2003), you can opt instead to claim a fixed mileage allowance for use of the car on business. The fixed allowance must not exceed the approved mileage allowance payments that apply to employees (see p. 92). If you use the approved allowance, you cannot claim capital allowances, though you may (unlike employees) still claim relief for interest on a loan taken out to buy the car. The option to use the approved allowance is made when you buy the car and applies until you stop using that car in your business. Opting for the approved allowance could save you tax if your car is fairly cheap (perhaps secondhand) and small/fuel efficient. It also saves paperwork because the only record you need to keep is your business mileage.

Not allowed
Travel between your home and business premises. Cost of buying a vehicle (see Capital allowances on p. 257). Parking fines, other fines.

Travel and subsistence

• Travel and subsistence	3.38 £	3.56 £

Normally allowed
Rail, air and taxi fares, hotel accommodation, cost of meals connected to an overnight stay whether included on your hotel bill or paid separately, modest additional expense of meals where your work is itinerant by nature (for example, commercial traveller) or during occasional journeys that are not part of your normal business pattern.

Not allowed
Cost of lunches and most other meals.

Advertising, promotion and entertainment

• Advertising, promotion and entertainment	3.39 £	3.57 £

Normally allowed
Advertising, mail-shots, free samples, gifts up to £50 a year to any client provided they promote your firm or its products or services and are not food, drink or tobacco.

Not allowed
Entertaining clients, business associates etc (only entertaining staff is allowed), gifts except those specifically allowed (see above).

Legal and professional costs

• Legal and professional costs	3.40 £	3.58 £

Normally allowed
Fees charged by accountants (including extra costs due to an Inland Revenue enquiry provided the enquiry does not reveal any negligent or fraudulent conduct), auditors, solicitors, surveyors, stocktakers and so on, professional indemnity premiums.

Not allowed
Legal costs of buying premises, equipment etc (treated as part of their cost –

see Capital allowances on p. 257), legal expenses on forming a company, cost of settling tax disputes, fines etc as a result of acting illegally.

Bad debts

• Bad debts	3.41 £	3.59 £

Normally allowed
Items you have sold or amounts you have invoiced but for which you no longer expect to be paid. A proportion of a bad debt given up under a voluntary arrangement. If in a later tax year you are paid, include the amount recovered in box 3.50 (other income/profits).

Not allowed
General reserve for bad debts.

Interest

• Interest	3.42 £	3.60 £

Normally allowed
Interest and arrangement fees for a business loan or overdraft.

Not allowed
The part of loan payments which represents capital repayments.

Other finance charges

• Other finance charges	3.43 £	3.61 £

Normally allowed
Charges on your business current account, credit card interest and fees, the interest element of hire purchase charges, leasing payments – but the amount you can claim is restricted in the case of a car whose retail price when new exceeded £12,000 unless it counts as environmentally friendly (see p. 259).

Not allowed
The part of any payment which represents capital repayment.

Depreciation and loss/(profit) on sale

• Depreciation and loss/(profit) on sale	3.44 £	3.62 £

Not allowed

None of these costs are allowable – instead you claim capital allowances (see p. 257). The figure you enter at 3.62 should exactly match the amount you put in box 3.44 – unless some of the costs relate to finance leases, in which case ask your tax office what you can deduct.

Other expenses

Normally allowed

Any expenses which you haven't found a place for in boxes 3.46 to 3.62. For example, any insurance premiums not included elsewhere, contributions to approved local enterprise agencies, training and enterprise councils, local enterprise councils and business link organisations, and part or all of subscriptions to trade or professional associations which secure some benefit for your business or to societies which have an arrangement with the Inland Revenue. Cost of your own training provided it is wholly and exclusively for business and updates your existing knowledge and skills.

• Other expenses	3.45 £ Put the total of boxes 3.30 to 3.45 in box 3.66 below	3.63 £	
		Total expenses	total of boxes 3.51 to 3.63 3.64 £
		Net profit/(loss)	boxes 3.49 + 3.50 *minus* 3.64 3.65 £

Not allowed

The non-business element of any expenses included in box 3.63. This includes, for example, ordinary clothing even if you bought it specially for business and would not normally wear it otherwise, buying a patent (see Capital allowances on p. 257), cost of computer hardware and any software costs not claimed in box 3.54 (see Capital allowances on p. 257), cost of your own training if it provides you with new skills (including initial training for operating a franchise) – claim Capital allowances instead, see p. 257.

Tax adjustments to net profit or loss

All the expenses which are not allowable are added together and the total entered in box 3.66. In the next box, you must enter the selling price of any goods which you took for personal use. These are added to your profits. If you are a farmer, box 3.67 is also the place to enter any compensation from the compulsory slaughter of animals that you have opted to spread forward from an earlier year to the year ending 5 April 2003. Similarly, if you wish to spread forward any compensation received in the year ending 5 April 2003, put the deduction in box 3.71 and a note in the Additional information box 3.116. See Help Sheet *IR224 Farmers and market gardeners*.

Tax adjustments to net profit or loss

	boxes 3.30 to 3.45	
• Disallowable expenses	**3.66** £	
• Adjustments (apart from disallowable expenses) that increase profits. Examples are goods taken for personal use and amounts brought forward from an earlier year because of a claim under ESC B11 about compulsory slaughter of farm animals	**3.67** £	
• Balancing charges (from box 3.23)	**3.68** £	
		boxes 3.66 + 3.67 + 3.68
Total additions to net profit (deduct from net loss)		**3.69** £
• Capital allowances (from box 3.22)	**3.70** £	
		boxes 3.70 + 3.71
• Deductions from net profit (add to net loss)	**3.71** £	**3.72** £
		boxes 3.65 + 3.69 *minus* 3.72
Net business profit for tax purposes (put figure in brackets if a loss)		**3.73** £

ADJUSTMENTS

So far, in completing the Self-employment supplement, you have entered figures for one particular accounting period. As explained on p. 252 this may not be the same as the period over which you are actually taxed which is known to the Inland Revenue as your basis period. After the first two or three years in business, your basis period (and the dates you enter in 3.74 and 3.75) will normally be the same as your accounting period. But in the early years of the business, or if you change your accounting date, you may have to enter different dates.

If your basis period does differ from your accounting period, you have to make an adjustment in box 3.77. Work this out by adding together and/or dividing the profits or losses for the relevant accounting periods. This is explained on p. 253 and in Help Sheet *IR222 How to calculate your taxable profits*. Remember to enter the adjustment in brackets if it is a deduction.

Overlap relief

In boxes 3.78 and 3.80, you should keep a record of the overlap profit (see p. 254) that you are carrying forward. You may be able to use part or all of it to reduce your profits or create a loss if you closed your business in the year ending 5 April 2003 (see p. 256) or you changed your accounting date (see

p. 256). Enter the amount of overlap profit you want to use in this way in box 3.79. See IR222 *How to calculate your taxable profits*.

Adjustments to arrive at taxable profit or loss

Basis period begins	3.74 / /	and ends	3.75 / /
Profit or loss of this account for tax purposes (box 3.26 or 3.73)			3.76 £
Adjustment to arrive at profit or loss for this basis period			3.77 £
• Overlap profit brought forward	3.78 £	• Deduct overlap relief used this year	3.79 £
• Overlap profit carried forward	3.80 £		
Averaging for farmers and creators of literary or artistic works *(see Notes, page SEN9, if you made a loss for 2002-03)*			3.81 £
Adjustment on change of basis			3.82 £

Farmers, authors, artists and similar creative workers whose income varies substantially from year to year can make a claim to be taxed on the average of their earnings from consecutive years. In box 3.81 enter the increase or reduction in your income as a result of the claim. See Help Sheets *IR224 Farmers and market gardeners* or *IR234 Averaging for creators of literary or artistic works*.

EXAMPLE

Sam started his business as a self-employed landscape gardener on 6 July 2002. His basis period for the tax year ending 5 April 2003 is the period between 6 July 2002 and 5 April 2003. He draws up his first set of accounts on 5 June 2003. In all the boxes up to 3.76 he enters the figures for his first accounting period, running to 5 June 2003. His profit in this accounting period was £8,000. Because he was only in business for 274 of the 365 days in the year to 5 April 2003, his profits for the tax year were $^{274}/_{365} \times$ £8,000 = £6,005. At box 3.77 he enters an adjustment (in brackets) of £8,000 − £6,005 = £1,995.

LOSSES

If you make a loss, there are several ways you can get tax relief on it.

Other income or gains for this year

Net profit for 2002-03 (if you made a loss, enter '0')		3.83 £
Allowable loss for 2002-03 (if you made a profit, enter '0')	3.84 £	
• Loss offset against other income for 2002-03	3.85 £	
• Loss to carry back	3.86 £	

Complete box 3.85 to set the loss against other income you have during the tax year ending 5 April 2003 – for example, from working for an employer or from your savings. If this does not use up all the loss, you can ask for the rest to be set against any taxable capital gains for tax year ending 5 April 2003. If any loss still remains, you can ask for relief on it to be given in some other way. The time limit for making this choice with respect to losses made in the accounting period being declared for the tax year ending 5 April 2003 is 31 January 2005.

Other income and gains for the previous year

• Loss to carry back	3.86 £

Complete box 3.86 to carry back the loss to the tax year ending 5 April 2002 to set against your income from any source for that year. If this does not use up the full loss, you can ask for the rest to be set against any capital gains for the tax year ending 5 April 2002. If some loss still remains, you can ask for relief on it to be given in some other way. The time limit for making this choice is 31 January 2005.

EXAMPLE

Sonja Frisk has been an antiques dealer for the last ten years. Normally, she makes a reasonable living but, in 2002, the sale of some expensive artifacts fell through and Sonja made a £7,000 loss for the tax year.

Sonja could set the remaining loss against other income which she had in the tax year ending 5 April 2003 from a part-time job lecturing in art history at the local university. Alternatively, she can carry back her loss to the tax year ending 5 April 2002, or carry it forward to set against future profits from her antiques business. She doesn't want to use her loss this year, because she will pay only 10 per cent tax on her lecturing income, compared with the 22 per cent top rate of tax she paid last year; nor is she keen to carry forward her loss because she does not expect to pay a higher rate of tax in future. She claims to carry back her loss to the year ending 5 April 2002. qualifying for tax relief of 22 per cent × £7,000 = £1,540.

> **TAX-SAVING IDEA**
> If your business is more or less a hobby, you can set off losses you make against other income but only *provided* you carry on the activity on a commercial basis with a view to realising a profit.

> **TAX-SAVING IDEAS**
> You do not have to make up your mind about how to get tax relief for your losses straightaway. You have a while to wait and see how your business affairs turn out. But the time limits for each option are strict, so don't delay so long that you miss them.

Other income for earlier years

You can ask for a loss made in the first four years of the business to be carried back and set against income (but not gains) for the previous three tax years – that is, those ending 5 April 2000, 2001 and 2002. The loss is set against the earliest year first. The time limit for this choice is also 31 January 2005.

Future profits

• Loss to carry forward (that is allowable loss not claimed in any other way)	3.87	£

Complete box 3.87 to carry the loss forward to set against your future profits from the same business. It will be set against the next profits you make with any remaining loss being rolled forward to set against the next profits and so on until the loss is completely used up. You have until 31 January 2009 to make this choice.

Closing down

If your business closed down during the tax year ending 5 April 2003, you have a further option. A loss you made during your last 12 months of trading can be set against your profits for the three previous tax years – that is you

> **TAX-SAVING IDEA**
> Where you set business losses against capital gains, the normal rule is that the maximum claim is the amount of tapered capital gain (see p. 111). But, for business losses made in the tax year ending 5 April 2005 onwards, you will set losses against capital gains before taper relief. And, for losses made in the tax years ending 5 April 2003 and 2004, you can elect for this treatment. Doing so produces a bigger reduction in the capital gain. You claim this relief in the Capital gains supplementary pages (see Chapter 23).

EXAMPLE

Jim Newall has profits for income tax purposes of £8,500 for the tax year ending 5 April 2003. These are also the profits on which his Class 4 NICs are based. They are calculated as follows:

Profit for Class 4 NICs purposes	=	£8,500
Less lower profit limit	=	£4,615
Amount chargeable (£8,500 – £4,615)	=	£3,885
Class 4 NICs at 7 per cent × £3,885	=	£271

can go back to the tax year ending 5 April 2000. The time limit for this choice is also 31 January 2009. For more information see Help Sheet *IR227 Losses.*

NATIONAL INSURANCE

Class 4 National Insurance contributions		
• Tick box 3.94 if exception or deferment applies	3.94	
• Adjustments to profit chargeable to Class 4 National Insurance contributions	3.95	£
Class 4 National Insurance contributions due	3.96	£

Running your own business, you will usually have to pay National Insurance contributions (NICs) both for yourself and for any people you employ. You will have to pay: Class 2 contributions at a flat-rate of £2 a week in the tax year ending 5 April 2003 and the year ending 5 April 2004. If your profits are less than £4,025 in the tax year ending 5 April 2003 (£4,095 in the year ending 5 April 2004), you can opt not to pay.

Class 2 NICs help you to qualify for certain state benefits, such as retirement pension and incapacity benefit, so it might be better to carry on paying even if your profits are low. Class 2 contributions are paid direct to the Inland Revenue, usually by direct debit.

You may also have to pay Class 4 contributions. Unlike other types of National Insurance, Class 4 contributions do not entitle you to any state benefits – they are simply a tax on profits which is collected along with your income tax. In the tax year ending 5 April 2003, Class 4 NICs were payable at a rate of 7 per cent on profits over £4,615 up to £30,420. There were no Class 4 NICs to pay on profits above the upper limit. (In the year ending 5 April 2004, Class 4 NICs are payable at a rate of 8 per cent on profits over £4,615 up to £30,940 and at a new rate of 1 per cent on profits above £30,940.) If your profits are less than the lower limit, you do not pay any Class 4 NICs at all.

> **TAX-SAVING IDEAS**
>
> - Losses can be used to reduce your Class 4 National Insurance contributions as well as your income tax bill.
> - And the treatment of losses is not necessarily identical: where, for income tax purposes, you elect for a loss to be set against income or gains other than profits from your business, that amount of loss is carried forward and set against future profits for Class 4 purposes.
> - If you're paying both Class 1 and Class 4 National Insurance on some of your income, ask to have the Class 4 liability deferred until you know precisely how much is due. Otherwise, you could end up paying too much in contributions.

A few groups of people are excluded from having to pay Class 4 NICs. They include people over state pension age (currently 60 for women and 65 for men), people under age 16 if they have been granted an exemption by the Inland Revenue (ask for form CA2835U available from Inland Revenue NICO [Deferment Unit], Longbenton, Newcastle upon Tyne NE98 1ZZ tel 08459 157141) and people who are not resident in the UK.

In some circumstances, you might have earnings which count as profits of your business but which have already had Class 1 NICs deducted. In other cases, you might have earnings both as an employee (on which Class 1 contributions are payable) and from self-employment. There is a cap on the overall amount you have to pay in National Insurance, so it may be that Class 4 NICs won't be payable after all. However, you usually don't know whether this is the case until after part of the Class 4 NICs would have become payable, so you can ask to have payment deferred until the position is known by contacting Inland Revenue NICO [Deferment Unit] at the address above or by downloading form CA72B from www.inlandrevenue.gov.uk.

If you are either excluded from paying Class 4 NICs or your tax office has agreed that you can defer paying them, you should tick the box at 3.94 and put 0 in boxes 3.95 and 3.96. In all other cases, leave box 3.94 blank. If you have any losses from the year ending 5 April 2003 or previous years which have not yet been set against profits chargeable to Class 4 contributions enter them in box 3.95 because they can reduce your profits used for working out Class 4 NICs (as well as reducing your income tax liability). If you have paid interest for business purposes but it has not been deducted in working out your profits for income tax purposes, you might be able to deduct it for Class 4 NICs purposes. If this applies enter the amount of interest also in box 3.95.

Box 3.96 invites you to write down the amount you owe in Class 4 NICs. You don't have to do this sum yourself. Provided you send in your tax return by the 30 September deadline, you can leave the box blank and let your tax office do the sums. If you prefer to work out your Class 4 NICs yourself, there is a calculator included in the notes accompanying your Self-employment supplement. (The calculator is not suitable if you run more than one business, see Help Sheet *IR220 More than one business.*)

Class 2 and Class 4 contributions are not allowable expenses and can't be deducted when working out your profits for income tax purposes. If you have employees, you have to pay employer's Class 1 NICs for them if they earn more than the primary threshold (£89 a week for the tax years ending 5 April 2003 and 2004). In this case, the amount you pay counts as an allowable expense (see p. 268).

COMPANY OR SELF-EMPLOYMENT?

The 2002 Budget announced both a reduction in corporation tax for small companies and an increase in National Insurance contributions on profits and earnings. As a result, running your business as a company and paying yourself partly in dividends (on which there is no National Insurance) could save you thousands of £s in tax compared with remaining self-employed. Not surprisingly, many small businesses are deciding to incorporate. Before joining the rush, get advice from an accountant and bear in mind the following:

- incorporating means ending your self-employment business which could trigger a large tax bill for the year you close down (see p. 256)
- might you be caught by the IR35 rules (see p. 211)? If so, incorporating could mean more not less tax to pay
- the procedures for running a company are more formal than self-employment. This may mean more time spent on administration, higher accountant's fees, and less convenient access to the money your business makes
- the government might make further changes in future that reduce the relative tax advantages of operating as a company.

PARTNERSHIP

CHAPTER 19

Q4 Were you in partnership?	YES	PARTNERSHIP

If you are in business with one or more partners, you should answer YES to Q4 in the basic tax return and fill in the Partnership supplement. There are two versions:

- short version. Use this if the partnership income is from trading profits or interest from bank or building society accounts which has already been taxed at the savings rate. This version will be adequate for most partners
- full version. If your partnership earnings are more complex because you have untaxed investment income, foreign income or income from land and property, for example, you'll need to complete this longer supplement.

The partnership should already have provided you with a Partnership Statement summarising your share of the profits, losses and other income. If you received the full statement, you need the full version of the supplementary pages; if you received a short statement, you need only the short supplement. If you haven't received a Partnership supplement or you need the full version, contact the Inland Revenue Orderline (see p. 147).

You and your fellow partners are jointly responsible for the partnership tax return, although one partner may be nominated to deal with it. This is a separate document from the partnership supplement. Profits are calculated on the return as if the partnership were a single person using largely the same rules as for a self-employed person (see Chapter 18). How profits are shared between partners depends on your partnership agreement.

Once the partner dealing with the tax return has worked out the taxable profits for the partnership as a whole, he or she must show each partner's share of the profits, losses and tax suffered on the Partnership statement at the end of the Partnership return. The Partnership statement gives each individual partner the information needed to complete their own Partnership supplement. Each partner is then responsible for the tax on their own share of the profits.

Each partner is treated as if they were carrying on a business on their own, and the short version of the Partnership supplement is very similar to the Adjustments to arrive at taxable profit and loss and Class 4 National Insurance sections of the Self-employment supplement (see pp. 274 and 275). The other sections of the supplement simply summarise your share of any tax that the partnership has already suffered. For this reason, we have not gone through the Partnership supplement in detail.

Becoming a partner

Partnership details			
Partnership reference number		Description of partnership trade or profession	
4.1		**4.2**	
• Date you started being a partner (if during 2002-03)	**4.3** / /	• Date you stopped being a partner (if during 2002-03)	**4.4** / /

When you join a partnership, the normal opening rules described on pp. 252–6 apply. The period on which your tax is based is likely to be different from the accounting year for the partnership. The dates you put in boxes 4.5 and 4.6 should reflect how the opening year rules apply to you.

The opening year rules may result in overlap profits (see p. 254) on which you can eventually claim tax relief either when you leave the partnership or, possibly, if the partnership accounting date is changed.

Once the special opening year rules have worked through, you are taxed on the normal current year basis. The period on which your tax is based will then be the same as the accounting year of the partnership, so you put the start date of the partnership year in box 4.5 and the end date in box 4.6.

Ceasing to be a partner

If you leave a partnership you are treated as if you are closing down your own business. The normal closing rules apply (see p. 256), including the claiming of tax relief on any overlap profits carried forward from the opening years or a change of accounting date.

Partnerships providing personal services

If your partnership hires out your services to client companies and, in the absence of the partnership, your work would effectively amount to that of an employee, you may be caught by the 'IR35 rules' described on p. 211. Ask the Orderline (see p. 147) to send you Help Sheet *IR222 How to calculate your taxable profits*, which explains the adjustments you need to make.

LAND AND PROPERTY

CHAPTER 20

Q5 Did you receive any rent or other income from land and property in the UK? YES LAND & PROPERTY

If you ticked the YES box against Q5 on page 2 of the tax return, you will need the Land and property supplementary pages. Many people renting out the odd room in their home may have to do little more than tick one box on the first page. But there is also space for details of more substantial lettings businesses and for income from holiday homes.

If you take in lodgers in your home, providing meals and other services, this may amount to a form of business (but see The Rent a Room scheme below) and details should be entered on the Self-employment supplementary pages (see Chapter 18). Income from property abroad is entered on the Foreign pages (see Chapter 21).

The documents you need
You will need details of the rents you have received and any receipts or invoices for expenses. With furnished holiday lettings, you will also need records of the periods the properties were available for letting out.

If any of these properties is jointly owned, remember to enter only your share from these documents when filling in the tax return.

THE RENT A ROOM SCHEME

Are you claiming Rent a Room relief for gross rents of £4,250 or less?
(Or £2,125 if the claim is shared?)
Read the Notes on page LN2 to find out
- whether you can claim Rent a Room relief; and
- how to claim relief for gross rents over £4,250

Yes

If 'Yes', tick box. If this is your only income from UK property, you have finished these Pages

The Rent a Room scheme applies to rent from letting out furnished accommodation in your home and income from providing any related services, such as providing meals or doing your lodger's laundry. In the normal way you would pay tax on any profit you make – in other words, the income you get less allowable expenses you incur. If instead you opt for the Rent a Room scheme, the first slice of the income is tax-free, but you are not allowed to deduct any expenses.

> **TAX-SAVING IDEA**
> If you make a profit from taking in lodgers and your income from the lettings is £4,250 or less in the year ending 5 April 2003, there will be no tax to pay on this income if you opt for the Rent a Room scheme. If your gross income from the lettings is more than £4,250 but the expenses and allowances you can claim come to £4,250 or less, you will pay less tax if you opt for the Rent a Room scheme. Using the Rent a Room scheme can save you administration because, for tax purposes, you need only keep records of your income not any expenses.

The scheme can apply only to rooms you let in your only or main home (see p. 56). It doesn't matter whether you own the home or you yourself are a tenant (though bear in mind that you may need permission from a mortgage lender or landlord before taking in lodgers). The scheme may not apply to rooms let as offices or for other business purposes. And you cannot claim Rent a Room relief if you yourself are not living in the property because, say, you have gone abroad or moved into job-related accommodation.

Under the scheme, for the year ending 5 April 2003, the first £4,250 of such income (without any expenses deducted) is tax-free. If anyone else living in the same home is letting out another room or you are jointly letting out room(s) with one or more other people, you each get £2,125 tax-free. The amount of Rent a Room relief has been unchanged since April 1997 and remains unchanged for the tax year ending 5 April 2004.

> **EXAMPLE**
> Natalie Lean lets out three rooms in her house, bringing in a total of £150 a week in rent. This means her gross rental income for the tax year beginning 6 April 2003 will be £7,800, on which she could claim expenses and allowances of £2,350.
>
> If the rental income is taxed as normal property income, she will pay tax on £7,800 – £2,350 = £5,450. But if she claims the Rent a Room relief, she will pay tax on the excess of the gross rental income of £7,800 over £4,250 – that is, on £3,550.
>
> Rent a Room relief means Natalie will pay tax on £1,900 less income.

Unless you made a loss on the letting (in other words, your expenses came to more than the income), it will be worth claiming Rent a Room relief if your gross income from the letting(s) is £4,250 or less. Tick the YES box if this is your only letting income. There is nothing more to enter – leave the rest of the Land and property pages blank.

In all other cases, which boxes you complete depends on how much profit or loss you made from the letting(s) in the year ending 5 April 2003:

- if you made a loss, follow the instructions for Other property income (see p. 296)
- if the expenses and allowances you can deduct from your letting income come to more than £4,250 (or £2,125 if you are sharing the relief), follow the instructions for Other property income (see p. 293)
- if the deductions you can make from your letting income come to £4,250 (£2,125) or less, opt for the Rent a Room scheme by putting your income in box 5.20 on page 2 and the Rent a Room relief you are claiming (either £4,250 or £2,125) in box 5.35. Don't enter any expenses in boxes 5.24 to 5.30 and don't claim any other deductions in boxes 5.36 (capital allowances) or 5.37 (wear and tear allowance).

FURNISHED HOLIDAY LETTINGS

Is your income from furnished holiday lettings?
If not applicable, please turn over and fill in Page L2 to give details of your property income — **Yes** — If 'Yes', tick box and fill in boxes 5.1 to 5.18 before completing Page L2

If you have no income from short-term furnished lettings, turn over to page L2 and to p. 291.

Tax benefits of furnished holiday lettings

Income from furnished holiday lettings is treated differently from other forms of property income, to reflect the fact that it is a form of business for many owners. This offers several tax benefits:

- you can claim capital allowances on plant and equipment (see p. 257)
- losses can be set off against other income or gains for the same or previous tax year and losses in the first four years of the business can be deducted from other income from the previous three years (see p. 290)
- it counts as relevant earnings for tax relief on pension contributions (p. 74)
- you can claim the special business reliefs for capital gains tax (p. 132).

To count as furnished holiday lettings, the property must normally meet all the following conditions for the tax year ending 5 April 2003:

- be available for letting to the general public on a commercial basis (that is, with a view to a profit) for at least 140 days
- actually let for at least 70 of those days
- not occupied for more than 31 days in a row by the same person for at

> **WHAT INCOME IS TAXED?**
>
> Income from land and property (other than that dealt with under the Rent a Room scheme) is all taxed in the same way – irrespective of its type. All income from land and property in the UK is added together. You pay tax on the income after deduction of allowable expenses, interest paid on loans to buy or improve the properties and losses from letting out property in the past. You can also claim allowances for some equipment you buy.
>
> The tax you pay in a tax year is based on the property income and expenditure during that year. If you make up accounts for your property business for the year ending 5 April, the figures in your accounts will be the ones to use in filling in your tax return.
>
> But if your accounting year runs to different dates, you will have to use two sets of accounts to work out what your property income and expenditure was for the tax year (see p. 252).

least seven months of the year. (The seven months need not be continuous.)

If you first started letting the property during the tax year ending 5 April 2003, these conditions must be satisfied for the first 12 months of letting. If you finished letting the property during that tax year, the conditions must have been met for the 12 months ending with the last letting. If you own more than one furnished holiday letting, you can average out the letting for 70 days rule between all of them.

Income

Furnished holiday lettings		
• Income from furnished holiday lettings	5.1	£

Enter the total income from all your furnished holiday lettings in the UK for the tax year ending 5 April 2003 – before any deductions such as agents' commission. Include any income for services provided to tenants, such as cleaning, linen hire and use of additional facilities. Also include any money received from insurance policies for loss of rent.

Expenses

■ ***Expenses*** (furnished holiday lettings only)

If your total property income, including that from furnished holiday lettings, is less than £15,000, enter your total expenses in box 5.7, as Other expenses – you don't need to give details of individual expenses. If your total property income is over this limit, you need to list expenses separately:

Rent, rates, insurance, ground rents etc

• Rent, rates, insurance, ground rents etc.	5.2	£

Enter the amount of rent, business rates, council tax, water rates, ground rent and insurance premiums on the furnished holiday lettings (including for insurance against loss of rents) in box 5.2.

Repairs, maintenance and renewals

• Repairs, maintenance and renewals	5.3	£

Claim in box 5.3. Any work that prevents the property deteriorating is a repair – such as painting and damp treatment. You can't claim here the cost of improvements, additions or extensive alterations. If such work made repairs unnecessary you used to be able to claim part of the outlay equal to what the repairs would have cost, but this concession was withdrawn from 6 April 2001 onwards.

TAX-SAVING IDEA

The Inland Revenue accepts that work which once counted as an improvement to a property may over time and due to technological advances now be accepted as a repair and so count as an allowable expense. The example it gives is replacing old windows with double glazing. If you are replacing an old feature with a modern equivalent, try claiming and ask your tax office to confirm that the expense is allowable.

If you aren't claiming capital allowances for the furniture, fixtures and fittings, you can claim a renewals deduction for the cost of replacing them. If the new items are better, you cannot claim the full cost. And if any of the old items are sold, the proceeds should be deducted from the amount you claim.

Finance charges

• Finance charges, including interest	5.4	£

Enter in box 5.4 the cost of any loan you took out to buy the property – including interest paid and charges for setting up the loan.

Legal and professional costs

• Legal and professional costs	5.5 £	

You can claim legal and professional expenses for a letting of less than a year, including fees for agents, surveyors and accountants and commission. You can also claim such costs when renewing the lease for a longer letting provided it is for less than 50 years. But you cannot claim expenses incurred in the first letting of a property for more than a year. Nor can you claim costs of registering title to land, getting planning permission or in connection with the payment of a premium on renewal of a lease. Enter the total in box 5.5.

Cost of services provided

• Costs of services provided, including wages	5.6 £	

You can claim as an expense the cost of services such as gardening, cleaning and porterage. You can't claim the cost of your own time, but you can claim the cost of paying other people such as a member of your family.

Enter the total in box 5.6. If you are paid for any services you provide, this should be included as part of the income in box 5.1.

Other expenses

		total of boxes 5.2 to 5.7
• Other expenses	5.7 £	5.8 £

Other expenses include advertising costs, stationery, telephone calls, rent collection and travel to the property when solely for the letting.

Add together the figures in boxes 5.2 to 5.7 and enter the total in box 5.8.

Net profit

	box 5.1 *minus* box 5.8
Net profit (put figures in brackets if a loss)	5.9 £

Net profit is income minus expenses. Deduct the figure in box 5.8 from that in box 5.1 and put the amount in box 5.9, in brackets if it is a loss.

Tax adjustments

■ *Tax adjustments*	
• Private use	5.10 £

Private use

If a furnished holiday letting is partly used for your own enjoyment or that of friends staying rent-free, this counts as private use. Part of the costs must be apportioned to this private use, and cannot be claimed as an expense. For example, if it was available for letting for nine months of the year and used by you for the rest of the time, you can claim only three-quarters of the costs of owning it. (You can still claim the full costs of letting it out as expenses.)

There are two ways to make an adjustment to reflect private use. You can enter the appropriate share of the costs in boxes 5.2 to 5.7, but let your tax inspector know what you've done. Or, better, you enter the costs in full in these boxes and enter in box 5.10 a figure for private use which is deducted from the total.

Capital allowances and balancing charges

		box 5.10 + box 5.11
• Balancing charges	5.11 £	5.12 £
• Capital allowances	5.13 £	
• Tick box 5.13A if box 5.13 includes enhanced capital allowances for environmentally friendly expenditure	5.13A	

You can claim capital allowances for the cost of buying furniture, machinery such as a lawnmower or equipment such as a water pump. If you get rid of an item on which you have claimed capital allowances, a balancing charge may be added to your profits, reflecting the sale proceeds or the second-hand value. There's more on p. 257 about capital allowances and balancing charges. You might also find it useful to get Help Sheet *IR250 Capital allowances and balancing charges in a rental business* from the Orderline (see p. 147).

Enter the amount of any capital allowances you are claiming for the tax year ending 5 April 2003 in box 5.13 and the amount of any balancing charge in box 5.11. Add the figures in boxes 5.10 and 5.11 together and enter the total in box 5.12.

If you are claiming first-year capital allowances on something which counts as environmentally friendly spending (see table on p. 259), tick box 5.13A.

Profit for the year (copy to box 5.19). If loss, enter '0' in box 5.14 and put the loss in box 5.15		boxes 5.9 + 5.12 *minus* box 5.13 **5.14** £
Loss for the year (if you have entered '0' in box 5.14)	boxes 5.9 + 5.12 *minus* box 5.13 **5.15** £	

Total boxes 5.9 and 5.12 and subtract the amount in box 5.13. If the answer is a negative number, you have made a tax loss on your furnished holiday lettings. Enter 0 in box 5.14 and put the amount of the loss in box 5.15. If you have made a profit, enter it in box 5.14.

Losses for the year

Any loss in box 5.15 can be used to reduce the amount of tax you pay on other income or capital gains in the tax year ending 5 April 2003 or earlier tax years:

- other income for the tax year ending 5 April 2003 (enter the amount you wish to claim in box 5.16)
- capital gains for the same tax year – include the amount you wish to claim in the total you enter in box F4 or column K2 of the Capital gains supplementary pages (see p. 316)
- income and gains for earlier tax years – enter the amount you wish to claim in box 5.17. If you have already claimed to offset this loss, still include it here but make a note of the amount in the Additional information box on page 9 of the basic tax return.

• Loss offset against 2002-03 total income	**5.16** £
• Loss carried back	see Notes, page LN4 **5.17** £
• Loss offset against other income from property (copy to box 5.38)	see Notes, page LN4 **5.18** £

If you haven't used all the loss in box 5.15, you can set off what remains against other property income for the tax year ending 5 April 2003. Enter what is left in box 5.18 and copy it into box 5.38 on page L2 of the Land and property supplementary pages.

OTHER PROPERTY INCOME

All your rental and other income from property (except rents within the Rent a Room scheme – see p. 283) is added together and treated as the proceeds of a single rental business. You are treated in this way whether you have, say, a single buy-to-let property or a whole string of flats and houses.

Income

Other property income		
■ *Income*		
	copy from box 5.14	
• Furnished holiday lettings profits	5.19	£

Copy the figure for profits on furnished holiday lettings from box 5.14 to box 5.19.

Rents and other income from land and property

				Tax deducted
• Rents and other income from land and property	5.20	£	5.21	£

Enter in box 5.20 the total income from all your lettings in the UK except furnished holiday lettings for the tax year ending 5 April 2003 – before any deductions such as agents' commission. Include the following:

- rent you will receive after 5 April 2003 which is payment in arrears for the tax year ending 5 April 2003 (equally, leave out any rent received in arrears this year that was included in last year's return, and any rent received on or before 5 April 2003 which is payment in advance for rent for periods after 5 April 2003)
- any income for services provided to tenants, such as cleaning, gardening or porterage
- any money received from insurance policies for loss of rent
- ground rent and feu duties
- grants from local authorities for repairs (you can claim the cost of repairs as an expense)
- payments for using your land – for example, to shoot or graze.

If any tax has been deducted from the income before you get it, enter the total in box 5.21. The figure you enter in box 5.20 should be the before-tax amounts – so should include the amount in box 5.21.

If you own and let the property jointly with someone else, enter only your share of the income in box 5.20, and your share of the expenses lower down. If you only know your share of the profit after expenses, enter this in box 5.20 or any loss in box 5.29. Tick box 5.46 and give the name and address of the person who keeps the records for the shared property in the Additional information box on page 9 of the main tax return.

Chargeable premiums, reverse premiums

• Chargeable premiums	5.22 £	
• Reverse premiums	5.22A £	boxes 5.19 + 5.20 + 5.22 + 5.22A 5.23 £

If you receive a premium from a tenant in return for granting a lease, you will have to pay income tax on part of it if the lease lasts 50 years or less (and capital gains tax on the rest). Any work the tenant agrees to do for you on being granted a lease counts as a premium.

If you are paid the premium in instalments, the total premium is still taxable in the year the lease is granted. But if paying in one go would cause you hardship, you can ask your tax inspector to allow you to pay by yearly instalments. The maximum number of instalments is eight (or the number of years you are getting the premium over, if less).

The proportion on which you will have to pay income tax is calculated as follows:

$$\frac{51 - \text{number of years of the lease}}{50}$$

So if the lease is a 20-year one, the proportion of the premium which is taxable as income is:

$$\frac{51 - 20}{50} = \frac{31}{50}$$

Enter the taxable amount in box 5.22.

A lease for more than 50 years is treated as capital rather than business income. There is no income tax to pay, but capital gains tax may be due (see p. 318).

If the property you let out is one you are yourself letting and you received a payment or other benefit, such as a contribution towards fitting out the property, to persuade you to take it on, this is a reverse premium. If actual money has been laid out by the landlord, it is taxed as income. Give the amount in

EXAMPLE

Miriam Patel has divided most of her house into furnished rooms which she lets out, providing cleaning. The total yearly income is £9,640 but she can deduct these expenses:

- a proportion of the outgoings on the house (council tax, water rates, gas, electricity and insurance) which add up to £3,400 a year. Miriam is letting out three-quarters of the house and claims this proportion
- the cost of cleaning (cleaner's wages plus materials) – £1,300 a year
- an allowance for wear and tear of the furniture and furnishings – Miriam claims the actual cost of replacement (£500 for this year).

Thus Miriam's tax bill would be calculated as follows:

Total rent received		£9,640
Less expenses		
Three-quarters of the outgoings of £3,400 a year	£2,550	
Cost of cleaning	£1,300	
Cost of replacing furniture and furnishings	£500	
Total allowable expenses		£4,350
Taxable rental income		£5,290

If Miriam does the cleaning, no allowance can be made for her time. But if she pays someone else to do the work (her mum, say), she can claim this cost as an allowable expense.

box 5.22A – if you are not sure whether you have received a reverse premium, ask your tax inspector or your business adviser.

Add the figures in boxes 5.19, 5.20, 5.22 and 5.22A together and enter the total in box 5.23.

Expenses

■ ***Expenses*** (do not include figures you have already put in boxes 5.2 to 5.7 on Page L1)

• Rent, rates, insurance, ground rents etc.	5.24 £	
• Repairs, maintenance and renewals	5.25 £	
• Finance charges, including interest	5.26 £	
• Legal and professional costs	5.27 £	
• Costs of services provided, including wages	5.28 £	total of boxes 5.24 to 5.29
• Other expenses	5.29 £	5.30 £

If your total property income, including income from furnished holiday lettings, for the tax year ending 5 April 2003 is less than £15,000, go to box 5.29 and enter your total expenses in it (but excluding any expenses relating to furnished holiday letting which you should have put in box 5.7 on page 1). If your total property income is over this limit, you need to list the expenses incurred in the tax year ending 5 April 2003 separately.

The details of what expenses you can claim in boxes 5.24 to 5.29 are given under Furnished holiday lettings on pp. 286–8. Note that with furnished property, you can claim a renewals deduction in box 5.25 for the cost of replacing furniture, fixtures and fittings, but not if you are already claiming a wear and tear allowance on the property (see below).

Don't include any expenses you have already claimed in boxes 5.2 to 5.7.

Add together the figures in boxes 5.24 to 5.29 and enter the total in box 5.30.

Net profit (put figures in brackets if a loss)	box 5.23 *minus* box 5.30 **5.31** £

Subtract the figure in box 5.30 from that in box 5.23 to find the net profit or loss on the letting. Enter the figure in box 5.31, in brackets if it is a loss.

Tax adjustments

■ *Tax adjustments*		
• Private use	**5.32** £	
• Balancing charges	**5.33** £	box 5.32 + box 5.33 **5.34** £

Box 5.32 is where you enter a figure for any private use of the property, in the same way as for furnished holiday lettings (see p. 289).

Any balancing charges (see p. 289) should be put in box 5.33. Add together the amounts in boxes 5.32 and 5.33 and put the total in box 5.34.

Enter in box 5.35 any tax-free amount you are claiming under the Rent a Room scheme (see p. 283). Otherwise leave it empty.

If you want to claim capital allowances (see p. 257), enter the amount in box 5.36. You can't claim capital allowances on items used in a property let as a furnished home (unless it is a furnished holiday letting). You can instead claim a renewals deduction for the cost of replacing such items (in box 5.25 above). Or you can claim a wear and tear allowance in box 5.37 of 10 per cent of the rent less service charges and local taxes. Once you have chosen a method, you can't switch. And if you have been using a different method of allowing for wear and tear agreed with your tax inspector before 6 April 1976, you can carry on using it.

• Rent a Room exempt amount	5.35 £		
• Capital allowances	5.36 £		
• Tick box 5.36A if box 5.36 includes a claim for 100% capital allowances for flats over shops	5.36A		
• Tick box 5.36B if box 5.36 includes enhanced capital allowances for environmentally friendly expenditure	5.36B		
• 10% wear and tear	5.37 £		
• Furnished holiday lettings losses (from box 5.18)	5.38 £	boxes 5.35 to box 5.38	5.39 £

Usually, capital allowances let you claim only part of your costs in the year you incurred them. But you can claim a 100 per cent capital allowance to cover in full any amount you have spent in the year to 5 April 2003 renovating or converting the space over a shop or other commercial property into flats for rent, provided certain conditions are met. The property must have been built before 1980, all or most of the ground floor must be for business use, it must have no more than five floors and the upstairs part must originally have been constructed primarily for residential use. The flats must pass a value test with the rents not exceeding given limits. The limits are set at £350 a week for a two-room flat in Greater London and £150 a week elsewhere rising to £480 a week for a four-room flat in Greater London and £300 a week elsewhere. Flats with five or more rooms do not qualify. 'Room' does not include kitchens, bathrooms and small hallways. If the figure you put in box 5.36 includes a claim for 100 per cent capital allowances for this purpose, tick box 5.36A. If you don't claim the full 100 per cent first year allowance, you can claim writing down allowance of 25 per cent in subsequent years.

If you are claiming first-year capital allowances on something which counts as environmentally friendly spending (see table on p. 259), tick box 5.36B.

You should already have filled in box 5.38 if you wish to set off a loss on furnished holiday lettings against other property income (see box 5.18).

In box 5.39 enter the total of boxes 5.35, 5.36, 5.37 and 5.38.

Adjusted profit (if loss enter '0' in box 5.40 and put the loss in box 5.41)		boxes 5.31 + 5.34 *minus* box 5.39 **5.40** £
Adjusted loss (if you have entered '0' in box 5.40)	boxes 5.31 + 5.34 *minus* box 5.39 **5.41** £	
• Loss brought forward from previous year		**5.42** £
Profit for the year		box 5.40 *minus* box 5.42 **5.43** £

Add the figures in boxes 5.31 and 5.34 together and subtract the figure in box 5.39. If the answer is a negative number, you have made a tax loss on your property interests. Enter 0 in box 5.40 and put the amount of the loss in box 5.41. There are several ways that a tax loss on property income can be used to reduce your tax bill (see boxes 5.44 to 5.46, below).

If you have made a profit, enter it in box 5.40. You can reduce this – and the amount of tax you pay on your property income – if you made a loss on property income from the tax year ending 5 April 2002. Enter the total loss from that year in box 5.42, and subtract it from the figure in box 5.40.

If the answer is a negative number, enter 0 in box 5.43 and put the balance in box 5.45. If the answer is more than zero, you have made a taxable profit on your property income for the tax year ending 5 April 2003.

Losses

• Loss offset against total income (read the note on page LN8)	**5.44** £
• Loss to carry forward to following year	**5.45** £

You can deduct a property income loss from other forms of income for the tax year ending 5 April 2003 but only in certain circumstances.

- If you have claimed capital allowances in box 5.36. Even then, the maximum loss you can set off in this way is restricted. See the notes accompanying the Land and property supplement for how to calculate and claim this relief
- If you have land used for agriculture and the loss is due to certain agricultural expenses. If this applies, ask the Orderline (see p. 147) to send you Helpsheet *IR251 Agricultural land*.

Enter the amount of loss you wish to deduct in this way in box 5.44. Alternatively, a loss which reflects an excess of capital allowances over balancing charges can be carried over to next year and set against your income for the tax year ending 5 April 2004. If this is what you would like to do, make a note of the figure to enter in the 2004 tax return.

Finally, any other unused losses can be carried over to deduct from future profits from property – enter these in box 5.45. If the figure in box 5.43 is 0 you will have already entered the right figure in box 5.45. If the figure in box 5.40 is 0, you find the figure to enter in box 5.45 by adding together the figures in boxes 5.41 and 5.42 and subtracting the figure in box 5.44.

• Tick box 5.46 if these Pages include details of property let jointly	5.46
• Tick box 5.47 if **all** property income ceased in the year to 5 April 2003 **and** you don't expect to receive such income again, in the year to 5 April 2004	5.47

Tick box 5.46 if you own and let property jointly with someone else – and give the name and address of the person who keeps the records in the Additional information box on page 9 of the basic tax return.

Tick box 5.47 if, during the year ending 5 April 2003, you stopped getting any income from property – for example, you sold all your rental properties – and you do not expect to have any property income in the year ending 5 April 2004.

FOREIGN

CHAPTER 21

Q6 Did you have any taxable income from overseas pensions or benefits, or from foreign companies or savings institutions, offshore funds or trusts abroad, or from land and property abroad or gains on foreign insurance policies? YES

Have you or could you have received, or enjoyed directly or indirectly, or benefited in any way from, income of a foreign entity as a result of a transfer of assets made in this or earlier years? YES

Do you want to claim foreign tax credit relief for foreign tax paid on foreign income or gains? YES

FOREIGN

If you ticked any of the three YES boxes at Q6 on page 2 of the basic tax return, you will need the supplementary pages called Foreign. These have space to give details about your foreign savings, pensions and benefits, property income and other investment income from abroad. Earnings from work abroad should be entered in the Employment, Self-Employment or Partnership pages of the tax return as appropriate, though you will need to use page 3 of the Foreign pages to claim any tax credit relief (see below). Similarly, details of capital gains on overseas transactions should be entered in the capital gains supplement, though you will need to use page 3 of the Foreign pages to claim any tax credit relief (see below).

Note that anywhere other than England, Scotland, Wales and Northern Ireland counts as 'foreign', so you should include, for example, interest from accounts held in the Channel Islands or Republic of Ireland on the Foreign pages.

This chapter tells you how to fill in the Foreign pages, and about the expenses and allowances you can claim. But the tax treatment of people who live abroad is beyond the scope of this guide. If this applies to you, seek professional advice from your bank, accountant or tax adviser.

How foreign income is taxed

Income from abroad is taxable in the UK, even if you have already paid foreign tax on it. You can deduct any foreign tax paid from the income before working out your UK tax bill – so you pay UK tax only on what you get after paying foreign tax.

But in most cases, you can instead claim a deduction from your UK tax bill to reflect the foreign tax paid, known as foreign tax credit relief. This is likely to mean paying less in UK tax than if you simply deduct the foreign tax from the gross income before working out the tax bill.

However, working out the amount of tax credit relief can be complicated and this guide assumes you are leaving the calculations to your tax inspector. If you feel up to the calculations, you can use the guidance notes sent out by the Inland Revenue to calculate your tax credit relief and thus your UK tax bill on such income.

> **EXAMPLE**
>
> Bill Livingstone made £2,500 after expenses last year letting out his villa in Freedonia. He paid the equivalent of £400 tax on this to the Freedonian tax authorities.
>
> In calculating his UK tax, he could have simply deducted the £400 of Freedonian tax from the £2,500 and paid tax on £2,100. Since he paid tax on the income at the basic rate of 22 per cent, the tax bill would have been 22% × £2,100 = £462.
>
> But he claimed tax credit relief, so the full £2,500 was taxable at 22 per cent – £550 in tax. He could then deduct the £400 of Freedonian tax, making his UK tax bill just £150.

Note that if the amount of foreign tax is adjusted, you must notify your tax inspector if it means any deduction for that tax was bigger than it should have been.

What income is taxed

The instructions below are for people who are domiciled in the UK and resident or ordinarily resident here. Their foreign income is taxed on an arising basis – when they get it or it is credited to them, regardless of whether or when it is brought back to the UK. You should enter the amounts you got in sterling, using the exchange rate on the date the income arose.

There are different rules for people who are not domiciled or not ordinarily resident in the UK – see Chapter 24 for how this is determined. If either applies, you will need to fill in the Non-residence supplementary pages (see p. 329). And your foreign income will be taxed on a remittance basis (ie only when income is brought into the UK rather than when it arose) – on the Foreign pages, enter the amounts of income received in the UK and the equivalent share of any foreign tax deducted from it.

Tax-free foreign income

The following types of foreign income are tax-free in the UK:

- pensions paid by Germany or Austria to the victims of Nazi persecution

and to pensioners who have fled from persecution
- the extra foreign pension paid to you if you have been retired because you were disabled by injury on duty or by a work-related illness
- any part of a pension from overseas that reduces the amount of tax-free UK war widows' and dependants' pensions
- social security benefits which are similar to UK benefits that are tax-free – child benefit, maternity allowance, guardian's allowance, child's special allowance, bereavement payments, incapacity benefit (only for the first six months if it began on or after 13 April 1996), attendance allowance, disability living allowance and severe disablement allowance.

A tenth of overseas pensions funded by an overseas employer or pension fund is tax-free in the UK unless it is taxed on a remittance basis (see p. 299).

Income stuck in a foreign country

In some cases, you will be unable to remit foreign income to the UK because it arises in a country which has exchange controls or is short of foreign exchange. If so, you can claim that the income should not after all be taxed in the year ending 5 April 2003. If income is unremittable, you will not be able to give all the information asked for on the pages of this supplement. In column A, enter the country and tick the box to show the income is unremittable. In column B, enter the amount of the income in foreign currency (delete the £ sign). In column D, enter the amount of any foreign tax paid on the income, again in the foreign currency concerned. Leave columns C and E blank.

The documents you need

You will need to gather together dividend vouchers for overseas shares, bank statements for overseas bank accounts, pension advice notes, foreign property bills – as well as details of any foreign tax paid.

FOREIGN SAVINGS

On page F1 give details of foreign interest and other savings income for the tax year ending 5 April 2003 unless you are taxed on a remittance basis (see p. 299). Savings taxed on a remittance basis go on page F2.

Enter each source of income on a separate line. If any of these types of income is from joint holdings, enter your share only. In column A give the name of the country where the income arose. In column B, give the amount of income before deducting any foreign tax or UK tax but after subtracting any income which is unremittable. In columns D, enter the amount of any foreign tax paid. If the income is unremittable, see *Income stuck in a foreign country* above.

Foreign savings

Fill in columns A, B, D and E, and tick the box in column E if you want to claim foreign tax credit relief.

	Country A	tick box if income is unremittable ▼	Amount before tax B	Foreign tax D	Amount chargeable E	tick box to claim foreign tax credit relief ▼
■ *Interest, and other income from overseas savings* - see Notes, page FN4			£	£	£	
			£	£	£	
			£	£	£	

Under double taxation agreements signed between the UK and more than 100 countries, tax should be deducted from investment income by the foreign country at a reduced rate which is then taken into account in calculating your UK tax bill. If the figure in column D is more than you should have paid under such an agreement, ask the foreign tax authority for a refund of the excess.

The amount you enter in column E depends on whether you wish to claim foreign tax credit relief (see p. 305):

- if you intend to claim it, enter the amount from column B and tick the box
- if you are not claiming tax credit relief, enter the figure from column B less any foreign tax from column D.

			£	£	£	
					total of column above 6.1 £	

Add the figures in column E and enter the total in box 6.1.

Enter the same information for dividends received for the tax year ending 5 April 2003 unless you are taxed on a remittance basis (see p. 299) The following should not be included:

> **TAX-SAVING IDEA**
>
> Some countries, such as Jersey, Guernsey and the Isle of Man, pay gross interest on savings (in other words, without deducting any tax). If you are a UK taxpayer, you must declare this interest and pay UK tax on it. But there can be a delay between earning the interest and paying the tax. For example, if interest was paid or credited on 30 April 2003 and you pay tax through self-assessment, the tax is not due until 31 January 2005. In the meantime, you can earn extra interest on the uncollected tax.

- distributions by a foreign company in the form of shares (but enter any cash alternative you took instead)
- stock dividends from foreign companies
- bonus shares from a scrip issue by a foreign company
- capital distributions – for example, the return of your capital or distributions in the course of a liquidation.

		£	£	£	
				total of column above	
			6.2	£	

Add the figures for dividends in column E and enter the total in box 6.2.

Foreign savings income taxable on the remittance basis and foreign income from overseas pensions or social security benefits, from land and property abroad, chargeable premiums or income/benefits received from overseas trusts, companies and other entities

On page F2, give the same information for foreign pensions, social security benefits and property income. And if you are taxed on your foreign income on a remittance basis (see p. 299), this is where you give details of foreign interest, dividends and other savings income. In addition to columns A, B, D and E, you need to enter in column C any UK tax deducted from certain types of income.

Pensions and social security benefits

Exclude pensions and benefits which are free of UK tax – see p. 300. If only part of a payment is free of UK tax, give the amount which is not exempt in column E.

INCOME FROM FOREIGN LAND AND PROPERTY

Income from overseas property is taxed in much the same way as that from UK property (see p. 283). You can deduct expenses including the cost of managing the property and collecting the income (for example, paying an agent). If you buy equipment, you may be able to claim a capital allowance or some other form of deduction (see p. 294). And you can deduct loan interest on the property.

As for UK property, there are certain expenses you cannot claim. These include personal expenses – such as the costs incurred while the property is not let. Nor can you claim any loss you make when you sell the property.

There is space on page F2 of the Foreign supplement for details of the income and tax paid on overseas property and land. But before you fill this in, you must turn to page F4 and complete a copy of it for each property, giving details of the income, expenses and other deductions for the tax year ending 5 April 2003. Then complete page F5. If your foreign income is taxed on a remittance basis (see p. 299), you do not need to complete pages F4 and F5.

OTHER OVERSEAS INCOME

This is where you give details of miscellaneous other types of overseas income. If you have these complex investments, you should take specialised tax advice.

- Disposals of holdings in offshore funds, income from non-resident trusts and benefits received from overseas trusts, companies and other entities - *see Notes, page FN11.* **6.5** £

Offshore funds

The income from an offshore fund should be entered as savings income on page F1 of the foreign pages. Here you must give details of any gain made on cashing in part or all of your investment unless the fund qualifies as a distributor fund – one which distributes most of its income as dividends. This is to stop investors rolling up income in offshore funds to create capital gains and so reduce their tax bills.

If the fund does not count as a distributor fund, enter the gain in box 6.5. If you have received an equalisation payment from a distributor fund, you should enter the part of the gain taxable as income in box 6.5. The taxable amount will be shown on the voucher given to you by the fund manager.

The government is currently reviewing the regime for taxing offshore funds and intends to make changes in the 2004 Finance Act.

Income from non-resident trusts

If you are entitled to the income from a trust that is not resident in the UK, enter the amount from foreign sources in box 6.5. Any of the trust's income from UK sources should have been entered in the appropriate boxes of the Income part of the tax return as if it had been paid direct to you.

Any income paid to you from a non-resident trust at the discretion of the trustees should be entered in box 6.5.

Income received by trusts or companies abroad

You may have transferred assets with the result that income becomes payable to a company, trust or other entity based abroad. If you or your husband or wife may at any time enjoy that income (say, because you are shareholders of the company or beneficiaries of the trust), or you receive or are entitled to receive a capital sum (including a loan) in connection with the transfer, the income or capital sum is taxable as income and should be entered on page F2 and included in boxes 6.3 and 6.3A or 6.4 and 6.4A unless you are ticking box 6.5A (see below).

If someone else makes a transfer to the company, trust or other entity described above, you are taxed on the income or other benefit to the extent that the company has 'unexpended income'. This means income that has not already passed to someone else or been spent by the company, trust or other entity. In this case, put the amount in box 6.5 unless you are ticking box 6.5A (see below).

In either case, give details of the assets transferred and the name and address of the company, trust or other entity concerned in box 6.39 on page F5.

If you have these complex types of investments, you should take specialised tax advice.

If you can show that the purpose of the transfer of assets was not to avoid tax, you won't need to give details here. Tick box 6.5A.

Foreign life insurance policies

	Number of years	Tax treated as paid	Gains(s)
• Gains on foreign life insurance policies etc. - *see Notes page FN12.*	6.6	6.7 £	6.8 £

Give details here of any gains you have made on foreign life insurance policies – whether because the policy has come to an end or because you have drawn some benefit from it. Enter the number of years you have held the policy in box 6.6 and the gain in box 6.8.

Most such gains are simply added to your taxable income because no foreign tax has been paid on them. If foreign tax has been deducted, you may be able to get a 'credit for notional basic rate tax' which means the gain will be taxed only at the difference between the basic and higher rate in the same way as a UK life insurance policy gain (see p. 174). Enter the amount of any notional income tax credit in box 6.7.

FOREIGN TAX CREDIT RELIEF

With all types of foreign income, you can simply deduct any foreign tax already paid from the income before working out the UK tax bill. But you are likely to pay less UK tax if you claim foreign tax credit relief which reduces the UK tax bill to reflect the foreign tax already paid.

This section is for calculating tax credit relief on all your foreign income, including that from investments, pensions, benefits and property already entered above. But you can also claim the relief on foreign income from employment, self-employment and partnerships which you will have entered elsewhere on the tax return.

Foreign tax credit relief for foreign tax paid on employment, self-employment and other income

See Notes, page FN14

Enter in this column the Page number in your Tax Return from which information is taken. Do this for each item for which you are claiming foreign tax credit relief ▼	Country **A**	Foreign tax **D**	Amount chargeable **E**	tick box to claim foreign tax credit relief ▼
		£	£	
		£	£	
		£	£	

First you must enter details of these other forms of foreign income. Give the country the income arose in, the amount of foreign tax paid on it and the gross amount of the income before deduction of foreign tax. In the first column, give the page number of the tax return where the income is fully reported.

Box 6.9 gives you room to enter the amount of foreign tax credit relief you wish to claim on all of your foreign income. This is only for people who want to do the sums themselves – if you don't want to get involved in the calculations, go on to the next section.

If you want to work out your tax credit relief, you need to use the Foreign Tax Credit Relief Working Sheet on pages FN18 to FN23 of the Notes on Foreign. There are full instructions on pages FN15 to FN16, and all the data you need to complete it on the following pages. You won't be able to complete the working sheet until you have completed most of the rest of the tax return. Some of the figures you have to enter on it are drawn from the Tax Calculation Guide which you use to work out your overall tax bill.

- If you are calculating your tax, enter the total foreign tax credit relief on your income in box 6.9
  - see Notes, pages FN15 and FN16.

6.9 £

Fill in a separate working sheet for each item of foreign income you wish to claim relief for. Enter the total amount you wish to claim in box 6.9.

The bottom half of the page is for details of capital gains you wish to claim foreign tax credit relief on. Help Sheet *IR261 Foreign Tax Credit Relief: Capital Gains* tells you what to enter and how to do the sums if you wish to calculate the tax credit relief on your foreign gains.

Foreign tax credit relief for foreign tax paid on chargeable gains reported on your Capital Gains Pages

See Notes, page FN15

Amount of gain under UK rules	Period over which UK gain accrued	Amount of gain under foreign tax rules	Period over which foreign gain accrued	Foreign tax paid D	tick box to claim foreign tax credit relief ▼
£	*days*	£	*days*	£	
£	*days*	£	*days*	£	
£	*days*	£	*days*	£	

- If you are calculating your tax, enter the total foreign tax credit relief on your gains in box 6.10
  - see Notes, page FN15.

6.10 £

If you have calculated the tax credit relief on your capital gains, enter the total in box 6.10.

TRUSTS

CHAPTER 22

Q7 Did you receive, or are you deemed to have, income from a trust, settlement or the residue of a deceased person's estate?	YES	TRUSTS ETC

If you ticked the YES box at Q7 on page 2 of the basic tax return, you will need the supplementary page called Trusts etc. You should give details about taxable income from trusts and other forms of settlement such as a transfer of assets, and from the estates of people who have died. In some cases, you may have to give details of income from trusts you have set up. Even though the money has been paid to someone else, it may be treated as yours.

Do not enter any details in this supplement about income from a 'bare trust' – a trust to which you have an absolute right to both the income and assets. You are treated as the owner of the assets and any income or gains from them. You should enter income from a bare trust in the sections of the basic tax return and other supplements that deal with the particular type of income concerned.

The documents you need

With a payment from a trust or an estate, the trustees or personal representatives should have given you a form R185 setting out the details. There are different versions of the forms for interest in possession trusts, for other trusts and for estates.

If you have directly or indirectly provided funds for a settlement and are not sure whether the income will be treated as yours, Help Sheet *IR270 Trusts and settlements – income treated as the settlor's* should help. Ask the Orderline (p. 147).

INCOME FROM TRUSTS AND SETTLEMENTS

Income paid out by trusts and other forms of settlement in the tax year ending 5 April 2003 comes with a tax credit which reflects the amount of tax already deducted from it or deemed to have been paid on it. What you receive is the net (after-tax) amount of income. To find the gross (before-tax) amount, you need to add back the tax credit. You can find out the amount of the tax credit from certificate R185 or similar statement the trustees should give you.

How trust income is taxed

The amount of the tax credit depends on the type of trust:

- trust with an interest in possession where you have the 'absolute right' to the income from the trust. The tax credit will be at the rate of 20 per cent of the grossed-up amount of interest; 10 per cent of the grossed-up amount of share dividends and unit trust distributions; and for other sorts of income, such as rents or royalties, it will be at the basic rate of tax – 22 per cent for the tax year ending 5 April 2003
- a discretionary trust where the trustees have discretion about paying out the income. The tax credit will be at the 'rate applicable to trusts', which is 34 per cent of the grossed-up income
- accumulation and maintenance trusts – the income also comes with a tax credit of 34 per cent.

If the tax credit, other than the 10 per cent credit on share dividends and similar income, is more than the amount of tax you would have paid if the grossed-up income had come direct to you, you can claim a rebate. For example, if you get interest from a trust and your income – including the grossed-up trust income – is too low to pay tax, you could reclaim all the tax credit which comes with it. With a discretionary trust, anyone not liable to higher rate tax can reclaim part of the tax credits.

Higher rate taxpayers will have to pay extra tax on income from either sort of trust. With a discretionary trust, this would be an extra 6 per cent of the grossed-up amount (the difference between the 40 per cent higher rate and the 34 per cent tax credit that comes from the trust).

Trust income that might be treated as yours

If you have directly or indirectly provided funds for a settlement, the income from those funds may be treated as yours – even though you haven't received it.

The sorts of trust which might produce an income that would be treated as yours include:

- a trust from which you, your husband or wife or children can benefit
- a trust that has lent or repaid money to you or your spouse
- a trust where the capital would come back to you if the beneficiaries died before becoming entitled to it.

TAX-SAVING IDEA

If you want to give a child more capital and their income is approaching the limit at which it will be treated as yours, think about gifts in investments such as National Savings Children's Bonus Bonds, National Savings Certificates which produce a tax-free return or paying into a stakeholder pension scheme for your child.

EXAMPLE

Gerry Hall received £250 from a discretionary trust in the tax year ending 5 April 2003, which comes with a tax credit of £128.79. He pays tax at no more than the basic rate (even when the grossed-up trust payment of £378.79 is added to his income). So he should have paid tax on the payment at the basic rate of 22 per cent only – a tax bill of 22 per cent of £378.79, or £83.33. He is thus entitled to a rebate of: £128.79 – £83.33 = £45.46

This treatment might also apply if you make some investments on behalf of your children unless they have reached 18 or they are married – for example, opening a savings account in their names. Any income from such investments is treated as yours unless it is £100 a year or less before tax. This exception applies to gifts from each parent, so a child can have up to £200 a year before tax in income from gifts from both parents without a problem.

You can't get round this by giving the funds to someone else who passes them on to your child. You would still have indirectly provided the funds and the income would be yours. The same would be true if you settled some money on a friend's child in return for him doing the same for you.

This income should be included as your own in Q10 in the basic tax return and not entered on the Trusts etc pages unless you create a proper trust.

Enter the income from trusts in the tax year ending 5 April 2003 in boxes 7.1 to 7.12. Also include here any income from trusts or settlements which is treated as yours even though you haven't received it. For discretionary trusts, put the actual amount received in box 7.1, the tax credit in box 7.2 and the gross income in box 7.3 (this should be the sum of boxes 7.1 and 7.2). For income from a trust with an interest in possession on which the tax credit is at the 22 per cent basic rate, give the same details in boxes 7.4 to

TAX-SAVING IDEA

Reclaim some or all of the tax credit that comes with income from trusts if it is more than you would have paid if the income had come straight to you. Unless you pay tax at the higher rate, you will always be entitled to a rebate on income from a discretionary trust.

7.6. For savings income on which the tax credit is 20 per cent, enter the details in boxes 7.7 to 7.9. For dividends and distributions where the tax credit is 10 per cent, enter the details in boxes 7.10 to 7.12.

Income from trusts and settlements

■ *Income taxed at:*

	Income receivable	Tax paid	Taxable amount
• the 'rate applicable to trusts'	7.1 £	7.2 £	7.3 £
• the basic rate	7.4 £	7.5 £	7.6 £
• the lower rate	7.7 £	7.8 £	7.9 £
• the dividend rate	7.10 £	7.11 £	7.12 £

You don't need to enter the following here:

- ◆ scrip dividends or foreign income dividends received from a trust with an interest in possession and paid by UK companies, authorised unit trusts or open-ended investment companies – give details of these on page 3 of the basic tax return (see p. 164)
- ◆ income from foreign sources paid to you by a trust with an interest in possession – give details on the Foreign supplementary pages (see p. 298)
- ◆ income from a discretionary trust where the trustees are not resident in the UK – this should also go on the Foreign pages.

INCOME FROM ESTATES

Income from the estates of deceased persons

■ *Income bearing:*

	Income receivable	Tax paid	Taxable amount
• basic rate tax	7.13 £	7.14 £	7.15 £
• lower rate tax	7.16 £	7.17 £	7.18 £
• repayable dividend rate	7.19 £	7.20 £	7.21 £
• non-repayable basic rate tax	7.22 £	7.23 £	7.24 £
• non-repayable lower rate tax	7.25 £	7.26 £	7.27 £
• non-repayable dividend rate	7.28 £	7.29 £	7.30 £

You do not pay income tax on anything you inherit from a dead person. And if you have inherited something which then produces an income, such as money in a bank savings account or properties that produce rent, you should enter the interest or other income in the appropriate part of the main tax return. You might receive interest along with a legacy because, say, there has been a delay between your inheriting the item and it being handed over. Do not include the interest on these pages – it should be entered under Q10 on the basic tax return.

However, you should give details in this section of the tax return of income you receive from the estate while it is being wound up by the personal representatives – the executors or administrators. You would be entitled to this income if you were a residuary beneficiary – the person or one of the people who gets what is left after all the specific bequests and legacies have been made.

Such income will come with a tax credit in the same way as a trust with an interest in possession. For most types of income, this tax will be repayable if it is more than you would have paid; but the tax is not repayable for some types of income such as gains on life insurance policies and UK dividends.

The statement supplied by the personal representatives – tax certificate R185 (Estate income) – will show you the rate the income has been taxed at and whether it is repayable. Enter the details for the tax year ending 5 April 2003 in boxes 7.13 to 7.30. Give the name of the estate and the total amount paid to you in the Additional information box at the bottom of the page.

In some cases, income accrued during the life of the dead person and paid into the estate after their death will come to you after being taken into account in calculating the inheritance tax bill on the estate. There is a special tax relief that stops you having to pay higher rate tax on such income – ask your tax inspector for details.

Income from foreign estates

If you get income from a foreign estate, it will not have borne full UK tax – either because the personal representatives are outside the UK tax net or because the estate is that of someone who died while domiciled outside the UK and has income from non-UK sources. In this case, enter the full amount of such income in both boxes 7.13 and 7.15. Don't enter anything in box 7.14, even if some foreign tax has been deducted.

If the foreign estate has some income from UK sources, it will have paid some UK tax. In this case, you can reduce the amount entered in boxes 7.13 and 7.15 by the following amount:

$$\frac{\text{net amount of income subject to UK tax}}{\text{total estate income less UK tax}} \times \text{total estate income before UK tax}$$

Foreign tax paid

• total foreign tax for which tax credit relief not claimed	7.31	£

If you have been paid income from an estate which has already been taxed in a foreign country, you may end up paying two lots of tax on it: tax in the foreign country and tax in the UK. You may be able to reduce the amount of UK tax you pay on the income to reflect the foreign tax paid – this is known as tax credit relief.

To claim tax credit relief – which will usually be worthwhile – leave box 7.31 blank and make your claim on the Foreign supplementary pages (see p. 298).

If you don't want to claim tax credit relief – which can be quite complicated – you can instead deduct the foreign tax you have paid from the income. Enter the amount in box 7.31.

CAPITAL GAINS

CHAPTER 23

Q8	Capital gains - read the guidance on page 7 of the Tax Return Guide.		
	• If you have disposed of your only or main residence do you need the Capital Gains Pages?	YES	
	• Did you dispose of other chargeable assets worth more than £15,400 in total?	YES	
	• Were your total chargeable gains more than £7,700 or do you want to make a claim or election for the year?	YES	CAPITAL GAINS

If you have ticked any of the three YES boxes in Q8 on page 2 of the basic tax return, you will need the supplementary pages called Capital gains. These ask for details of taxable gains you have made on buying and selling assets such as shares, unit trusts and property. You may also have to report a taxable gain even though you haven't sold something – if you give it away, for example. And if you have made a loss on such assets, you should give details here also, since it might reduce your overall tax bill now or in the future.

This chapter tells you how to fill in the Capital gains supplementary pages. Chapter 10 explains how the tax works in detail with examples of the sometimes complicated calculations needed to fill in these pages. It also explains how to claim all the reliefs and allowances to minimise your capital gains tax bill.

The documents you need

You will need details of anything you have spent on buying or selling or maintaining the value of assets. With shares and unit trusts, you need any paperwork relating to share issues while you owned them or company reorganisations.

For assets owned on 31 March 1982, you may also need details of their value on that date (see p. 115). Use catalogues, press advertisements or stock market share price records to value them.

With assets that are jointly owned, you need enter only your share of any gains. With a husband and wife, the gain or loss is split 50:50 between them unless they have told their tax inspectors that the asset is not owned equally (see p. 108).

CHARGEABLE GAINS AND ALLOWABLE LOSSES

The first page of the Capital gains pages has space at the top for you to write your name and the tax reference you will find on the front of your basic tax return. What you do next depends on what transactions you carried out in the year ending 5 April 2003.

If you have only made relatively straightforward transactions in quoted shares or securities, including unit trusts, you can use the simple grid on page CG1 (see opposite). But you cannot use this page if any of the shares were held at 31 March 1982, or you are able to claim taper relief on any of the gains made, or you want to claim any other tax relief that would reduce your gains other than indexation allowance.

If your transactions are more than just quoted shares, or you can claim taper relief, or you want to claim reliefs such as reinvestment relief, you must fill in pages CG2 to CG6 instead (see p. 318).

In some circumstances, you may need to give details of capital gains or losses even though you haven't disposed of the assets they relate to in the tax year ending 5 April 2003. For example, if you have been given something and agreed to take over the gain from its previous owner (hold-over relief), you have to pay tax on that gain if you become non-resident within six years of the end of the tax year in which the gift was made (see p. 131). Include any gains made by a trust that are treated as your gains because you are the settlor and, for example, you or your husband or wife can benefit from the trust.

Include anything you have been given as a result of the reconstruction or takeover of a company, building society or mutual insurance company (see p. 128). But you don't need to enter any details of disposals of assets on which gains are tax-free. Thus you should leave out possessions which are worth £6,000 or less when you disposed of them – these are known as chattels (see p. 117). However, if you made a loss on the disposal of a chattel, you should give details since it could be used to reduce your tax bill.

PAGE CG1: QUOTED SHARES AND SECURITIES ONLY

A Enter details of quoted shares or other securities disposed of	B Tick box if estimate or valuation used	C Enter the date of disposal	D Disposal proceeds	E Gain or loss after indexation allowance, if due (enter loss in brackets)	F Further information, including any elections made
1		/ /	£	£	
2		/ /	£	£	

This page is for giving details of each taxable disposal of quoted shares and other securities made during the tax year ending 5 April 2003. 'Quoted shares and other securities' means:

- shares or securities of a company which are quoted on the London Stock Exchange (including its subsidiary techMARK) throughout the period you held them. This does not include UK shares quoted on the Alternative Investment Market, Ofex or Tradepoint
- shares or securities of a company listed on an overseas recognised stock exchange throughout the period you held them. This includes NASDAQ. It used also to include shares quoted on European junior markets, such as NADAQ Europe (formerly EASDAQ), the Nouveau Marché and Neue Markt Frankfurt. But from 28 November 2001, these no longer count as recognised exchanges. Do not enter here any shares listed on these exchanges that you bought before 28 November 2001 – use pages CG2 and CG3 instead
- units in a unit trust which was UK authorised throughout the period you held them
- shares in a company which was an open-ended investment company (oeic) throughout the period you held them.

If you are likely to run out of space on page CG1, make photocopies before filling it in. Put your name and tax reference on each sheet.

Column A: Give details to identify the shares or unit trusts – the name of the company or unit trust fund manager, types of shares or units and the number disposed of.

Column B: Tick this box if your figures include any estimates or valuations. This would be the case if the shares or securities were acquired from or disposed of to a connected person (see p. 111). Give details of why you have used an estimate in column F, or on page CG7 if there is not enough space.

Column C: Enter the date you disposed of the shares or securities, in numerical form (so 24 August 2002 would be 24/08/02).

Column D: Enter the total disposal proceeds, including any cash or other asset to be received in the future. But if the disposal was a gift or a sale to a connected person you should enter the market value of the asset (see p. 111).

Column E: Enter the net gain or loss after any indexation allowance you are claiming. Put losses in brackets. See Chapter 10 for how to work out the gain or loss and indexation allowance.

Column F: Give any other relevant details on the disposal, including if it is a disposal of part of a larger holding of shares (p. 113) or if you have exchanged shares in a company takeover or reconstruction.

You don't have to submit the calculations done to reach any of these figures – but you can if you want to. There's space on page CG7 to give details.

Total gains	**F1** £	*Total your gains in column E and enter the amount in box F1*
Total losses	**F2** £	*Total your losses in column E and enter the amount in box F2*

Add all your gains in column F and enter the total in box F1. Add all your losses and enter the total in box F2.

Net gain/(loss)	box F1 *minus* box F2 **F3** £	*If your net gains are below £7,700* ***or*** *you have a net loss, there is no liability. If you have a net loss, please fill in the losses summary on Page CG8 otherwise carry*

Subtract your total losses in box F2 from your total gains in box F1 and enter the answer in box F3. If the amount in box F3 is more than £7,700, continue to box F4.

If the amount in box F3 is £7,700 or less, there is no capital gains tax to pay – enter the amount in box F7 and box 8.7 on page CG8. Leave box 8.8 on page CG8 blank. If the amount in box F3 is a net loss, go to p. 323 and fill in the Capital losses summary on page CG8.

minus income losses set against gains	**F4** £

There are losses on several types of income you can deduct from a net chargeable gain if you haven't enough income to set them off against:

- any trading losses from self-employment (p. 276) or a partnership
- losses from furnished holiday lettings (p. 290)
- certain expenses incurred in the seven years after you have closed a business which would have been allowable against business income (post-

cessation expenditure) – for example bad debts, costs of rectifying faulty work (p. 191)

- certain expenses incurred by employees up to six years after they have left their jobs (post-employment deductions) – for example, insurance premiums for policies that pay out against claims of faulty work.

If you have such losses, you can enter them in box F4 up to the amount in box F3.

	box F3 *minus* box F4 **F5** £	*If your gains are now below £7,700, there is no liability; copy box F5 to box F7 and complete Page CG8. Otherwise, carry on to box F6*

Subtract the amount in box F4 from the amount in box F3 and enter the result in box F5. If the amount in box F5 is more than £7,700, continue to box F6.

If the amount in box F5 is £7,700 or less, there is no capital gains tax to pay – enter the amount in box F7 and box 8.7 on page CG8. Leave box 8.8 on page CG8 blank.

minus losses brought forward	**F6** £	*Enter losses brought forward up to the **smaller** of either the total losses brought forward or the figure in box F5 **minus** £7,700*

You deduct any allowable losses left over from previous tax years from the amount in box F5 (see p. 118). If you have enough losses held over, you must reduce your total taxable gains to £7,700, the amount that is tax-free for the tax year ending 5 April 2003.

If your losses from previous years are not big enough to reduce the amount in box F5 to £7,700, enter the full amount carried over in box F6. If your losses from previous years are more than enough to reduce the amount in box F5 to £7,700 enter in Box F6 the amount that subtracted from the amount in box F5 will leave exactly £7,700.

Total taxable gains	box F5 *minus* box F6 **F7** £	*Copy this figure to box 8.7 on Page CG8 (if F7 is blank because there is no liability, leave 8.7 blank).*

Subtract the amount in box F6 from the amount in box F5 and enter the result in box F7. This is your total taxable gains for the year ending 5 April 2003. Copy this figure to box 8.7 on page CG8 and fill in the rest of that page. If there is any additional information you need to give, there is space on page CG7.

PAGES CG2 AND CG3: DISPOSALS OF MORE THAN QUOTED SHARES

Complete these pages if you have made disposals which include land, homes or unquoted shares either on their own or in addition to quoted shares and securities. Also fill in these pages if you are disposing of shares or securities held at 31 March 1932, or on which you are claiming taper relief or any other tax relief other than indexation allowance.

Your 2002-03 Capital Gains Tax liability

A Brief description of asset	AA* Type of disposal. Enter Q, U, L, T or O	B Tick box if estimate or valuation used	C Tick box if asset held at 31March 1982	D Enter the later of date of acquisition and 16 March 1998	E Enter the date of disposal	F Disposal proceeds	G Enter details of any elections made, reliefs claimed or due and state amount (£)
Gains on assets which are either wholly business or wholly non-business							
1				/ /	/ /	£	

Losses Description of asset	Type of * disposal. Enter Q, U, L or O	Tick box if estimate or valuation used	Tick box if asset held at 31March 1982	Enter the later of date of acquisition and 16 March 1998	Enter the date of disposal	Disposal proceeds	Enter details of any elections made, reliefs claimed or due and state amount (£)
13				/ /	/ /	£	

You will see there is space to give details of ten disposals that resulted in gains (two where the asset was used for both business and non-business purposes) and four that produced allowable losses. If you are likely to run out of space, make photocopies of pages CG2 and CG3 before filling them in. Put your name and tax reference on each extra sheet you submit.

Column A: Give details to identify the asset – the address of the property, for example, or the name of the company with shares, the type of share and the number disposed of.

Column AA: Enter one of the following letters in this column:

- Q for quoted shares or securities (for what these are, see p. 315)

- U for unquoted shares or securities
- L for land or property
- T for a trust gain treated as yours because you are the settlor if you have opted to set personal losses against these gains (see Tax-Saving Idea). Fill in all the columns except B to F. If you are not claiming personal losses against these gains, do not enter them here. Instead enter them at lines 11 and 12 with the total in box 8.4 (see p. 323)
- O for other assets (for example, chattels or goodwill).

> **TAX-SAVING IDEA**
>
> From 6 April 2003 onwards, where gains made by a trust are attributed to you as settlor, any capital losses you personally have made which cannot be used against personal gains must be set against the trust gains. For the tax years ending 5 April 2001, 2002 and 2003, you can choose whether to use your personal losses in this way (instead of carrying them forward) and you have until 31 January 2005 to make this election. Work out the tax due with and without the election and opt for whichever method produces the lowest bill. The losses are set against the trust gains after deducting any trust losses but before deducting taper relief. Then the taper relief that the trustees would otherwise have applied is set against the net trust gains attributed to you. See Inland Revenue Help Sheet IR277 *Trusts with settlor interest: taper and losses* for more information. For guidance on when trust gains are attributable to the settlor, see Inland Revenue Help Sheets IR294 *Trusts and capital gains tax* and IR299 *Non-resident trusts and capital gains tax*.

Column B: Tick this box if your figures include any estimates or valuations. This would be the case if you owned the asset on 31 March 1982 when you need to estimate its value on that date (p. 115). Transactions with connected people also involve market valuations (see p. 111). Give details of why you have used an estimate in column G, or on page CG7 if there is not enough space.

Column C: Tick if you owned the asset on 31 March 1982 – there are special rules for calculating the gains and losses on such assets (see p. 115). Also tick if you are treated as having owned it then – for example, if your spouse did and has since given it to you.

Column D: Enter the date you acquired the asset if it was after 16 March 1998. If it was on or before 16 March 1998, enter that date. Give the date in numerical form (so 24 August 2002 would be 24/08/02).

Column E: Enter the date you disposed of the asset, in numerical form.

Column F: Enter the total disposal proceeds, including any cash or other asset to be received in the future. But if the disposal was a gift or a sale to a connected person you should enter the market value of the asset (see p. 111).

If you have been given the right to something in the future in return for the disposal, this should also be included unless it would be taxed as income (for example, dividends or royalties). If it is not clear what you will get in the future – as with a share of any profits – include an estimate in the disposal proceeds. When that uncertain part is finally paid, this will count as another disposal – the right to the share of the profits will have been exchanged for real cash. There will then be another capital gain or loss to report at that time.

Column G: If you wish to claim any tax relief on the gain other than indexation allowance, give details here plus the amount claimed. These include private residence relief on your only or main home (p. 56), retirement relief when you retire from a business (p. 133) and rebasing relief (p. 116). Also say here if you are making any claim that defers the tax such as hold-over relief (p. 131), capital gains deferral relief (p. 132) or roll-over relief (p. 134). Special claim forms may be needed in addition to the tax return.

Column H: Enter in the *Gains* section the net gain after any indexation allowance or other relief, but before losses and taper relief. Enter any losses in the *Losses* section lower down the page. If the assets are for mixed business and non-business use, split the gains and losses appropriately.

H Chargeable Gains after reliefs but before losses and taper	I Enter 'Bus' if business asset	J Taper rate	K Losses deducted			L Gains after losses	M Tapered gains (gains from column L x % in column J)
			K1 Allowable losses of the year	K2 Income losses of 2002-03 set against gains	K3 Unused losses b/f from earlier years		
£		%	£	£	£	£	£
£		%	£	£	£	£	£
£		%	£	£	£	£	£

Add all your gains in column H and enter the total in box 8.1. Add all your losses and enter the total in box 8.2. Subtract the amount in box 8.2 from the amount in box 8.1. Provided you have no trust gains attributed to you not already dealt with by setting off of personal losses (see p. 319), continue with page CG3 unless any of the following applies:

- If the answer is £7,700 or less, you have no capital gains tax to pay in the tax year ending 5 April 2003. Enter the answer in box 8.3 and in box 8.7 on page CG8. Enter 0 in box 8.4. Give any information needed on pages CG4 to CG6 and turn to page CG8.
- If the answer is more than £7,700 and you have enough losses brought forward from a previous year to reduce your gains to £7,700, you have no capital gains tax to pay. Enter in box 8.6 the amount of losses from previous years needed to achieve this and enter £7,700 in box 8.3 and in box 8.7 on page CG8. Enter 0 in box 8.4. Give any information needed on pages CG4 to CG6 and turn to page CG8.
- If the answer is a minus amount, your allowable losses are greater than your chargeable gains. You have no capital gains tax to pay – enter 0 in boxes 8.3, 8.4 and 8.7 on page CG8. Give any information needed on pages CG4 to CG6 and turn to page CG8.

Column I: Enter 'Bus' in this colum in the appropriate row if the asset was a business asset or used partly for business after 5 April 1998.

Column J: This column is for the taper rate on the disposal – the percentage of the net gain that is taxable after deducting taper relief. So if the rate of taper relief is 15 per cent, the taper rate is 85 per cent. Taper relief came into effect only from 1998 onwards (see p. 119). To find the taper rate you should use, see the table on p. 120.

Column K: This column is for entering any losses to be deducted from net gains – with three possible sources.

Column K1: Enter allowable losses from the tax year ending 5 April 2003. Allocate these against the gains on assets with the highest taper rates first. If you still have some losses unused after doing that, allocate the rest against the gains on the assets with the next highest taper rates.

> **TAX-SAVING IDEA**
>
> Normally a capital loss must be set against gains made in the same tax year even if that means some or all of your tax-free allowance (£7,700 in the year ending 5 April 2003) is wasted. However, a loss made on a disposal to a 'connected person' (see p. 111) must be carried forward until it can be set against gains on disposals to the same connected person. Therefore, you can avoid wasting your tax-free allowance by selling or giving the loss-making asset to a connected person (which could include a trust of which you are the settlor).

Suppose, for example, you have a net gain of £10,000 with a taper rate of 100 per cent and another of £10,000 with a taper rate of 85 per cent. You have an allowable loss of £15,000. You should allocate £10,000 of the loss to the gain with a taper rate of 100 per cent, the highest taper rate. The remaining £5,000 of the loss should be allocated to the gain with the taper rate of 85 per cent. That leaves a net gain of £5,000 with a taper rate of 85 per cent. If you allocated the loss the other way – £10,000 to the gain with a taper rate of 85 per cent – you would be left with a net gain of £5,000 with a taper rate of 100 per cent, and a higher tax bill.

Note that you must deduct the losses so long as there are gains to deduct them from – you can't hold losses from the same tax year back even if your total gains are going to end up below the tax-free allowance of £7,700 for the tax year ending 5 April 2003.

Column K2 is for entering losses on several types of income you can deduct from a net chargeable gain if you haven't enough income to set them off against. The income losses that can be used in this way are the same as those listed for box F4 on p. 000.

If you have such losses, you don't have to deduct them here – and you should not if deducting them means you would lose the benefit of your £7,700 tax-free allowance for the tax year ending 5 April 2003.

Column K3 is for losses carried forward from earlier tax years. Again you shouldn't deduct more than you need to reduce your total gains to the tax-free allowance of £7,700 for the tax year ending 5 April 2003.

Add the losses claimed in column K2 and enter the total in box 8.5. Add the losses claimed in column K3 and enter the total in box 8.6.

Column L: For each asset, subtract the losses in Columns K1, K2 and K3 from the net gain in Column J and enter the result in Column L. This is the gain after losses.

Column M: For each asset, multiply the amount in Column L by the taper rate in Column J and enter the result in Column M. This is the tapered gain on the disposal.

So if the gain after losses is £10,000 and the taper rate is 95 per cent, the tapered gain on disposal would be:

£10,000 × 95% = £9,500

Add the gains in column M and enter the total in box 8.3.

		11 **Attributed gains from UK resident trusts where no election has been made for the set off of personal losses** (see page CGN4) *(enter the name of the Trust on Page CG7)*	£
	Losses arising	12 **Attributed gains from non UK resident trusts where no election has been made for the set off of personal losses** (see page CGN4) *(enter the name of the Trust on Page CG7)*	£

Enter any trust gains attributable to you as settlor if you have not elected to set personal losses against them (see p. 319). Give the name of the trust on page CG7 and details of how the gains have been attributed to you.

		Total of attributed gains where no election has been made (total of rows 11 and 12)	8.4 £
	£	**Total taxable gains** (after allowable losses and taper relief)	box 8.3 + box 8.4 £

Add the amounts of attributed gains and enter the total in box 8.4.

Add the amount in box 8.3 to the amount in box 8.4 to find your total taxable gains. Enter the answer in the box and copy it to box 8.7 on page CG8. Complete pages CG4, CG5 and CG6 for all disposals not involving quoted shares or securities.

You don't have to submit the calculations done to reach these figures – but you can if you want to. There's space on page CG7 to give details.

PAGES CG4 TO CG6: FURTHER INFORMATION

These pages are for giving extra details needed for any transactions in unquoted shares or securities, land and property or other assets. Each page has room for two such transactions – if you need more space, make copies.

PAGE CG7: ADDITIONAL INFORMATION

This page is for any extra details you need to give.

PAGE CG8: CHARGEABLE GAINS AND ALLOWABLE LOSSES

Start by completing the first few boxes which summarise what you have already filled in.

If you have used an estimate or valuation in listing any of your gains or losses, there will be a tick in column B on page CG1 or CG2. Tick YES in the first line if there are any ticks in column B.

Chargeable gains and allowable losses	
Once you have completed Page CG1, or Pages CG2 to CG6, fill in this Page.	
Have you 'ticked' any row in Column B, 'Tick box if estimate or valuation used' on Pages CG1 or CG2 or in Column C on Page CG2 'Tick box if asset held at 31 March 1982'?	YES
Have you given details in Column G on Pages CG2 and CG3 of any Capital Gains reliefs claimed or due?	YES
Are you claiming, and/or using, any clogged losses (see Notes, page CGN11)?	YES

If you have filled in pages CG2 and CG3 and have claimed any tax relief on a gain other than indexation allowance in column G, tick YES in the second line.

Enter from Page CG1 or column AA on Page CG2:	
• the number of transactions in quoted shares or other securities	box Q
• the number of transactions in other shares or securities	box U
• the number of transactions in land and property	box L
• the number of gains attributed to settlors	box T

Enter the number of transactions in the five main categories:

- Box Q – quoted shares and securities (for what these are, see p. 315)
- Box U – unquoted shares or securities
- Box L – land or property
- Box T – gains from trusts attributed to you as settlor
- Box O – any other assets.

If you have filled in page CG1, all the transactions should be 'Q' – quoted shares or securities. If you have filled in pages CG2 and CG3, each transaction is categorised in column AA.

Total taxable gains (from Page CG1 **or** Page CG3)	8.7 £

Enter the total taxable gains from Box F7 on page CG1 or from the total taxable gains box on page CG3, bottom right.

Your taxable gains *minus* the annual exempt amount of £7,500 (leave blank if '0' or negative)	box 8.7 *minus* £7,500 8.8 £

Subtract £7,700 from the amount in box 8.7 and enter the result in box 8.8. This is the net amount of chargeable capital gains you have to pay tax on in the tax year ending 5 April 2003.

Additional liability in respect of non-resident or dual resident trusts (see Notes, page CGN6)	8.9	£

This is where you give details if you have benefited directly or indirectly from non-resident or dual resident trusts. You may be liable to capital gains tax on anything you receive from the trust – whether it be cash, a loan or an asset. You need to give details in box 8.9 of the amount of tax due on what you have received in the tax year ending 5 April 2003. To work this out, use the calculator on Help Sheet *IR301 Calculation of the increase in tax charge on capital gains from non-resident, dual resident and immigrant trusts*. Enter the name of the trust (and its tax reference if you know it) on page CG7.

CAPITAL LOSSES

This part of the Capital gains supplementary pages helps you keep track of your allowable losses. It summarises the losses you have made in the year ending 5 April 2003 and how you have used them. And it lists losses from previous years and whether these have been used. The information will be useful when you come to fill in next year's tax return.

There are some losses that can only be set against gains of certain types – called 'clogged losses'. These are losses on:

- Disposals to connected persons (see p. 111). These losses can only be set against gains on disposals to the same connected person
- Assets transferred to you after 15 June 1999 by trustees when you become absolutely entitled to settled property. These losses can only be set against gains on the same asset or an asset derived from that asset and have to be used before any other losses.

If you have clogged losses, make a copy of page CG8 for each one and keep separate records for each one. This will help you use them at the right time. Keep each copy until the clogged losses have been fully used up.

This year's losses

Capital losses	
(If your loss arose on a transaction with a connected person, see page CGN14, you can only set that loss against gains you make on disposals to that same connected person. See the notes on clogged losses on page CGN11.)	
■ *This year's losses*	
• Total (normally from box 8.2 on Page CG3 or box F2 on Page CG1. But, if you have clogged losses, see Notes, page CGN10)	8.10 £

The first few boxes are for losses for the tax year ending 5 April 2003. Enter in box 8.10 the total allowable losses for the year – the figure from box F2 on page CG1 or box 8.2 on page CG3.

• Used against gains (total of column K1 on Page CG3, or the smaller of boxes F1 and F2 on Page CG1)	8.11 £

Enter in box 8.11 the amount of the allowable losses for the tax year ending 5 April 2003 used to reduce your chargeable gains in that year. This is the total of the amounts entered in column K1 on Page CG3, or the smaller of boxes F1 and F2 on Page CG1.

• Used against earlier years' gains (generally only available to personal representatives, see Notes, page CGN11)	8.12 £

Personal representatives clearing up the estate of someone who has died and completing the tax return for the part of the tax year up to the date of that person's death can carry unused losses back to earlier tax years and effectively claim a tax rebate for the estate (see p. 119). Enter any amount this applies to in box 8.12.

• Used against income (only losses of the type described on page CGN9 can be used against income)	8.13A £	amount claimed against income of 2002-03	
	8.13B £	amount claimed against income of 2001-02	box 8.13A + box 8.13B 8.13 £

If you have made losses on shares in unquoted trading companies, you can set them off against income from the same tax year or the previous tax year. For more information, see Help Sheet *IR286 Negligible value claims and income tax losses for shares you have subscribed for in qualifying trading companies* and *IR297 Enterprise Investment Scheme and Capital Gains Tax*.

If you make such a claim, enter the amount claimed against income for the tax year ending 5 April 2003 in box 8.13A, and the amount against the previous tax year in box 8.13B. Add boxes 8.13A and 8.13B and enter the total in box 8.13.

• This year's unused losses	box 8.10 *minus* (boxes 8.11 + 8.12 + 8.13)	**8.14** £

Add the amounts in boxes 8.11, 8.12 and 8.13 and subtract the total from the amount in box 8.10. Enter the result in box 8.14 – this is the total unused losses for the tax year ending 5 April 2003 which can be carried forward to future tax years.

Earlier years' losses

■ ***Summary of earlier years' losses***	
• Unused losses of 1996-97 and later years	**8.15** £

The next few boxes record what has happened to losses carried forward from previous tax years. Enter in box 8.15 the amount carried over from the tax year ending 5 April 1997 and later tax years. You can find the figures you need on last year's tax return – the one for the 2001–02 tax year. Add the figures in boxes 8.14 and 8.15 of that tax return to fill in box 8.15 on this year's tax return.

• Used this year (losses from box 8.15 are used in priority to losses from box 8.18) (column K3 on Page CG3 or box F6 on Page CG1)	**8.16** £

Enter in box 8.16 the amount of the losses from box 8.15 used this year – these losses must be used before losses from earlier years. The figure is the amount in box F6 on page CG1 or the total in column K3 on page CG3 – if none of these losses have been used, put 0 in box 8.16.

• Remaining unused losses of 1996-97 and later years	box 8.15 *minus* box 8.16	**8.17** £

Subtract the amount in box 8.16 from the amount in box 8.15 and enter the result in box 8.17. This is the remaining unused losses from the tax year ending 5 April 1997 and later years.

• Unused losses of 1995-96 and earlier years	**8.18** £

Enter in box 8.18 the total of any unused losses from the tax year ending 5 April 1996 and earlier tax years. You can find this figure in box 8.12 of last year's tax return – the one for the 2001–02 tax year.

• Used this year (losses from box 8.15 are used in priority to losses from box 8.18) (column K3 on Page CG3 or box F6 on Page CG1)	box 8.6 *minus* box 8.16 (or box F6 *minus* box 8.16)	**8.19** £

Box 8.19 records the mount of losses from the tax year ending 5 April 1996 and earlier tax years used in the tax year ending 5 April 2002. It can be found by subtracting the amount in box 8.16 or box F6 from the amount in box 8.6. If box 8.6 and box F6 are blank, put 0 in this box.

Total of unused losses to carry forward

Finally, the tax return has space to note down the totals of losses you can carry forward to future tax years.

• Carried forward losses of 1996-97 and later years	box 8.14 + box 8.17 8.20 £

Add the amounts in boxes 8.14 and 8.17 and enter the total in box 8.20. This is the amount of losses for the tax year ending 5 April 1997 and later tax years you can carry forward.

• Carried forward losses of 1995-96 and earlier years	box 8.18 *minus* box 8.19 8.21 £

Subtract the amount in box 8.19 from the amount in box 8.18 and enter the result in box 8.21. This is the amount of losses for the tax year ending 5 April 1996 and earlier tax years you can carry forward.

NON-RESIDENCE

CHAPTER 24

Q9	Are you claiming that you were not resident, or not ordinarily resident, or not domiciled, in the UK, or dual resident in the UK and another country, for all or part of the year?	YES	NON-RESIDENCE ETC

If you are a resident of the UK, you are liable for UK tax on all your income whether it comes from within the UK or abroad. But, if you count as a non-resident, there is no UK tax on your income from abroad, only on any income which originates in the UK.

If you want to claim non-residence (or non-domicile) for the tax year ending 5 April 2003, you need to fill in the Non-residence Supplement which you can get through the Orderline (see p. 147). You are likely to need this if:

- you are normally a UK resident but you are working abroad for an extended period
- you have been a UK resident but you are going to live abroad permanently or indefinitely – for example because you are retiring abroad
- you have been resident elsewhere but you are based in the UK for now or you have returned for permanent residence.

This guide cannot give you all the detail you may need so you should consult a professional adviser. See also Inland Revenue booklet *IR20 Residents and Non-Residents etc*. At the time of writing, the government was consulting on possible changes to the rules regarding domicile and residence. However, the rules described here apply for the tax year ending 5 April 2003.

Residency is not defined in the tax legislation, but it has been the subject of much case law. Broadly, it means the place where you usually live. Because different countries use different criteria to decide who is resident, it is possible to count as a resident of more than one country at the same time, in which case you could pay two lots of tax on the same income. However, the UK has double taxation agreements with many countries to avoid this situation.

In general, payment of UK taxes depends on whether or not you were resident during the particular tax year in question. Occasionally, it may hinge on where you are ordinarily resident. Again, there is no hard and fast definition, but basically your ordinary residence is the country you are resident in year after year, which you use as your base, returning to it for extended periods, and probably where you have an established home.

Your domicile can be the key to whether or not there is tax on foreign income and gains you receive and any inheritance tax to pay on your estate when you die. Your country of domicile is the place which you consider to be your permanent home and where you would intend to end your days. You can have only one country of domicile and it is not necessarily the country in which you are resident or ordinarily resident. Claims for foreign domicile should be made as soon as possible on form DOM1.

Note that even if you are non-resident for tax purposes, you might still be able to claim the UK personal tax allowances to set against your income from UK sources, for example, if you are a citizen of a Commonwealth country or a European country within the European Economic Area (this includes the UK), a Crown employee (or a widow or widower of someone who was a Crown employee) or employed by a UK missionary service.

A word of warning: there are Inland Revenue concessions which might apply to you. You can claim the concessions, providing you don't use them simply as a means of avoiding tax. If the Inland Revenue suspects that tax avoidance is your main motive, it will refuse you the concession.

How do you count as being non-resident?

If you have generally been considered as a UK resident, to count as non-resident for tax purposes, you need to pass all four of the following tests:

- the motive test
- the absent for a whole tax year test
- the 183 days test
- the 91 days test.

The notes which accompany the Non-residence supplement include a calculator which will help you to work out whether you pass all these tests.

The motive test

You will pass this test if you leave the UK to work full-time, providing the other tests are also met. Whether or not your job is full-time is judged, first, by comparing your hours with the norm in the UK, but if your job is less structured it will be assessed on its own merits and in the light of what is normal for your type of work and the country you are going to. You could also count as working full-time if you have two or more part-time jobs.

By concession, if you count as non-resident because of your work abroad, your wife or husband, if they go with you, will also count as non-resident, providing they pass the other tests.

Another way to pass the test is if you go abroad to live permanently or at least indefinitely. The Inland Revenue will want evidence that this is your intention – for example, that you have bought a home abroad or you are going to marry someone in another country. If you still have a UK home, it wants to know how that fits with your plans to live overseas. Once you've lived abroad for three years, it will be accepted that you are non-resident.

If you can't pass this test at the time you go away, the situation can be reviewed later on, if new evidence of your motive becomes available or once you have been abroad for three years.

The absent for a whole tax year test

To count as non-resident for a tax year, if you work abroad, your job must last for at least a whole tax year and you must be out of the country for the whole tax year or longer, except for visits within the other rules (see below). Similarly, if you go to live abroad permanently or indefinitely, you must be out of the country for at least a whole tax year.

By concession, in the year you leave and the year you return, you can count as non-resident for just part of the year, provided that year is part of a longer period of non-residency. If you want to claim this split year treatment, you must give details of your date of arrival in or departure from the UK in box 9.25 or box 9.26 of the supplementary pages.

The 183 days test

You will always count as resident for the tax year if you spend 183 days or more in the UK. There are no exceptions to this rule. For example, if you make visits back home during a period working abroad, the total of your visits during any tax year must come to less than 183 days if you are not to lose your status as a non-resident. For the purposes of this rule and the next, the days on which you travel do not count as days spent in the UK.

The 91 days test

In addition to the 183 days test, the average time you spend in the UK must come to less than 91 days in a tax year. This is worked out over the period since you left until you have been away for four tax years. After that it is worked out over the most recent four tax years. You are allowed to ignore periods you had to spend in the UK for reasons beyond your control – for example, because someone in your family was ill.

Mobile workers

You might have the sort of job that takes you on frequent trips abroad, possibly working abroad all week and just returning home to the UK for weekends. Even if you pass the 183 and 91 days tests, the Inland Revenue takes the view that you are unlikely to count as non-resident, if your home and domestic life continue to be UK-based. It argues that, in these circumstances, you have not genuinely left the UK. In the past, the Revenue may have granted non-resident status to people in these circumstances and it has indicated that it might review these cases if there is reason to believe that the earlier decision was not based on a full disclosure of all the relevant facts.

How do you count as being non-domiciled in the UK?

Your domicile is relevant only if it will affect the tax you must pay, so unless you fall into one of the following categories, you do not need to fill in boxes 9.27 to 9.31, and you should also leave box 9.5 blank. The tax areas which might be affected are where:

- you have income or gains from foreign investments which you will not be bringing in full into the UK
- you are claiming UK tax relief on contributions to a foreign pension scheme made out of earnings from a non-UK resident employer
- the costs of travelling between the UK and your normal home have been paid by your employer
- you worked abroad for a non-UK employer and have not brought all the earnings into the UK.

You can have only one domicile at a time and there are three ways in which it can be established: by birth, by dependency or by choice. From birth, you normally have the domicile of your father – that is not necessarily

> **TAX-SAVING IDEAS**
>
> If you go to work or live abroad, make sure your trips back home average less than 91 days a year and come to less than 183 days in any single tax year to avoid paying UK taxes on your overseas income.
>
> Taking a long lease of three years on a home abroad would help to show that you intended to live abroad permanently.
>
> If you are returning permanently to the UK after a period of non-residence abroad and you have been saving through an offshore roll-up fund, make sure you sell your investment before you become a UK resident again. If you don't, you will become liable for tax on the rolled-up income.

the same as the country in which you were born. If the domicile of the person on whom you are dependant changes, so will yours. Similarly, if you become dependant on someone else of a different domicile, your own domicile will fall into line with that. Women no longer acquire their husbands' domicile on marriage. Once you reach the age of 16, you have the right to choose a new domicile but the change is not easily made. You would need to show that you had settled in the new country of domicile with a view to staying there permanently. Your home, business interests, social and family ties, and the form of any will would all be relevant, but other factors could also be just as important.

KEEPING AN EYE ON YOUR TAX AFFAIRS

CHAPTER 25

Self-assessment means you can control your own tax affairs, and make sure you don't pay a penny more than you should. But even if you do all the sums, there are several forms the Inland Revenue will send you that you need to check to make sure you aren't paying too much.

This chapter looks at three of the most important forms:

- the Tax Calculation which your tax inspector issues after you send in your tax return – correcting any mistakes and setting out his or her calculations of your tax bill
- the PAYE Coding Notice sent to people who work for someone else – this tells your employer how much tax to deduct from your pay
- the Statement of Account sent to anyone who has a tax liability following submission of a self-assessment tax return.

TAX CALCULATION

Once you have sent in your tax return, the Inland Revenue checks through it for any obvious errors – such as arithmetical mistakes or failing to copy figures correctly from one part to another. You will be sent a Tax Calculation (form SA302) only if the Inland Revenue has corrected your own calculation or if you have asked the Inland Revenue to work out your tax bill for you. The Tax Calculation form tells you the result of this process, the total tax the inspector thinks you owe and the amount of any payments on account you have to make. Check this carefully as soon as it arrives and challenge your tax inspector if you don't agree with the figures.

The first page of the Tax Calculation form summarises the figures:

- first it says if there are any corrections to your tax return – if there are, they will be listed on the back of the first page
- then it tells you the total amount of income tax plus capital gains tax owed for the tax year – the calculation will be set out on the second sheet

- lastly it says what the tax inspector calculates as the two payments on account you have to make towards the next year's tax bill and what balancing payment, if any, is due (see p. 21). These are shown on the front of the first page.

If you have calculated your own tax bill, checking the Tax Calculation form is straightforward. It is simply a matter of comparing the figures you worked out on the Tax Calculation Guide with the inspector's calculation. If you have left it to the tax inspector to do the sums, you will need a copy of your tax return and a calculator to check the figures.

If there is anything you don't understand on the Tax Calculation form, write or phone your tax office for clarification. And if you disagree with the tax inspector's figures, do the same – otherwise you will be expected to pay up.

PAYE CODING NOTICE

This form sets out the calculations your tax inspector has made in setting your PAYE code for the tax year. In the year ending 5 April 2002, 6 per cent of Coding Notices were incorrect, so it is important to check the calculation. Your employer will use the code to work out how much tax should be deducted from your pay. People with two jobs should have two PAYE codes – and two Coding Notices.

If you have retired, any pensions you get from an occupational pension scheme or personal pension will also have tax deducted from them before you receive the money. Again, you should have a PAYE code for each one if you have more than one substantial pension.

Your PAYE code reflects the amount of allowances your tax inspector estimates you can set against your earnings in the current tax year. It may also be adjusted to collect tax on fringe benefits and income such as freelance earnings, odd pensions and savings interest. The amounts are based on information given in your tax return, by your employer and by other organisations that send details of payments to the Inland Revenue.

Your employer usually makes various other adjustments to your gross pay to arrive at the take-home amount. These can include deduction of National Insurance, student loan repayments, pension contributions and donations to charity through payroll giving. They may also include an addition to your pay if you qualify for the working tax credit, which is a social security benefit delivered through the PAYE system if you are an employee. But none of these deductions or additions is reflected in your PAYE tax code – your employer follows separate administrative procedures for making these adjustments.

Children's tax credit, if you qualified, used to be reflected in your PAYE code. But, from 6 April 2003, it is replaced by child tax credit, a state benefit paid direct to the child's main carer and not through PAYE.

If you have been given the correct code or codes, you will have paid the right amount of tax on your income by the end of the tax year. But if there has been a mistake, you may pay too much and have to wait for a rebate. And although paying too little tax may seem attractive, you will have to make up any underpayment in the following tax year – often in one go if it is £2,000 or more. So it makes sense to check your PAYE code carefully whenever you receive a Coding Notice.

Checking a Coding Notice

The main figures on a PAYE Coding Notice are in two columns. The first lists the allowances that are to be set off against this income to reduce the tax bill on it. If this is your main source of income, the Coding Notice should normally list all your allowances unless they are specifically to be set

EXAMPLE

Harriet Svensen checks her Coding Notice for the 2003–04 tax year – the one ending 5 April 2004. This is the code for her main job with Viking Electronics. She first sees that she has been given the right tax allowances for the year:

- £4,615 personal allowance
- £2,150 married couple's allowance (see p. 48)
- £60 a year for her subscription to her professional body.

This makes total allowances of £6,825. The following amounts are deducted from this:

- £150 for Harriet's membership of a local sports club paid by the company
- £2,560 for the benefit of her company car
- £1,170 married couple's allowance restriction to keep to 10 per cent the tax relief a basic rate taxpayer, such as Harriet, gets on the allowance (see p. 339).

Thus Harriet has total deductions of £3,880. Harriet's tax-free amount for the year is £6,825 − £3,880 = £2,945. Her tax code is found by dropping the last digit to get 294: the letter to be added is T, because she has a company car (see p. 341). So Harriet's code is 294T.

Inland Revenue

PAYE Coding Notice

Tax code for tax year 2003/04

P2(T)

Mrs S H SVENSEN
143 WENDOVER ROAD
LONDON
SW14 5NJ

Please keep all your coding notices. You may need to refer to them if you have to fill in a tax return. Please also quote your tax reference and National Insurance number if you contact us.

HM INSPECTOR OF TAXES
LONDON PROVINCIAL 24
GRAYFIELD HOUSE
5 BANKHEAD AVENUE
SIGHTHILL
EDINBURGH EH11 4AE

Inland Revenue office phone: 0131 453 7200	Date of issue: 12 JAN 2003
Tax reference: 976/52425	National Insurance number: YR 61 53 51 C

Your tax code for the year shown above is 294T

This tax code is used to deduct tax payable on your income from

VIKING ELECTRONICS

If you move to another job, your new employer will normally continue to use this tax code. The tax code is worked out as follows:

The **'See note'** columns below refer to the numbered notes in the leaflet **'Understanding Your Tax Code'**. This tells you about the **letter part** of your tax code.

Check that your details are correct. If you think they're wrong, or you have any questions, ask me (my details are above).

This coding notice replaces any previous notice for the year.

See note	Your tax allowances	£
01	PERSONAL ALLOWANCE	4615
02	MARRIED ALLOWANCE	2150
10	PROFESSIONAL SUSBCRIPTIONS	60
A	**Total allowances**	6825

See note	Amounts taken away from your total allowances	£
30	BENEFITS IN KIND	150
30	CAR BENEFIT	2560
25	MARRIED ALLOWANCE RESTRICTION	1170
B	**Total deductions**	3880

C **Your tax free amount for the year is £** 2945 **, making your tax code** 294T **see example overleaf**

If necessary we will use this box to give you further information about your tax code

P2(T) BS10/02

EXAMPLE

Gerry Walker pays £500 gross (before-tax relief) into a stakeholder pension scheme in the tax year ending 5 April 2004. Since the basic rate of tax for the tax year is 22 per cent, he gets basic rate tax relief of 22 per cent of £500 = £110. So he actually hands over £500 – £110 = £390.

But Gerry pays tax at the higher rate, so he is entitled to tax relief of 40 per cent of £500 = £200. The extra £90 (£200 – £110) is given by increasing his tax allowances by £225, since 40 per cent of £225 is £90.

off against other types of income (for example, against rents or freelance income).

The second column lists amounts that will be deducted from your allowances in order to collect extra tax. For example, if you have taxable fringe benefits, their taxable value will normally be in this column. So will other sources of untaxed income, such as freelance earnings, taxable state pensions and benefits and income from savings that have not been taxed.

Checking the entries is very straightforward – the Inland Revenue guide sent out with notices explains the headings. Start by making sure you have all the allowances and deductions you're entitled to in the first column. Some allowances and deductions won't be included for basic rate taxpayers where they get tax relief directly. For example, you get tax relief at the basic rate on contributions to a personal pension (including a stakeholder scheme) by paying lower premiums (see p. 75). If you pay tax at the higher rates, there will be an entry on your Coding Notice to give you the extra relief, as the following example shows. Higher rate tax relief can also be given in this way on gifts to charity – Gift Aid (see p. 195).

Then check the amounts to be taken away from your tax allowances in the second column. These include the **Allowance restriction** for tax allowances restricted to tax relief at 10 per cent only – now applying only to married couple's allowance and maintenance relief for people born before 6 April 1935. You will have been given these allowances and credit in the first column, but the PAYE system would then give you tax relief at your top rate of tax. This will be the right amount of tax relief if you pay tax at the 10 per cent lower rate of tax only. But if your top rate is the 22 per cent basic rate or the 40 per cent higher rate, you would get too much tax relief. The allowance restriction recovers the extra tax relief you would get if this happened.

EXAMPLE

Harriet (see example on p. 336) is married to Bill who is ten years older than her and was born before 6 April 1935. He qualifies for the married couple's allowance but the couple have transferred the full basic amount of £2,150 to Harriet (see p. 48). In her Coding Notice, this amount appears in the left-hand column. But the allowance is meant to give only 10 per cent tax relief, which in Harriet's case would be £215. If £2,150 is simply deducted from Harriet's income, it would give her tax relief at her top rate of 22 per cent – in other words, relief of 22% × £2,150 = £473. This is £473 − £215 = £258 too much.

Harriet's tax inspector corrects this with a tax credit restriction of £1,170, shown in the right-hand column of the Notice. By deducting £1,170 from the allowance, tax of 22% × £1,170 = £257.40 is collected which is, give or take a few pence, the amount of the excess relief that would otherwise have been given.

The tax inspector found out how much to deduct as a tax credit restriction by taking the excess relief and dividing it by Harriet's top rate of tax: £258 ÷ 22% = £1,172.73 which is rounded down to £1,170.

If you expect your top rate of tax to have changed in this tax year, this restriction might be too large or too small. If so, tell your Tax Inspector so the right amount of tax is deducted through PAYE.

Untaxed interest collects tax on interest you are expected to get during the tax year which will not have tax deducted from it first – for example, from NS&I investment account (see below). If you are a basic rate taxpayer, the amount entered here will be less than you actually get. This is because you pay tax on interest at 20 per cent only (p. 5) but tax is deducted from your earnings at 22 per cent for the tax year which began on 6 April 2003. This entry will avoid collecting too much tax on it.

Higher rate tax adjustment collects extra higher rate tax due on interest,

EXAMPLE

Gerry Walker gets £200 of interest from his NS&I Investment Account in the tax year ending 5 April 2004. He should pay tax of 20 per cent of £200 = £40. But he is a basic rate taxpayer, so adding £200 to his taxable income would collect too much – 22 per cent of £200 = £44.

Gerry's tax inspector adds £182 to Gerry's income with an untaxed income deduction from his PAYE code. This will collect the right amount, since 22 per cent of £182 = £40.

EXAMPLE

Betty Pinder pays tax at the higher rate and receives £1,000 of interest. This is paid after deduction of tax at 20 per cent: 20 per cent of £1,000 is £200, so she receives £1,000 – £200 = £800 of savings income net.

But Betty should have paid tax at 40 per cent on the gross amount – 40 per cent of £1,000 = £400. So she owes another £400 – £200 = £200. To collect this £200, a higher rate tax adjustment of £500 is made: by adding £500 to Betty's taxable income, she will pay 40 per cent of £500 = £200 on her income taxed under PAYE.

dividends and some other sorts of income which are paid after deduction of tax which covers any basic rate tax due.

If you have underpaid less than £2,000 of tax in a previous tax year, the Inland Revenue will normally try to collect this by a **Tax underpaid** adjustment to your PAYE code. For example, if you owe £500 and pay tax at the basic rate of 22 per cent, your tax inspector will add £2,273 to your taxable income to collect it: 22 per cent of £2,273 = £500.

Calculating your PAYE code

Total deductions are subtracted from total allowances to find the amount of income covered by the PAYE code which can be tax-free during the tax year. This is then converted into a PAYE code – normally by knocking off the last figure and adding one of the following letters, depending on your allowances and tax rate:

L – personal allowance at the rate for those aged under 65 only
P – personal allowance for those aged 65-74 only
Y – personal allowance for the over-75s only
V – personal allowance for those aged 65–74 and married couple's allowance for those born before 6 April 1935 and aged under 75, paying tax at the basic rate.

So if your only tax allowance is the single person's allowance for people under 65 of £4,615 and you have £160 deductions for fringe benefits, your total tax-free amount for the year will be £4,615 – £160 = £4,455. Your code is found by knocking off the last figure to give you 445, and adding L because you get only the single person's allowance. Your PAYE code will be 445L.

When it comes to deducting tax from your pay, the employer's tax tables will say that an employee with a code of 445L was entitled to tax-free pay during the tax year of £4,459 – divided equally over the year.

The letters after the number mean that if the main allowances change, your PAYE code can be adjusted by your employer or pension provider. So if, say, an increase to the under-65 personal allowance is announced in the Budget (usually in March but occasionally in April), everyone with an L code automatically gets the extra tax-free pay generally from their May pay packet onwards.

T codes
If the code ends in the letter T, your tax position is more complicated – you may be getting other allowances, for example, blind person's allowance. You could also get it if you have fringe benefits such as a company car, or have asked for it because you don't want your employer to know what allowances you are entitled to. Changes cannot be made automatically if you have this sort of code and you will have to wait longer for the tax office to make the adjustments.

K codes
If the amount of deductions is more than your allowances, you will have a PAYE code that begins with a K. This is calculated as follows:

- subtract the deductions from the allowances – the answer will be a negative number
- take the last figure off the number
- reduce that number by one
- put a K in front of the answer to give a PAYE code.

K codes have to be recalculated every time the tax allowances change or there is some alteration in your circumstances.

PAYE codes with more than one source of income
There are special PAYE codes which don't have numbers or which have numbers which don't stand for tax allowances. These are mainly used for deducting tax from second or third sources of income:

- BR – this income is all to be taxed at the basic rate. This is where other sources of income have had all your allowances set against them and used up the amount of income which is taxed at the lower rate
- D – this income is all to be taxed at the higher rate. This is where other sources of income have had all your allowances set against them and used up the amount of income which is taxed at the lower and basic rates
- OT – you are not entitled to any tax-free pay, but this source of income is to be taxed first at the starting rate, then the basic rate and perhaps eventually the higher rate

> **EXAMPLE**
>
> Rasheed Patel is a single man, and his only tax allowance is the personal allowance of £4,615. However, he has a company car with a taxable value of £4,850, so his tax-free amount for the year is £4,615 – £4,850 = – £235.
>
> His PAYE code is therefore found by dropping the last digit to get 23. Then he subtracts 1 to get 22 – giving a code of K22. With a PAYE code of K22, Rasheed would have £229 added to his pay for the year before the tax was worked out (instead of having some allowances deducted).

- NT – this income should be paid without any tax being deducted, perhaps because it is less than your tax-free allowances.

STATEMENT OF ACCOUNT

If you have income of £500 or more in a tax year from being self-employed, from letting out property or from investments which pay out income without deduction of tax, you will normally have to make two payments of tax on account against your final tax bill for the year. However, there will be no need to make such payments if most of your tax – 80 per cent or more – is deducted from your income at source.

If you do have to make payments on account, the first is due on 31 January during the tax year, the second by 31 July after it has finished. The amounts are based on the income you got in the previous tax year.

Shortly before a payment is due, you will receive a Statement of Account showing the amount to pay. So, if you ask the Inland Revenue to work out your tax bill, you'll get statements in December and June. If you work out your own tax bill, you'll get statements in June and usually shortly after the end of the tax year, but just a Tax return and payment reminder in December.

You must pay the tax requested on the Statement of Account by the right date – paying late could mean an interest charge (see p. 22). So it is vital to check the statement. If it demands more than you should pay in the current tax year, you can ask for the payments to be reduced. But you must do this before the date the payment is due. This section of the guide tells you how to check a statement and how to claim a reduction.

If you are registered with the Inland Revenue's online service (see p. 16), from

Inland Revenue **Self Assessment - Statement of Account**

Statement Number 999 Sheet 1 of 1

Tax Reference 99999 99999
Employer Reference 999/XXXXXXXXXXXXX

Statement Date 19 June 2003

999999 999999 999

MR J SMITH
99 THE MALL
NEWTONTHORPE
PRESTON
LANCS
PR9 99Z

Issued by
AREA DIRECTOR
INLAND REVENUE PRESTON
999 WEST AVENUE
PRESTON
LANCS
PR9 99Z

Telephone 01999 999999

Payment Enquiries: Telephone 01274 999999

Amount to pay £1594.87 *see details below*

Date	Description	Amount	Summary
31 JAN 02	1st payment on account due for year 02/03	1450.00	
	From payment £500.00 made 11 JUN 03	500.00 CR	
	From payment £450.00 made 12 JUN 03	450.00 CR	
	From payment £400.00 made 14 JUN 03	400.00 CR	
	Total credits	1350.00 CR	
	Plus interest up to 19 JUN 03	44.87	
	Balance		144.87
	Balance as at 19 JUN 03		144.87
Becoming due			
31 JLY 03	2nd payment on account due for year 01/02	1450.00	
	Balance		1450.00
	Amount to pay		**1594.87**

Interest is running on the balance at the date of this statement, so to avoid further interest you should pay this now. A further amount, as shown, is becoming due. You will be charged interest if you pay late.

SA300 (Shipley) BMSD 9/01

▼ **Please detach payslip here** when making payment direct to the Accounts Office or by Girobank ▼

Girobank Trans cash
Girobank plc Bootle Merseyside GIR 0AA

Inland Revenue **Payslip**

bank giro credit

158
208
24

Reference: 99999 99999K

Credit account number: 610 5041

Amount due (no fee payable at PO counter): £ 1594.87

CHEQUE ACCEPTABLE

By transfer from Alliance & Leicester / Giro account number

MR J SMITH

Signature ____________ Date ____________

For official use only

Cashier's stamp and initials

BANK OF ENGLAND
HEAD OFFICE COLLECTION A/C
INLAND REVENUE

CASH

CHEQUES

£

10-50-41

SA300 (Shipley)

▼ *Please do not fold this payslip or write or mark below this line* ▼

9999999999K &9999999999 999999999 74 X

Spring 2003 onwards you should be able to view your Statements of Account online.

How to reduce your payments on account

If you think your tax bills for the types of income covered by a Statement of Account will be lower than in the previous year, you can claim to make a lower payment on account than the Inland Revenue is asking for. This might happen if your income has dropped – for example, you have received less in rent, profits from your business or on the investment income which is received without deduction of tax. Or your tax bill might be less because you have become newly eligible for an allowance or can claim higher deductions against your income – for example, you have started to pay large pension contributions.

If this is the case, work out your expected tax bill for this tax year carefully. Then calculate how this should be divided between the two payments on account. If you should be paying less than the Inland Revenue is asking for, make your claim to pay less on Inland Revenue form SA303. You may have received a copy with your Statement of Account – otherwise ask your tax office for a copy or download one from the Inland Revenue website. You must send this back before the payment on account is due.

If later you realise you could pay still less, you can make a further claim – as long as it is before the payment is due. If you discover after making the first payment that it was too much, you can reduce the second payment on account to compensate.

It is probably better to pay slightly more rather than too little in your payments on account. If you pay too much, you will get interest on it; if you pay too little, you will pay interest. There are penalties in the form of fines if you are caught trying to hoodwink your tax inspector in the amounts you pay. And provided you make the payments on account demanded on time, there is normally no interest to pay even if your tax bill turns out to have been much higher.

TAX-FREE INCOME

Income from a job
Check with your employer if you are uncertain about whether any of these forms of income is taxable

- work-related expenses reimbursed to you by your employer and covered by an agreement with the Inland Revenue that they do not need to be declared (see p. 219)
- some fringe benefits, such as canteen meals and Christmas parties provided for all staff, mileage allowance up to the authorised rates if you use your own transport for business, special clothes for the job and subscriptions to approved professional societies (see p. 89)
- foreign service allowances paid to diplomats and other servants of the Crown
- goods and services your employer lets you have cheaply (see p. 89)
- miners' free coal or cash allowances in lieu of coal
- long-service awards so long as they are not in cash and are within set limits (see p. 91)
- awards from approved suggestions schemes (see p. 92)
- payments for moving because of your job, within set limits (see p. 92)
- genuine personal gifts – for example, wedding presents.

Income on leaving a job
Check with your ex-employer

- gratuities from the armed forces
- payments relating to certain foreign service
- lump-sum compensation for an injury or disability that means you can no longer do the job
- tax-free lump sum instead of part of a pension and certain other ex gratia payments on retirement or death
- up to £30,000 of other compensation on leaving a job, including statutory redundancy payments, pay in lieu of notice (provided receiving it was not part of your contract of employment or customary) and counselling and outplacement services (see p. 224).

Pensions and benefits
Check with the organisation paying the pension or benefit

- state pension Christmas bonus and winter fuel allowance
- war widows' and orphans' pensions and equivalent overseas pensions
- bereavement payment
- certain compensation payments and pensions paid to victims of Nazi persecution
- war disablement pensions
- additional pensions paid to holders of some bravery awards such as the Victoria Cross
- the part of a pension paid to a former employee who retires because of a disability caused by injury at work or a work-related illness which is in excess of the pension paid to an employee who retires on normal ill-health grounds
- income support paid to people aged 60 or over, single parents with a child under 16 and those staying at home to look after a severely disabled person. Part of income support paid to unemployed people may be tax-free – see your statement of taxable benefits (p. 169)
- jobfinder's grant, most youth training scheme allowances, employment rehabilitation and training allowances, back to work bonus
- housing benefit and council tax benefit
- improvement and renovation grants for your home
- payments from the social fund
- maternity allowance (but statutory maternity pay is taxable)
- child benefit, one-parent benefit, school uniform grants
- additions for dependent children paid with a state pension or social security benefit
- guardian's allowance
- student grants and educational maintenance allowance
- incapacity benefit for first 28 weeks (and if paid to replace invalidity benefit)
- industrial disablement benefits
- disability living allowance
- attendance allowance
- working tax credit and child tax credit although the amount you get is reduced if your before-tax income exceeds certain thresholds (see p. 12).

Investment income
If in doubt, check with the organisation paying the income

- interest on National Savings & Investment (NS&I) Certificates (and Ulster Savings Certificates if you normally live in Northern Ireland),

NS&I Children's Bonus Bonds

- interest and terminal bonuses on bank and building society Save-As-You-Earn (SAYE) schemes
- first £70 of interest each year from NS&I Ordinary Account (£140 for married couples with a joint account)
- income from an individual savings account (ISA) – see p. 81
- income from a personal equity plan (PEP) – see p. 83
- interest on a tax-exempt special savings account (TESSA) kept open for the full five years – see p. 84
- dividends on ordinary shares in a venture capital trust (see p. 87)
- part of the income paid by an annuity (other than a pension annuity)
- amount paid out from certain friendly society policies
- loan interest paid to members of a credit union.

Other tax-free income

If in doubt, check with the organisation paying out the money

- what you receive in maintenance payments from a former spouse
- up to £4,250 a year of income from letting out a furnished room in your only or main home – the rent a room scheme (p. 283)
- income you get for fostering children up to certain limits
- gambling winnings (as long as it is not your business)
- lottery winnings
- premium bond prizes
- income from qualifying life insurance policies that pay out on death – for example, mortgage protection policies, family income benefit policies
- income from insurance policies to cover mortgage payments if you are sick or unemployed
- income from income protection policies you yourself pay for, creditor insurance and some long-term care policies
- pay-outs under some accident insurance policies (usually group ones)
- interest on a delayed settlement for damages for personal injury or death
- compensation for being wrongly sold a personal pension
- interest on a tax rebate.

GROSSING-UP TABLES

APPENDIX B

Some forms of income are paid net – after some tax has been deducted from them. For example, 20 per cent tax is normally deducted from the interest on savings accounts in banks and building societies before it is paid out to you or added to your account (unless it is a tax-exempt special savings account or individual savings account). In working out your tax bill, you may need to know how much the income was before the tax was deducted – the gross income.

You can find the gross income by grossing-up the net income using the ready reckoners below. With most forms of savings income, tax will have been deducted at 20 per cent, so that is the rate in the first ready reckoner. The second is for grossing-up income where tax has been deducted at the basic rate of 22 per cent (or payments where tax relief has been deducted at 22 per cent). The third is for grossing-up income which comes with a tax credit of 10 per cent – share dividends and unit trust distributions.

If the tax rates change the tables here will not apply, but you can use the following formula to work out the grossed-up income:

$$\text{Amount paid to you net} \times \left(\frac{100}{100 - \text{rate of tax}}\right)$$

So, looking back to the tax year ending 5 April 2000, the basic rate was 23 per cent. If you had received £50 after tax, you could have found the grossed-up amount as follows:

$$\text{£}50 \times \left(\frac{100}{100 - 23}\right)$$

$$= \text{£}50 \times \frac{100}{77}$$

$$= \text{£}64.94$$

Grossing-up at 20 per cent

Net amount	*Gross amount*	*Net amount*	*Gross amount*	*Net amount*	*Gross amount*
£	£	£	£	£	£
1	1.25	10	12.50	100	125.00
2	2.50	20	25.00	200	250.00
3	3.75	30	37.50	300	375.00
4	5.00	40	50.00	400	500.00
5	6.25	50	62.50	500	625.00
6	7.50	60	75.00	600	750.00
7	8.75	70	87.50	700	875.00
8	10.00	80	100.00	800	1,000.00
9	11.25	90	112.50	900	1,125.00
				1,000	1,250.00

EXAMPLE

Gary Loudon receives building society interest of £1,793 in the tax year ending 5 April 2003. He must gross up this net interest at 20 per cent as follows:

	Net income	*Gross income*
	£1,000	£1,250.00
	£700	£875.00
	£90	£112.50
	£3	£3.75
TOTAL	£1,793	£2,241.25

Grossing-up at 22 per cent

Net amount	*Gross amount*	*Net amount*	*Gross amount*	*Net amount*	*Gross amount*
£	£	£	£	£	£
1	1.28	10	12.82	100	128.21
2	2.56	20	25.64	200	256.41
3	3.85	30	38.46	300	384.61
4	5.13	40	51.28	400	512.82
5	6.41	50	64.10	500	641.03
6	7.69	60	76.92	600	769.23
7	8.97	70	89.74	700	897.44
8	10.26	80	102.56	800	1,025.64
9	11.54	90	115.38	900	1,153.85
				1,000	1,282.05

EXAMPLE

Peggy Cronin receives net income of £4,375 in the tax year ending 5 April 2003, from which tax has been deducted at the basic rate of 22 per cent. She finds the gross income as follows:

	Net income	*Gross income*
	£4,000	£5,128.21
	£300	£384.61
	£70	£89.74
	£5	£6.41
TOTAL	£4,375	£5,608.97

Grossing-up at 10 per cent

Net amount	*Gross amount*	*Net amount*	*Gross amount*	*Net amount*	*Gross amount*
£	£	£	£	£	£
1	1.11	10	11.11	100	111.11
2	2.22	20	22.22	200	222.22
3	3.33	30	33.33	300	333.33
4	4.44	40	44.44	400	444.44
5	5.56	50	55.56	500	555.56
6	6.67	60	66.67	600	666.67
7	7.78	70	77.78	700	777.78
8	8.89	80	88.89	800	888.89
9	10.00	90	100.00	900	1,000.00
				1,000	1,111.11

EXAMPLE

Belinda Gaspari receives share dividends worth £1,297 in the tax year ending 5 April 2003. She must gross-up the net dividends at 10 per cent for this tax year:

	Net income	*Gross income*
	£1,000	£1,111.11
	£200	£222.22
	£90	£100.00
	£7	£7.78
TOTAL	£1,297	£1441.11

USEFUL LEADLETS

APPENDIX C

You can get all these leaflets free from your tax office or any tax enquiry centre (look in The Phone Book under 'Inland Revenue'). Most are also available from *www.inlandrevenue.gov.uk* or by calling 08459 000404.

Introductions to self-assessment

SA/BK3	Self-assessment. A guide to keeping records for the self-employed
SA/BK4	Self-assessment. A general guide to keeping records
SA/BK6	Self-assessment. Penalties for late tax returns
SA/BK7	Self-assessment. Surcharges for late payment of tax
SA/BK8	Self-assessment. Your guide
IR2013	Record-keeping for self assessment

General guides to the Inland Revenue

IR37	Appeals against tax, etc
IR73	Inland Revenue investigations: how settlements are negotiated
IR141	Open government
IR160	Inland Revenue enquiries under self-assessment: how settlements are negotiated
IR167	Charter for Inland Revenue taxpayers
IR2012	Paying self assessment electronically
AO1	How to complain about the Inland Revenue
COP1	Putting things right when we make mistakes
COP10	Information and advice
COP11	Enquiries into tax returns by local tax offices
CSS1	Customer Service Standards

Income tax for particular groups

IR33	Income tax and school leavers
IR41	Income tax and job seekers
IR60	Students and the Inland Revenue
IR115	Income tax, National Insurance contributions and childcare
IR121	Income tax and pensioners
IR170	Blind person's allowance

Tax credits

WTC1	Child tax credit and working tax credit. An introduction
WTC5	Child tax credit and working tax credit. Help with the cost of childcare
WTC/AP	Child tax credit and working tax credit: how to appeal against a tax credit decision or award
WTC/E6	Working tax credit paid with wages

Income tax and international issues

IR20	Residents and non-residents – liability to tax in the UK
IR138	Living or retiring abroad?
IR139	Income from abroad? A guide to UK tax on overseas income
IR140	Non-resident landlords, their agents and tenants

Income tax – general

IR1	Extra-statutory concessions (plus supplement with latest concessions)
IR45	What to do about tax when someone dies
IR46	Clubs, societies and voluntary associations
IR65	Giving to charity by individuals
IR90	Tax allowances and reliefs
IR122	Volunteer drivers
IR131	Statements of practice (plus supplement)
IR144	Income tax and incapacity benefit
IR153	Tax exemption for sickness or unemployment insurance payments
IR178	Giving shares and securities to charity

Savings, investments, pensions and property

IR2	Occupational pension schemes – a guide for members
IR3	Personal pension schemes (including stakeholder pension schemes) – a guide for members
IR68	Accrued income schemes. Taxing securities on transfer
IR78	Looking to the future. Tax reliefs to help you save for retirement
IR87	Letting and your home
IR110	A guide for people with savings
IR137	The Enterprise Investment Scheme
IR150	Taxation of rents – a guide to property income
IR152	Trusts – an introduction
IR169	Venture Capital Trusts
IR2007	Capital allowances for flats over shops
IR2008	ISAs, PEPs and TESSAs
P/TXB/1	Taxback. Are you paying too much tax on your savings?
–	Community investment tax relief schemes. A brief guide for investors

Employees

480	Expenses and benefits. A guide for tax
IR16	Share acquisitions by directors and employees. Explanatory notes
IR34	PAYE. Pay As You Earn
IR97	Approved save as you earn share option schemes
IR101	Approved company share option plans. An outline for employees
IR124	Using your own vehicle for work
IR134	Income tax and relocation packages
IR136	Income tax and company vans
IR143	Income tax and redundancy
IR145	Low-interest loans provided by employers
IR172	Income tax and company cars
IR176	Tax, National Insurance contributions and green travel
IR177	Share incentive plans and your entitlement to benefits
IR2002	Share incentive plans. A guide for employees
IR2006	Enterprise management incentives. A guide

Self-employed

P/SE/1	Thinking of working for yourself?
CWL2	National Insurance Contributions for self-employed people
IR56	Employed or self-employed? A guide for tax and National Insurance
IR72	Investigations. The examination of business accounts
CA02	National insurance for self-employed people with small earnings
CA72	National insurance contributions – deferring payment

Employers

480	Expenses and benefits. Tax guide
490	Employee travel. A tax and NICs guide for employers
IR59	Collection of student loans – a guide for employers
IR64	Giving to charity by businesses
IR69	Expense payments and benefits in kind. How to save yourself work
IR109	Employer compliance reviews and negotiations
IR155	PAYE settlement agreements
NE1	First steps as a new employer
NE3	New and small employers. Support with your payroll
COP3	Reviews of employers' and contractors' records

Capital gains tax

CGT1	Capital gains tax – an introduction

Inheritance tax

IHT2	Inheritance tax on lifetime gifts
IHT3	Inheritance tax. An introduction

IHT8* Alterations to an inheritance following a death
IHT11* Payment of inheritance tax from National Savings or British Government Stock
IHT13* Inheritance tax and penalties
IHT14* Inheritance tax. The personal representative's responsibilities
IHT15* Inheritance tax. How to calculate the liability
IHT16* Inheritance tax. Settled property
IHT17* Inheritance tax. Businesses, farms and woodlands
SV1* Shares Valuation. An introduction

*Available from the Capital Taxes Orderline 0845 234 1000 or the three Capital Taxes Offices:
England and Wales: Ferrers House, PO Box 38, Castle Meadow Road, Nottingham, NG2 1BB
Scotland: Meldrum House, 15 Drumsheugh Gardens, Edinburgh EH3 7UG
Northern Ireland: Dorchester House, 52-58 Great Victoria Street, Belfast BT2 7QL

Business Economic Notes
These give information on how tax inspectors approach particular businesses such as travel agents, road hauliers, hairdressers and funeral directors. You can download them free from the Inland Revenue website:
www.inlandrevenue.gov.uk/bens/index/htm

INDEX

C

D

G

H

T

U

V

W

Y

Z